Data Sovereignty

Data Sovereignty

*From the Digital Silk Road to
the Return of the State*

Edited by
ANUPAM CHANDER AND HAOCHEN SUN

Oxford University Press is a department of the University of Oxford. It furthers the University's objective of excellence in research, scholarship, and education by publishing worldwide. Oxford is a registered trade mark of Oxford University Press in the UK and certain other countries.

Published in the United States of America by Oxford University Press
198 Madison Avenue, New York, NY 10016, United States of America.

© Oxford University Press 2023

Some rights reserved. No part of this publication may be reproduced, stored in a retrieval system, or transmitted, in any form or by any means, for commercial purposes, without the prior permission in writing of Oxford University Press, or as expressly permitted by law, by licence or under terms agreed with the appropriate reprographics rights organization.

This is an open access publication, available online and distributed under the terms of a Creative Commons Attribution – Non Commercial – No Derivatives 4.0 International licence (CC BY-NC-ND 4.0), a copy of which is available at http://creativecommons.org/licenses/by-nc-nd/4.0/.

You must not circulate this work in any other form and you must impose this same condition on any acquirer.

Library of Congress Cataloging-in-Publication Data
Names: Chander, Anupam, editor. | Sun, Haochen, editor.
Title: Data sovereignty : from the digital silk road to the return of the state /
Anupam Chander, Haochen Sun.
Description: New York : Oxford University Press, 2023. |
Includes bibliographical references and index. | Identifiers: LCCN 2023032525 |
ISBN 9780197582794 (hardback) | ISBN 9780197582817 (epub) |
ISBN 9780197582800 (updf) | ISBN 9780197582824 (online)
Subjects: LCSH: Internet—Law and legislation. | Data protection—Law and legislation. |
Data transmission systems—Law and legislation. | Digital media—Law and legislation. |
Privacy, Right of. | Computer networks—Law and legislation.
Classification: LCC K564.C6 D35 2023 |
DDC 343.09/944—dc23/eng/20230914
LC record available at https://lccn.loc.gov/2023032525

DOI: 10.1093/oso/9780197582794.001.0001

Printed by Integrated Books International, United States of America

Note to Readers
This publication is designed to provide accurate and authoritative information in regard to the subject matter covered. It is based upon sources believed to be accurate and reliable and is intended to be current as of the time it was written. It is sold with the understanding that the publisher is not engaged in rendering legal, accounting, or other professional services. If legal advice or other expert assistance is required, the services of a competent professional person should be sought. Also, to confirm that the information has not been affected or changed by recent developments, traditional legal research techniques should be used, including checking primary sources where appropriate.

(Based on the Declaration of Principles jointly adopted by a Committee of the American Bar Association and a Committee of Publishers and Associations.)

You may order this or any other Oxford University Press publication by visiting the Oxford University Press website at www.oup.com.

Contents

List of Contributors	xiii

Introduction: Sovereignty 2.0	1
Anupam Chander and Haochen Sun	
I. Defining Digital Sovereignty	4
II. The Rise of Digital Sovereignty	7
A. China: Inventing Digital Sovereignty	8
B. The EU: Embracing Digital Sovereignty	13
C. Russia: Promoting the Runet	14
D. The United States: Digital Sovereignty by Default	16
E. The Global South: Avoiding Data Colonialism	18
III. How Digital Sovereignty Is Different	20
A. Always Global	21
B. Against Corporations	22
C. More Control	23
D. Enables Protectionism	24
IV. Digital Sovereignty and the Russian Invasion of Ukraine	27
V. The Plan for This Volume	29

PART I RETHEORIZING DIGITAL SOVEREIGNTY

1. Two Visions for Data Governance: Territorial vs. Functional Sovereignty	35
Frank Pasquale	
I. Introducing Functional Sovereignty	37
II. Asserting Functional Sovereignty	40
III. Conclusion	47
2. A Starting Point for Re-thinking "Sovereignty" for the Online Environment	49
Dan Svantesson	
I. Introduction	49
II. The Point of Departure: Sovereignty Applies Online, but How?	50
III. Three Examples Showcasing the Messy State of Sovereignty	53
A. Sovereignty and Law Enforcement Access to Data	53
B. Sovereignty and Content Removal Orders	54
C. Sovereignty and Peacetime Cyber Espionage	54

vi CONTENTS

IV. Sovereignty and the Four Functions of International Law	55
V. The Binary Nature of the Current Concept of Sovereignty	57
VI. Sovereignty = "State" + "Exclusiveness"?	58
VII. Sovereignty— Rule or Principle?	59
VIII. "State Dignity"—the Core of Sovereignty	64
A. Sovereignty Anchored in State Dignity—A Brief Illustration	67
IX. Digital/Data Sovereignty—Political Slogan or Anchored in International Law?	69
X. Concluding Remarks	70

3. Digital Sovereignty as Double-Edged Sword   72
Anupam Chander and Haochen Sun

I. Introduction	72
II. What Is Digital Sovereignty For?	72
III. The Double-Edged Sword of Digital Sovereignty	75
A. Speech	77
B. Privacy	80
C. National Security	82
IV. Conclusion	87

4. From Data Subjects to Data Sovereigns: Addressing the Limits of Data Privacy in the Digital Era   89
Anne SY Cheung

I. Introduction	89
II. Data Subjects vs. Data Sovereigns	91
III. Data Privacy in the Time of Pandemic	96
A. The Challenge of Non-Personalized Data	96
B. From Tracking the Pandemic to Tracking Individuals	98
C. The Illusory Promise of Consent	105
IV. Beyond Privacy: From Data Subjects to Data Sovereigns	107
V. Conclusion	111

PART II TECHNOLOGY AND ECONOMIC INSTITUTIONS

5. Digital Sovereignty + Artificial Intelligence   115
Andrew Keane Woods

I. Introduction	115
II. How Digital Sovereignty Might Influence AI	119
A. Three Models	120
B. Implications	123
III. How AI Might Influence Digital Sovereignty?	125
A. Three Models	125
B. Implications	130

CONTENTS vii

IV. Key Variables		131
	A. Access to Training Data	131
	B. Industrial Policy	132
	C. National Laws and Norms	133
	D. Attitudes toward AI-Powered Machines	134
V. Conclusion		136

6. **Taobao, Federalism, and the Emergence of Law, Chinese Style** 137
Lizhi Liu and Barry R. Weingast

I. Introduction		137
II. Development and Legal Market Infrastructure		141
III. Federalism, Chinese Style: Delegation and the Origins of Chinese Political and Economic Reform, 1981–1993		143
IV. Taobao and Law, Chinese Style		145
	A. Evolution of Law, Chinese Style	146
	B. Taobao Creates a Market	147
	C. Taobao's Private Legal System	148
V. Taobao and the Evolution of Federalism, Chinese Style: Recentralization		152
	A. Decentralization and the Incomplete Common Market	153
	B. Taobao and the Formation of a Common Market	154
	C. Taobao and Recentralization	155
VI. Conclusion		157

7. **Leveling the Playing Field between Sharing Platforms and Industry Incumbents: Good Regulatory Practices?** 159
Shin-Yi Peng

I. Introduction: Increasing Regulatory Fragmentation		159
II. A Case Study: Regulating the Sharing Economy and Its "Enemies"		160
	A. Innovation: The Sharing Platforms	160
	B. Competition: The Incumbents	162
	C. Regulation: Dynamic and Divergent Approaches	164
III. Regulatory Cooperation on Platform Regulations: Good Regulatory Practices?		168
	A. Regulatory Cooperation Trends in the Regional Trade Agreements	168
	B. Good Regulatory Practices for Platform Regulations?	172
IV. Conclusion: Regulatory Cooperation and Sovereignty		176

8. **The Emergence of Financial Data Governance and the Challenge of Financial Data Sovereignty** 178
Giuliano G. Castellano, Ēriks K. Selga and Douglas W. Arner

I. Introduction		178
II. The Datafication of Finance		180
III. Financial Data Governance and General Data Governance		182
	A. Regulating Financial Data	183
	B. The Evolution of Data Governance Styles	185

viii CONTENTS

IV. Open Banking	187
V. Financial Data Governance Strategies	191
A. Property-Based: United States	192
B. Rights-Based: European Union	193
C. Shared Resource: China	196
D. Hybrid Models	199
VI. Financial Data Sovereignty: Localization vs. Globalization	202
A. Regulatory Fragmentation	202
B. Territorialization and Data Localization	205
VII. The Data Sovereignty Challenge	207

PART III TRADE REGULATION

9. Data Sovereignty and Trade Agreements: Three Digital Kingdoms 213
   Henry Gao

I. Data Sovereignty	214
II. Data Sovereignty and Trade Agreements	218
III. United States: The Firm Sovereignty Model	221
A. Firm Sovereignty	221
B. Privacy as a Consumer Right	222
C. Security as a Business Risk	223
D. Trade Agreements	224
IV. China: The State Sovereignty Model	225
A. Data Sovereignty	225
B. Trade Agreements	226
C. Personal Information Protection	227
D. "Important Data" and "Core Data"	228
V. EU: The Individual Sovereignty Model	231
A. The GDPR	231
B. Digital Sovereignty	232
C. Data Flow and Localization	234
D. Trade Agreements	235
VI. Why the Differences?	236
VII. Conclusion	238

10. Data Governance and Digital Trade in India: Losing Sight of the Forest for the Trees? 240
    Neha Mishra

I. Introduction	240
II. Data Governance in India: Multiple Narratives, Multiple Frameworks	243
A. Underlying Ideas of Data Governance	243
B. Policy Goals in Data Governance Instruments	245
C. The "Data Governance Complex" in India	249

CONTENTS   ix

III. Data Governance and Influences on Digital Trade
Policies in India   256
   A. The Nexus of Data Governance and Digital Trade   256
   B. Digital Trade Policies Reinforce the Data Governance Complex   258
   C. India in the Global Digital Trade Framework   261
IV. Conclusion   263

11. Creating Data Flow Rules through Preferential Trade
Agreements   264
Mira Burri
   I. Introduction   264
  II. Digital Trade Provisions in PTAs   267
   A. Developments over Time   267
   B. Overview of Data-Related Rules in PTAs   267
 III. Different PTA Templates for Digital Trade Governance   275
   A. The U.S. Template   275
   B. The Digital Trade Agreements of the European Union   284
   C. The RCEP   289
 IV. Conclusion   290

PART IV   DATA LOCALIZATION

12. Personal Data Localization and Sovereignty along Asia's
New Silk Roads   295
Graham Greenleaf
   I. Types of "Data Sovereignty" and "Data Localization"   296
  II. China, Russia, and Near Neighbors on the New Silk Roads   299
   A. China's Data Localizations   300
   B. Russia's Data Localizations   304
   C. Comparison of Chinese and Russian Localizations   306
 III. South Asia: Three Bills Include Localizations   308
   A. Regional Agreements   308
   B. India   309
   C. Sri Lanka   311
   D. Pakistan   312
   E. Comparison of South Asian Provisions   315
 IV. Central Asia: Five Laws Include Some Localizations   316
   A. International and Regional Agreements   318
   B. Data Localization Measures in National Laws   319
   C. Local Processing and Storage (Loc #1 and #2)   320
   D. Data Export Conditions and Prohibitions (Loc #3 and #4)   321
   E. Extraterritoriality and Local Representation (Loc #5 and #6)   323
   F. "Outsourcing Exemptions"   323
   G. Comparison of Central Asian Provisions   323

X CONTENTS

V.	How Relevant Are Free Trade Agreements?	324
	A. Adequacy and the GATS	324
	B. The Comprehensive and Progressive Agreement for Trans-Pacific Partnership (CPTPP)	326
	C. The Regional Comprehensive Economic Partnership (RCEP)	328
	D. FTAs and the Future of Data Localization	329
VI.	Conclusion	329

13. **Lessons from Internet Shutdowns Jurisprudence for Data Localization** 332

Kyung Sin Park

I.	Motivations of Data Localization	335
	A. Cybersecurity—Protection (Control) of Domestic People	335
	B. Nurturing Domestic Digital Players and Tax Revenues	336
II.	Trade Rules Applied to Data Localizations	337
	A. Applicability of Trade Rules	337
	B. Trade-Rules-Based Arguments against Data Localization	340
III.	Regulating Internet Shutdowns through Human Rights Norms	343
	A. United Nations	347
	B. UN Special Rapporteurs on Freedom of Expressions	348
	C. Joint Declarations of Special Rapporteurs on Freedom of Expression	350
	D. Europe	352
	E. Turkish Domestic Courts	356
	F. Americas	358
	G. Brazil Domestic Courts	360
	H. Africa	362
	I. Asia	363
IV.	Adaptation of the Internet Shutdown Jurisprudence for Data Localization	365
	A. Synthesis of Jurisprudence on Internet Shutdowns	365
	B. Adaptation to Data Localization	366
V.	Conclusion	370

14. **European Digital Sovereignty, Data Protection, and the Push toward Data Localization** 371

Theodore Christakis

I.	The Push Toward Data Localization in Europe	373
II.	The Need to Better Understand the Reasons behind Calls for Data Localization	374

CONTENTS   xi

III. The Influence of the *Schrems II* Judgment of the CJEU   376
   A. The Starting Point: Data Localization Is Not in the GDPR's DNA   376
   B. Calls for Data Localization After *Schrems II*   377
   C. Initial EDPB Guidance: Toward De Facto Data Localization   378
   D. The New Model SCC's and EDPB's Final Guidance:
      A Degree of Room for a Risk-Based Approach?   382
   E. Intensification of Enforcement of *Schrems II* by European
      DPAs and Rejection of a Risk-Based Approach   383
IV. Conclusion   385

List of Contributors

Douglas W. Arner, Kerry Holdings Professor in Law, University of Hong Kong Faculty of Law

Mira Burri, Professor of International Economic and Internet Law and Managing Director Internationalization, University of Lucerne Faculty of Law

Giuliano G. Castellano, Associate Professor and Deputy Director, Asian Institute of International Financial Law, University of Hong Kong Faculty of Law

Anupam Chander, Scott K. Ginsburg Professor of Law and Technology, Georgetown University Law Center

Anne SY Cheung, Professor of Law, University of Hong Kong Faculty of Law

Theodore Christakis, Professor of International and European Law, University Grenoble Alpes

Henry Gao, Professor of Law, Singapore Management University Faculty of Law

Graham Greenleaf, Professor of Law and Information Systems, UNSW Australia Faculty of Law

Lizhi Liu, Assistant Professor, McDonough School of Business, Georgetown University

Neha Mishra, Assistant Professor, Geneva Graduate Institute

Kyung Sin Park, Professor of Law, Korea University Law School and Co-Founder and Executive Director, Open Net Korea

Frank Pasquale, Professor of Law, Cornell Tech and Cornell Law School

Shin-yi Peng, Distinguished Professor of Law, National Tsing Hua University

Ēriks K. Selga, PhD Candidate, University of Hong Kong Faculty of Law

Haochen Sun, Professor of Law, University of Hong Kong Faculty of Law

Dan Svantesson, Professor of Law and Co-Director, Centre for Commercial Law, Bond University Faculty of Law

Barry R. Weingast, Senior Fellow, Hoover Institution and Ward C. Krebs Family Professor, Department of Political Science, Stanford University

Andrew Keane Woods, Milton O. Riepe Professor of Law and Distinguished Legal Scholar, the University of Arizona James E. Rogers College of Law

Introduction

Sovereignty 2.0

Anupam Chander and Haochen Sun

The Internet was supposed to end sovereignty. "Governments of the Industrial World, you weary giants of flesh and steel, you have no sovereignty where we gather," John Perry Barlow famously declared.[1] Sovereignty would prove impossible over a world of bits, with the Internet simply routing around futile controls.[2] But reports of the death of sovereignty over the Internet proved premature. Consider recent events:

- In late 2020, on the eve of what was to be the world's biggest initial public offering (IPO) ever, the Chinese government scuttled the listing of fintech provider Ant Group. Before the failed offering, Ant's CEO, Jack Ma, had made what some saw as a veiled critique of the government: "We shouldn't use the way to manage a train station to regulate an airport. . . . We cannot regulate the future with yesterday's means."[3] Chastened after Beijing's intervention, Ant announced that it would "embrace regulation," and Chinese netizens declared Jack Ma duly "tamed."[4]
- In June 2021, France fined Google $593 million for failing to follow an order to negotiate with news publishers to compensate them for displaying snippets of the publishers' news items before linking to them.[5]

---

[1] *See* John P. Barlow, *The Declaration of the Independence of Cyberspace*, ELEC. FRONTIER FOUND. (July 16, 2021), https://www.eff.org/cyberspace-independence.

[2] As John Gilmore famously announced, "The Net interprets censorship as damage and routes around it." *See* Philip Elmer-DeWitt, *First Nation in Cyberspace*, TIME, Dec. 6, 1993, at 62.

[3] Lily Kuo, *"Jack Ma Is Tamed": How Beijing Showed Tech Entrepreneur Who Is Boss*, GUARDIAN (Nov. 4, 2020), https://www.theguardian.com/business/2020/nov/04/jack-ma-ant-group-is-tamed-social-media-reacts-after-china-blocks-ipo.

[4] *Id.*

[5] *See* Gaspard Sebag, *Google Told to Pay for News with Ultimatum and $593 Million Fine*, BLOOMBERG (July 13, 2021), https://www.bloomberg.com/news/articles/2021-07-13/google-said-to-be-fined-593-million-by-french-antitrust-agency?sref=CrGXSfHu.

2   INTRODUCTION

- In July 2021, Luxembourg's privacy regulator fined Amazon $887 million for data protection violations.[6]
- European Union (EU) authorities are simultaneously investigating Google's ad technology, Apple's App Store, Facebook's Marketplace, and Amazon's use of data from its third-party sellers.[7] Even Facebook Dating receives unwanted attention from the British competition authority.[8]
- The technology giants are not safe even at home, as Ant discovered. In the home of most of the world's largest Internet companies, the U.S. Federal Trade Commission (FTC) seeks to compel Facebook to divest WhatsApp and Instagram, while investigating Amazon for competing with merchants that use its platform.[9] The federal government and all but two U.S. states are bringing antitrust claims against Google,[10] and the U.S. Justice Department is investigating Apple's App Store.[11]
- Assertions of digital sovereignty are hardly limited to Western nations. After Twitter deleted the Nigerian president's tweets warning of a new civil war, the Nigerian government in June 2021 simply banned Twitter from the country. On the eve of an election in January 2021, Uganda went even further, ordering a complete shutdown of the Internet, with President Yoweri Museveni explaining that Facebook had deleted pro-government accounts as manipulative.[12] Uganda followed the example of Zimbabwe, which responded to anti-government protests in 2019 by shuttering the Internet.[13]

---

[6] *See* Taylor Telford, *E.U. Regulator Hits Amazon with Record $887 Million Fine for Data Protection Violations*, WASH. POST (July 30, 2021), https://www.washingtonpost.com/business/2021/07/30/amazon-record-fine-europe/.

[7] *See* Sam Schechner & Parmy Olson, *Google Faces EU Antitrust Probe of Alleged Ad-Tech Abuses*, WALL ST. J. (June 22, 2021), https://www.wsj.com/articles/google-faces-eu-antitrust-probe-of-alleged-ad-tech-abuses-11624355128.

[8] *See* Press Release, U.K. Competition & Mkts. Auth., CMA Investigates Facebook's Use of Ad Data (June 4, 2021), https://www.gov.uk/government/news/cma-investigates-facebook-s-use-of-ad-data.

[9] Press Release, Fed. Trade Comm'n, FTC's Bureau of Competition Launches Task Force to Monitor Technology Markets (Feb. 26, 2019), https://www.ftc.gov/news-events/press-releases/2019/02/ftcs-bureau-competition-launches-task-force-monitor-technology.

[10] *See* Press Release, Dep't of Justice, Justice Department Sues Monopolist Google for Violating Antitrust Laws (Oct. 20, 2020), https://www.justice.gov/opa/pr/justice-department-sues-monopolist-google-violating-antitrust-laws.

[11] *See* Leah Nylen, *Apple's Easy Fide from U.S. Authorities May be Over*, POLITICO (June 24, 2020), https://www.politico.com/news/2020/06/24/justice-department-anti-trust-apple-337120.

[12] *See* Stephen Kafeero, *Uganda Has Cut Off Its Entire Internet Hours to Its Election Polls Opening*, QUARTZ AFRICA (Jan. 13, 2021), https://qz.com/africa/1957137/uganda-cuts-off-internet-ahead-of-election-polls-opening/.

[13] *See Zimbabwe Imposes Internet Shutdown Amid Crackdown on Protests*, AL JAZEERA (Jan. 18, 2019), https://www.aljazeera.com/news/2019/1/18/zimbabwe-imposes-internet-shutdown-amid-crackdown-on-protests.

The state (both nation-state as well as nearly every U.S. state) strikes back.[14] When Thomas Hobbes imagined an "Artificial Man" in the form of a state,[15] he was not picturing Facebook. But the reality is that modern leviathans like Facebook and Google, and even Reddit, Spotify, and Twitter, exercise enormous power over daily life. Increasingly, governments across the world have sought to bring these companies under their control. While China pioneered data sovereignty, it is now the demand of governments from Australia to Zimbabwe. The era of countries unsure whether they had the power to regulate the Internet is over.

Consider, for example, Vietnam's 2018 Law on Cybersecurity, which explicitly declares as its goal the protection of "national cyberspace." Its definition of security includes not just national security, but explicitly also "social order and safety, and the lawful rights and interests of organizations and individuals in cyberspace."[16] While there may be no official signs that one is "Now Entering Vietnamese Cyberspace" to greet visitors, the government clearly believes that Vietnamese cyberspace is not some metaphysical place outside its control.

In February 2022, Vietnam's Southeast Asian neighbor Cambodia suspended its plans to route all Internet traffic into or out of the country through an Internet gateway. Human Rights Watch declared that the true purpose of this infrastructure plan was to "tighten the noose on what remains of internet freedom in the country."[17] Even while suspending its plans, the Cambodian government defended itself, arguing that its goals were to "strengthen national security and tax collection as well as to maintain social order and protect national culture."[18] At the same time, the government insisted, without

---

[14] For a round-up of some recent enforcement actions faced by the biggest technology companies, *see* Joe Panettieri, *Big Tech Antitrust Investigations: Amazon, Apple, Facebook and Google Updates*, CHANNELE2E (Dec. 24, 2021), https://www.channele2e.com/business/compliance/big-tech-antitrust-regulatory-breakup-updates/.

[15] THOMAS HOBBES, LEVIATHAN (1651) ("[A]s men, for the atteyning of peace, and conservation of themselves thereby, have made an Artificiall Man, which we call a Common-wealth; so also have they made Artificiall Chains, called Civill Lawes, which they themselves, by mutuall covenants, have fastned at one end, to the lips of that Man, or Assembly, to whom they have given the Soveraigne Power; and at the other end to their own Ears.").

[16] Vietnam Law of Cybersecurity, art. 6.

[17] Human Rights Watch, *Cambodia Should Scrap Rights-Abusing National Internet Gateway*, May 16, 2022, https://www.hrw.org/news/2022/05/16/cambodia-should-scrap-rights-abusing-national-internet-gateway.

[18] Cambodian Ministry of Foreign Affairs, *Clarification by the Spokesperson of the Ministry of Foreign Affairs and International Cooperation on the National Internet Gateway Establishment*, Feb. 15, 2022, https://www.mfaic.gov.kh/posts/2022-02-15-Press-Release-Clarification-by-the-Spokesperson-of-the-Ministry-of-Foreign-Affairs-and-International-Cooperation-o-10-50-07.

4 INTRODUCTION

evidence, that such national Internet gateways "prevail in almost all countries around the world."

Against this backdrop, scholars are sharply divided about the increasing assertion of what is called variously "data sovereignty" or "digital sovereignty." Some scholars see it as a natural extension of traditional Westphalian sovereignty to the 21st century.[19] They are joined by other scholars, often from the Global South, who support data sovereignty in order to repulse imperial ambitions for data colonialism, a barricade against the exploitative and extractive practices of Western (and Chinese) technology giants.[20] Other scholars, however, worry that data sovereignty will break the Web apart, jeopardizing its numerous global benefits.[21] As Mark Lemley astutely laments, "The news you see, the facts you see, and even the maps you see change depending on where you are."[22]

This introduction proceeds as follows. Part I reviews some prominent definitions of "digital sovereignty" and "data sovereignty." Part II reviews the rise of digital sovereignty, focusing on four influential jurisdictions (the United States, China, the European Union, and Russia) and also the developing world. Part III describes some ways in which digital sovereignty is different than ordinary terrestrial sovereignty. Part IV considers the struggle for control of cyberspace that followed the Russian invasion of Ukraine. Part V concludes with a sketch of the plan for the volume that follows.

I. Defining Digital Sovereignty

At first glance, the term "sovereignty" over parts of the Internet may seem entirely out of place. After all, one of the prerequisites for the recognition of the sovereignty of a state in international law is the exercise of power over a

---

[19] *See, e.g.*, Andrew Keane Woods, *Litigating Data Sovereignty*, 128 YALE L.J. 328, 366–71 (2018) (arguing that we should "embrace [] sovereign differences" rather than opt for a single set of rules everywhere).

[20] *See* Renata Avila Pinto, *Digital Sovereignty or Digital Colonialism*, 27 SUR - INT'L J. HUM. RTS. 15, 23–24 (2018); Nick Couldry & Ulises A. Mejias, *Data Colonialism: Rethinking Big Data's Relation to the Contemporary Subject*, 20 TELEVISION & NEW MEDIA 336, 337 (2019); *cf.* JULIE E. COHEN, BETWEEN TRUTH AND POWER: THE LEGAL CONSTRUCTIONS OF INFORMATIONAL CAPITALISM 51 (2019) (noting the distributive nature of the construction of a "biopolitical public domain," where raw data is a resource to be processed).

[21] *See* Mark A. Lemley, *The Splinternet*, 70 DUKE L.J. 1397, 1427 (2021) ("[W]e should fight hard not to give up the Internet for an information superhighway, particularly one that's controlled by our national governments.").

[22] *Id.* at 1409.

territory.[23] Andrew Woods grounds his definition of "data sovereignty" in three core elements of state sovereignty: "(1) supreme control; (2) over a territory; (3) independent from other sovereigns."[24] The tension between the notion of "digital sovereignty" and the territorial foundation for sovereignty disappears when one recognizes that in order to exercise control over any territory, it is increasingly necessary to exercise control over the online activities available in that territory. This insight connects place and cyberspace. Woods writes that, in order to control data within their borders to the exclusion of other states, "states can command considerable control over the internet if only because they control the physical components of the network within their borders" through "an impressive arsenal of tools."[25] Dan Svantesson rightly observes that sovereignty should not have to be all or nothing, and so perhaps Woods's requirement of exclusivity is unnecessarily strict for a claim of data sovereignty.[26] For Woods, a state's data sovereignty powers include powers to compel compliance ("leav[ing] companies and their users free to design and use the internet as they see fit, as long as they comply when the government comes knocking") and powers to control the means of compliance ("the state tells internet firms how to operate").[27] It seems clear that multiple states are able to order the same firm how to operate, with occasional conflicts in approaches.[28]

Ke Xu divides sovereignty in cyberspace into three layers: the physical layer (sovereignty over physical Internet infrastructure and activities), the code layer (sovereignty over domain names, Internet standards, and regulations), and the data layer.[29] Like Hobbes, Luciano Floridi begins by theorizing individual sovereignty, which he defines in 21st-century terms as "self-ownership, especially over one's own body, choices, and data,"[30] and

---

[23] Article 1 of the Montevideo Convention on Rights and Duties of States provides as follows: "The state as a person of international law should possess the following qualifications: (a) a permanent population; (b) a defined territory; (c) government; and (d) capacity to enter into relations with the other states."

[24] Woods, *supra* note 19, at 360.

[25] *Id.* at 360–61.

[26] Dan Svantesson, "*A Starting Point for Re-thinking 'Sovereignty' for the Online Environment*," chapter in this volume.

[27] Woods, *supra* note 19, at 364.

[28] One prominent dispute involving a possible conflict—the Microsoft dispute with the U.S. authorities over data held in Ireland—did not create a hard conflict of laws because Ireland did not explicitly claim that transferring the data to the United States would be illegal under Irish law. United States v. Microsoft Corp., 138 S. Ct. 1186 (2018).

[29] Ke Xu, *Data Security Law: Location, Position and Institution Construction*, 3 BUS. & ECON. L. REV. 52, 57 (2019).

[30] Luciano Floridi, *The Fight for Digital Sovereignty: What It Is, and Why It Matters, Especially for the EU*, 33 PHIL. & TECH. 369, 371 (2020).

6 INTRODUCTION

then extends this to "digital sovereignty," which he defines as the "control of data, software (e.g., AI), standards and protocols (e.g., 5G, domain names), processes (e.g., cloud computing), hardware (e.g., mobile phones), services (e.g., social media, e-commerce), and infrastructures (e.g., cables, satellites, smart cities)."[31]

Data sovereignty, as argued by Paul Rosenzweig, may also be framed as a question: Which sovereign controls the data?[32] The core issue is one of jurisdiction, which is, of course, complicated by the borderless nature of the Internet.[33] "In short, the question is: 'Whose law is to be applied?'"[34] Rosenzweig argues that physical location is, as a practical matter, critical: "Where the servers are and where the data is stored will, in the end, likely control whose law applies. As they say, 'geography is destiny.'"[35] Certainly, the physical control over the network made possible through Internet service providers that route data is a key to digital sovereignty, at least where foreign corporations do not comply on other grounds.

We will use the term "digital sovereignty" to mean the application of traditional state sovereignty over the online domain,[36] or simply "sovereignty in the digital age."[37] Digital sovereignty should be defined broadly to cover a state's sovereign power to regulate not only cross-border flow of data through uses of Internet filtering technologies and data localization mandates, but also speech activities (e.g., combating fake news) and access to technologies. We use the term in a descriptive way to describe efforts by governments to assert control over online activities, often instantiated through actions targeted at Internet intermediaries. Notably, academics and news media are more likely to speak in terms of "data sovereignty" than "digital sovereignty," as a search of the database ProQuest shows:[38]

---

[31] *Id.* at 370–71.

[32] *See* Paul Rosenzweig, *The International Governance Framework for Cybersecurity*, 37 Can.-U.S. L.J. 405, 421 (2012).

[33] *See id.*

[34] *Id.* at 422.

[35] *Id.*

[36] This accords with the French Senate investigatory committee report, which defines digital sovereignty as the "capacity of the state to act in cyberspace." Le Devoir De Souveraineté Numérique: Ni Résignation, Ni Naïveté, Senat (2019), http://www.senat.fr/fileadmin/Fichiers/Images/redaction_multimedia/2019/2019_Infographies/20191004_infog_Souverainete_numerique_021019.pdf.

[37] Paul Timmers, *Challenged by "Digital Sovereignty,"* 23(6) J. Internet L. 1, 18 (2019).

[38] This search run on ProQuest on July 16, 2021, updates an analysis by Stephane Couture & Sophie Toupin, *What Does the Notion of "Sovereignty" Mean When Referring to the Digital?*, 21 New Media & Soc'y 2305, 2306 (2019). Note that the "other" category includes newspapers, trade journals, magazines, reports, blogs, books, and working papers.

	Data Sovereignty		Digital Sovereignty	
	Academic	Other	Academic	Other
2019– June 30, 2023	919	2672	224	1465

It is possible to draw a distinction between "data sovereignty" and "digital sovereignty," where "data sovereignty" refers to control over data, including through data protection law, competition law, and national security law. This definition would make data sovereignty a subset of digital sovereignty. But the relationship between "data sovereignty" thus defined and broader issues such as content moderation quickly becomes difficult to disentangle. Stopping information from flowing across borders, for example, implicates speech and commerce, as well as data governance. Indeed, a distinction between dominion over "data" and dominion over the "digital" is hard to sustain. *In framing this book, we have chosen to use both* "data sovereignty" and "digital sovereignty," recognizing that the term is sometimes used distinctly with "data sovereignty" and sometimes interchangeably. Indeed, we ourselves began the project using the term "data sovereignty," and then adopted the broader term in the course of writing in order to ensure that we captured the breadth of the topic.

II. The Rise of Digital Sovereignty

In this part, we review the effort to attain digital sovereignty in a few key jurisdictions. The review reveals at least three different motivations for assertions of digital sovereignty. First, governments demand digital sovereignty to better protect their population—seeking, for example, to remove material deemed illegal under their laws or to protect the rights of citizens in the digital domain. This often takes the form of regulating foreign corporations that intermediate data flows for the local population. Second, governments seek digital sovereignty in an effort to grow their own digital economy, sometimes by displacing foreign corporations, from fintech to social media. Third, governments seek digital sovereignty to better control their populations—to limit what they can say, read, or do.

8 INTRODUCTION

A. China: Inventing Digital Sovereignty

In the mid-1990s, when the world started coming online, China's Ministry of Public Security inaugurated its "Golden Shield Project," 金盾工程, which has been described as "a far-ranging attempt to harness emerging information technologies for policing."[39] Henry Gao observed that Chinese digital sovereignty evolved through different phases—physical controls and then controls over the software layer and content.[40] In other words, it went up the Internet stack.[41] As James Fallows wrote in a classic Western account of "the Great Firewall of China," "[i]n China, the Internet came with choke points built in."[42] China takes a multifaceted approach to exerting digital sovereignty, which includes controlling its physical infrastructure, regulating content, balancing negative economic impacts, and building international support for its conception of digital sovereignty.[43] The most prominent aspect of China's physical infrastructure innovation is the "Great Firewall," which is used by the government to block access to content for users in China.[44] However, sometimes the firewall causes collateral impact on Internet freedom beyond China's borders through domain name system pollution, where Chinese domain name servers accidentally serve foreign users, thus inadvertently blocking access to websites by users in other countries.[45]

In 2010, the Chinese State Council officially declared its support for "Internet sovereignty" (*wangluo zhuquan* or 网络主权) in a white paper entitled "The Internet in China." The white paper declared, "Within Chinese territory the Internet is under the jurisdiction of Chinese sovereignty. The Internet sovereignty of China should be respected and protected."[46] The link

---

[39] Lorand Laskai, *Nailing Jello to the Wall, in* JANE GOLLEY, LINDA JAIVIN, & LUIGI TOMBA, CONTROL 192, 194 (2017).

[40] Henry Gao, *Data Regulation with Chinese Characteristics, in* BIG DATA AND TRADE 245, 248 (ed. Mira Burri, 2021) (noting that 1996 and 1997 Chinese "regulations all focused on the Internet hardware," while attention was paid later to software and content).

[41] The architecture of the Internet is often described as consisting in stacked layers, from the physical infrastructure to the applications and uses that run atop that infrastructure. *See* Christopher S. Yoo, *Protocol Layering and Internet Policy*, 161 U. PA. L. REV. 1707, 1742 (2013).

[42] James Fallows, *The Connection Has Been Reset*, ATLANTIC (Mar. 2008), https://www.theatlantic.com/magazine/archive/2008/03/the-connection-has-been-reset/306650/.

[43] Anqi Wang, *Cyber Sovereignty at Its Boldest: A Chinese Perspective*, 16 OHIO ST. TECH. L.J. 395, 403 (2020); *Protecting Internet Security*, CHINA.ORG, http://www.china.org.cn/government/whitepaper/2010-06/08/content_20207978.htm (last visited Jan. 14, 2022).

[44] *See* Wang, *supra* note 43, at 408, 439.

[45] *See id.* at 408, 439–41; Robert McMillan, *China's Great Firewall Spreads Overseas*, COMPUTERWORLD (Mar. 25, 2010), https://www.computerworld.com/article/2516831/china-s-great-firewall-spreads-overseas.html [https://perma.cc/E2U5-FBHP] (archived Jan. 9, 2022).

[46] *See* Wang, *supra* note 43, at 397.

to territoriality seems to be both a nod to international law and also part of a long-standing Chinese Communist Party official approach to international relations that pledged non-interference in the internal affairs of foreign countries.[47] In 2015, President Xi explained that "respecting cyber-sovereignty" meant "respecting each country's right to choose its own internet development path, its own internet management model, its own public policies on the internet, and to participate on an equal basis in the governance of international cyberspace — avoiding cyber-hegemony, and avoiding interference in the internal affairs of other countries."[48]

China escalated the tech cold war. The Cybersecurity Administration of China opened investigations into the data transfer practices of Chinese tech giant Didi immediately following that company's New York Stock Exchange listing. It then ordered Didi removed from Chinese app stores.[49] Even though Didi's stock price plummeted, Chinese media celebrated the "rise of data sovereignty."[50]

China's conception of digital sovereignty is rooted, Anqi Wang writes, in traditional notions of territorial sovereignty[51] and officially justified by concern for national and ideological security.[52] China supports a "state-centric multilateralism" model of Internet governance,[53] which holds that states, not private sector actors like the Internet Corporation for Assigned Names and

---

[47] *See* Anupam Chander, *The Asian Century?*, 44 U.C. DAVIS L. REV. 717, 727 (2011) (noting the Five Principles for Peaceful Coexistence, including "mutual non-interference in each other's internal affairs").

[48] *See* Wang, *supra* note 43, at 397; Franz-Stefan Gady, *The Wuzhen Summit and the Battle Over Internet Governance*, DIPLOMAT (Jan. 14, 2016), https://thediplomat.com/2016/01/the-wuzhen-summit-and-the-battle-over-internet-governance/; Bruce Sterling, *Respecting Chinese and Russian Cyber-Sovereignty in the Formerly Global Internet*, WIRED (Dec. 22, 2015), https://www.wired.com/beyond-the-beyond/2015/12/respecting-chinese-and-russian-cyber-sovereignty-in- the-formerly-global-internet/ [https://perma.cc/K743-B5VD] (archived Jan. 9, 2022).

[49] *See* Jacky Wong, *Didi and the Big Chill on China's Big Data*, WALL ST. J. (July 5, 2021), https://www.wsj.com/articles/didi-and-the-big-chill-on-chinas-big-data-11625479452 (subscription required).

[50] *See* Li Qiaoyi & Hu Yuwei, *Chinese Regulator Orders App Stores to Remove Didi, Shows Resolve to Enhance Data Protection*, GLOBAL TIMES (July 4, 2021), https://www.globaltimes.cn/page/202107/1227778.shtml ("Ride-hailing firms manage large amounts of data regarding national transport infrastructure, flows of people and vehicles, among other types of information that involve national security, according to Dong. The rise of 'data sovereignty' versus the U.S. government's vigilance against Chinese firms ought to be a wake-up call for national security awareness to be given priority when it comes to fundraising plans in areas that might pose threats to China's national security, Dong told the Global Times on Sunday.").

[51] *See* Wang, *supra* note 43, at 397.

[52] *See id.* at 424 (explaining China views cybersecurity as another national security domain alongside land, sea, air, and space).

[53] *Id.* at 443–44.

10 INTRODUCTION

Numbers (ICANN), should be driving Internet governance.[54] In contrast, the "bottom-up multi-stakeholderism" subscribed to by the United States and other Western countries[55] holds that the private sector and civil society should remain key players in Internet governance.[56] The Western "information freedom" approach to the Internet[57] is perceived as a threat to "Chinese ideological security" and a tool of cultural imperialism.[58] The Chinese government instead seeks to use the Internet to consolidate party control, maintain social order, and proliferate desirable Socialist and Confucian values such as "'patriotism,' 'loyalty to the communist party,' 'dedication to one's work,' 'honesty,' [and] 'filial piety,'" to "develop a cohesive, Socialist nation."[59] President Xi affirmed this vision in 2016, stating, "we must . . . strengthen positive online propaganda, foster a positive, healthy, upward and benevolent online culture, use the Socialist core value view and the excellent civilizational achievements of humankind to nourish people's hearts and nourish society."[60]

China sees U.S. Internet infrastructure hegemony as a threat to its digital sovereignty.[61] In 2016, President Xi stated, "the fact that [the internet's] core technology is controlled by others is our greatest hidden danger."[62] Accordingly, the government has been investing heavily in research and development of Internet technology[63] and "territorializing critical infrastructure"[64] to escape Western technical and physical network dependence. Part of this effort has been a proliferation of Critical Information Infrastructure (CII) regulations,[65] including data localization regulations through the 2017 Cybersecurity Law (CSL).[66] Not only does Article 37 of the CSL require that data and personal information originating in China be stored within China,

---

[54] *See id.* (explaining that China opposes the current system where a U.S. corporation, ICANN (Internet Corporation for Assigned Names and Numbers), controls root ownership).

[55] *Id.* at 399.

[56] *See id.* at 444.

[57] *Id.* at 400.

[58] *Id.* at 406.

[59] *Id.* at 407.

[60] *Xi Jinping Gives Speech at Cybersecurity and Informatization Work Conference*, CHINA COPYRIGHT & MEDIA (Apr. 19, 2016), https://chinacopyrightandmedia.wordpress.com/2016/04/19/xi-jinping-gives-speech-at-cybersecurity-and-informatization-work-conference/ [https://perma.cc/JH49-FMJM] (archived Jan. 9, 2022).

[61] *See* Wang, *supra* note 43, at 404–05 (explaining that China perceives U.S. corporate and civil society control over domain names and U.S.-made infrastructure as favoring U.S. interests).

[62] *Id.* at 405.

[63] *See id.* at 434, 436.

[64] *Id.* at 435.

[65] *See id.* at 436–37.

[66] *See id.* at 408, 456.

but CII operators must also undergo "security assessments" before that data can be transferred abroad.[67] (The first such security assessment—against the ride-hailing company Didi—is described below.)

Content regulation and censorship is another integral component of China's "information sovereignty" on the Internet.[68] Though China's approach to content regulation is more extreme than in other countries,[69] it rejects accusations that its cyber sovereignty policies simply mask authoritarian control.[70] Instead, the government claims to censor "subversive," "harmful," "obscene," or "malicious" content while welcoming "kind criticism."[71] Content control remains a clear goal. In 2017, the Cyber Administration of China (CAC) asserted that "Online positive publicity must become bigger and stronger, so that the Party's ideas always become the strongest voice in cyberspace."[72] The Theoretical Studies Center Group of CAC also commented in the Communist Party magazine Qiushi that "[w]e must . . . steadily control all kinds of major public opinion; dare to grasp, dare to control, and dare to wield the bright sword; refute erroneous ideas in a timely manner" to "prevent mass incidents and public opinion from becoming online ideological patterns and issues."[73]

Some of the measures China takes to regulate content and maintain a "clear cyberspace"[74] include blocking virtual private network (VPN) access, algorithms that divert searches, the Real Name Registration Policy,[75]

---

[67] *See id.* at 456–57; Willem Gravett, *Digital Neo-Colonialism: The Chinese Model of Internet Sovereignty in Africa*, 20 AFR. HUM. RTS. L.J. 125, 130 (2020) (data on Chinese users must be hosted on Chinese mainland); *Cross-Border Data Transfers: CSL vs. GDPR*, REED SMITH (Jan. 2, 2018), https://www.reedsmith.com/en/perspectives/2018/01/cross-border-data-transfer-csl-vs-gdpr [https://perma.cc/HXT2-73TD] (archived Jan. 9, 2022); Samm Sacks, *China's Cybersecurity Law Takes Effect: What to Expect*, LAWFARE BLOG (June 1, 2017, 10:56 AM), https://www.lawfareb log.com/chinas-cybersecurity-law-takes-effect-what-expect [https://perma.cc/2GWM-VYST] (archived Jan. 9, 2022).

[68] *See* Wang, *supra* note 43, at 452.

[69] *See id.* at 466.

[70] *See id.* at 416.

[71] *Id.* at 422. President Xi commented that "to build a well-functioned Internet public sphere is not to censor all negative comments and only endorse a single perspective; it is to welcome, investigate, and learn lessons from the kind criticism but reject those comments which turn things upside down, mix the black with the white, spread rumors with malicious intentions, commit crimes and override the Constitution." *Id.* at 416.

[72] Elsa Kania, Samm Sacks, Paul Triolo, & Graham Webster, *China's Strategic Thinking on Building Power in Cyberspace*, NEW AM. (Sept. 25, 2017), https://www.newamerica.org/cybersecurity-ini tiative/blog/chinas-strategic-thinking-building-power-cyberspace; Wang, *supra* note 43, at 453; Gravett, *supra* note 67, at 131.

[73] Wang, note 43, at 455–56.

[74] *Id.* at 455.

[75] *Id.* at 456; Gravett, *supra* note 67, at 130 (describing a 2017 law that makes social media companies register users with their real names).

12 INTRODUCTION

and making domain name service providers responsible for content by their clients through a 2017 update to Article 28 of the Measures for the Administration of Internet Domain Names Law.[76] However, standards for what information is "erroneous" or in violation of the law remain unclear.[77] The government also introduced an "Interview Mechanism," which functions as a warning to websites and companies hosting prohibited content before sanctions, fines, or criminal prosecutions are pursued.[78] Such interviews incentivize self-correction and willing removal of censored content by allowing websites to stay up and avoid fines or harsher penalties like closure.[79]

Through its "Digital Silk Road," which adopts one of the authors' framing of the Internet as the "Electronic Silk Road,"[80] China has sought to advance its digital trade connections with developing countries across the world. This part of China's Belt and Road Initiative promotes collaboration between China and developing countries in critical Internet infrastructure projects, e-commerce, and artificial intelligence (AI).[81] By increasing developing African and Eurasian nations' Internet access,[82] as well as their dependence on Chinese technology, China acquires soft power while creating new markets for Chinese technology exports and e-commerce.[83] Many Western governments have expressed concern that China's grip on developing nations' Internet infrastructure could leave them vulnerable to possible surveillance by either China or local governments.[84] Thus, even as the Chinese government worries about foreign influences via the Internet, many other governments worry about the Chinese government exerting its influence via the Internet. China looms especially large in the geopolitics that are driving many assertions of digital sovereignty.

---

[76] *See* Wang, note 43, at 457–58.
[77] *See id.*
[78] *See id.* at 459–61, 464.
[79] *See id.* at 460–61, 464.
[80] ANUPAM CHANDER, THE ELECTRONIC SILK ROAD (2013).
[81] *See* Wang, *supra* note 43, at 441.
[82] *See id.* at 416–17.
[83] *See id.* at 447; Gravett, *supra* note 67, at 131 (international consensus building).
[84] *See* Wang, *supra* note 43, at 441–42.

B. The EU: Embracing Digital Sovereignty

Nowhere have calls for digital sovereignty been more intense than in Europe. As early as 2006, President Jacques Chirac of France called on Europeans to develop an indigenous information search capacity to respond to "the global challenge posed by Google and Yahoo."[85] As early as 2010, the French government was sounding the alarm about the loss of sovereignty in the face of foreign technology firms. François Fillon, then prime minister, observed that with respect to cloud computing, "North Americans dominate this market, which nevertheless constitutes an absolutely major stake for the competitiveness of our economies, for sustainable development and even, I dare say it, for the sovereignty of our countries."[86] Among the strategies the government adopted was the promotion of "*le cloud souverain*"—the "sovereign cloud"—through partnerships with cloud computing enterprises to support domestic employment, among other goals.[87] In 2013, the French government detailed efforts to "build a France of digital sovereignty," including the desire to make to "make France the world leader" in the field of "Big Data."[88]

EU digital sovereignty has been expressed perhaps most fully through a robust assertion of data protection law. The EU's data protection law covers not only companies based in the EU but also foreign companies that target

---

[85] CHANDER, *supra* note 80, at 40.

[86] Pierre Noro, *Le Cloud Souverain Est De Retour: Généalogie D'une Ambition Emblématique De La Souveraineté Numérique En France*, SCIENCESPO: CHAIRE DIGITAL, GOUVERNANCE ET SOUVERAINETÉ (July 20, 2020), https://www.sciencespo.fr/public/chaire-numerique/2020/07/20/cloud-souverain-genealogie-ambition-emblematique-souverainete-numerique/ (speech by Prime Minister François Fillon on broadband and the digital economy, Jan. 18, 2010).

[87] The French government then invested in two French cloud projects. *See* Delphine Cuny, *"Cloud" à la Française: Fleur Pellerin Justifie les Deux Projets Concurrents*, LA TRIBUNE (Oct. 2, 2012), https://www.latribune.fr/technos-medias/informatique/20121002trib000722485/cloud-a-la-francaise-fleur-pellerin-justifie-les-deux-projets-concurrents.html. Germany too has pursued a similar data sovereignty strategy by establishing local cloud centers for the storage of government information. *See* Andrew D. Mitchell & Jarrod Hepburn, *Don't Fence Me In: Reforming Trade and Investment Law to Better Facilitate Cross-Border Data Transfer*, 19 YALE J.L. & TECH. 182, 189 (2017).

[88] *See* MINISTÈRE DU REDRESSEMENT PRODUCTIF [MINISTRY OF ECON. REGENERATION], THE NEW FACE OF INDUSTRY IN FRANCE 51 (2013), available at https://www.economie.gouv.fr/files/nouvelle_france_industrielle_english.pdf [hereinafter NEW FACE OF INDUSTRY] (cited in Anupam Chander & Uyên P. Lê, *Data Nationalism*, 64 EMORY L.J. 677, 690–91 (2015)). President François Hollande announced the national innovation program on September 12, 2013, with a plan that used the term "sovereignty" no less than a dozen times. *See* Nicholas Vinocur, *Hollande Turns to Robots, Driverless Cars to Revive French Industry*, REUTERS (Sept. 12, 2013), https://www.reuters.com/article/france-industry/hollande-turns-to-robots-driverless-cars-to-rev ive-french-industry-idUSL5N0H73T020130912.

14 INTRODUCTION

EU residents and process information about them. This extraterritorial application of law has made the EU into an Internet-regulatory superpower.[89]

The German government announced in July 2020 that it would "establish digital sovereignty as a leitmotiv of European digital policy."[90] The European Commission similarly declared its intention to "strengthen its digital sovereignty and set standards, rather than following those of others."[91]

C. Russia: Promoting the Runet

Russia has embraced digital sovereignty as official policy, even seeking to create an entirely separable Russian Internet, dubbed the "Runet." This reflects a u-turn in policy from early years when the Russian government embraced the Internet as a means to transform the country from reliance on natural resources. In the wake of the Arab Spring, the Russian government began to assert greater control of the Internet, recognizing the Internet's demonstrated potential to help bring down governments.[92] Today, Russia's official policy is to create a "sovereign Runet"—a Russian Internet where the Russian government exercises "more control over what its citizens can access."[93] In 2019, Vladimir Putin signed a "Sovereign Internet" bill into law, gaining broad powers to monitor and control traffic on the Russian Internet through hardware and software controls installed in Russian telecommunications infrastructure and even to restrict the global Internet in certain

---

[89] ANU BRADFORD, THE BRUSSELS EFFECT: HOW THE EUROPEAN UNION RULES THE WORLD (2020) (noting that "the EU remains an influential superpower that shapes the world in its image"); Anupam Chander, Margot E. Kaminski, & William McGeveran, *Catalyzing Privacy*, 105 MINN. L. REV. 1733, 1734 (2021) (explaining that the GDPR's effectuation "positioned the European Union as the world's privacy champion.").

[90] TOGETHER FOR EUROPE'S RECOVERY, PROGRAMME FOR GERMANY'S PRESIDENCY OF THE COUNCIL OF THE EU 2020 8 (2020), available at https://www.eu2020.de/blob/2360248/978a43ce1 7c65efa8f506c2a484c8f2c/pdf-programm-en-data.pdf.

[91] *A Europe Fit for the Digital Age*, EUR. COMMISSION, https://ec.europa.eu /info/strategy/priorities-2019-2024/europe-fit-digital-age_en (last visited Jan. 15, 2022) [https://perma.cc/RJ6Z-FKB7] (archived Jan. 15, 2022). The German Presidency of the EU Council declared in 2020, "Europe must bolster its digital sovereignty to effectively respond to future challenges, guarantee livelihoods and ensure the security of its citizens." *See Expanding the EU's Digital Sovereignty*, EU2020, https://www.eu2020 .de/eu2020-en/eu-digitalisation-technology-sovereignty/2352828 (last visited Jan. 14, 2022).

[92] *See* Alexandra V. Orlova, *"Digital Sovereignty," Anonymity and Freedom of Expression: Russia's Fight to Re-Shape Internet Governance*, 26 U.C. DAVIS J. INT'L L. & POL'Y 225, 228 (2020).

[93] *See* Jane Wakefield, *Russia "Successfully Tests" Its Unplugged Internet*, BBC NEWS (Dec. 24, 2019), https://www.bbc.com/news/technology-50902496 [https://perma.cc /QK3E-2668] (archived Jan. 9, 2022) (quoting Professor Alan Woodward as saying that the Runet would keep Russian citizens "within their own bubble").

cases.[94] Ironically, given prolific Russian interventions in elections abroad, Russian demands for a sovereign Internet are driven in part by claims of "information warfare" waged by Western countries against the Russian government.[95] One of the goals of the Runet is to protect the Russian internet from "external negative influences."[96]

Russia employs a common and highly controversial tactic for implementing digital sovereignty: data localization.[97] Law No. 242-FZ, which came into effect in 2015, requires data operators to ensure that the recording, systematization, accumulation, storage, update/amendment, and retrieval of personal data of citizens of the Russian Federation are made using databases located in the Russian Federation.[98] In 2015, a Russian court blocked LinkedIn from the country for failure to localize data. In 2020, Russian regulators fined Facebook, Google, and Twitter for refusing to store their data in Russia, with Facebook paying the $53,000 penalty in 2021.[99] In 2021, Russia's Internet regulator Roskomnadzor throttled traffic to Twitter after Twitter failed to delete posts urging children to take part in anti-government protests.[100] Roskomnadzor has also threatened to throttle Google's traffic if it refuses to localize data.[101]

---

[94] *See* Ksenia Koroleva, Ulrich Wuermeling, & Tim Wybitul, *RuNet Law Comes into Force: What Is Next*, JDSUPRA (Nov. 27, 2019), https://www.jdsupra.com/legalnews/runet-law-comes-into-force-what-is-next-72937/.

[95] Orlova, *supra* note 92, at 231.

[96] *See The Ministry of Telecom and Mass Communications: Government Agencies and Telecom Operators Are Ready to Ensure Stable Operation of the Runet*, TASS (Dec. 23, 2019), https://tass.ru/ekonomika/7407631.

[97] For an argument that data localization both undermines domestic development and increases the power of local authoritarians, *see generally* Anupam Chander & Uyên P. Lê, *Data Nationalism*, 64 EMORY L.J. 677 (2015).

[98] *See* Federal'nyy zakon No. 242-FZ ot 21 iyulya 2014 g. O vnesenii izmeneniy v nekotoryye zakonodatel'nyye akty Rossiyskoy Federatsii v chasti, kasayushcheysya obnovleniya poryadka obrabotki personal'nykh dannykh v informatsionno-telekommunikatsionnykh setyakh [Federal Law No. 242-FZ of July 21, 2014 on Amending Some Legislative Acts of the Russian Federation in as Much as It Concerns Updating the Procedure for Personal Data Processing in Information-Telecommunication Networks], FEDERAL'NYY ZAKON [FZ] [Federal Law] 2014, No. 242-FZ, art. 18 § 5.

[99] *See* Adrian Shahbaz, Allie Funk, & Andrea Hackl, *Special Report 2020: User Privacy or Cyber Sovereignty?*, FREEDOM HOUSE, https://freedomhouse.org/report/special-report/2020/user-privacy-or-cyber-sovereignty (last visited Jan. 14, 2022); *Facebook Pays Russia $50K Fine For Not Localizing User Data*, MOSCOW TIMES (Nov. 26, 2020), https://www.themoscowtimes.com/2020/11/26/facebook-pays-russia-50k-fine-for-not-localizing-user-data-a72152.

[100] *See* Madeline Roache, *How Russia Is Stepping Up Its Campaign to Control the Internet*, TIME (Apr. 1, 2021), https://time.com/5951834/russia-control-internet/.

[101] *See Roskomnadzor Orders Twitter and Facebook to Localize Russian Users' Data by July 1*, MEDUZA (May 26, 2021), https://meduza.io/en/news/2021/05/26/roskomnadzor-orders-twitter-and-facebook-to-localize-russian-users-data-by-july-1.

16   INTRODUCTION

Russia has domestic versions of key Internet tools, including a browser, cloud computing service, maps, search engine, messaging service, and two social networks, most of which are owned by the Russian companies Yandex and Mail.ru. An antitrust case brought by Yandex against Google had ended with the requirement that Russians could choose Yandex's search engine on Android devices. Local alternatives to foreign apps reduce the costs of blocking those foreign apps. In 2022, rather than seeking the support of international authorities to clamp down on information online about its invasion of Ukraine, Russia turned to its domestic internet controls. In March 2022, the Russian Internet regulator, Roskomnadzor blocked access to Facebook on grounds that it discriminated against Russia, including by blocking RT and Sputnik across the European Union. A Russian court upheld the ban, concluding that Meta was carrying out extremist activities, though it exempted Meta's WhatsApp "due to its lack of functionality for the public dissemination of information." Shortly thereafter, Russia blocked Google News for linking to information that it considered "inauthentic" about the Ukraine invasion.

D. The United States: Digital Sovereignty by Default

One nation is more likely to criticize digital sovereignty than to explicitly embrace it: the United States.[102] This is because the United States is in the unique position of being home to many of the world's leading technology firms. This means that during the ordinary course of regulating its companies, the United States exercised digital sovereignty from the start. The U.S. FTC, for example, cited GeoCities for privacy failures as early as 1998.[103] There was never a moment when the United States did not exercise digital sovereignty,

---

[102] *See* Stephane Couture & Sophie Toupin, *What Does the Notion of "Sovereignty" Mean When Referring to the Digital?*, 21 NEW MEDIA & SOC'Y 2305, 2313 (2019) ("Within the United States, digital sovereignty (or related terms) usually have negative connotations across the political spectrum."). For example, the U.S. Ambassador to the European Union, Anthony Gardner, cautioned the EU in 2015: "The calls from some Member States, however, to promote so-called digital sovereignty, discriminatory regulation, or forced data localization will not help Europe to maintain and extend its leadership in the global digital economy." *See Remarks for TABC Conference: Perspectives on the EU's Digital Single Market Strategy – The Transatlantic Perspective*, U.S. MISSION TO THE EUROPEAN UNION (Sept. 15, 2015), https://useu.usmission.gov/remarks-tabc-conference-perspectives-eus-digital-single-market-strategy-transatlantic-perspective-2/.

[103] *FTC, GeoCities Settle on Privacy*, CNET (Aug. 13, 1998), https://www.cnet.com/tech/services-and-software/ftc-geocities-settle-on-privacy/; GeoCities, 127 F.T.C. 94 (1999).

THE RISE OF DIGITAL SOVEREIGNTY   17

and thus the United States never had to go out of its way to assert it: it was a natural consequence of the geography of the Internet.[104]

The dominance of American technology firms does not mean that the United States has not faced controversies along the way. The first Digital Millennium Copyright Act prosecution was strikingly brought against a Russian, who happened to be visiting the United States for the Def Con conference in 2002.[105] The United States accused the Russian programmer of selling tools that broke through Adobe's e-book security. Jennifer Granick, a leading digital rights advocate, argued at the time that the United States should not impose its interpretation of copyright law on foreign nations.[106]

The U.S. government has routinely seized domain names of sites that violate domestic law in part because top-level domain names are indexed on a domain name server in Virginia. Karen Kopel, writing in a student note in 2013, observed:

> Since its inception over two and a half years ago, [US federal] Operation In Our Sites has seized 1,719 domain names of which over 690 have been forfeited, ranging from websites selling allegedly counterfeit luxury goods, sports memorabilia, and pharmaceuticals, to websites that host copyrighted music, movies, TV shows, software, and websites that only link to this content.[107]

But these enforcement actions, Kopel suggests, lack sufficient process and may infringe on free speech concerns.[108]

The fact that the largest Internet companies are based in the United States also means that data about Americans are typically stored in the United States. This allows prosecutors to use traditional judicial processes within

---

[104] Anupam Chander, *Law and the Geography of Cyberspace*, 6 W.I.P.O.J. 99, 101–02 (2014).

[105] *See generally* United States v. Elcom Ltd., 203 F. Supp. 2d 1111 (N.D. Cal. 2002); Robert Lemos, *Russian Crypto Expert Arrested at Def Con*, CNET (Mar. 2, 2002), https://www.cnet.com/news/russ ian-crypto-expert-arrested-at-def-con/. The DMCA criminalizes the sale of tools that break encryption protecting copyrighted works, such as DVDs and e-books.

[106] *See* Matt Richtel, *Russian Company Cleared of Illegal Software Sales*, N.Y. TIMES (Dec. 18, 2002), https://www.nytimes.com/2002/12/18/business/technology-russian-company-cleared-of-illegal-software-sales.html [https://perma.cc/S6NB-WJKF] (archived Jan. 9, 2022) (quoting Jennifer Granick as saying that the acquittal of the Russian company in the case was "good for democracy: people in other countries can make determinations about what is right and wrong for themselves.").

[107] Karen Kopel, *Operation Seizing Our Sites: How the Federal Government is Taking Domain Names Without Prior Notice*, 28 BERKELEY TECH. L.J.859, 860 (2013).

[108] *Id.* at 885–93.

18   INTRODUCTION

the country to access the data, subject to Fourth Amendment and statutory protections. But when U.S. prosecutors sought information stored in Ireland on Microsoft servers, Microsoft protested that this was beyond the statutory authority of prosecutors.[109] Congress intervened to amend the law to grant authority to prosecutors to use judicial process to require companies to produce data held abroad.[110]

But earlier enforcement efforts against Internet enterprises do not seem to compare with the regulatory demands that resound today across the political spectrum in the United States. If there ever was a laissez-faire era for U.S. Internet regulation,[111] that era is distinctly over.[112]

At the same time, the U.S. government remains concerned that foreign efforts to assert digital sovereignty can be a guise for old-fashioned protectionism. For example, the U.S. government's 2021 report on "foreign trade barriers" cites EU digital sovereignty practices as possibly "unfairly target[ing] large U.S. service suppliers and hamper[ing] their ability to provide innovative, Internet-based services in the EU."[113]

E. The Global South: Avoiding Data Colonialism

Even as access to the Internet has grown dramatically,[114] many governments in the Global South worry about being left behind in the digital economy. Digitization, whether led by foreign or domestic firms, has, of course, proven critical to their economic growth, giving individuals information about markets and opportunities that was hard to obtain previously. Yet, foreign companies have an outsized presence in their digital lives. Developing nations fear recapitulating colonialism, specifically, of being both the raw

---

[109] *In re* Warrant to Search a Certain E–Mail Account Controlled & Maintained by Microsoft Corp., 829 F.3d 197, 204–05 (2d Cir. 2016).

[110] USA CLOUD Act, 18 U.S.C. § 2713, *et seq.* (2012).

[111] For a comparative history of U.S. Internet regulation, *see generally* Anupam Chander, *How Law Made Silicon Valley*, 63 EMORY L.J. 639 (2014).

[112] *See* John Cassidy, *Will Joe Biden and Lina Khan Cut the Tech Giants Down to Size?*, NEW YORKER (June 21, 2021), https://www.newyorker.com/news/our-columnists/will-joe-biden-and-lina-khan-cut-the-tech-giants-down-to-size.

[113] U.S. TRADE REPRESENTATIVE, 2021 NATIONAL TRADE ESTIMATE REPORT ON FOREIGN TRADE BARRIERS 216 (2021).

[114] About half of the world's people now have Internet access. *Individuals Using the Internet*, WORLD BANK, https://data.worldbank.org/indicator/IT.NET.USER.ZS.

materials (now in the form of data) and markets for Western manufacture (in the form of processed information).[115]

In 2021, South Africa published a draft "National Data and Cloud Policy" that explicitly seeks to "promote South Africa's data sovereignty."[116] The draft policy laments that "data generated in Africa and South Africa is mostly stored in foreign lands and, where stored locally, is owned by international technology giant companies."[117] It seeks to reverse that through a data localization mandate: "All data classified/identified as critical Information Infrastructure shall be processed and stored within the borders of South Africa."[118] The draft policy also announces, "[d]ata generated in South Africa shall be the property of South Africa, regardless of where the technology company is domiciled."

In fact, in its recently released "Digital Transformation Strategy for Africa (2020–2030)," the African Union envisions "data sovereignty" as one of its policy priorities.[119] It, too, suggests data localization as a strategy to promote data sovereignty: "Even though Africa is at the moment less restrictive, soon it will be necessary to ensure localization of all personal data of Africa's citizens."[120] In Senegal, President Macky Sall hopes to "guarantee[] Senegalese digital sovereignty" by building a data center within the country with the help of a Chinese loan and Huawei equipment and technical assistance.[121] This is part of China's Digital Silk Road effort, tying countries to China through technology.

After Twitter deleted a tweet by President Muhammadu Buhari that some saw as threatening violent reprisal against protestors, the Nigerian government simply banned Twitter from the country.[122] In the battle between

---

[115] *See* Angelina Fisher & Thomas Streinz, *Confronting Data Inequality*, 60 COLUM. J. TRANSNAT'L L. 829, 831 (2022).

[116] South Africa Dept. of Comm. & Digital Tech., Invitation to Submit Written Comments on the Proposed National Data and Cloud Policy 11, Apr. 1, 2021.

[117] *See Data Generated in SA Is the Property of SA, Says New Draft Govt Policy – And Cops Need Access*, BUS. INSIDER SA (Apr. 6, 2021), https://www.businessinsider.co.za/a-draft-national-data-and-cloud-policy-demands-data-sovereignty-for-south-africa-2021-4.

[118] South Africa Dept. of Comm. & Digital Tech., *supra* note 116, at 27.

[119] THE DIGITAL TRANSFORMATION STRATEGY FOR AFRICA (2020–2030), AFRICAN UNION 11 (2020), https://au.int/en/documents/20200518/digital-transformation-strategy-africa-2020-2030.

[120] *Id.*; *see* Halefom H. Abraha, *How African Countries Can Benefit From the Emerging Reform Initiatives of Cross-border Access to Electronic Evidence*, CROSS-BORDER DATA FORUM (July 6, 2020), https://www.crossborderdataforum.org/how-african-countries-can-benefit-from-the-emerging-ref orm-initiatives-of-cross-border-access-to-electronic-evidence/.

[121] Dan Swinhoe, *Senegal to Migrate All Government Data and Applications to New Government Data Center*, DATA CTR. DYNAMICS (June 23, 2021), https://www.datacenterdynamics.com/en/news/senegal-to-migrate-all-government-data-and-applications-to-new-government-data-center/.

[122] *Nigerian Govt Accuses Twitter of Double Standards, Supporting Secessionists*, BUS. STANDARD (June 3, 2021), https://www.business-standard.com/article/international/nigerian-govt-accu

20 INTRODUCTION

developing states and big tech, Nigeria shows that a government willing to forgo a platform that it or its citizens use can still win. In the non-Western parts of the world (including both developing countries and the former Soviet Bloc nations), assertions of digital sovereignty are more likely to include shutdowns of a website or even the Internet. Governments may be more likely to turn to complete shutdowns of a site or even the Internet generally (through disabling cell services) if they feel that a foreign platform will not otherwise comply with its censorship demands.

Indigenous peoples are also seeking digital sovereignty. Indigenous data sovereignty "deals with the right and ability of tribes to develop their own systems for gathering and using data and to influence the collection of data by external actors."[123] For example, the Māori Data Sovereignty Network seeks to ensure that Māori peoples have sovereignty over the "data produced by Māori or that is about Māori and the environments we [the Māori] have relationships with."[124]

III. How Digital Sovereignty Is Different

Digital sovereignty is not merely the assertion of sovereignty online. The last few decades have taught us that the Internet changes the nature of sovereignty in a variety of ways. First, because of the global nature of the Internet, digital sovereignty almost always has global implications, whether it involves speech regulation, privacy, consumer protection, competition concerns, or law enforcement; thus, digital sovereignty can create significant roadblocks to one of the Internet's key virtues—its empowering of global connections. Second, because the digital sphere is intermediated by corporations, the

---

ses-twitter-of-double-standards-supporting-secessionists-121060300481_1.html. The tweet in question stated: "Many of those misbehaving today are too young to be aware of the destruction and loss of lives that occurred during the Nigeria civil war. Those of us in the fields for 30 months, who went through the war, will treat them in the language they understand," the president tweeted on Tuesday night." *Id.*

[123] Christopher B. Chaney, *Data Sovereignty and the Tribal Law and Order Act*, 65-APR FED. LAW. 22, 23 (2018); *see also* Aila Hoss, *Exploring Legal Issues in Tribal Public Health Data and Surveillance*, 44 S. ILL. U. L.J. 27, 38 (2019); Rebecca Tsosie, *Tribal Data Governance and Informational Privacy: Constructing "Indigenous Data Sovereignty"*, 80 MONT. L. REV. 229, 229–30 (2019) ("Data sovereignty describes the right of a nation to 'govern the collection, ownership and application of data' concerning the tribe or its members and to control data that is housed within tribal territory.").

[124] Lida Ayoubi, *Intellectual Property Commercialisation and Protection of Mātauranga Māori in New Zealand Universities*, 28 N.Z. U. L. REV. 521, 553 (2019).

assertion of digital sovereignty typically occurs vis-à-vis corporations, not governments. Third, because daily life is increasingly permeated by the Internet, digital sovereignty can offer governments surveillance tools that far exceed any history has previously provided. Fourth, because of the dominance of U.S .technology companies globally, governments can readily weaponize digital sovereignty to serve protectionist goals.

A. Always Global

Unless one cuts off the local Internet from the global Internet (a possibility that China, Iran, North Korea, and Russia are working toward in different measures), the regulation of the Internet almost inevitably involves foreign actors.[125] Consider a French court's order to Yahoo! in 2000 to stop permitting French residents to access Nazi materials. Yahoo! responded by banning these materials across the world.[126] The EU's General Data Protection Regulation (GDPR) does not regulate the processing of personal information about a US person in a transaction in the United States, but yet Microsoft and numerous other companies have chosen to apply at least parts of the GDPR to their practices worldwide.[127] Anu Bradford labels this the "Brussels Effect."[128] While David Johnson and David Post famously argued that the global nature of the Internet made any sovereign assertion illegitimate,[129] Jack Goldsmith demonstrated that inter-jurisdictional conflicts

---

[125] *Cf.* Jennifer Daskal, *Borders and Bits*, 71 VAND. L. REV. 179, 185 (2018) (observing "the transnational nature of both data and the companies that regulate our data"). Jennifer Daskal argues that the differences "between data and its tangible counterpart," in particular, data's mobility, interconnectedness, and divisibility, demonstrate the difficulties of applying traditional jurisdictional frameworks to internet problems. Jennifer Daskal, *The Un-territoriality of Data*, 125 YALE L.J. 326, 365–78 (2015).

[126] Yahoo! Inc. v. La Ligue Contre Le Racisme Et L'Antisemitisme, 433 F.3d 1199, 1205 (9th Cir. 2006) (Fletcher, J.) ("Yahoo's new policy eliminates much of the conduct prohibited by the French orders.").

[127] *See* Julie Brill, *Microsoft's Commitment to GDPR, Privacy and Putting Customers in Control of Their Own Data*, MICROSOFT ON THE ISSUES (May 21, 2018), https://blogs.microsoft.com/on-the-iss ues/2018/05/21/microsofts-commitment-to-gdpr-privacy-and-putting-customers-in-control-of-their-own-data/ [https://perma.cc/SV9F-U9M9] (archived Jan. 9, 2022) ("we will extend the rights that are at the heart of GDPR to all of our consumer customers worldwide").

[128] Anu Bradford, *The Brussels Effect*, 107 Nw. U. L. REV. 1, 3 (2012) ("Unilateral regulatory globalization occurs when a single state is able to externalize its laws and regulations outside its borders through market mechanisms, resulting in the globalization of standards.").

[129] *See* David R. Johnson & David Post, *Law and Borders-the Rise of Law in Cyberspace*, 48 STAN. L. REV. 1367, 1375 (1996) ("Territorial regulation of online activities serves neither the legitimacy nor the notice justifications. There is no geographically localized set of constituents with a stronger and more legitimate claim to regulate it than any other local group.").

22   INTRODUCTION

are not new with the Internet and that international law has tools to manage them.[130] Paul Berman goes further to argue that pluralist approaches to governance should be normatively welcome as they better express contemporary conditions.[131]

Digital sovereignty increasingly means regulating not only one's citizens alone but also foreigners—typically firms offering services across the world. In order for law to be meaningful in a world of Internet globalization, states must regulate foreign entities. It is this necessarily extraterritorial[132] exercise of jurisdiction that increases the difficulty, complexity, and risk of digital sovereignty.

At the same time, excessive assertions of digital sovereignty can tear the Internet apart, relegating all to national spaces for commerce and speech, where once individuals could transact and speak with each other across the world. The specter of the 193 nations of the United Nations—and other sub- and supra-national jurisdictions as well—regulating the internet at the same time seems daunting indeed. Instead of being the world's most-free-speech zone, the Internet may become the world's most-unfree zone, merely a conglomeration of the censorship and rules of all the jurisdictions in the world.

B. Against Corporations

Where sovereignty has historically been asserted in relation to foreign states, digital sovereignty is equally or perhaps more likely to be asserted against foreign corporations. Foreign corporations are the ones that are dealing directly with their residents—collecting data, offering services, and moderating speech. Jennifer Daskal observes that much of transnational Internet governance "is largely being mediated by the private parties that hold and manage our data."[133] She writes, "It is these companies that increasingly determine whose rules govern and, in key ways, how they are interpreted and applied."[134] Writing about digital sovereignty, Lucien Floridi observes, "The most visible clash is between companies and states."[135]

---

[130] *See generally* Jack L. Goldsmith, *Against Cyberanarchy*, 65 U. CHI. L. REV. 1199 (1998).
[131] *See* Paul Schiff Berman, *The Globalization of Jurisdiction*, 151 U. PA. L. REV. 311, 490 (2002).
[132] The application of the term "extraterritorial" is itself open to debate, as some would argue that the exercise of jurisdiction against companies located abroad that are operating in one's jurisdiction is in fact an exercise simply of territorial jurisdiction.
[133] Daskal, *supra* note 125, at 185.
[134] *Id.*
[135] *See* Floridi, *supra* note 30, at 371.

Indeed, the European Parliament's study of digital sovereignty explicitly rests its call for digital sovereignty on this ground: "Strong concerns have been raised over the economic and social influence of non-EU technology companies, which threatens EU citizens' control over their personal data, and constrains both the growth of EU high-technology companies and the ability of national and EU rule-makers to enforce their laws."[136] Much of the enforcement activity under the GDPR is, accordingly, targeted at corporations. Much as some U.S. residents worry about the exploitation of their data by U.S. companies, India worries that foreign companies are benefiting from local data—the 21st-century version of serving as the source of raw materials for the manufacturers of the Global North.[137]

C. More Control

As Neil Richards observes, "[we] are living in an age of surveillance. The same digital technologies that have revolutionized our daily lives over the past three decades have also created ever more detailed records about those lives."[138] Those digital technologies can be utilized by the state. Michael Birnhack and Niva Elkin-Koren worry about what they called "the invisible handshake" between the government and corporations: "Whether the Big Brother we distrust is government and its agencies, or multinational corporations, the emerging collaboration between the two in the online environment produces the ultimate threat."[139]

In *Seeing Like a State*, historian James C. Scott argues that increases in what he calls "legibility" (the ability of the state to better understand its population) were a critical part of large governmental projects.[140] Scott sees this legibility, when combined with hubris, as leading to failed schemes—but increases in legibility could also lead to greater control. The digital world

---

[136] *See* EUR. PARLIAMENTARY RES. SERV., DIGITAL SOVEREIGNTY FOR EUROPE 1 (2020), https://www.europarl.europa.eu/RegData/etudes/BRIE/2020/651992/EPRS_BRI(2020)651992_EN.pdf.

[137] *Mukesh Ambani Says "Data Colonisation" as Bad as Physical Dolonisation*, ECON. TIMES (Dec. 19, 2018), https://economictimes.indiatimes.com/news/company/corporate-trends/mukesh-ambani-says-data-colonisation-as-bad-as-physical-colonisation/articleshow/67164810.cms?utm_source%3Dtwitter_web%26utm_medium%3Dsocial%26utm_campaign%3Dsocialsharebuttons.

[138] Neil M. Richards, *The Dangers of Surveillance*, 126 HARV. L. REV. 1934, 1936 (2013).

[139] Michael D. Birnhack & Niva Elkin-Koren, *The Invisible Handshake: The Reemergence of the State in the Digital Environment*, 8 VA. J.L. & TECH. 6, 3 (2003).

[140] *See generally* JAMES C. SCOTT, SEEING LIKE A STATE: HOW CERTAIN SCHEMES TO IMPROVE THE HUMAN CONDITION HAVE FAILED (1998).

24 INTRODUCTION

enlarges governmental legibility dramatically, even more so when the government gains access to information collected by private companies. The legibility that Internet companies seek into their users for commercial purposes, which Julie Cohen observes,[141] can be exploited by the state as well.

Scott argues that mid-20th-century failures of government planning resulted from hubris, with the planners "forgetting that they were mortals and acting as if they were gods."[142] For Scott, the absence of representative institutions reduces resistance to these large planning measures. Scott's government planners were largely well-intentioned, with noble goals of a more egalitarian society.[143] We should be mindful that digital regulators, whether well-intentioned or not, should not wield unchecked power. This will require both a vigorous civil society and laws that are designed with appropriate checks for governmental abuse.

D. Enables Protectionism

When President of the European Commission Jean-Claude Juncker proposed the "Digital Single Market" policy in 2015, he focused on promoting European innovation—but not through protectionist applications of regulation: "Today, we lay the groundwork for Europe's digital future. I want to see pan-continental telecom networks, digital services that cross borders, and a wave of innovative European start-ups."[144] Günther Oettinger, then a member of the European Commission for Budget and Human Resources, explained that "[t]he digital single market can be a win-win" for both European and Silicon Valley firms.[145] Andrus Ansip, the European Commissioner for Digital Single Market from 2014 to 2019, similarly suggested, "[t]he digital single market will provide opportunities for trade, investment, innovation

---

[141] JULIE E. COHEN, BETWEEN TRUTH AND POWER: THE LEGAL CONSTRUCTIONS OF INFORMATIONAL CAPITALISM 38 (2019).

[142] SCOTT, *supra* note 52, at 342.

[143] *Id.* at 346.

[144] Hamza Shaban, *European Union Unveils Digital Single Market Plan*, BUZZFEED NEWS (May 6, 2015), https://www.buzzfeednews.com/article/hamzashaban/european-union-unveils-digital-single-market-plan; *see* David O'Sullivan, *Stop the Hysteria: Of Course, Europe Wants an Open Internet*, WIRED (Apr. 30 2015), https://www.wired.com/2015/04/eu-ambassador-on-open-internet/.

[145] Hamza Shaban, *EU Digital Commission to Silicon Valley: Relax*, BUZZFEED NEWS (Sept. 25, 2015), https://www.buzzfeednews.com/article/hamzashaban/eu-digital-commissioner-to-silicon-valley-relax.

not only for Europe, but globally—also, for the United States."[146] Fredrik Persson, chairman of the Confederation of Swedish Enterprise cautioned that European efforts toward digital sovereignty "should not create a European fortress that pulls up the drawbridge to the outside world."[147] In March 2021, German Chancellor Angela Merkel, Danish Prime Minister Mette Frederiksen, Estonian Prime Minister Kaja Kallas, and Finnish Prime Minister Sanna Marin sent a joint letter to European Commission President Ursula von der Leyen encouraging European efforts for digital sovereignty but cautioning that the EU should avoid protectionist strategies to build digital sovereignty: "Digital sovereignty is about building on our strengths and reducing our strategic weaknesses, not about excluding others or taking a protectionist approach."[148] Many European leaders have explicitly disavowed protectionism, instead embracing the coexistence of foreign and domestic technology companies.

Other voices within the EU, however, portray issues of digital sovereignty as a zero-sum geopolitical struggle. In 2019, French President Emmanuel Macron declared, "[t]he battle we're fighting is one of sovereignty." He continued, "[i]f we don't build our own champions in all new areas—digital, artificial intelligence—our choices . . . will be dictated by others."[149] The European Parliament's study of digital sovereignty echoes this: "EU policymakers have identified a potential dependence on foreign technology as presenting a risk to Europe's influence."[150]

The European Parliament's study goes on to argue that the dominance of foreign Internet platforms in the EU is itself a hallmark of the loss of European sovereignty. The study explains: "[L]arge online platforms (mostly non-EU based) are increasingly seen as dominating entire sectors of the EU economy and depriving EU Member States of their sovereignty in areas such

---

[146] Hamza Shaban, *Digital Single Market Isn't Anti-American, Says EU Commissioner*, BUZZFEED NEWS (May 28, 2015), https://www.buzzfeednews.com/article/hamzashaban/digital-single-market-isnt-anti-american-says-eu-commissione.

[147] Christakis, *supra* note 26, at 58.

[148] *See Estonia, EU countries propose faster 'European digital sovereignty'*, ERR NEWS (Feb. 3, 2021), https://news.err.ee/1608127618/estonia-eu-countries-propose-faster-european-digital-sovereignty.

[149] Kenneth Propp, *Waving the flag of digital sovereignty*, ATLANTIC COUNCIL (Dec. 11, 2019), https://www.atlanticcouncil.org/blogs/new-atlanticist/waving-the-flag-of-digital-sovereignty/ . It might be noted that this concern about too-powerful-foreign-corporations is uncomfortably coupled with the hope that these national champions will themselves be globally successful.

[150] EUR. PARLIAMENTARY RES. SERV., DIGITAL SOVEREIGNTY FOR EUROPE 1 (2020), https://www.europarl.europa.eu/RegData/etudes/BRIE/2020/651992/EPRS_BRI(2020)651992_EN.pdf.

26 INTRODUCTION

as copyright, data protection, taxation or transportation." But this argument seems misplaced. It is like arguing that because people drive Toyota cars on U.S. roads, Americans no longer control their streets. As long as the cars are regulated by local law, the fact that they might be built abroad should not undermine sovereignty.

Some see a zero-sum game with respect to the Internet with winners and losers. In 2020, Thierry Breton, the European Union's Commissioner for Internal Market, expressed confidence that EU companies would beat their American counterparts: "The winners of today will not be the winners of tomorrow."[151] At times, however, the European approach to digital sovereignty seems to be focused on replacing U.S. enterprises with European ones, a classic protectionist strategy. Commissioner Breton seeks to ensure that "European data will be used for European companies in priority, for us to create value in Europe."[152]

Even while seeking to rein in the power of U.S. tech titans, some in the EU seem to covet their own. In June 2021, "French President Emmanuel Macron announced the objective of having '10 companies worth €100 billion by 2030' in Europe . . . after he received . . . recommendations to encourage the emergence of digital giants in Europe."[153] Some in the EU wish to create their own "European digital champions."[154] Regulatory actions in the digital space are especially amenable to protectionist use because the largest players in the industry are often foreign-owned corporations. Whether justified or not, some saw Facebook's hand in the Trump administration's targeting of largely Chinese-owned TikTok.[155]

---

[151] Foo Yun Chee, *This Is the EU's Plan to Compete with Silicon Valley*, WORLD ECON. F. (Feb. 20, 2020), https://www.weforum.org/agenda/2020/02/eu-data-market-technology-silicon-valley.

[152] FRANCES BURWELL & KENNETH PROPP, THE EUROPEAN UNION AND THE SEARCH FOR DIGITAL SOVEREIGNTY: BUILDING "FORTRESS EUROPE" OR PREPARING FOR A NEW WORLD? 6 (2020).

[153] *See* Mathieu Pollet, *Macron Wants Europe to Have 10 Tech Giants Worth €100 Billion by 2030*, EURACTIV (June 16, 2021), https://www.euractiv.com/section/digital/news/macron-wants-eur ope-to-have-10-tech-giants-worth-e100-billion-by-2030/.

[154] *See* Theodore Christakis, "European Digital Sovereignty": Successfully Navigating between the "Brussels Effect" and Europe's Quest for Strategic Autonomy 89 (Dec. 2020) (e-book published by the Multidisciplinary Institute on Artificial Intelligence/Grenoble Alpes Data Institute), https://papers. ssrn.com/sol3/papers.cfm?abstract_id=3748098.

[155] Georgia Wells, Jeff Horwitz, & Aruna Viswanatha, *Facebook CEO Mark Zuckerberg Stoked Washington's Fears About TikTok*, WALL ST. J. (Aug. 23, 2020), https://www.wsj.com/articles/faceb ook-ceo-mark-zuckerberg-stoked-washingtons-fears-about-tiktok-11598223133#:~:text=Zuc kerberg%20told%20Georgetown%20students%20that,American%20values%20and%20technologi cal%20supremacy.

IV. Digital Sovereignty and the Russian Invasion of Ukraine

We can see the critical role of digital sovereignty by examining the digital battle that erupted upon the Russian invasion of Ukraine. The 2022 invasion was accompanied by a simultaneous struggle over digital control, both within Ukraine and Russia. On February 28, 2022, with 200,000 Russian troops within his country, Ukrainian Minister of Digital Transformation Mykhailo Fedorov sent an urgent plea to ICANN, the California-based body that manages the global Internet domain name system. Citing Russian disinformation, hate speech, the promotion of violence online, and cyber-attacks, he asked ICANN to revoke the domains ".ru.," ".рф," and ".su"—the Russian and (former) Soviet top level domains. Fedorov simultaneously wrote to RIPE Network Coordination Centre (RIPE NCC), a regional Internet registry based in Amsterdam, asking it to cancel all Internet addresses allocated to Russians. He hoped to wipe Russia off the Internet.

ICANN responded that it "does not control internet access or content," and that, in any case, its goal was "to ensure that the Internet works, not . . . to stop it from working." RIPE NCC, too, while condemning the "violent actions" against Ukraine, rejected the request, arguing that the Internet address registry should not be "used to achieve political ends." Strikingly, it cited Dutch law. If the Internet authorities had indeed removed Russian domain names or Internet addresses, faith in those authorities might have been eroded, as countries would begin wondering if they would be the next target of such actions. It would make those authorities clearly geopolitical actors.

Instead of global and regional Internet authorities, the struggle over the Russian Internet would shift to the Internet companies that provide so much of the infrastructure of the modern economy. Private U.S. enterprises were willing to take more active steps. YouTube suspended Russian state-supported media channels, while Google suspended most of its commercial services in Russia, including advertising. But Google continued to provide Russians with free services such as search, Gmail, and YouTube, and to support the Android operating system. Twitter expanded its labeling of Russian state-owned media to include tweets by third parties referencing such media. It followed EU sanctions banning such media within the EU. Like some other newspapers, the *Washington Post* lifted its paywall for users in Russia and Ukraine, hoping to make its high-quality information about the conflict more readily available.

28   INTRODUCTION

Meta established a special operations center including Russian and Ukrainian speakers to respond more quickly to issues. It expanded third-party fact-checking capacity in Russian and Ukrainian languages and offered financial support to Ukrainian fact-checking partners. Meta labeled Russian state-controlled media outlets, stopped algorithmically recommending them, and, in accordance with EU sanctions, stopped distributing them within the European Union. In March 2022, Meta made a controversial change to its hate speech policy, temporarily allowing violent speech such as "death to the Russian invaders." While Meta's goal was to avoid removing posts by "ordinary Ukrainians expressing their resistance and fury at the invading military forces," it left the company open to the charge that it permitted calls for violence against Russian soldiers when it would not allow such calls against others. As mentioned above, later in March 2022, the Russian Internet regulator, Roskomnadzor blocked access to Facebook and Instagram.

The Telegram app, which claims a quarter of Russia's population as users, took a more equivocal path, permitting both Russian propaganda and criticism. Founded by a Russian, Pavel Durov, and his brother, Telegram is now operated by Durov from Dubai. In 2018, Russia had sought to ban Telegram for allegedly refusing to hand over encryption keys, but then lifted the ban after the company, according to the Russian government, agreed to help it combat terrorism and extremist content. In 2021, the founder of a rival messaging app warned Telegram users that Telegram could read in plain text all of the messages they had ever sent. Telegram is not end-to-end encrypted by default, unlike alternatives like WhatsApp and Signal.

These major developments following the Russian invasion of Ukraine thus reveal some key elements of digital sovereignty. First, controlling the local Internet carries global implications. Both Russia and Ukraine sought to influence global actors, both public and private, to achieve their political goals. Ukraine's efforts to banish Russia from the global Internet threatened core functions, and would, if successful, have raised alarms across the world at the control wielded by obscure, unelected institutions.

Second, Internet enterprises hold incredible power, and any government that hopes to regulate its territory must be able to regulate those enterprises. The power of Internet companies includes the ability to promote or censor information. No denial of service cyberattack against digital infrastructure is necessary when the corporation itself denies service.

Third, when governments can coopt the power of Internet companies, they gain an awesome power that can be abused. For example, Internet enterprises can be ordered to promote the official version of the truth and censor all else. Having ejected Facebook, the Russian government could turn to the homegrown alternative it controlled—Vkontakte, which operates the country's most popular social media network and email service. In 2021, state-owned enterprise Gazprom had gained control over VKontakte, and a new CEO, Vladimir Kiriyenko, was installed. After the Russian invasion, the United States and the EU placed Kiriyenko on the sanctions list because he "supports Vladimir Putin's aim for greater control over the internet."[156]

V. The Plan for This Volume

This volume provides a comprehensive and systematic account of digital sovereignty. It grew out of the conference, "Data Sovereignty along the Digital Silk Road," organized by the editors and hosted virtually by Georgetown University and the University of Hong Kong in January 2021.

Consisting of four parts, the volume adds new theoretical perspectives on digital sovereignty and explores the cutting-edge issues it raises. Drawing mainly on various theories concerning political economy, international law, human rights, and data protection, the first part reconsiders the nature and scope of digital sovereignty. Frank Pasquale first puts forward an important idea "functional sovereignty" that highlights how large technology companies exert their authority to govern the Internet and use of digital data often in parallel to the territorial sovereign power that a government wields. To understand and tackle the nature and scope of this "functional sovereignty" is of paramount importance given that it has created a new digital political economy and affected the functioning of our liberal democracy. Revealing problems with the state boundary-based notions of sovereignty, Dan Svantesson attempts to reconceptualize sovereignty in the digital age as a political power to confront assaults on "state dignity." This theoretical approach would divert us from the state boundary-based thinking to examine the seriousness of societal effects (e.g., leakage of personal data) caused by assaults such as cyberattack. The own chapter follows, arguing that digital sovereignty has a double-edged nature. While governments must exercise it to promote citizens' freedom and welfare, governments can also abuse this

---

[156] Morgan Meaker, *How the Kremlin Infiltrated Russia's Facebook*, WIRED, June 1, 2022 7:00 AM, https://www.wired.com/story/vk-russia-democracy/.

30 INTRODUCTION

power, causing harms to citizens and our democratic institutions. We call for checks and balances to regulate a government's assertion of its digital sovereignty. Anne Cheung closes this section by presenting self-sovereignty as a new theoretical basis to enhance protection of personal data. Responding to the problems exposed by the COVID-19 pandemic, she demonstrates that this approach can empower individuals to better protect their data in multiple ways.

The second part of the volume discusses major challenges at the intersection of digital sovereignty and new technological developments in sectors such as AI, e-commerce, and the sharing economy. Andrew Woods takes the lead to explore how the digital sovereignty policies and attitudes adopted in China, European Union, and the United States would impact their respective development of the AI technology. He also considers some major factors such as access to training data for us to better understand the relationship between digital sovereignty and AI. Lizhi Liu and Barry Weingast examines unique roles that China's e-commerce sector has played in improving the building blocks of its legal market infrastructure. They demonstrate that Taobao's internal operations for contract enforcement and dispute resolution have promoted China's institutional structure of economic governance. Given the growing importance of the sharing economy, Shin-yi Peng considers how regional trade agreements could deal with divergent domestic approaches to regulating sharing platforms such as Uber and Airbnb. She concludes that current regulatory practices and regulatory cooperation championed by those agreements cannot do much to harmonize the divergent regulatory approaches and encourages trade negotiators to seek new avenues of international cooperation. With a dynamic account of data and data governance in the digital finance sector, Giuliano Castellano, Ēriks Selga, and Douglas Arner identify three different financial data governance strategies that the United States, the European Union, and China have adopted based on their own policies toward market institutions and the protection of individual and public interests in data. They also discuss how the global financial market should cope with challenges posed by regulatory fragmentation and localization requirements for financial data.

As trade regulation is increasingly intertwined with digital sovereignty, the third part of the volume explores various issues and developments in the national, regional, and international regulation of data flow. Based on a study of various domestic rules governing cross-border flows of data, Henry Gao puts forward three models of constructing data sovereignty in this regard, namely the United States' firm sovereignty model, China's state sovereignty model, and the EU's individual sovereignty model. He also considers how the different trade protection policies adopted by these countries have shaped their own regime of data governance. With a closer look at the underlying ideas, policy goals, and regulatory complexities of India's data governance, Neha Mishra reveals why India has built this nationalist regime that mainly supports its domestic digital economy. This reality, as she further shows, has largely prevented India from negotiating trade rules dealing with cross-border data flows. Mira Burri examines the extent to which preferential trade agreements, mainly concluded by the European Union and the United States with their respective trade partners, have developed regional rules governing cross-border flows of data and set up temples for further rule-making. As data governance becomes the focal part of trade negotiations, she calls for increased regulatory cooperation and legal innovation in making such rules regionally and internationally.

The fourth part of the volume presents data localization as a major form of assertion of digital sovereignty, examining its promise and pitfalls in the process of trade liberalization, data regulation, and human rights protection. Graham Greenleaf first shows that the data localization mandate normally entails six distinct forms of legal regulation, ranging from storing and processing data locally to the prohibition of exporting data. He then studies data privacy laws in the major countries along the modern "Silk Roads", finding that China, Russia, and three South Asian countries adopted all six forms of data localization and five Central Asian countries only regulate data exports. Kyung Sin Park explores the tension between data localization requirements and human rights protection norms. Internet shutdowns, as he demonstrates, can produce data localization effects that may harm the protection of human rights such as free speech and privacy. Theodore Christakis examines the rise of data localization requirements in the EU and identifies the factors contributing to this rise. He then shows how the Court of Justice of the European Union's 2020 *Schrems II* ruling has rendered such requirements more stringent.

Taken together, the brilliant contributions to this volume demonstrate both the urgency and complexity of digital sovereignty.

PART I
RETHEORIZING DIGITAL SOVEREIGNTY

1

Two Visions for Data Governance

Territorial vs. Functional Sovereignty

Frank Pasquale

Large Internet platforms wield extraordinary (and often unchecked) power. When it comes to decisions about monetizing videos on YouTube in the United States, for example, Google has the final word.[1] The "law of Amazon" has similarly forceful effect with respect to a vast range of disputes between buyers and sellers on its platform. Meta's content moderation is a de facto governance of communications and content on WhatsApp, Instagram, and Facebook.[2] Platforms regularly avoid responsibility for disinformation spread on their networks, or even violent attacks plotted on them, despite repeated warnings about these dangers from scholars and civil society.

In the United States, a long-standing technocratic policy consensus in favor of maintaining these cessions of authority to platforms, and perhaps even expanding them, has only recently been challenged. The fragmentation of U.S. authority also complicates nascent efforts to reverse course, ensuring that even if Congress passes, and the president signs, legislation to amend and limit Section 230 of the Communications Decency Act (or similar reforms), courts stand ready to apply free expression doctrine in order to create similar immunities for platforms.

---

[1] I realize that the more accurate characterization here, under current corporate structures, would be to refer to Alphabet (as parent company). However, in the public mind, the entity has been best known as Google, and I recognize this common parlance here. *See also* Jake Barnes, *One Trademark per Source*, 18 TEX. INTELL. PROP. L.J. 1 (2009) (arguing for limits on the ability of firms to obscure or disguise common ownership by proliferating trademarks of goods and services they market). While the functional sovereigns of the Internet can likely block constructive ideas like Barnes's from being adopted in the United States, other jurisdictions may be able to assert territorial sovereignty and implement them.

[2] I use Meta here, despite the concerns expressed in note 1 above, because it conveniently distinguishes between the original firm (Facebook) and two acquisitions that have been key to Mark Zuckerberg's control of important social media. Meta also connotes the firm's current pivot to a "metaverse" strategy, whereas Alphabet does not convey a similar substantive shift in aspiration.

Frank Pasquale, *Two Visions for Data Governance* In: *Data Sovereignty*. Edited by: Anupam Chander and Haochen Sun, Oxford University Press. © Oxford University Press 2023. DOI: 10.1093/oso/9780197582794.003.0002

36 TWO VISIONS FOR DATA GOVERNANCE

In the United States, once unquestioned powers of federal and state governments are being eroded by courts, libertarian culture, and a chaotic public sphere that renders widespread agreement on facts and values increasingly difficult. Strong federal regulation of the commercial dimensions of platform power remains unlikely in the U.S., even as the E.U. forges ahead with several important measures.[3] The resulting erosion of public governmental power gives rise to "functional sovereignty" in the U.S., as firms control forums and online spaces that government is too weak and divided to regulate. When the Supreme Court's expansive interpretations of the First Amendment throw into question systematic government initiatives to structure and regulate old and new media, it is up to broadcast and technology firms to decide whether to permit insurrectionary organizing, hate campaigns, or the viral spread of lies about election integrity and vaccine safety. Similarly, platforms for merchants and videos have taken on a larger role in resolving online disputes as consumer protections shrivel in the wake of one-sided terms of service and increasingly out-of-reach courts. The governance of data in the U.S. continues to be primarily based on so-called contracts (imposed in a one-sided way by large firms onto their users), and only secondarily by weak and underenforced privacy laws (as well as rules permitting or mandating certain forms of access to information, like the California Consumer Privacy Act).[4] To be sure, regulatory efforts are belatedly intensifying in the United States as a revitalized Federal Trade Commission (FTC) begins to make up for years of minimalist approaches to privacy and competition law. But even Lina Khan's FTC finds itself sandbagged in the courts regularly, and the rise of the Major Questions Doctrine creates even more artillery for conservative judges to use when they are skeptical of what agency initiatives.

In such a complex politico-legal landscape, a key question for courts and policymakers will be how far to permit functional sovereignty to expand. This chapter examines this emerging question, particularly in light of the evolving climate, health, and politico-economic crises evident at the present

---

[3] While some Republican political leaders indicate interest in regulating social networks, Republican judicial appointees are may well declare unconstitutional strong legislation in this direction, at both the state and federal level. Reminiscent of William Connolly's social theory of the evangelical-capitalist resonance machine, this arrangement allows for populist appeals to voters who are contemptuous of the "woke elites" they believe run large technology firms, while simultaneously reassuring large corporate donors that a more classically conservative judiciary will overturn much information regulation as violative of the First Amendment.

[4] Frank Pasquale, *Privacy, Antitrust, and Power*, 20 GEO. MASON L. REV. 1009 (2013).

conjuncture. Part II explores governmental and corporate power, mapping their expansions to territorial and functional sovereignty (respectively). Part III interprets a series of moves in platform data governance as functional sovereignty, identifying efforts by large multinational corporations to assert their authority to decide how to resolve controversies and exercise power, regardless of territorial sovereigns' preferences. Part IV concludes with reflections on the comparative desirability of functional and territorial sovereignty. The deep paradox here is that the ostensibly "freedom-favoring" aspects of the erosion of territorial sovereignty may not disperse power, but instead merely transfer it, in less legitimate forms, to less accountable actors.

I. Introducing Functional Sovereignty

Neil Walker defines sovereignty as "the discursive form in which a claim concerning the existence and character of a supreme ordering power for a particular polity is expressed, which supreme ordering power purports to establish and sustain the identity and status of the particular polity *qua* polity and to provide a continuing source and vehicle of ultimate authority for the juridical order of that polity."[5] In other words, sovereignty is more than the ability to order affairs in a given space. Rather, theorists and advocates tend to invoke the term in order to both claim and valorize the power of an authority to command obedience. When the aspirational form of liberal democratic governance is the Habermasian ideal speech situation, shaped by the "unforced force of the better reason," or its deliberative democratic or republican American cousins, insistence on territorial sovereignty may seem a crude relic, or a path to absolutism.[6] Nevertheless, the term still has resonance for many, and cannot be gainsaid as a useful descriptive designation of a condition of unquestioned authority.

Most discussions of sovereignty in the realms of legal and political theory assume that the entity claiming sovereignty is a government of a territory. For example, the Brexit slogan "take back control" presumed an external

---

[5] Neil Walker, *Late Sovereignty in the European Union, in* SOVEREIGNTY IN TRANSITION 6 (Neil Walker ed., 2003).

[6] DON HERZOG, SOVEREIGNTY, RIP (dismissing the classical conception of sovereignty as utterly out of place in contemporary governance). For deliberative democratic ideals, *see* JURGEN HABERMAS, THE THEORY OF COMMUNICATIVE ACTION VOL. 2: SYSTEM AND LIFEWORLD (1985); MICHAEL SANDEL, DEMOCRACY'S DISCONTENT (1998); AMY GUTMANN & DENNIS THOMPSON, WHY DELIBERATIVE DEMOCRACY? (2004); Frank Michelman, *Law's Republic*, 97 YALE L. REV. 1493 (1988).

38 TWO VISIONS FOR DATA GOVERNANCE

power leeching away the potency and scope of the British government's prerogatives.[7] In practical politics, sovereignty has become a buzzword for nationalists asserting the power of local governments vis-à-vis supranational entities (like the EU or NATO) or global capital markets.[8]

There is, however, another "pretender to the throne," usurping contemporary states' sovereignty: multinational corporations.[9] Once countries join the World Trade Organization or treaties like the Berne Convention, they face several limits on their ability to regulate firms. International trade regimes' may encase corporation-favoring legal rules like Investor-State Dispute Settlement. The revenues of megafirms already exceed the budgets of many nations.[10] And where states may find that administrative processes and courts constrain their executives' decisions to act, corporations' boards are prone to exercise much less control on their chief executives.

The bureaucratic torpor of so many states is reduced in private, for-profit corporations, and this rapidity of response is a particularly potent force multiplier in an era of social acceleration.[11] Deregulation and preemption of state law also permits the expansion of corporate power: when state authority contracts, private parties fill the gap. That power can feel just as oppressive, and have effects just as pervasive, as governance by bureaucrats. As the great legal realist Robert Lee Hale stated, "There is government whenever one person or group can tell others what they must do and when those others have to obey or suffer a penalty."[12] Hale's work was an inspiration for many regulatory initiatives aimed at taming the worst business practices.

The standard justification for firms' power is a variation on Albert O. Hirschman's dichotomy of exit and voice: workers and consumers may not have much say in how the firm is run, but the exit option is always available. Hence many prominent advocates of laissez-faire have argued that capital is

---

[7] For an early analysis of this potential backlash dynamic, *see* GLYN MORGAN, THE IDEA OF A EUROPEAN SUPERSTATE (2005).

[8] Paolo Gerbaudo & Francesco Screti, *Reclaiming Popular Sovereignty: The Vision of the State in the Discourse of Podemos and the Movimento 5 Stelle*, 24 JAVNOST: THE PUBLIC 4, 320–35 (2017).

[9] DAVID ROTHKOPF, POWER INC.: THE EPIC RIVALRY BETWEEN BIG BUSINESS AND GOVERNMENT—AND THE RECKONING THAT LIES AHEAD (2013).

[10] For a thoughtful exposition of the process of "encasement" of market orders via international agreements (to be contrasted with Polanyian embedding of markets in a supportive social order), *see* QUINN SLOBODIAN, GLOBALISTS (2019); *see also* NANCY MCLEAN, DEMOCRACY IN CHAINS (2017) (on the constitutionalization of pro-business rules).

[11] On social acceleration, *see* WILLIAM E. SCHEUERMAN, LIBERAL DEMOCRACY AND THE SOCIAL ACCELERATION OF TIME (2020); HARTMUT ROSA, THE SOCIAL ACCELERATION OF TIME: A NEW THEORY OF MODERNITY (2016).

[12] ROBERT LEE HALE, FREEDOM THROUGH LAW—PUBLIC CONTROL OF PRIVATE GOVERNING POWER (1952).

INTRODUCING FUNCTIONAL SOVEREIGNTY   39

not coercive: to the extent sovereignty in capitalism exists at all, it is the sovereignty of the consumer casting "dollar votes" that matters. On this view, markets are a free and equilibrating play of incentives and choices.

To philosopher Elizabeth Anderson, however, to say "that wherever individuals are free to exit a relationship, authority cannot exist within it . . . is like saying that Mussolini was not a dictator, because Italians could emigrate."[13] Of course, emigrating from a nation-state is very difficult and often impossible for those who most want to do so. But what about the customer of a firm that is a monopoly or near-monopoly? Or the user of an Internet service with decades of data about their interactions, all tailored to help ensure the most targeted and useful search results? Or the buyers and sellers on a platform where the vast majority of their potential counterparties operate?

All these imbalances create a dynamic that makes Hirschman's classic "exit" option far less tenable. Where voice is necessary, we often expect some stake in governance (no matter how small). That, too, is denied by many firms to their users—shareholders and managers control the organization. Users' power is minuscule in comparison.

This governance role is particularly pronounced in the rise of platforms on the Internet. The platform business model is centered around data—gathering massive amounts of information about, say, riders and drivers (for transport platforms), employers and employees (for employment platforms), searchers and entities wanting to be found (for search engines). In many jurisdictions, platforms have fought both litigants' and governments' efforts to gain access to critical data about activities coordinated on the platform, as well as the platforms' own way of dealing with these activities.[14] Some constitutionalized claims—such as trade secrecy or free expression claims—successfully recruit the judiciary to declare the legislative and executive branches permanently disabled from making critical interventions to shape the platforms' actions in the public interest.[15]

---

[13] ELIZABETH ANDERSON, PRIVATE GOVERNMENT: HOW EMPLOYERS RULE OUR LIVES (AND WHY WE DON'T TALK ABOUT IT) (2017).

[14] *The only way to hold Facebook, Google, and others accountable: More access to platform data*, ALGORITHM WATCH (2020).

[15] Zhang v. Baidu (2013); Langdon v. Google, (2007); For a more general perspective on the First Amendment's deregulatory impact, *see* Julie Cohen, *The Zombie First Amendment*; Amy Kapczynski, *The Lochnerized First Amendment and the FDA: Toward a More Democratic Political Economy*, 118 COLUM. L. REV. 7 (2018); Amanda Shanor, *The New* Lochner, 133 WIS. L. REV. (2016).

40 TWO VISIONS FOR DATA GOVERNANCE

II. Asserting Functional Sovereignty

In his 1978 book *The Antitrust Paradox*, Robert Bork poured scorn on decades of U.S. antitrust enforcement, for two central reasons.[16] First, he considered it indeterminate; it was too difficult for business owners to plan future acquisitions and strategy based on under-developed, under-specified doctrine. Second, Bork believed that bigness was very often a sign of efficiency and success. The more market shares a firm had, the more customers had spent their dollar votes, as consumer sovereigns over markets, to elevate the firm.[17] To Bork, antitrust enforcement against powerful firms had a strong whiff of punishing the successful. Just as his conservative *confreres* opposed steeply progressive income taxes targeting millionaires and billionaires, so too they found megafirms to be sympathetic, even heroic actors, as they concentrated market power.

The Silicon Valley entrepreneur and Facebook and Palantir investor Peter Thiel took this Borkian ideal further in his book *Zero to One*.[18] For Thiel, systems like patent (which allow the inventor to monopolize use of her or his or its invention for a term of years) or scale-driven network effects in data collection or social networks (which generate massive returns via user lock-in) incentivize leaps in innovation. According to the political theorist Corey Robin, this ideal of admiration for the bold innovator finds its roots in both Macaulay's "Great Man" theory of history, and in Friedrich Nietzsche's hypostatization of the *ubermensch*, or superman.[19] Such theories legitimize Mark Zuckerberg's role as a kind of World President of a large swathe of social media, appointing (without constraint from a Senate) the quasi-justices of a Free Expression Supreme Court for the Facebooked World (under the

---

[16] Parts of this section earlier appeared in *From Territorial to Functional Sovereignty: The Case of Amazon*, LAW AND POLITICAL ECONOMY BLOG, Dec. 6, 2017; and in Frank Pasquale, *Digital Capitalism: How to Tame the Platform Juggernauts*, FES: WISODirekt, at https://library.fes.de/pdf-files/wiso/14444.pdf.

[17] The concept "consumer sovereignty" has been attributed to William Harold Hutt. To continue the law and political economy theme, we might analogize this normative affirmation as "output legitimacy," echoing Fritz Scharpf's theory of legitimacy distinct from "input legitimacy," which examines the procedures leading to decisions. Chicago School antitrust's focus on output (price, quantity, and theoretically quality) of goods and services as the critical maximands or desiderata of antitrust, is also distinct from the more structural and procedural foundations of many earlier and later approaches to competition policy.

[18] PETER THIEL, ZERO TO ONE (2014).

[19] Corey Robin, *Nietzsche's Marginal Children: On Friedrich Hayek*, THE NATION (2013), https://www.thenation.com/article/archive/nietzsches-marginal-children-friedrich-hayek/.

auspices of the "Facebook Oversight Board."). Megafirms may eventually give substance to a "nomos" for the earth.[20]

Key U.S. trade policies have fostered this ambition, as well as the extraordinary deference the U.S. government now must give "expressive" firms. Under current First Amendment doctrine, the power of private firms like Google, Apple, Twitter, Amazon, and Facebook is extraordinary, whether they are conceived as media (with expansive First Amendment protections) or a form of "intermedia" (like cable companies, which can also assert free speech rights). It is strange to hear U.S. conservatives complain about these powers so much recently, since they worked so strenuously to fill courts with judges and justices profoundly sympathetic to the free speech claims of corporations. But there is also a certain disingenuousness in some liberals' reply that "they're private firms, they can do whatever they want" to claims of censorship on the right. Had these platforms banned certain liberal or left politicians or causes, there would be justified anger and calls for government regulation—perhaps even for the "must-carry" regulations I proposed in 2016.[21] If implemented, these must-carry regulations would amount to a re-assertion of the prerogatives of territorial sovereigns over the functional sovereigns of new media.

Functional sovereignty is not limited to the Internet and characterizes developments in several data-intensive industries. Concentration is paying dividends for the largest banks in the United States (widely assumed to be too big to fail), and major health insurers (the last hope of neoliberals who want the insurers to use their bargaining power to reduce remarkably high U.S. healthcare costs). Like the digital giants, health insurance firms not only act as middlemen, but also aspire to capitalize on the knowledge they have gained from monitoring providers in order to supplant them and directly provide services. They aspire to govern, and not merely participate in, their respective sectors.

The core idea of antitrust is that the people, through government, can limit the size and power of economic entities, to require them to serve public ends. When the idea of the common good is discredited as hopelessly quaint and naive, it is easy to embrace rule by the largest corporations, granting them

---

[20] CARL SCHMITT, THE NOMOS OF THE EARTH IN THE INTERNATIONAL LAW OF JUS PUBLICUM EUROPAEUM (1950).

[21] Frank Pasquale, *Platform Neutrality: Enhancing Freedom of Expression in Spheres of Private Power*, 17 THEORETICAL INQUIRIES IN LAW 487 (2016).

functional sovereignty.[22] Nor has this horizon of functional sovereignty been merely theoretical. In areas they control, major digital firms are no longer market participants. Rather, they are market makers, able to exert what amounts to largely unaccountable regulatory control over the terms on which others can sell goods and services. Moreover, they aspire to displace more government roles over time, replacing the logic of territorial sovereignty with functional sovereignty in a wider array of human endeavors. In functional arenas from room-letting to transportation to commerce, persons will be increasingly subject to corporate, rather than democratic, control.

For example: the power of city regulators of short term stays wanes as Airbnb can use data-driven methods to effectively regulate room-letting, and then apartment- and house-letting.[23] Amazon came close to demanding special laws for its new headquarters when it set cities to compete for it, and a Georgia mayor even proposed creating a new town in the state and calling it "Amazon." Wisconsin established special judicial procedures for Foxconn.[24] Some vanguardists of functional sovereignty may suggest that online rating systems could replace state occupational licensure—so rather than having government boards license professionals, a platform like LinkedIn could collect star ratings on them. Presumably one-star physicians would be substantially cheaper than five-star ones, if market dynamics were allowed to fully take their course, further tiering health care and likely exacerbating health disparities.

This shift from territorial to functional sovereignty is creating a new digital political economy. Amazon's rise is instructive.[25] As Federal Trade Commission Chair Lina Khan has explained, "the company has positioned itself at the center of e-commerce and now serves as essential infrastructure for a host of other businesses that depend upon it."[26] The "everything store"

---

[22] Ajay Singh Chaudry & Raphael Chappe, *The Supermanagerial Reich*, L.A. REVIEW OF BOOKS (2016), https://lareviewofbooks.org/article/the-supermanagerial-reich/; DAVID KORTEN, WHEN CORPORATIONS RULE THE WORLD (1995); HARVEY COX, THE MARKET AS GOD (2016).

[23] Cliff Kuang, *An Exclusive Look at Airbnb's First Foray Into Urban Planning*, FAST COMPANY (2016), https://www.fastcompany.com/3062246/an-exclusive-look-at-airbnbs-first-foray-into-urban-planning.

[24] Sara Salinas, *A Georgia Mayor Wants to Build a New Town and Name It Amazon*, CNBC (2017), https://www.cnbc.com/2017/10/19/georgia-mayor-wants-amazons-second-headquarters-in-town-named-amazon.html; Scott Bauer, *Portions of Wisconsin's Foxconn Law Could be Unconstitutional, State Analysis Finds*, CHICAGO TRIBUNE (2017), https://www.chicagotribune.com/business/ct-foxconn-wisconsin-law-20170920-story.html.

[25] Lina M. Khan, *Amazon Bites Off Even More Monopoly Power*, N.Y. TIMES (2017), https://www.nytimes.com/2017/06/21/opinion/amazon-whole-foods-jeff-bezos.html.

[26] Lina M. Khan, *Amazon's Antitrust Paradox*, 126 YALE L. REV. 710 (2017).

may seem like just another service in the economy—a virtual mall. But when a firm combines tens of millions of customers with a "marketing platform, a delivery and logistics network, a payment service, a credit lender, an auction house . . . a hardware manufacturer, and a leading host of cloud server space," as Khan observes, it's not just another shopping option. It is aiming at becoming the "must-have" platform for serious sellers and buyers. With that power, it can increasingly force buyers to pay for ads to get the attention of shoppers. And as drives for efficiency leave buyers with less and less time to shop and money to spend, the lure of instant low prices is well-nigh irresistible. What small town stores found out during the rise of Walmart, small online retailers are discovering now: consumer loyalty is hard to maintain when survival is on the line, and a few dollars saved via Amazon may be the difference between making rent and being evicted.

Digital political economy helps us understand how platforms accumulate power. With online platforms, it is not a simple narrative of "best service wins." Network effects have been on the cyberlaw (and digital economics) agenda for over 20 years. Amazon's dominance has exhibited how network effects can be self-reinforcing. The more merchants there are selling on (or to) Amazon, the better shoppers can be assured that they are searching all possible vendors. The more shoppers there are, the more vendors consider Amazon a "must-have" venue. As crowds build on either side of the platform, the middleman becomes ever more indispensable. A new platform can enter the market—but until it obtains access to the 480 million items Amazon sells (often at deep discounts), why should the median consumer defect to it?

As artificial intelligence improves, the tracking of shopping into the Amazon groove will tend to become ever more rational for both buyers and sellers. Like a path through a forest trod ever clearer of debris, it becomes the natural default. To examine just one of many centripetal forces sucking money, data, and commerce into online behemoths, play out how the possibility of online conflict redounds in Amazon's favor. If you have a problem with a merchant online, do you want to pursue it as a one-off buyer? Or as someone whose reputation has been established over dozens or hundreds of transactions—and someone who can credibly threaten to deny Amazon hundreds or thousands of dollars of revenue each year? The same goes for merchants: the more tribute they can pay to Amazon, the more likely they are to achieve visibility in search results and attention (and perhaps even favor) when disputes come up. What Bruce Schneier said about security is increasingly true of commerce online: customers will want to be in the good graces

44 TWO VISIONS FOR DATA GOVERNANCE

of one of the neo-feudal giants who bring order to the online realm.[27] Yet few hesitate to think about exactly how the digital lords might use their data advantages against those they ostensibly protect.[28]

To better grasp these dynamics, consider Rory van Loo's characterization of the "corporation as courthouse"—that is, when platforms like Amazon run dispute resolution schemes to settle conflicts between buyers and sellers.[29] Van Loo describes both the efficiency gains that an Amazon settlement process might have over small claims court, and the potential pitfalls for consumers (such as opaque standards for deciding cases). Beyond such economic considerations, consider also the political and legal origins of e-commerce feudalism. For example, as consumer rights shrivel, it is rational for buyers to turn to Amazon (rather than overwhelmed small claims courts) to press their case. The evisceration of class actions, the rise of arbitration, boilerplate contracts—all these make the judicial system an increasingly vestigial organ in consumer disputes.[30] Individuals rationally turn to online giants for powers to impose order that libertarian legal doctrine stripped from the state.[31] And in so doing, they reinforce the very dynamics that led to the state's weakening in the first place.

This weakness became something of a joke when Amazon incited a bidding war for its second headquarters. Mayors abjectly begged Amazon to locate jobs in their jurisdictions. As readers of Richard Thaler's *The Winner's Curse* might have predicted, the competitive dynamics have tempted far too many to offer far too much in the way of incentives.[32] As journalist Danny Westneat confirmed:

---

[27] Bruce Schneier, *Feudal Security*, SCHNEIER ON SECURITY (2012), https://www.schneier.com/blog/archives/2012/12/feudal_sec.html.

[28] Ariel Ezrachi & Maurice E. Stucke, *Is Your Digital Assistant Devious?*, OXFORD L. STUD. Research Paper No. 52/2016, U. TENN. L. STUD. Research Paper No. 304 (2016), available at https://papers.ssrn.com/sol3/papers.cfm?abstract_id=2828117.

[29] Rory Van Loo, *The Corporation as Courthouse*, 33 YALE J. ON REG. 547 (2016).

[30] Herman Schwartz, *The Death of the Class-Action Lawsuit?*, THE NATION (2015), https://www.thenation.com/article/archive/the-death-of-the-class-action-lawsuit/; Jessica Silver-Greenberg & Robert Gebeloff, *Arbitration Everywhere, Stacking the Desk of Justice*, N.Y. TIMES (2015), https://www.nytimes.com/2015/11/01/business/dealbook/arbitration-everywhere-stacking-the-deck-of-justice.html; Margaret Jane Radin, BOILERPLATE: THE FINE PRINT, VANISHING RIGHTS, AND THE RULE OF LAW, (2012).

[31] Heather Boushey, *How the Radical Right Played the Long Game and Won*, N.Y. TIMES (2017), https://www.nytimes.com/2017/08/15/books/review/democracy-in-chains-nancy-maclean.html.

[32] RICHARD H. THALER, THE WINNER'S CURSE: PARADOXES AND ANOMALIES OF ECONOMIC LIFE (1991).

Chicago has offered to let Amazon pocket $1.32 billion in income taxes paid by its own workers.

Fresno has a novel plan to give Amazon special authority over how the company's taxes are spent.

Boston has offered to set up an "Amazon Task Force" of city employees working on the company's behalf.

Stonecrest, Georgia even offered to *cannibalize itself*, to give Bezos the chance to become mayor of a 345-acre annex that would be known as "Amazon, Georgia."[33]

Note that these maneuvers—what tax law scholar Tracey Kaye calls "corporate seduction" via tax and other incentives—are not new.[34] But as they accelerate, they mark a faster transfer of power from state to corporate actors.[35] The mayors are often in a weakened position because of a lack of revenue, and now they are succoring a corporate actor with a long history of fighting to push taxation even lower.[36] Similarly, the more online buyers and sellers are relying on Amazon to do their bidding or settle their disputes, the less power they have relative to Amazon itself. They are less like arms-length transactors with the company, than they are like subjects of a feudal lord, whose many roles include consumer and anti-fraud protection.[37]

Even the federal government may privatize critical procurement functions, relying on Amazon's giantism to extract deals that the Defense Department is itself unable to demand.[38] Procurement premised on public purpose could

---

[33] Danny Westneat, *This City Hall, Brought to You by Amazon*, SEATTLE TIMES (2017), Parts of this section earlier appeared in *From Territorial to Functional Sovereignty: The Case of Amazon*, LAW AND POLITICAL ECONOMY BLOG, Dec. 6, 2017, and in Frank Pasquale, *Digital Capitalism: How to Tame the Platform Juggernauts*, FES: WISODirekt, at https://library.fes.de/pdf-files/wiso/14444.pdf. https://web.archive.org/web/20230728215208; https://www.seattletimes.com/business/amazon/this-city-hall-brought-to-you-by-amazon/;

ASSOCIATED PRESS, *City Aims to Name New Town for Company: Amazon, Georgia*, CHICAGO TRIUBUNE (2017), https://www.chicagotribune.com/business/ct-biz-stonecrest-georgia-rename-amazon-20171003-story.html.

[34] Tracy A. Kaye, *The Gentle Art of Corporate Seduction: Tax Incentives in the United States and the European Union*, 57 KANSAS L. REV. 93 (2008).

[35] David Rothkopf, POWER, INC.: THE EPIC RIVALRY BETWEEN BIG BUSINESS AND GOVERNMENT—AND THE RECKONING THAT LIES AHEAD (2012).

[36] DEAN BAKER, THE CONSERVATIVE NANNY STATE, HOW THE WEALTHY USE THE GOVERNMENT TO STAY RICH AND GET RICHER (2006).; Arjun Kharpal & Silvia Amaro, *Amazon Is Ordered to Pay Nearly $300 Million by EU Over "Illegal Tax Advantage,"* CNBC (2017), https://www.cnbc.com/2017/10/04/amazon-eu-tax-bill-luxembourg-deal.html.

[37] Brad Littlejohn, *Big Tech and the Logic of Feudalism* 5(3) AMERICAN AFFAIRS 99 (2021).

[38] Jon D. Michaels, CONSTITUTIONAL COUP: PRIVATIZATION'S THREAT TO THE AMERICAN REPUBLIC (2017); David Dayen, *The "Amazon Amendment" Would Effectively Hand Government Purchasing Power Over to Amazon*, THE INTERCEPT (2017), https://theintercept.com/2017/11/02/amazon-amendment-online-marketplaces/.

46 TWO VISIONS FOR DATA GOVERNANCE

contribute to a Green New Deal.[39] When it is, instead, premised merely on the cheapest cost general contractor, it is an open invitation to continue the same unethical sourcing that has plagued so much other government purchasing.[40]

Solutions to Amazon's power will, no doubt, be hard to advance as a political matter. The firm has enormous political power, and is respected by many consumers for its extraordinary efficiencies. But understanding the bigger picture here is a first step toward understanding these efficiencies' costs. Political economy clarifies the stakes of Amazon's increasing power over commerce. We are not simply addressing dyadic transactions of individual consumers and merchants. Data access asymmetries will disadvantage consumers and merchants generally (and advantage Amazon as the middleman) for years to come.[41] Nor can we consider that power imbalance in isolation from the way Amazon pits cities against one another. Mastery of political dynamics is just as important to the firm's success as any technical or business acumen. And only political organization can stop its functional sovereignty from further undermining the territorial governance at the heart of democracy.[42]

Much the same could be said of other aspects of dominant digital platforms. Think, for instance, of long-standing demands by Apple and Google for 30 percent of the revenues earned by app developers selling via their app stores. This exaction has been lowered in varied small scale concessions since 2021, but the lack of a full accounting of the size of the fees generated relative to the costs of running their app stores is quite striking. This extraction of revenue might be thought of as a digital "tax," rather than a cost or fee, since it so clearly recalls the plenary authority of a state to demand some share of income from residents. When Arizona moved to regulate this power

---

[39] Christian Parenti, *The Big Green Buy, How Obama Can Use the Government's Purchasing Power to Spark the Clean-Energy Revolution*, THE NATION (2010), https://www.thenation.com/article/archive/big-green-buy/; The Green New Deal Group, *A Green New Deal*, NEW ECONOMIC FOUNDATION (2008), https://b.3cdn.net/nefoundation/8f737ea195fe56db2f_xbm6ihwb1.pdf.

[40] Rick Helfenbein, *How Government-Supported Forced Labor Is Undercutting American Manufacturers*, GOVERNMENT EXECUTIVES (2017), https://www.govexec.com/management/2017/10/how-government-supported-forced-labor-undercutting-american-manufacturers/141739/.

[41] Maurice E. Stucke & Allen P. Grunes, *Debunking the Myths Over Big Data and Antitrust*, U. TENN. L. STUD. Research Paper No. 276 (2015), https://papers.ssrn.com/sol3/papers.cfm?abstract_id=2612562.

[42] Stacy Mitchell & Olivia Lavecchia, *Amazon's Stranglehold: How the Company's Tightening Grip on the Economy Is Stifling Competition, Eroding Jobs, and Threatening Communities*, INST. LOCAL SELF-RELIANCE (2016), https://ilsr.org/amazon-stranglehold/.

III. Conclusion

The lesson here is not that there is only one, true way to govern life online. The state cannot micromanage every aspect of platforms, and they should be free to innovate in genuinely productive ways. When states become authoritarian, their governance of platforms becomes just as questionable as platforms' functional sovereigny. Indeed, there are many valid concerns that robust territorial sovereignty may give unaccountable states too much power in many areas of social relations. But the opposite approach, elevating functional over territorial sovereignty in key areas of Internet and data governance, may ultimately lead to similar concerns, by enabling the rise of reactionary political movements and unaccountable centers of private power.

The functional sovereignty of very large technology platforms is now tending to discredit its primary ideological justification: that a democratic state must not control too much of what information industries do. In some areas large Internet platforms micromanage users, but in other important spheres something close to anarchy reigns. This leadership vacuum renewed the relevance of a classic paradox identified by Karl Popper in *The Open Society and its Enemies*:

> [T]he paradox of tolerance: Unlimited tolerance must lead to the disappearance of tolerance. If we extend unlimited tolerance even to those who are intolerant, if we are not prepared to defend a tolerant society against the onslaught of the intolerant, then the tolerant will be destroyed, and tolerance with them.[44]

Popper also mentions a "paradox of democracy, or more precisely, of majority rule; i.e. the possibility that the majority may decide that a tyrant should rule."[45] One can model the rise of the functional sovereignty of

---

[43] Jerod McDonald-Evoy, *How Apple and Google killed an Arizona bill aimed at their app store profits*, AZ MIRROR, Sept. 7, 2021, at https://www.azmirror.com/2021/09/07/how-apple-and-google-killed-an-arizona-bill-aimed-at-their-app-store-profits/.

[44] Popper, *The Open Society and its Enemies: The Spell of Plato* 226 n.4 (1945).

[45] *Id.*

technology platforms in the United States as the start of a strange interaction between Popper's paradoxes of tolerance and democracy (which are themselves reminiscent of Plato's theory of regimes in Book VIII of the *Republic*). Majorities have elected representatives who have let the platforms rule important aspects of social and political life capriciously. That caprice and corresponding neglect of public values have enabled antidemocratic forces to spread lies about the 2020 election, which have in turn rationalized efforts around the country to tilt election laws in antidemocratic ways. Only the willfully naive believe the persons who demand tolerance for the spread of the 2020 election lies will be consistent civil libertarians if they take power—witness, for instance, how many of them simultaneously push to ban critical race theory in schools. Thus illiberal forces have found the United States' declining territorial and rising functional sovereigns unwilling or unable to rebuff their repeated efforts to push public policies in directions that culminate in a hollowing of democracy, including gerrymanders and vote-counting procedures that are so extremely one-sided they are undermining the state's democratic legitimacy.[46]

A state that is constitutionally disabled from preventing widespread and effective disinformation campaigns on matters of utmost public concern (such as the validity of elections, and the safety of vaccines in a world-historical pandemic), or plots to disrupt its electoral process, is not a state capable of preserving its own traditions of rights and freedom, much less credibly promoting them elsewhere. Given that the January 6, 2021, insurrection ended an over 150-year-long U.S. tradition of peaceful transitions of presidential power, U.S. leaders should reflect on what are the baselines of societal consensus and intermediary responsibility that are necessary for a democracy to function.

The first steps toward regaining true territorial sovereignty over data in the United States are clear. Revitalized leadership at the Federal Trade Commission and Department of Justice are taking steps toward reversing decades of concentration of corporate power. Courts must quickly defer to agencies that have developed reasonable, statutorily authorized steps toward mitigating wicked problems now being inadequately addressed by functional sovereigns. And policymakers must learn from abroad, translating just initiatives for territorial sovereignty into an American idiom of democratized governance of economy and society.

---

[46] Steven Simon & Jonathan Stevenson, *How Do We Neutralize the Militias*, N.Y. REV. BOOKS, Aug. 19, 2021.

2

A Starting Point for Re-thinking "Sovereignty" for the Online Environment

Dan Svantesson*

I. Introduction

There is a surprisingly thin line between finding a solution that suits everyone and finding a solution that suits no one. In the concept of "sovereignty," as currently applied online, we find an example falling into the latter of these options—while superficially appealing to many, "sovereignty" as applied actually suits no one when analyzed in detail. The same is even more true of the related sub-concepts such as "digital sovereignty" and "data sovereignty" that so often are touted these days.

This chapter draws attention to how the traditional binary conception of sovereignty—in the sense of an act either violating sovereignty, or not—is incompatible, or at least a poor fit, with the realities of the interconnected online environment. In this context it will be argued that the time has come to challenge the reliance on binary distinctions such as this, and the related binary distinction between territorial on the one hand and extraterritorial on the other.

Having analyzed these matters in detail, this chapter proceeds to advance a conception of sovereignty anchored in the notion of "state dignity." The application of this conception of sovereignty is then illustrated.

---

* Work on this chapter was supported by ERDF "CyberSecurity, CyberCrime and Critical Information Infrastructures Center of Excellence" (No. CZ.02.1.01/0.0/0.0/16_019/0000822). I am also grateful for having had the opportunity to discuss the concept of sovereignty in detail with my colleagues (Steven Freeland, Samuli Haataja, Danielle Ireland-Piper, Wendy Bonython, Jonathan Crowe, Rebecca Azzopardi, and Nathan Mark) within Bond University's "Technology and Jurisdiction Research Team," and my colleagues Anna-Maria Osula and Radim Polčák within the CyberSecurity, CyberCrime and Critical Information Infrastructures Center of Excellence at Masaryk University. Those discussions have helped develop my understanding of sovereignty. However, the views expressed here are of course mine alone.

Dan Svantesson, *A Starting Point for Re-thinking "Sovereignty" for the Online Environment* In: *Data Sovereignty.* Edited by: Anupam Chander and Haochen Sun, Oxford University Press. © Oxford University Press 2023. DOI: 10.1093/oso/9780197582794.003.0003

50 A STARTING POINT FOR RE-THINKING "SOVEREIGNTY"

Finally, before reaching a few concluding remarks, some issues with the concepts of "data sovereignty" and "digital sovereignty" are highlighted.

Thus, this chapter addresses two separate, but related, questions:

(1) What does the current concept of sovereignty entail for the online environment; and

(2) How could anchoring the concept of "sovereignty" in a notion of "state dignity" help create order and harmony online?

II. The Point of Departure: Sovereignty Applies Online, but How?

While it has not always been so,[1] today, it is uncontroversial to suggest that sovereignty applies online. In fact, this is one of the few things upon which there is widespread consensus.[2] But the value of this apparent consensus is superficial indeed given that those who say *that* sovereignty applies online generally do not engage with the considerably more difficult question of *how* sovereignty applies online. This raises a most severe question: What if the reality is that the reason why we do not have an answer to the "how question" is that sovereignty cannot be applied in a meaningful manner online? The very prospect of this being the case shows the primitive level we currently are at and how badly we need more expertise directed at this question.[3]

Another clear indicator of the messiness of this area of law is found in the sheer number of sovereignty-related concepts that are being thrown around in the debates. A recent book chapter of high quality and great value is illustrative. Chapter 3 of Buchan's excellent book *Cyber Espionage and International Law* is titled "Cyber Espionage and the Rules of Territorial Sovereignty, Non-Intervention and the Non-Use of Force."[4] That chapter alone makes reference

---

[1] John Perry Barlow, *A Declaration of the Independence of Cyberspace*, ELECTRONIC FRONTIER FOUNDATION (Feb. 8, 1996), https://www.eff.org/cyberspace-independence.

[2] *See, e.g.*, U.N. General Assembly, *Report of the Group of Governmental Experts on Developments in the Field of Information and Telecommunications in the Context of International Security*, U.N. Doc. A/ 68/ 98 (June 24, 2013), https://undocs.org/A/68/98; U.N. General Assembly, *Final Substantive Report*, U.N. Doc. A/AC.290/2021/CRP.2 (Mar. 10, 2021), https://front.un-arm.org/wp-content/uploads/2021/03/Final-report-A-AC.290-2021-CRP.2.pdf.

[3] *See further* Dan Svantesson, *Is International Law Ready for the (Already Ongoing) Digital Age? Perspectives from Private and Public International Law*, in INTERNATIONAL LAW FOR A DIGITAL WORLD (Marjolein J. Busstra et al. eds., 2020).

[4] RUSSELL BUCHAN, CYBER ESPIONAGE AND INTERNATIONAL LAW 48–69 (2018).

to no less than 12 sovereignty-related concepts: typically without devoting any time to distinguishing them from each other or to discussing how they relate to each other.[5] Buchan's valuable book is only one example of this issue, and with such a plethora of related and undefined concepts in use, the risk of commentators speaking at cross-purposes is obvious.

More broadly, in the survey that formed the base for the *Internet & Jurisdiction Global Status Report 2019*,[6] several interviewed experts emphasized the concern that, in the Internet jurisdiction field, legal concepts are old fashioned and outdated. Furthermore, one of the survey questions posed the claim that we already apply the right legal concepts to address cross-border legal challenges on the Internet. Among the surveyed experts, 46 percent either disagreed or strongly disagreed, 36 percent indicated that they neither agreed nor disagreed, and only 18 percent either agreed or strongly agreed.

This, it is submitted, hints at what may be termed "artificial (i.e., manmade) regulatory challenges" in that the frameworks and concepts—including the concept of sovereignty—being applied are insufficient to address the issues with which we are confronted. In general, it seems that international lawyers are looking at all changes taking place in today's world through the lenses of vested concepts such as extraterritoriality, sovereignty, etc. They want the world to be guided by reference to these concepts. Yet it should perhaps be the other way round—the concepts we use should be guided by how the world in fact is. While we of course ought to make use of those concepts that truly remain useful, we must also be prepared to let concepts develop over time and indeed to develop new concepts if reality so requires. In other words, the inadequacy of the tools may cause regulatory challenges preventing, or at least limiting, progress.

It seems to me that the Internet jurisdiction debate—including as it relates to sovereignty—these days is focused on tackling the most imminent day-to-day issues (some of the "genuine regulatory challenges"[7]), at the expense

---

[5] The following concepts are mentioned: "territorial sovereignty," "sovereign right," "sovereign decision," "sovereign state," "sovereign equality," "state sovereignty," "sovereign authority," "sovereign cyber infrastructure," "sovereign prerogative," "sovereign physical territory," "sovereign competence," and "sovereign government." Thus, despite the already large number of sovereignty-related terms used, they do not include the concepts of "digital sovereignty," "data sovereignty," "information sovereignty," "informational sovereignty," or "technology sovereignty" commonly seen today.

[6] DAN SVANTESSON, INTERNET & JURISDICTION GLOBAL STATUS REPORT 2019 (2019), https://www.internetjurisdiction.net/news/release-of-worlds-first-internet-jurisdiction-global-status-report.

[7] In the context of applying international law to Internet activities or situations, there are numerous instances of competing legitimate interests; state A's protection of free speech may be difficult

of attention being directed at the underlying conceptual mess: that is, the mentioned "artificial regulatory challenges." This is of course natural given the very real impact these challenges have for society. However, real progress can only be made where we also tackle the "artificial regulatory challenges"— the current mess is harmful and needs to be eliminated as much as possible.

At any rate, perhaps it can be assumed that the descriptor sovereign, or sovereignty, does not always add much substance. However, for the purpose of conceptual clarity, it would no doubt be of value to map out, and gain consensus on, matters such as:

- What turns a "right" into a "sovereign right" and a "decision" into a "sovereign decision"?
- What is the relationship between "sovereign authority," "sovereign prerogative," and "sovereign competence"?
- Does "territorial sovereignty" correspond to the "sovereign physical territory," and how does "sovereign cyber infrastructure" fit within that?
- If there is a need to write out terms such as "sovereign state" and "sovereign government," does that mean that there can be a "non-sovereign state" and a "non-sovereign government"?

Regrettably, not all these questions can be addressed within the scope of this chapter. Here, it will have to suffice to work from a regurgitation of the conventional wisdom regarding sovereignty such as the omnipresent statement from *Island of Palmas*: "Sovereignty in the relations between States signifies independence. Independence in regard to a portion of the globe is the right to exercise therein, to the exclusion of any other State, the functions of a State"[8] and standard statements in scholarly works such as that:

> The corollaries of the sovereignty and equality of states are: (a) a jurisdiction, prima facie exclusive, over a territory and the permanent population living there; (b) a duty of non-intervention in the area of exclusive

---

to reconcile with state B's restrictions on hate speech, and so on. On a slightly more general level, we may observe that broad claims of jurisdiction may unreasonably interfere with the rights of people in other states, while restrictive approaches to jurisdiction may render a victim without realistic access to justice. Thus, the difficulties we experience in applying international law to the Internet stem from the fact that the "genuine regulatory challenges" we need to work with are both numerous and go to the depth of involving the most fundamental legal notions.

[8] Island of Palmas (Neth. v. U.S.), 2 R.I.A.A. 829 (Perm. Ct. Arb. 1982).

jurisdiction of other states; and (3) the ultimate dependence upon consent of obligations arising whether from customary law or from treaties[.][9]

Put simply, conventional thinking treats the concept of sovereignty as a binary concept of independence and exclusiveness as to the right to control access to and egress from their territory, and exclusiveness as to the right to perform governmental functions within their territory.

III. Three Examples Showcasing the Messy State of Sovereignty

As already hinted at, the application of sovereignty to the online environment is characterized by uncertainty and inconsistency. Further evidence that this is so may be gained by considering and contrasting a selection of examples of how sovereignty is manifested online. I will here restrict myself to three illustrative examples.

A. Sovereignty and Law Enforcement Access to Data

Imagine a scenario in which a law enforcement agency in state A arrests a citizen of state A in state A and takes possession of the suspect's computer. Via the computer, the law enforcement agency downloads the suspect's files stored on a server in state B. Is this a violation of state B's sovereignty?

Traditionally, investigative measures such as this are viewed as an aspect of enforcement jurisdiction and territorially restricted. Thus Crawford, for example, expresses a commonly held belief when he proclaims: "Persons may not be arrested, a summons may not be served, police or tax investigations may not be mounted, orders for production of documents may not be executed, on the territory of another state, except under the terms of a treaty or other consent given."[10]

---

[9] JAMES CRAWFORD, BROWNLIE'S PRINCIPLES OF PUBLIC INTERNATIONAL LAW 457 (8th ed. 2012).

[10] *Id.* at 479. Elsewhere, I have questioned Crawford's claim and pointed to the weakness of the sources upon which he relies for his claim. DAN SVANTESSON, SOLVING THE INTERNET JURISDICTION PUZZLE 165–66 (2017) [hereinafter SVANTESSON, SOLVING THE INTERNET JURISDICTION PUZZLE]. Furthermore, as can be seen both in the US's CLOUD Act and in the current e-evidence reform in the European Union, Crawford's claim no longer reflects current state practice. Indeed, for some time, I have advocated that we ought to recognize "investigative jurisdiction" as a distinct category. Dan Svantesson, *Extraterritoriality in the Context of Data Privacy Regulation*, 7 MASARYK U. J.L. & TECH.

Thus, conventional thinking suggests that the scenario above involves a violation of sovereignty.

B. Sovereignty and Content Removal Orders

The scenario above demonstrated that cross-border *access* to data may be seen to violate sovereignty under traditional conceptions of sovereignty. Against that background, one may have assumed that cross-border *removal* of data would be viewed as an even more severe violation of sovereignty under traditional conceptions. However, that does not appear to be the case.

Imagine that a court in state A orders a party in state B to delete content held by it on servers in state B. The content is lawful under the laws of state B, but threatened with contempt of court, the party in state B complies with the order. Is this a violation of state B's sovereignty?

I have not been able to find any support in international law literature for treating this as a violation of sovereignty. Further, I have found no evidence of states expressly approaching this as a violation of sovereignty.[11] Yet clearly the forced deletion mandated by state A in the form of a court order (backed up with a threat of a contempt of court order) is more invasive than is the mere access to data by foreign law enforcement.

C. Sovereignty and Peacetime Cyber Espionage

The inconsistency and uncertainty continue if we consider how traditional conceptions of sovereignty approach peacetime cyber espionage. Imagine, for example, that in times of peace, state A hacks into a computer system of state B. Data of national security relevance are copied by state A. Is this a violation of state B's sovereignty?

---

87 (2013); *see further* SVANTESSON, SOLVING THE INTERNET JURISDICTION PUZZLE, *supra* note 10, at 165–67.

[11] However, perhaps, e.g., the Court of Justice of the European Union hinted at a sovereignty issue in this context in Case C-507/17, Google LLC v. Commission nationale de l'informatique et des libertés (CNIL), ECLI:EU:C:2019:772 (Sept. 24, 2019) and in Case C-18/18, Eva Glawischnig-Piesczek v. Facebook Ireland Ltd. ECLI:EU:C:2019:821 (Oct. 3, 2019).

The general consensus seems to be that there is no general consensus as to whether the scenario above involves a violation of sovereignty.[12]

IV. Sovereignty and the Four Functions of International Law

Building on what I have articulated elsewhere,[13] I argue that international law fulfills at least four different roles. International law is (1) a tool to decide legal disputes; (2) a tool to provide a framework to control, to guide, and to plan life out of court; (3) a tool to express and communicate the values of those who created the law; and (4) a tool—a surface or a playing board—on which political adversaries recognize each other as such and pursue their adversity in terms of something shared.[14]

If the above is accepted, it may be enlightening to consider the extent to which the concept of sovereignty, as tradition would have us apply it, performs in relation to these four functions. First, it is clear from decisions such as *Island of Palmas*[15] that—at least on some occasions—sovereignty may be "successfully"[16] used as a tool to decide legal disputes in disputes relating

---

[12] *Compare, e.g.*, Ybo Buruma, *International Law and Cyberspace - Issues of Sovereignty and the Common Good, in* INTERNATIONAL LAW FOR A DIGITAL WORLD (Marjolein J. Busstra et al., 2020); BUCHAN, *supra* note 4, at 48–69; Jared Beim, *Enforcing a Prohibition on International Espionage*, 18 CHICAGO J. INT'L L. 647 (2018).

[13] Dan Svantesson, *A Jurisprudential Justification for Extraterritoriality in (Private) International Law*, 13 SANTA CLARA J. INT'L L. 517, 551–52 (2015) [hereinafter Svantesson, *A Jurisprudential Justification for Extraterritoriality in (Private) International Law*]. *See further* SVANTESSON, SOLVING THE INTERNET JURISDICTION PUZZLE, *supra* note 10, at 129–32.

[14] The first two of these roles may be derived from Hart: "The principal functions of the law as a means of social control are not to be seen in private litigation or prosecutions, which represent vital but still ancillary provisions for the failures of the system. It is to be seen in the diverse ways in which the law is used to control, to guide, and to plan life out of court." H.L.A. HART, THE CONCEPT OF LAW 40 (3d ed. 2012). The third role, I articulated in Svantesson, *A Jurisprudential Justification for Extraterritoriality in (Private) International Law, supra* note 13, at 551–52. The fourth role was articulated by Koskenniemi: "[It] is international law's formalism that brings political antagonists together as they invoke contrasting understandings of its rules and institutions. In the absence of agreement over, or knowledge of the 'true' objectives of political community—that is to say, in an agnostic world—the pure form of international law provides the shared surface—the only such surface—on which political adversaries recognise each other as such and pursue their adversity in terms of something shared, instead of seeking to attain full exclusion—'outlawry'—of the other. In this sense, international law's value and its misery lie in its being the fragile surface of political community among states, other communities, individuals who disagree about their preferences but do this within a structure that invites them to argue in terms of an assumed universality." MARTTI KOSKENNIEMI, THE POLITICS OF INTERNATIONAL LAW 266 (2011).

[15] Island of Palmas (Neth. v. U.S.), 2 R.I.A.A. 829 (Perm. Ct. Arb. 1982).

[16] The word successfully here should not be misunderstood. I do not mean to comment on the quality of the decisions that are rendered based on the current application of the concept of sovereignty.

56 A STARTING POINT FOR RE-THINKING "SOVEREIGNTY"

to activities in the "real," physical, world. This does not, however, necessarily translate well into the adjudication of disputes stemming from the online environment. Second, given the undisputable uncertainty associated with the concept of sovereignty, it seems reasonable to conclude that the concept performs poorly in its function as a tool to provide a framework to control, to guide, and to plan life out of court. Third, the noted uncertainty could also be seen as an indication that the concept of sovereignty, as currently applied, performs rather poorly in the function as a tool to express and communicate the values of those who created the law. However, it may here be added that, the fact that states so frequently opt to articulate their respective positions by reference to the concept of sovereignty suggests that the concept has a value in relation to this function. Fourth, not least given how widespread is its use, it seems equally clear that the concept of sovereignty—perhaps due to its inherent vagueness—is most successful in its function as a tool forming part of the surface or playing board on which political adversaries recognize each other as such and pursue their adversity in terms of something shared. Having said that, I hasten to acknowledge the inherent dangers associated with a relatively vague concept, such as sovereignty, being used for the third and fourth mentioned functions. The risk of misunderstandings and disagreements is obvious: misunderstandings and disagreements that may quickly escalate to dangerous levels.

Based on the above, we can rank the performance of the traditional concept of sovereignty in respect of the four functions of international law. From best to worst:

(1) The traditional concept of sovereignty is primarily a tool forming part of the surface or playing board on which political adversaries recognize each other as such and pursue their adversity in terms of something shared. In this role its vagueness and the uncertainty with which it is associated is both its most significant advantage and a major cause for concern.

(2) The traditional concept of sovereignty performs reasonably well as a tool to express and communicate the values of those who (i.e., the states) created the law. Also in this context its vagueness and the uncertainty with which it is associated is both its most significant advantage and a major cause for concern.

(3) The traditional concept of sovereignty performs reasonably well as a tool to decide legal disputes stemming from offline. However, its

vagueness and the uncertainty with which it is associated creates an unpredictable legal framework and makes it difficult to ensure consistency in its application. Further, its application to online disputes is less obvious.

(4) The traditional concept of sovereignty performs poorly as a tool to provide a framework to control, to guide, and to plan life out of court. Its vagueness and the uncertainty with which it is associated creates an unpredictable legal framework and increases the risk of misunderstandings and conflict.

If a concept performs poorly in all four of these functions, it can be seen as useless. But if it is (a) used sometimes as a tool to decide legal disputes and (b) frequently used as a tool to express and communicate values and as a tool forming part of the surface or playing board on which political adversaries recognize each other as such and pursue their adversity in terms of something shared, and at the same time (c) performs poorly as a tool to provide a framework to control, to guide, and to plan life out of court, then it is a dangerous concept indeed.

V. The Binary Nature of the Current Concept of Sovereignty

Like the (in a sense associated) binary distinction between territorial and extraterritorial, sovereignty as a binary concept is one of the most central concepts under stress in the online environment. This should not come as a surprise. Similar to how other binary simplifications, such as the distinction between day and night, work for certain purposes but are inadequate for other important purposes, binary simplifications of complex legal matters are bound to prove inadequate.

Much like how the day/night simplification has been supplemented by, for example, dusk and dawn, and indeed the many nuances in between catered for using the 24-hour clock, the sovereignty concept must adequately reflect the nuances involved. Thus, sovereignty as a binary concept has limited legal utility. For many purposes, it must be approached as a matter of degree: that is, "the act by state B is contrary to state A's sovereignty to an unacceptable degree." Only then can we start to apply it in a sensible manner online.

58 A STARTING POINT FOR RE-THINKING "SOVEREIGNTY"

Elsewhere, I have argued in favor of the following nuanced—non-binary—jurisprudential framework for jurisdiction, to replace the binary territorial/extraterritorial notion of jurisdiction:

In the absence of an obligation under international law to exercise jurisdiction, a state may only exercise jurisdiction where:

(1) there is a substantial connection between the matter and the state seeking to exercise jurisdiction;

(2) the state seeking to exercise jurisdiction has a legitimate interest in the matter; and

(3) the exercise of jurisdiction is reasonable given the balance between the state's legitimate interests and other interests.[17]

Space limitations prevent a detailed discussion of the framework here; however, I have discussed it in detail elsewhere.[18] At the minimum it should be noted that these are merely core principles on which more detailed jurisdictional rules and tests may be formulated. As is suggested below, perhaps this structure may prove to be of use also in relation to the concept of sovereignty.

VI. Sovereignty = "State" + "Exclusiveness"?

Looking at terms such as "sovereign right," "territorial sovereignty," "sovereign decision," "sovereign equality," "sovereign authority," "sovereign cyber infrastructure," "sovereign prerogative," "sovereign physical territory," and "sovereign competence," one possible definition of the concept of sovereignty is "state" plus "exclusiveness." Under such a definition, a "sovereign right," for example, means a state's right that is exclusive. However, such a definition raises several questions. First, is it truly correct to view sovereignty as something only states may possess? This is an important question, for example in relation to Indigenous peoples, but it is not a topic pursued further here.

We can now turn to the exclusiveness element emphasized in *Island of Palmas* ("Sovereignty in the relations between States signifies independence.

---

[17] Dan Svantesson, *A New Jurisprudential Framework for Jurisdiction: Beyond the Harvard Draft*, 109 AJIL UNBOUND 69 (2015).

[18] SVANTESSON, SOLVING THE INTERNET JURISDICTION PUZZLE, *supra* note 10; RADIM POLČÁK & DAN SVANTESSON, INFORMATION SOVEREIGNTY: DATA PRIVACY, SOVEREIGN POWERS AND THE RULE OF LAW (2017).

Independence in regard to a portion of the globe is the right to exercise therein, to the exclusion of any other State, the functions of a State."[19]), and in standard statements in scholarly works such as that by Crawford ("The corollaries of the sovereignty and equality of states are: (a) a jurisdiction, prima facie exclusive, over a territory and the permanent population living there"[20]). It is of course noteworthy that Crawford speaks of exclusiveness as being prima facie and does so specifically in the context of jurisdiction over a territory and the permanent population living there while *Island of Palmas* does so regarding the right to exercise the functions of a state within a portion of the globe.

Much could be made of these differences. However, my concern applies to both uses. Put simply, incorporating exclusives within the concept of sovereignty renders it unusable in the interconnected cyber context. We can call this the "exclusiveness trap." To my mind, we must avoid the "exclusiveness trap" without for that sake rendering the concept of sovereignty meaningless. Further below, I will seek to do so by anchoring the concept of sovereignty in the notion of state dignity; sovereignty being treated as a matter of degree, rather than something binary, can—I submit—take us out of the "exclusiveness trap."

VII. Sovereignty—Rule or Principle?

Attempts at applying the concept of sovereignty to the online environment have resulted in debates going to the very core of that concept.[21] Most prominently, there is a healthy debate as to whether sovereignty is itself *a binding rule* of international law, or rather *a principle* of international law that guides state interactions but does not dictate results under international law.

Most of the states that have expressed a view on the matter seem to have sided with the proposition that sovereignty is indeed a binding rule of international law, rather than merely a principle. Examples of states falling into this category include the Netherlands;[22]

---

[19] Island of Palmas (Neth. v. U.S.), 2 R.I.A.A. 829 (Perm. Ct. Arb. 1982).

[20] CRAWFORD, *supra* note 9, at 457.

[21] This section draws, and expands, upon Dan Svantesson, *"Lagom Jurisdiction"—What Viking Drinking Etiquette Can Teach Us about Internet Jurisdiction and Google France*, 12 MASARYK U. J.L. & TECH. 29 (2018).

[22] Letter from the Government of the Kingdom of the Netherlands, Minister of Foreign Affairs to Parliament 2 (July 2019), https://unoda-web.s3.amazonaws.com/wp-content/uploads/2020/02/appendix-Internaional-law-in-cyberspace-kingdom-of-the-netherlands.pdf.

60   A STARTING POINT FOR RE-THINKING "SOVEREIGNTY"

France;[23] Austria;[24] the Czech Republic;[25] Finland;[26] Iran;[27] and recently, Germany.[28] However, it must be noted that this apparent consensus is superficial indeed since the respective positions adopted among these states differ, or are silent, on the circumstances in which sovereignty is in fact violated.

The main proponents for sovereignty to be viewed as a principle rather than a rule are the United Kingdom and the United States. For example, the United Kingdom has articulated the position that sovereignty is "fundamental to the international rules-based system" but that there is no "specific rule or additional prohibition" for cyber activities that fall below the use of force and intervention thresholds,[29] and that "there is no such rule as a matter of current international law."[30] Furthermore, according to a US DoD memo, the law does not presently support the proposition that "sovereignty acts as a binding legal norm" relevant to cyber activities.[31] Yet other states have managed to adopt both of the views noted above. In late 2020, the New Zealand Foreign Affairs & Trade expressed its view on the matter and argued that:

---

[23] U.N. Secretary-General, *Developments in the Field of Information and Telecommunications in the Context of International Security: Report of the Secretary-General*, at 22–26, U.N. Doc. A/74/120 (June 24, 2019).

[24] Austria maintained that "a violation of the principle of State sovereignty constitutes an internationally wrongful act." U.N. Open-Ended Working Group, *Comments by Austria, Pre-Draft Report of the OEWG—ICT* (Mar. 31, 2020), https://front.un-arm.org/wp-content/uploads/2020/04/comments-by-austria.pdf.

[25] The Czech Republic noted that it considers "the principle of sovereignty as an independent right and the respect to sovereignty as an independent obligation." CZECH REPUBLIC, STATEMENT BY RICHARD KADLČÁK AT OPEN-ENDED WORKING GROUP ON DEVELOPMENTS IN THE FIELD OF INFORMATION AND TELECOMMUNICATIONS IN THE CONTEXT OF INTERNATIONAL SECURITY OF THE FIRST COMMITTEE OF THE GENERAL ASSEMBLY OF THE UNITED NATIONS (2020), https://www.nukib.cz/download/publications_en/CZ%20Statement%20-%20OEWG%20-%20International%20Law%2011.02.2020.pdf.

[26] According to Finland, sovereignty is "a primary norm of public international law, a breach of which amounts to an internationally wrongful act and triggers State responsibility." Ministry for Foreign Affairs, *Finland Published Its Positions on Public International Law in Cyberspace*, FINNISH GOVERNMENT (Oct. 15, 2020), https://valtioneuvosto.fi/en/-/finland-published-its-positions-on-public-international-law-in-cyberspace.

[27] *See* ISLAMIC REPUBLIC OF IRAN, DECLARATION OF GENERAL STAFF OF THE ARMED FORCES OF THE ISLAMIC REPUBLIC OF IRAN REGARDING INTERNATIONAL LAW APPLICABLE TO THE CYBERSPACE (2020), https://nournews.ir/En/News/53144/General-Staff-of-Iranian-Armed-Forces-Warns-of-Tough-Reaction-to-Any-Cyber-Threat.

[28] THE FEDERAL GOVERNMENT OF GERMANY, ON THE APPLICATION OF INTERNATIONAL LAW IN CYBERSPACE 4 (2021), https://www.auswaertiges-amt.de/blob/2446304/2ae17233b62966a4b7f16d50ca3c6802/on-the-application-of-international-law-in-cyberspace-data.pdf.

[29] Jeremy Wright, Attorney Gen. of the U.K., Speech at Chatham House Royal Institute for International Affairs: Cyber and International Law in the 21st Century (May 23, 2018), https://www.gov.uk/government/speeches/cyber-and-international-law-in-the-21st-century.

[30] *Id.*

[31] Memorandum from Jennifer M O'Connor, Gen. Counsel of the Dep't of Def., International Law Framework for Employing Cyber Capabilities in Military Operations 3 (Jan. 19, 2017).

SOVEREIGNTY—RULE OR PRINCIPLE? 61

11. The *principle of sovereignty* prohibits the interference by one state in the inherently governmental functions of another and prohibits the exercise of state power or authority on the territory of another state. In the physical realm, the principle has *legal effect through* the prohibition on the use of force, through the rule of non-intervention and also through *a standalone rule of territorial sovereignty.* [. . .]

12. In the cyber realm, the principle of sovereignty *is given effect through the prohibition* on the use of force and the rule of non-intervention. New Zealand considers that the standalone rule of territorial sovereignty also applies in the cyber context but acknowledges that further state practice is required for the precise boundaries of its application to crystallise.[32] (emphasis added)

Thus, the New Zealand view seems to be that sovereignty is a principle of international law, but that it has part of its legal effect through territorial sovereignty that, in contrast, New Zealand sees as a rule of international law.

The core of the current debate was neatly showcased in an excellent Symposium on Sovereignty, Cyberspace, and the Tallinn Manual 2.0 published in 2017 in the *American Journal of International Law Unbound*.[33] In their contribution, Gary P. Corn (a Staff Judge Advocate, United States Cyber Command) and Robert Taylor (a Former Principal Deputy General Counsel, U.S. Department of Defense) argue that:

Some argue that [. . .] sovereignty is itself a binding rule of international law that precludes virtually any action by one state in the territory of another that violates the domestic law of that other state, absent consent. However, law and state practice instead indicate that sovereignty serves as a principle of international law that guides state interactions, but is not itself a binding rule that dictates results under international law. While this principle of sovereignty, including territorial sovereignty, should factor into the conduct of every cyber operation, it does not establish an absolute bar against individual or collective state cyber operations that

---

[32] New Zealand Foreign Affairs & Trade, The Application of International Law to State Activity in Cyberspace (2020), https://www.mfat.govt.nz/assets/Peace-Rights-and-Secur ity/International-security/International-Cyber-statement.pdf. See also the recently articulated position of Switzerland that manages to—within the same paragraph—state that "Sovereignty is a foundational principle of international law." And that "Sovereignty is a binding primary rule of in-ternational law." (Federal Department of Foreign Affairs, Switzerland's position paper on the application of international law in cyberspace Annex UN GGE 2019/2021, https:// www.dfae.admin.ch/dam/eda/en/documents/aussenpolitik/voelkerrecht/20210527-Schweiz-Annex-UN-GGE-Cybersecurity-2019-2021_EN.pdf).

[33] Tom Ginsburg, *Introduction to Symposium on Sovereignty, Cyberspace, and Tallinn Manual 2.0*, 111 AJIL Unbound 205 (2017).

62 A STARTING POINT FOR RE-THINKING "SOVEREIGNTY"

affect cyberinfrastructure within another state, provided that the effects do not rise to the level of an unlawful use of force or an unlawful intervention.[34]

While stated in the context of state cyber operations, these observations have much broader impact, and indeed much broader appeal. In essence, Corn and Taylor argue that (a) sovereignty is an underlying principle that cannot be violated per se; (b) but that sovereignty, as expressed in the relatively clear proscriptions against unlawful use of force and unlawful interventions, can be violated; and that (c) everything else is a gray zone in relation to which the underlying principle of sovereignty tells us little or nothing.[35]

I agree with Corn and Taylor that sovereignty—at least currently—is an underlying principle that cannot be violated per se. As I have argued together with Polčák in a discussion of dignity and sovereignty (a topic to which I will reason to return in the below):

> The problem is that both of these concepts [sovereignty and privacy] too often are treated as rights on their own while they both actually consist of subsets of rights. For example, [. . .] sovereignty is protected by tools such as jurisdictional exclusiveness over the state's territory and the duty of non-interference placed on other states.[36]

However, in sharp contrast, Schmitt and Vihul point to international law cases where the activities in dispute where held to "only constituted violations of sovereignty, not unlawful interventions or uses of force"[37] and suggest that, in the light of such cases "no conclusion can be drawn other than that the principle of sovereignty operates as a primary rule of international law."[38] This is, unsurprisingly, in line with how the *Tallinn Manual 2.0 on the*

---

[34] Gary P. Corn & Robert Taylor, *Sovereignty in the Age of Cyber*, 111 AJIL UNBOUND 207, 208–09 (2017).

[35] Corn and Taylor state: "Through both custom and treaty, international law establishes clear proscriptions against unlawful uses of force and prohibits certain interventions among states. And while questions remain as to the specific scope and scale of cyber-generated effects that would violate these binding norms, the rules provide a reasonably clear framework for assessing the legality of state activities in cyberspace above these thresholds, including available response options for states. Below these thresholds, there is insufficient evidence of either state practice or opinio juris to support assertions that the principle of sovereignty operates as an independent rule of customary international law that regulates states' actions in cyberspace." *Id.* at 207–08.

[36] POLČÁK & SVANTESSON, *supra* note 18, at 63.

[37] Michael N. Schmitt & Liis Vihul, *Sovereignty in Cyberspace: Lex Lata Vel Non?*, 111 AJIL UNBOUND 213, 215 (2017).

[38] *Id.*

International Law Applicable to Cyber Operations approaches sovereignty.[39] Schmitt and Vihul also noted, in relation to their work on the Tallinn Manual 2.0: "In Tallinn Manual 2.0, we, together with the seventeen other members of the so-called 'International Group of Experts,' found that violations of sovereignty could be based on two different grounds: '(1) the degree of infringement upon the target state's territorial integrity; and (2) whether there has been an interference with or usurpation of inherently governmental functions.' "[40] I note in passing that also this may arguably be seen as a move away from treating so sovereignty as a binary concept.

While it may seem counterintuitive at a first glance, I suspect that the end result here is that Schmitt and Vihul give sovereignty a more limited scope of operation than do Corn and Taylor. After all, according to Schmitt and Vihul—assuming they are indeed endorsing the Tallinn Manual 2.0 definition just alluded to—violations of sovereignty must stem from one of the two different grounds they put forward, grounds that correspond with the conventional view of sovereignty. In contrast, while Corn and Taylor do not recognize sovereignty as a right that can be violated per se, they do see it as the foundation for two distinct rights—protection against the unlawful uses of force and unlawful interventions—which can be violated, as well as the foundation for a gray area.

Be that as it may, the fact that leading experts take so fundamentally different positions on such a central matter is no doubt telling in itself—also the very core concepts of international law remain in contention. And in the end, I suggest that the reality is that both Schmitt/Vihul and Corn/Taylor are wrong in part and right in part, although admittedly I remain closer to siding with Corn and Taylor.

On my reading of the *lex lata* ("the law as it exists"), sovereignty is no right capable of being violated per se, rather it is as Corn and Taylor note the foundation for the relatively clear proscriptions against unlawful use of force and unlawful interventions. In addition, the principle of sovereignty is the foundation for a selection of other recognized international wrongs to which Schmitt and Vihul,[41] as well as Spector,[42] direct our attention.

---

[39] Rule 4 states: "A State must not conduct cyber operations that violate the sovereignty of another State."

[40] Schmitt & Vihul, *supra* note 37, at 215.

[41] Schmitt & Vihul, *supra* note 37.

[42] Phil Spector, *In Defense of Sovereignty, in the Wake of Tallinn 2.0*, 111 AJIL UNBOUND 219 (2017).

In other words, at this stage only two rules have sprung from the principle of sovereignty; that is proscriptions against (a) use of force and (b) unlawful intervention. And in addition to those rules there are pockets of clarity in what otherwise is a gray zone. Those pockets are represented by the cases Schmitt, Vihul, and Spector mention but they do not currently form comprehensive and defined rules, and they certainly do not transform the underlying principle of sovereignty into a rule of international law capable of being violated as such.

There is one more point made by Corn and Taylor, to which I want to draw attention:

> The fact that states have developed vastly different regimes to govern the air, space, and maritime domains underscores the fallacy of a universal rule of sovereignty with a clear application to the domain of cyberspace. The principle of sovereignty is universal, but its application to the unique particularities of the cyberspace domain remains for states to determine through state practice and/or the development of treaty rules.[43]

This is a very important observation. Not only does it provide support for the idea that sovereignty is an underlying principle rather than a right per se, but it also highlights that whatever way sovereignty is dealt with in other areas, there is scope for applying it differently in the online environment. After all, if sovereignty takes the shape of *lex specialis* in other fields, it can do so on the Internet arena as well, should we conclude that that is the better option.

VIII. "State Dignity"—the Core of Sovereignty

Drawing upon the discussion above, it is possible to make at least eight significant observations:[44]

(1) The concept of sovereignty applies online;
(2) The current application of the concept of sovereignty—especially online—is uncertain, messy, and incoherent;

---

[43] Corn & Taylor, *supra* note 34, at 210.
[44] This section draws, and expands, upon POLČÁK & SVANTESSON, *supra* note 18.

(3) The traditional concept of sovereignty performs poorly as a tool to provide a framework to control, to guide, and to plan life out of court;

(4) The complexity and lacking conceptual refinement associated with sovereignty creates "artificial regulatory challenges," for example, in the form of legal uncertainty and commentators speaking at cross-purposes;

(5) Part of the problem stems from the traditional conception of sovereignty as binary. Instead, sovereignty should be treated as a matter of degree;

(6) Part of the problem stems from the conception of sovereignty as giving rise to exclusiveness. Sovereignty being treated as a matter of degree, rather than something binary, can take us away from the "exclusiveness trap";

(7) Currently, sovereignty is better viewed as a principle rather than a rule of international law; and

(8) There is a relatively widespread desire to treat sovereignty as a rule rather than a principle of international law.

In this section, I seek to promote the idea of anchoring sovereignty in the notion of "state dignity," an idea first presented in the 2017 book *Information Sovereignty–Data Privacy, Sovereign Powers and the Rule of Law* I co-authored with Polčák. Practical justifications for such a development are already alluded to in the above. However, I also have an ideological basis for promoting this change.

On its most fundamental level, the traditional basis of sovereignty is control, as in physical control. Support for this is plentiful, for example, in the thinking of 17th-century legal scholars, exemplified by Hugo Grotius (Hugo de Groot). Grotius stated that:

> It seems clear, moreover, that sovereignty over a part of the sea is acquired in the same way as sovereignty elsewhere, that is, [. . .] through the instrumentality of persons and territory. It is gained through the instrumentality of persons if, for example, a fleet, which is an army afloat, is stationed at some point of the sea; by means of territory, in so far as those who sail over the part of the sea along the coast may be constrained from the land no less than if they should be upon the land itself.[45]

---

[45] HUGO GROTIUS ON THE LAW OF WAR AND PEACE, at 112 (Stephen C. Neff ed., 2012).

66 A STARTING POINT FOR RE-THINKING "SOVEREIGNTY"

As the world has become increasingly "civilized," we should be able to undertake a shift from sovereignty as a territoriality-focused concept based on physical control to a more sophisticated normative concept based on mutual respect and the rules of international law.[46] In this we find an ideological basis for the advocated move from the current paradigm of sovereignty based on territory/control, to a paradigm of sovereignty anchored in "state dignity."

The starting point for the proposal is the following from the book I co-authored with Polčák:

> At least *de lege ferenda*, ['with a view to the future law'] it is tempting to suggest that [. . .] an infringement of sovereignty would only result in legal consequences where it impacts the dignity of the state in question. In this sense, the reference to dignity would work like a filter, sorting actions according to the level of infringement in which they result. In other words, the function would be similar to how the requirement of actual harm filters the severity of actions in relation to certain torts (such as injurious falsehood).
>
> The rationale for an approach such as that advanced above is that, [. . .] as states operate in a globalised world, absolute sovereignty is not possible. Where that is accepted, a filtering method is a necessity and dignity may be an effective way to achieve filtering.
>
> In saying this, we openly acknowledge that without a strict definition of dignity—and we argue that no matter how strict definition of dignity we manage to produce, it cannot cater for a level of guidance producing total certainty—imposing dignity as a filtering method will be no more precise than a 'wet finger in the air' type test. Nevertheless, it may well that that is as far as we can come, and it may be all we need [as a starting point].[47]

Skeptical voices will no doubt hasten to point out that, transferring focus to state dignity is little more than "kicking the can down the road." There is certainly merit in this concern. However, while the "can" that we "kicked" (i.e.,

---

[46] As noted by Khan: "[I]n recent years there are increasing signs that the traditional and rather categorical symbiosis between territory and power may no longer lay a legitimate claim for exclusivity. This is hardly deplorable since from an international law perspective, possession and transfer of territory have never been considered an end in itself. *L'obsession du territoire* of modern States was always meant to serve people, not vice versa." Daniel-Erasmus Khan, *Territory and Boundaries, in* THE OXFORD HANDBOOK OF THE HISTORY OF INTERNATIONAL LAW 225, 248 (Bardo Fassbender & Anne Peters eds., 2012) (footnote omitted).

[47] POLČÁK & SVANTESSON, *supra* note 18, at 64–65.

the traditional notion of sovereignty) was based on territoriality, the "can" we find "down the road" (i.e., sovereignty anchored in state dignity) is not. This is certainly a significant transformation that, I argue, of its own makes this venture worthwhile. Indeed, it may be that this is the greatest achievement of the proposal. However, there is also a significant flow on effect: that is, a violation of state dignity is then always a matter of degree. Consequently, this allows us to move away from the legal fiction of a binary concept of sovereignty imposed by the binary nature of territoriality.

Having said that, I stress that I see sovereignty anchored in state dignity as a useful approach also in relation to the non-territory-focused aspects of the traditional notion of sovereignty. Thus, also alleged violations, for example, of "sovereign equality" could be approached from the perspective of state dignity: that is, within the context of international relations, where one state acts in a manner that does not show sufficient regard to another states sovereign equality, it may be concluded that the victim state's dignity has been infringed upon.

A. Sovereignty Anchored in State Dignity—A Brief Illustration

So how would this sovereignty anchored in state dignity look in practice?[48] The following example may be illustrative. Imagine that a Light Sport Aircraft of one state (state A) accidentally enters the airspace of another state (state B). Now compare that situation to if the aircraft in question instead was a heavy military bomber. Why are these situations different? While we can, and indeed have, come up with all sorts of sophisticated legal doctrines for distinguishing these situations, on a practical level a key difference is that of the relative impact of state B's dignity. The military bomber poses a threat to

---

[48] Compare to Haataja's interesting discussion of entropy, the notion of informational violence, and the ontological equality principle (SAMULI HAATAJA, CYBER ATTACKS AND INTERNATIONAL LAW ON THE USE OF FORCE 59–61 (2019)); and Tsagourias's valuable work on reassessing what the principle of non-intervention entails in the cyber era (Nicholas Tsagourias, *Electoral Cyber Interference, Self-Determination and the Principle of Non-Intervention in Cyberspace, in* GOVERNING CYBERSPACE: BEHAVIOUR, POWER AND DIPLOMACY (Dennis Broeders and Bibi van den Berg eds., 2020)). See also Roguski's proposal for an intrusion-based approach to violations of territorial sovereignty (Przemysław Roguski, *Violations of Territorial Sovereignty in Cyberspace—an Intrusion-based Approach, in* GOVERNING CYBERSPACE: BEHAVIOUR, POWER AND DIPLOMACY (Dennis Broeders and Bibi van den Berg eds., 2020)). All this interesting recent scholarship points to a growing appetite to reconsider key international law concepts in the cyber context.

state B that the Light Sport Aircraft ordinarily does not. Furthermore, the intrusion by the bomber suggests that state A is not treating state B as an equal (sovereign equality) since no state can accept unauthorized overflights by foreign military. I argue that it is then not the intrusion, in a territorial sense, that is the issue. Rather, it is the impact on "state dignity" that really matters. And in this, I argue, we have identified the core issue in the concept of sovereignty.

Putting this in the cyber context, under my model the question is not, for example, whether a cyberattack "takes place" here or there so as to infringe sovereignty (as a binary concept). Rather the question is, to what degree (if at all) did the cyberattack infringe on the state dignity of the victim state. Consider, for example, that state A undertakes a cyberattack with serious societal implications—important research data are deleted, and patient records manipulated making it impossible to safely carry out medical procedures—in the victim state (state B). Under the conventional approach to sovereignty, we would presumably start by asking whether the affected cyber infrastructure was located on the territory of state B.

In contrast, under my state dignity-focused approach, it would not matter whether state B had used local cyber infrastructure or a cloud-based structure wholly or partly abroad—attention would be placed on the degree to which state A's action infringes state B's dignity. Another advantage is that my proposed structure also recognizes that an attack on 100 small soft targets may be a serious attack even if none of those targets individually meet the threshold of, for example, being critical infrastructure on the territory of the victim state.

It goes without saying that this is just a starting point. Much work remains for any modernization of the important concept of sovereignty so as to anchor it in the notion of state dignity. For example, we need to develop clarity as to what types of activities may constitute a violation of sovereignty as grounded in state dignity. In that context, I think we can possibly make use of the three principles of the jurisprudential framework for jurisdiction I mentioned in passing above; that is, we could take into account (1) substantial connection, (2) legitimate interest, and (3) interest balancing. Again, much work remains, and I am here merely offering a point of departure and pointing out a potentially fruitful direction.

We would also have to engage with the question of what are the potential implications of a violation of sovereignty anchored in the notion of state dignity. However, that is equally much a challenge under current definitions of sovereignty and not a topic that will be pursued here.

IX. Digital/Data Sovereignty—Political Slogan or Anchored in International Law?

Reference to the concepts such as "data sovereignty" and "digital sovereignty" appear frequently and in many different contexts at the moment. Put simply they have become "trendy." Unfortunately, however, it may be that they add little real value and rather add to the already existing messiness and complexity of the landscape described above.

In my view, the term "data sovereignty" is an odd construct indeed.[49] By squeezing together the concepts of "data" and "sovereignty," we are unavoidably imposing severe restrictions on at least one of them. Put simply, as far as law is concerned, making sense of the term "data sovereignty" requires a significant act of contortionism.

To see why this is so, we need only consider the personal nature of data and the public nature of sovereignty. For example, the personal control over data that data privacy laws typically ensure for individuals seems entirely incompatible with an idea of a state having sovereignty over the data generated within the country.

Turning to the concept of digital sovereignty we can note that, when we speak of digital versions of things—for example, digital contracts—we do well to make sure that we truly speak about digital versions of the underlying concept. That should be the case for "digital sovereignty" too. But looking at the widespread uses of the term digital sovereignty, it is clearly not the case. In my view, we ought to challenge any misappropriation of the terms such as "sovereignty."

At any rate, in the context of digital sovereignty, we do not necessarily have to face the obstacle outlined in relation to data sovereignty. However, digital sovereignty in the sense of independence, cyber resilience, self-determination, or indeed self-reliance is of course arguably contrary to the very goal, or idea, of a global Internet. Whether that is viewed as a significant issue or not will vary between those who see risks in Internet fragmentation/

---

[49] Traditionally, "data sovereignty" is frequently discussed in the context of Indigenous populations. *See further* Patrick Hummel et al., *Data Sovereignty: A Review*, BIG DATA & SOCIETY, Jan.–June 2021, at 12.

balkanization and those who see such developments as natural. I do not need to enter that quagmire here. Rather, in our context, to show the issue with the concept of digital sovereignty, it suffices to point to the fact that such digital sovereignty cannot be articulated as a right or even a principle of international law. It is merely an ambition, or a goal, of a mainly practical or ideological nature.

In the light of the above, it seems safe to conclude that, as currently used, neither the concept of "data sovereignty" nor the concept of "digital sovereignty," are anchored in the international law concept of sovereignty. Often, what people mean when they now speak of "digital sovereignty" and related concepts is simply "control." Thus, those who speak of digital sovereignty and data sovereignty merely make use of the weight and status that the term "sovereignty" lends to the underlying goals pursued under the banners of "digital sovereignty" and "data sovereignty."

Yet this does not render these concepts irrelevant for the state dignity-focused reform agenda alluded to above. In fact, while they lack conceptual value or merit, the widespread focus on "digital sovereignty" and "data sovereignty" may provide important momentum for such a reform.

X. Concluding Remarks

Sovereignty is now a popular buzzword. But it is often a poor choice for many of its current uses due to its status as a long-standing, complex, and controversial concept in international law. Furthermore, this chapter has sought to illustrate that, while there is widespread agreement that sovereignty applies online, there is equally widespread disagreement as to key questions such as how sovereignty applies online, and whether sovereignty is a rule or a principle under international law.

At least in part, these disagreements stem from the fact that traditional notions of sovereignty—anchored in territoriality as they are—are a poor fit for the online environment. Their binary nature and focus on exclusiveness are key obstacles to a meaningful application online.

In the above, I have sought to advance a concept of sovereignty anchored in the notion of "state dignity." This involves at least two dramatic changes to how we work with sovereignty. Under my proposal, sovereignty:

(1) must change from being approached as a territoriality-focused concept based on physical control to a more sophisticated normative concept focused on state dignity; and

(2) must change from being approached as a binary concept to being recognized as a matter of degree.

Much work is needed, and international law typically moves with the speed of a glacier. However, every journey must start somewhere. And, at the moment, with the hyped-up focus on vague and misused concepts like "data sovereignty" and "digital sovereignty," perhaps there is the right type of momentum for the type of reform I have advocated above. Time will tell.

3

Digital Sovereignty as Double-Edged Sword

Anupam Chander and Haochen Sun[*]

I. Introduction

Digital sovereignty is simultaneously a necessary incident of democratic governance and democracy's dreaded antagonist. Governments need to control the Internet's impact on their people. Yet, at the same time, control over the Internet offers governments enormous power over their residents' lives. In a sense, this is simply a 21st-century version of the insight of international law scholar Louis Henkin: sovereignty can insulate a government's worst ills from foreign intrusion.

Assertions of digital sovereignty thus carry a double edge—useful both to protect citizens and to control them. Digital sovereignty can magnify the government's powers by making legible behaviors that were previously invisible to the state. Thus, the same rule can be used to safeguard or repress—a feature that legislators across the Global North and South should anticipate through careful checks and balances.

II. What Is Digital Sovereignty For?

Digital sovereignty—the exercise of control over the Internet—is the ambition of the world's leaders, from Australia to Zimbabwe, seen as a bulwark against both foreign states and foreign corporations. Governments have

---

[*] The authors thank Kelly Chen, Kealey Clemens, Elizabeth Goodwin, Noelle Wurst, Ming Yi, and librarian Heather Casey for excellent research assistance. This chapter is adapted from a paper the authors first published in Volume 55 (2022) of the *Vanderbilt Journal of Transnational Law*.

Anupam Chander and Haochen Sun, *Digital Sovereignty as Double-Edged Sword* In: *Data Sovereignty*. Edited by: Anupam Chander and Haochen Sun, Oxford University Press. © Oxford University Press 2023. DOI: 10.1093/oso/9780197582794.003.0004

resoundingly answered first-generation Internet law questions of who, if anyone, should regulate the Internet. The answer: they all will. Governments now confront second-generation questions—not whether, but how to regulate the Internet.

Digital sovereignty is necessary to protect privacy, ensure consumer protection, promote competition, and enable law enforcement. Developing countries should seek to ensure that the digital economy does not leave them behind. However, even as scholars understandably seek to protect individual rights through digital sovereignty, they often neglect the critique that sovereignty can insulate human rights abuses from outside review. Away with the "S-word," the preeminent human rights theorist Louis Henkin cautioned.[1] We argue that Henkin's concern is even graver with respect to digital sovereignty, which presents a greater risk of totalitarian control. While digital sovereignty may well be a geopolitical necessity in opposition to both foreign governments and foreign corporations, digital sovereignty also allows a government to assert enormous powers over its own citizens, and thus deserves exacting scrutiny. This is the double-edged sword of digital sovereignty: it both enables the protection of residents and their control.

The ongoing tech wars between the United States and China, as this chapter shows, epitomize the double-edged sword of digital sovereignty. In 2020, the Trump administration issued a series of executive orders that had the effect of banning TikTok's and WeChat's operations in the United States on national security grounds.[2] While dealing with potential threats posed by China's collection of data through these platforms, the government turned a blind eye to the serious harm its orders had caused to speech protection.[3] The

---

[1] *See* Louis Henkin, *That "S" Word: Sovereignty, and Globalization, and Human Rights, et Cetera*, 68 FORDHAM L. REV. 1, 11 (1999) (observing that he "use[s] the word only to stop using it").

[2] *See* Anupam Chander, *Protecting the Global Internet from Technology Cold Wars*, COMMC'NS OF THE ACM 22 (Sept. 2021).

[3] *See* Eva Galperin, David Greene, & Kurt Opsahl, *TikTok Ban: A Seed of Genuine Security Concern Wrapped in a Thick Layer of Censorship*, ELEC. FRONTIER FOUND. (Aug. 4, 2020), https://www.eff. org/zh-hant/deeplinks/2020/08/tiktok-ban-seed-genuine-security-concern-wrapped-thick-layer-censorship [https://perma.cc/EAA4-6EXP] (archived Jan. 6, 2022) ("Banning Americans from using the TikTok app would infringe the First Amendment rights of those users to express themselves online."); Gregg Leslie, *TikTok and the First Amendment*, SLATE (Sept. 29, 2020), https://slate. com/technology/2020/09/tiktok-wechat-first-amendment-free-speech.html [https://perma.cc/B5YM-UHTM] (archived Jan. 6, 2022) (arguing that "the First Amendment should save TikTok [and WeChat]"); Shelly Banjo & Misyrlena Egkolfopoulou, *TikTok Teens Try To Trick Trump Campaign, Again*, BLOOMBERG (July 10, 2020), https://www.bloomberg.com/news/articles/2020-07-09/tik tok-teens-try-to-trick-trump-campaign-again [https://perma.cc/VR2S-AAJU] (archived Jan. 14, 2022) (reporting that users "believe Trump is trying to take TikTok away because of national security, but more to retaliate against activism on the app and all the videos about him that drag him through the mud").

upshot was that more than 100 million U.S. users[4] would have been muted on TikTok, a digital platform crucial for social activities during the COVID-19 pandemic and for politics on the eve of an election.[5] American courts reacted to the dark side of the U.S. government's assertions of digital sovereignty. The courts enjoined those sweeping orders against TikTok and WeChat because they "burden[ed] substantially more speech than is necessary to serve the government's significant interest in national security."[6]

This chapter surveys the various ways in which states are asserting digital sovereignty. It argues that digital sovereignty is not merely a 21st-century extension of traditional sovereignty, necessary to discipline the corporations that have enormous power in our lives, but also that digital sovereignty is especially susceptible to hijacking by abusive governments. It explores this double-edged sword of digital sovereignty through recent regulatory interventions.

This argument helps explain a puzzling feature of discussions of digital sovereignty: observers generally welcome digital sovereignty efforts by governments in the Global North but deplore such efforts by governments in the Global South.[7] In the former case, digital sovereignty is recognized as the government protecting citizens—either from foreign governments or corporations. In the latter case, digital sovereignty is seen as the government hijacking the Internet to protect itself. This disparity is true across a range of issues, from content moderation, to data privacy, to data localization, to

---

[4] Alex Sherman, *TikTok Reveals Detailed User Numbers for the First Time*, CNBC (Aug. 24, 2020), https://www.cnbc.com/2020/08/24/tiktok-reveals-us-global-user-growth-numbers-for-first-time. html ("More than 100 million Americans are monthly active users today, the company said earlier this month. The company also revealed it has more than 50 million daily U.S. users.").

[5] *See* Taylor Lorenz, *This Is Why You Heard About TikTok So Much in 2020*, N.Y. TIMES (Feb. 26, 2021), https://www.nytimes.com/2020/12/31/style/tiktok-trends-2020.html (discussing how TikTok transformed business, entertainment, news, activism, and social connection in 2020).

[6] U.S. WeChat Users All. v. Donald J. Trump, 488 F. Supp. 3d 912, 928 (N.D. Cal. 2020); *see also* TikTok Inc. v. Donald J. Trump, President of the United States, 490 F. Supp. 3d 73 (D.D.C. 2020).

[7] For example, when India ordered MasterCard to stop issuing new cards in the country because of a failure to comply with requirements to store the data in India, reports in the media criticized the curb as "egregious." *See* Andy Mukherjee, *Sorry, No Mastercard? Digital Trade Needs Rules*, BLOOMBERG OP. (July 15, 2021), https://www.bloomberg.com/opinion/articles/2021-07-15/india-s-data-clampdown-on-mastercard-shows-need-for-biden-digital-trade-deal [https://perma.cc/FMA5-NEX5] (archived Jan. 7, 2022). Similar concerns about the transfer of data abroad, when raised in Europe, have often been seen as privacy protective (whether justified or not). Hong Kong recently real-name SIM card registration introduced to much alarm. But real-name SIM card registration is already a feature in some 155 countries, including Australia, France, and Germany. *See A List of Mandatory 'Real Name' Prepaid SIM Card Registration Country?*, BUZZSIM, https://buzzsim.com/mandatory-real-name-registration-for-prepaid-sim-card-in-different-countries/ [https://perma.cc/77QK-NAMT] (archived Jan. 7, 2022); *Timeline of SIM Card Registration Laws*, PRIVACY INT'L (Apr. 21, 2021), https://privacyinternational.org/long-read/3018/timeline-sim-card-registration-laws [https://perma.cc/9ZAU-CG44] (archived Jan. 7, 2022).

national security. The double-edged nature of digital sovereignty also means that sometimes only the negative possibilities of digital regulations are perceived. The American government, academics, and media have rightly observed how the Chinese government's assertions of digital sovereignty beefed up its political control and trampled on human rights through measures such as Internet filtering, digital surveillance, and data misuse. This sometimes means that aspects of these laws that protect citizens' rights are not recognized as such. Notably, China has been actively protecting citizens' data privacy rights through waves of legislative proposals, regulatory measures, and judicial decisions (though there are dangers in this exercise as observed in this chapter).

Our argument exposes a difficulty in one popular framing of digital sovereignty as an effort to thwart Chinese technology dominance on the grounds that Chinese technology inherently promotes greater authoritarian controls. We agree that technologies are never neutral, and they can be more or less adaptable for authoritarian purposes. However, this framing of an ethical North vs. an unethical South obscures the fact that regulatory systems everywhere have to be better prepared for the abuses of technology by governments keen on maintaining their power. The recent revelations of the widespread use by countries in Europe and across the world of spyware by Israeli surveillance provider NSO dramatize this concern. There is no need for a government to adopt Chinese technologies[8] if one can buy spyware off the shelf from Western suppliers.

We argue for digital sovereignty, but within a system of checks and balances, and limited to protect the virtues of the global Internet. Digital sovereignty is both necessary and dangerous. It is both merely an incident to popular sovereignty and its *bête noire*.

III. The Double-Edged Sword of Digital Sovereignty

Digital sovereignty can grant governments extensive powers over the companies that collect unprecedented amounts of data over us. This part examines a number of ways in which that power can lend itself to abuse. Even

---

[8] *See* Paul Mozur, Jonah M. Kessel, & Melissa Chan, *Made in China, Exported to the World: The Surveillance State*, N.Y. Times (Apr. 24, 2019), https://www.nytimes.com/2019/04/24/technology/ecuador-surveillance-cameras-police-government.html. [https://perma.cc/4KZX-7VGL] (archived Jan. 9, 2022).

well-intentioned law—in the examples discussed here that are designed to protect against abusive speech or to protect privacy or national security—can be prone to abuse. This part offers examples of this possibility, noting that these rules can be implemented, interpreted, or enforced in ways that favor powerful politicians.

As much as sovereignty is often necessary for democratic governance, it can also immunize oppression. Louis Henkin acerbly noted that the "most common use of the word 'sovereignty' may be in sovereign immunity—immunity from law, immunity from scrutiny, immunity from justice."[9]

This dual nature may explain what appears to be a double standard in judging digital sovereignty acts by different countries. That is, the same norm could be used to help ensure that foreign companies protect the rights of local citizens, or it could be used to threaten those foreign companies when they don't follow the demands of an authoritarian government. For example, when Russia passes a "grounding law" that requires Internet companies with more than 500,000 daily visitors to open offices in Russia,[10] that seems distinctly more dangerous[11] than EU obligations for maintaining a local representative.[12] Even the Indian government's demand that Twitter appoint local grievance officers leaves open the possibility of retaliation against such officers for failure to abide by government orders.[13] The intermediary rules requiring local grievance officers seem to have been instituted by

---

[9] *See* Henkin, *supra* note 1, at 13.

[10] *See Putin Signs Into Law Bill on "Grounding" Google, Facebook, Other IT Giants in Russia*, INTERFAX (July 1, 2021), https://interfax.com/newsroom/top-stories/72163/ [https://perma.cc/GT73-H42J] (archived Jan. 9 2022).

[11] *See* Vittoria Elliott, *New Laws Requiring Social Media Platforms to Hire Local Staff Could Endanger Employees*, REST OF WORLD (May 14, 2021), https://restofworld.org/2021/social-media-laws-twitter-facebook/#:~:text=Jason%20Pielemeier%2C%20policy%20director%20of,refuse%20to%20take%20government%20orders.

[12] Regulation (EU) 2016/679 of the European Parliament and of the Council of 27 April 2016, art. 27, 2016 O.J. (L 119), 1 (requiring local representative of foreign data controllers or processors that lack a local establishment).

[13] *See* Saritha Rai & Upmanyu Trivedi, *Twitter to "Fully Comply" with India Internet Rules*, BLOOMBERG (July 8, 2021), https://www.bloomberg.com/news/articles/2021-07-08/twitter-pledges-to-fully-comply-with-india-internet-rules?sref=ExbtjcSG&mc_cid=3a6c8a29f1&mc_eid=18fe0b3837. The rules require three officers, all of whom must be Indian residents: A chief compliance officer "responsible for ensuring compliance" with local legislation and regulation, "a nodal person of contact for 24×7 coordination with law enforcement agencies and officers," and a grievance officer who will be responsible for all functions mentioned under the grievance redressal mechanism. *See also Modi Govt Announces New Rules to Tighten Oversight Over Social Media, Digital Media Platforms, Streaming Services*, WIRE (In.) (Feb. 25, 2021), https://thewire.in/government/modi-govt-announces-new-rules-to-tighten-oversight-over-social-media-digital-media-platforms-streaming-services [https://perma.cc/TDB2-LNMR] (archived Jan. 9 2022).

Prime Minister Narendra Modi's government following its displeasure with Twitter.[14]

A. Speech

1. NetzDG (Germany)

Germany's Network Enforcement Act of 2018 (popularly known as "NetzDG") requires social media companies with two million or more users to remove "manifestly unlawful" speech within 24 hours after user complaint, with limited exceptions. Repeat failures can lead to fines of up to 50 million euros. "In effect, the NetzDG conscripts social media companies into governmental service as content regulators," Diana Lee writes.[15] Germany's broad criminal law related to speech makes this even more risky than it might be elsewhere: "It can be a criminal offense in Germany to call another person a 'jerk,' or even to use the informal du, or 'thou,' to communicate a lack of respect for the recipient," Lee notes, quoting research by James Whitman.[16] NetzDG specifies 22 offenses that require such rapid deletion, including libel, defamation, sedition, and calls for violence. As Lee notes, "[i]n close cases, social media companies will likely err on the side of caution in order to avoid penalties under the NetzDG."[17] Many worry about the possibility of over-blocking content, given the penalties for noncompliance with the takedown obligation.[18]

By requiring incredibly rapid takedowns, such laws "virtually require the use of upload filters," as Hannah Bloch-Wehba argues.[19] Bloch-Wehba observes that automated content moderation "preserv[es] the centralization and dominance of large technology companies," thereby making

---

[14] Aditya Kalra & Sankalp Phartiyal, *India Plans New Social Media Controls after Twitter Face-Off*, REUTERS (Feb. 24, 2021, 10:19 AM), https://www.reuters.com/article/us-india-tech-regulation/india-plans-new-social-media-controls-after-twitter-face-off-idUSKBN2AO201.

[15] Diana Lee, *Germany's NetzDG and the Threat to Online Free Speech*, MEDIA FREEDOM & INFO. ACCESS CLINIC (Oct. 10, 2017), https://law.yale.edu/mfia/case-disclosed/germanys-netzdg-and-threat-online-free-speech.

[16] *Id.* (quoting James Q. Whitman, *Enforcing Civility and Respect: Three Societies*, 109 YALE L.J. 1279, 1297 (2000)).

[17] *Id.*

[18] Amelie Heldt, *Reading Between the Lines and the Numbers: An Analysis of the First NetzDG Reports*, 8(2) INTERNET POL'Y REV. 1, 5 (2019).

[19] Hannah Bloch-Wehba, *Automation in Moderation*, 53 CORNELL INT'L L.J. 41, 69 (2020). She notes for example that Google's NetzDG transparency report "documents how it uses hashing, fingerprinting, and automated flagging technologies to try to identify unlawful content more quickly." *See also id.* at 70.

78 DIGITAL SOVEREIGNTY AS DOUBLE-EDGED SWORD

"surveillance cheaper and easier for law enforcement."[20] She worries that social media companies will internalize the political goals of enforcers to avoid enforcement actions: "Platforms adapt their content moderation rules and practices to conform to regulators' preferences, both to comply and to avoid new regulations."[21] Annemarie Bridy elaborates, worrying about the "troubling dynamic in which platform executives seek to appease government actors—and thereby to avoid additional regulation—by suppressing speech in accordance with the prevailing political winds."[22] Facebook's "X-check" internal process, which exempts some high-profile users, including politicians, from the automated application of its rules, further demonstrates this dynamic.[23]

NetzDG is being replaced with the European Union's Digital Services Act.

2. Eva Glawischnig-Piesczek v. Facebook Ireland Limited (European Union)

Can an Internet company be liable if it refuses to remove a post calling a member of Parliament a "corrupt oaf" and a "fascist"?[24] Possibly, according to the Court of Justice of the European Union (CJEU). An Austrian politician had sued Facebook because it had refused to remove a post containing those offensive terms used against her. The case wound its way to the CJEU, which held that the EU's E-Commerce Directive[25] did not preclude liability on Facebook's part for refusing to remove this content. The E-Commerce Directive provides protections for "information society services." Article 15 provides, in part: "Member States shall not impose a general obligation on providers, when providing [information society services], to monitor the information which they transmit or store, nor a general obligation actively to seek facts or circumstances indicating illegal activity."[26] Recital 47 of the

---

[20] *Id.* at 46.

[21] *Id.*

[22] Annemarie Bridy, *Moderation's Excess*, JOTWELL (Mar. 27, 2020), https://cyber.jotwell.com/moderations-excess/.

[23] Jeff Horwitz, *Facebook Says Its Rules Apply to All. Company Documents Reveal a Secret Elite That's Exempt*, WALL. ST. J. (Sept. 13, 2021), https://www.wsj.com/articles/facebook-files-xcheck-zuckerberg-elite-rules-11631541353 (last visited Jan. 9, 2022).

[24] The specific terms were "lousy traitor of the people" ("miese Volksverräterin"), "corrupt oaf" ("korrupter Trampel"), and a member of a "fascist party" ("Faschistenpartei"). Luc von Danwitz, *The Contribution of EU Law to the Regulation of Online Speech the Glawischnig-Piesczek Case and What It Means for Online Content Regulation*, 27 MICH. TECH. L. REV. 167, 171 (2020).

[25] Directive 2000/31/EC of the European Parliament and of the Council of 8 June 2000 on Certain Legal Aspects of Information Society Services, in Particular Electronic Commerce, in the Internal Market, 2000 O.J. (L 178) 1.

[26] *Id.* at art. 15.

E-Commerce Directive, however, permits monitoring obligations in a specific case—such as the one in *Glawischnig-Piesczek*.[27] The CJEU went further to conclude that the Austrian court could not only order the deletion of the particular post, but also prevent any post with content that is "equivalent" across Facebook sites "worldwide."[28]

The demand to remove posts "having equivalent meaning" across Facebook worldwide seems to require automated systems that are likely to produce significant errors.[29] Even this chapter might not pass such a filter! And the decision to allow an Austrian court to order a global removal, in the context of criticism (warranted or not) of a politician, no less, will embolden other states to demand the same. The assertion of Austrian law across the world seems difficult to justify, even more so on matters involving political speech. The CJEU's sustaining of the Austrian court's power to order the removal of the post would have been easier to defend if it did not include all "equivalent" posts, and if it was limited to Austria (or perhaps the EU). But the underlying law may make it difficult to call out politicians who are actually corrupt or fascist—because of worries that they may sue.

At the same time, Facebook's defense in the case that Facebook was governed by either Irish law (because of its European headquarters) or U.S. law (because of its global headquarters), but not Austrian law, was itself an attack on Austrian digital sovereignty, which both Austria and the CJEU properly rebuffed. After all, as long as speech law has not been harmonized across the EU, to subject Austrians to Irish speech law based on the jurisdictional choices of Facebook would be to do an end run around Austrian law.[30]

---

[27] Felipe Romero Moreno, *"Upload Filters" and Human Rights: Implementing Article 17 of the Directive on Copyright in the Digital Single Market*, 34 INT'L REV. L., COMPUTERS & TECH. 153, 154 (2020).

[28] Case C-18/18, Eva Glawischnig-Piesczek v. Facebook Ireland Ltd., ECLI:EU:C:2019:821, ¶ 53 (Oct. 3, 2019).

[29] *See* NATASHA DUARTE, EMMA LLANSÓ, & ANNA LOUP, MIXED MESSAGES? THE LIMITS OF AUTOMATED SOCIAL MEDIA CONTENT ANALYSIS (2017); *see also* Emma Llansó, *No Amount of "AI" in Content Moderation Will Solve Filtering's Prior-Restraint Problem*, 7 BIG DATA & SOC'Y 1 (2020).

[30] *See* CHANDER, *supra* note 2, at 34 (2013) (arguing that "public policy objectives cannot easily be evaded through a simple jurisdictional sleight of hand or keystroke").

80 DIGITAL SOVEREIGNTY AS DOUBLE-EDGED SWORD

B. Privacy

1. Justice Reform Act (France)

In 2016, lawyer and machine-learning expert Michaël Benesty analyzed French asylum decisions by judges, revealing that some judges rejected almost all asylum requests while others accepted most.[31] The study caused a furor in France, and led to a law that criminalized any such studies, punishable by up to five years in prison.[32] The new Article 33 of the Justice Reform Act reads, "No personally identifiable data concerning judges or court clerks may be subject to any reuse with the purpose or result of evaluating, analyzing or predicting their actual or supposed professional practices."[33] Such a law makes it more difficult to scrutinize the judicial process and to identify judges that might be hostile to particular claims.

2. Data Protection/Didi (China)

On June 30, 2021, Didi, the ride-hailing firm based in Beijing, went public on the New York Stock Exchange.[34] On July 2, the Cyberspace Administration of China (CAC) announced a cybersecurity review of Didi, and on July 4, it ordered the Didi app removed from Chinese app stores.[35] The cybersecurity review was aimed at "preventing national data security risks, maintaining national security and safeguarding public interests."[36] CAC ordered the app

---

[31] Malcolm Langford & Mikael Rask Madsen, *France Criminalises Research on Judges*, VERFASSUNGSBLOG (June 22, 2019), https://verfassungsblog.de/france-criminalises-research-on-jud ges/ [https://perma.cc/25VH-WYJF] (archived Jan. 9 2022).

[32] *See France Bans Judge Analytics, 5 Years in Prison for Rule Breakers*, ARTIFICIAL LAW. (June 4, 2019), https://www.artificiallawyer.com/2019/06/04/france-bans-judge-analytics-5-years-in-pri son-for-rule-breakers/ [https://perma.cc/2BWD-8SGQ] (archived Jan. 9, 2022). One British commentator observes that "the old law against 'Scandalising the Judiciary' was only recently abolished in England & Wales, which shows that judges over here have not always liked to be scrutinized too closely either." *See also id.*

[33] Jason Tashea, *France Bans Publishing of Judicial Analytics and Prompts Criminal Penalty*, ABA J. (June 7, 2019, 12:51 PM), https://www.abajournal.com/news/article/france-bans-and-creates-crimi nal-penalty-for-judicial-analytics (quoting translation by Rebecca Loescher) [https://perma.cc/ 2JRP-GDYD] (archived Jan. 9 2022) (original text available at https://www.legifrance.gouv.fr/jorf/ article_jo/JORFARTI000038261761?r=LEGAIp0IBR [https://perma.cc/BE5F-5QP6] (archived Jan. 9 2022)).

[34] Kate Conger & Raymond Zhong, *Didi, the Chinese Ride-Hailing Giant, Makes Its Debut on Wall Street*, N.Y. TIMES (June 30, 2021), https://www.nytimes.com/2021/06/30/technology/didi-wall-str eet-initial-public-offering.html [https://perma.cc/Z9PX-FR7V] (archived Jan. 9 2022).

[35] *See* Zhijing Yu, Vicky Liu, & Yan Luo, *China Initiates Cybersecurity Review of Didi ChuXing and Three Other Chinese Mobile Applications*, COVINGTON: INSIDE PRIVACY (July 6, 2021), https://www. insideprivacy.com/international/china/china-initiates-cybersecurity-review-of-didi-chuxing-and-three-other-chinese-mobile-applications/ [https://perma.cc/MWD8-SBEJ] (archived Jan. 9, 2022).

[36] *Id.*

removal because it found that the app was "illegally collecting and using personal information."[37] For the cybersecurity review, the CAC relied on the Cybersecurity Law of 2017 and the Measures on Cybersecurity Review issued thereunder in 2020.

Chinese commentators explained the cybersecurity review as being motivated by the "hypothetical scenario of the US coercing Chinese firms to submit data . . . citing the US government's track record of stopping at nothing to forcing businesses to surrender."[38] A Chinese Foreign Ministry spokesperson lent support to this concern, arguing that "it is the US that forces companies to open 'back doors' and illegally obtain user data."[39] Zuo Xiaodong, the vice president of the China Information Security Research Institute, similarly stated, "[i]n the listing process in the US, some important data and personal information held by Chinese companies may be revealed due to the US regulation request."[40] The focus was the requirement that companies registered with the U.S. Securities and Exchange Commission have to make available their audit records to the Public Company Accounting Oversight Board.

The concerns are similar, at least on one level, to those expressed by the CJEU with respect to data transfers to the United States. After all, there the European court cited Executive Order 12333, Section 702 of the Foreign Intelligence and Surveillance Act, and Presidential Policy Directive 28 to argue that U.S. law did not sufficiently protect the data of foreigners from American governmental surveillance.[41] In that sense, the Didi enforcement order could be seen as an effort to protect the personal data of Chinese residents. Indeed, in July 2022, the Chinese authorities fined Didi $1.2 billion for excessive collection of personal information and for security risks in its operations. But at the same time, the Didi enforcement effort—the first application of the cybersecurity review—was also a warning to Chinese companies about who the boss is.

---

[37] *See id.*
[38] Li Qiaoyi & Zhang Hongpei, *3 More Internet Firms Scrutinized Amid Rising Data Security Concern*, GLOBAL TIMES (China) (July 5, 2021, 11:28 PM), https://www.globaltimes.cn/page/202 107/1227899.shtml.
[39] *Id.*
[40] *Id.*
[41] *See* Case C-311/18, Data Prot. Comm'r v. Facebook Ireland Ltd., ECLI:EU:C: 2020:559, ¶¶ 182– 84 (July 16, 2020).

82 DIGITAL SOVEREIGNTY AS DOUBLE-EDGED SWORD

C. National Security

1. TikTok Ban (United States)

On July 31, 2020, President Donald Trump announced on Air Force One that "as far as TikTok is concerned, we're banning them from the U.S."[42] A flurry of executive orders would follow. On August 6, 2020, President Trump issued two parallel executive orders targeting TikTok and another Chinese-owned app, WeChat,[43] followed by another order requiring ByteDance, the Beijing-based owner of TikTok, to divest its U.S. TikTok subsidiary following a national security review by the Committee on Foreign Investment in the United States (CFIUS).[44] Through TikTok, the president argued, the Chinese government could secretly compile compromising data about Americans, enabling blackmail.[45] The Trump administration seemed to be relying on a frighteningly broad provision of the Chinese National Intelligence Law, Article 7, which states that "any organization or citizen shall support, assist, and cooperate with state intelligence work according to law." The Trump administration also argued that the Chinese government would use the app to censor American speech or to disseminate propaganda. TikTok had indeed been caught suspending an American teenager who cleverly used an eyelash tutorial to criticize the Chinese government's treatment of Uyghur Muslims.[46] Facing a furor, TikTok apologized for what it described as an error

[42] Riya Bhattacharjee, Amanda Macias, & Jordan Novet, *Trump Says He Will Ban TikTok Through an Executive Action*, CNBC (July 31, 2020), https://www.cnbc.com/2020/07/31/trump-says-he-will-ban-tiktok-through-executive-action-as-soon-as-saturday.html.

[43] Executive Order on Addressing the Threat Posed by TikTok, Exec. Order No. 13,942, 85 Fed. Reg. 48,637 (Aug. 6, 2020) ("any person, or with respect to any property, subject to the jurisdiction of the United States" would be prohibited from transacting with ByteDance Ltd., the Chinese owner of TikTok, or any of its subsidiaries); Executive Order on Addressing the Threat Posed by WeChat, Exec. Order No. 13,943, 85 Fed. Reg. 48,641 (Aug. 6, 2020) (order prohibits "any transaction *that is related to WeChat* . . . with TenCent Holdings Ltd., Shenzhen, China, or any subsidiary of that entity . . .") (emphasis added); Proclamation No. 10,061, 84 Fed. Reg. 51,295 (Sept. 27, 2019) (ordering ByteDance to divest all of its rights and interests in any assets or property used to enable or support the operation of TikTok in the United States, and "any data obtained or derived from TikTok or Music.ly application users in the United States" within 90 days); Press Release, U.S. Dep't of Com., Commerce Department Prohibits WeChat and TikTok Transactions to Protect the National Security of the United States (Sept. 18, 2020), https://2017-2021.commerce.gov/news/press-releases/2020/09/commerce-department-prohibits-wechat-and-tiktok-transactions-protect.html.

[44] *See* Pres. Proc. No. 10,061, 84 Fed. Reg. 51,295 (ordering ByteDance to divest all of its rights and interests in any assets or property used to enable or support the operation of TikTok in the United States, and "any data obtained or derived from TikTok or Music.ly application users in the United States" within 90 days).

[45] *See* TikTok Inc. v. Trump, 490 F. Supp. 3d 73, 77 (D.D.C. 2020).

[46] *See* Paige Leskin, *TikTok Issues Public Apology for Suspending the Account of the Teen Behind the Viral Chinese Takedown Video Disguised as a Makeup Tutorial*, Bus. Insider (Nov. 2019), https://www.businessinsider.com/tiktok-apology-china-muslims-viral-video-feroza-aziz-suspend-politics-2019-11.

and restored her account. Since that time, posts with the hashtag #uyghur have garnered 82.5 million views on the app.[47]

President Trump announced the TikTok ban some three months before the election, pointing his fingers at an alleged insidious foreign plan to infiltrate the United States. He declared that if his opponent won the election, "You're going to have to learn to speak Chinese."[48] But when federal courts saw the government's secret evidence against TikTok, they sided with TikTok, preliminarily enjoining the TikTok and WeChat bans.[49] Judge Carl Nichols, a Trump appointee to the federal bench, halted the TikTok ban despite the government's claims that it posed a national security threat.[50] In a second case, Judge Wendy Beetlestone declared the government's concerns "hypothetical."[51] Notably, the CFIUS divestiture order, however, remains in limbo, with TikTok's legal challenge suspended during ongoing negotiations between the company and the U.S. government.

The national security rationales conveniently justified actions that targeted a platform that had proved particularly troublesome to the president.[52] Trump borrowed even more of the authoritarian Internet playbook than might be obvious: like authoritarians everywhere, he sought to silence his critics. TikTok had already proven a thorn in his side, with comedian Sarah Cooper using the platform to lampoon him, and teens coordinating via TikTok to claim tickets to his rally so as to leave the arena mostly empty.[53] TikTok, after all, was the one massive social media platform in the United States that he had not mastered. If he had banned Twitter, Facebook,

---

[47] Authors' independent search on TikTok app on May 10, 2021. TikTok no longer reports views of a hashtag, so an update of this figure is unavailable.

[48] Kevin Liptak, *Trump Says Americans Will Have to Learn Chinese if Biden Wins but Offers Little Condemnation of Beijing*, CNN (Aug. 11, 2020, 1:58 PM), https://www.cnn.com/2020/08/11/politics/trump-china-biden-learn-chinese/index.html.

[49] *See* U.S. WeChat Users All v. Trump, 488 F. Supp. 3d 912, 928 (N.D. Cal. 2020) ("On this limited record, the prohibited transactions burden substantially more speech than is necessary to serve the government's significant interest in national security, especially given the lack of substitute channels for communication.").

[50] *See* TikTok Inc. v. Trump, 490 F. Supp. 3d 73, 85 (D.D.C. 2020) ("the specific evidence of the threat posed by Plaintiffs, as well as whether the prohibitions are the only effective way to address that threat, remains less substantial").

[51] Marland v. Trump, 498 F. Supp. 3d 624, 642 (E.D. Pa. 2020).

[52] *See* Stuart Emmrich, *Is Sarah Cooper the Reason Donald Trump Wants to Ban TikTok?*, VOGUE (Aug. 1, 2020), https://www.vogue.com/article/is-sarah-cooper-the-reason-donald-trump-wants-to-ban-tik-tok. Under this theory, the WeChat ban would be merely collateral damage, as it would be odd to target TikTok without also banning this other popular Chinese-owned app.

[53] Chander, *supra* note 2, at 24.

84   DIGITAL SOVEREIGNTY AS DOUBLE-EDGED SWORD

or YouTube, he would have lost a channel to reach millions of his followers directly.[54]

In 2021, a new president would revoke the TikTok and WeChat bans, ordering instead a broad review of access to U.S. persons' sensitive data by foreign adversaries.[55] President Biden said that such a review would be based on "rigorous, evidence-based analysis and should address any unacceptable or undue risks consistent with overall national security, foreign policy, and economic objectives, including the preservation and demonstration of America's core values and fundamental freedoms."[56] Coupling the rescission of the prior order with this statement suggests that the earlier executive orders failed to meet those standards.

The failure of the TikTok ban in 2020 is a sign of healthy checks and balances, but the fact that it occurred shows that such checks and balances are necessary. The willingness of federal courts to refuse to meekly accept the president's claim of a national security emergency is heartening. This is also a story of a Congress that had anticipated abuses; courts that enjoined the TikTok and WeChat bans relied on the fact that Congress had provided protections for speech from the otherwise broad emergency economic powers that Congress granted to the president.[57]

---

[54] *See* Adam Conner, *Trump's Facebook Account Should Never Be Reinstated Because We Know What He'd Use It For,* NBC (May 3, 2021, 7:07 PM), https://www.nbcnews.com/think/opinion/trump-s-facebook-account-should-never-be-reinstated-because-we-ncna1266182 (former President Trump maintained roughly 32 million Facebook followers); Trump Tweets Can't Be Brought Back To Life on Twitter, BBC (Apr. 8, 2021), https://www.bbc.com/news/technology-56675272 [https://perma.cc/DDL2-JCG5] (archived Jan. 9, 2022) (Former President Trump maintained roughly 90 million Twitter followers); Donald J. Trump, YOUTUBE, https://www.youtube.com/channel/UCAql2DyG U2un1Ei2nMYsqOA (last visited Jan. 9, 2022) [https://perma.cc/23RF-YWX7] (archived Jan. 9, 2022) (former President Trump maintained roughly 2.7 million subscribers on his frozen YouTube channel).

[55] *See* Executive Order on Protecting Americans' Sensitive Data from Foreign Adversaries, Exec. Order No. 14,034, 86 Fed. Reg. 31,423 (June 9, 2021) [hereinafter Protecting Americans' Sensitive Data]; *see* Kim Lyons, *Biden Revokes Trump Executive Order That Targeted Section 230,* VERGE (May 15, 2021), https://www.theverge.com/2021/5/15/22437627/biden-revokes-trump-executive-order-section-230-twitter-facebook-google [https://perma.cc/HM23-C5AR] (archived Jan. 9, 2022). The Biden administration has not yet withdrawn the CFIUS executive order requiring divestiture but does not seem to be enforcing that order.

[56] Protecting Americans' Sensitive Data, *supra* note 55.

[57] *See* TikTok Inc. v. Trump, 490 F. Supp. 3d 73, 80 (D.D.C. 2020) ("IEEPA's informational-materials limitation deprives the President of authority to regulate or prohibit—'directly or indirectly,' 'regardless of format or medium of transmission,' and 'whether commercial or otherwise'—the importation or exportation of 'informational materials.'") (citing 50 U.S.C. § 1702(b)(3)); Marland v. Trump, 498 F. Supp. 3d 624, 637 (E.D. Pa. 2020) ("With the Berman Amendment, however, Congress modified IEEPA to expressly 'exempt the regulation of informational materials from the Executive's congeries of powers.'") (citation omitted). Judge Laurel Beeler relied on the First Amendment to protect against possible executive overreach, concluding, "On this limited record, the prohibited transactions burden substantially more speech than is necessary to serve the government's significant interest in

THE DOUBLE-EDGED SWORD OF DIGITAL SOVEREIGNTY 85

In late 2022, some US. State governments and then the federal government banned TikTok on government devices, citing national security concerns. And in 2023, the state of Montana banned TikTok entirely within the state, though that ban has been challenged both by TikTok and by TikTok influencers.

2. NSO Spyware for Hire (Israel)

In July 2021, Amnesty International revealed that some 50 thousand individuals in more than 45 countries—including 14 heads of state[58] and numerous journalists—were the target of phone hacking using software sold by the NSO Group.[59] For example, an "investigation suggests the Hungarian government of Viktor Orbán appears to have deployed NSO's technology as part of his so-called war on the media, targeting investigative journalists in the country as well as the close circle of one of Hungary's few independent media executives."[60] In 2021, the iPhones of U.S. Embassy employees working in Uganda were reportedly hacked using spyware developed by the NSO Group.[61]

NSO is hardly the only Western company implicated in the sale of repressive technologies. The Israeli company Cellebrite has been implicated in oppression by governments across the world, but still managed to do a two-and-a-half billion dollar IPO in New York in 2021.[62] Its IPO prospectus warned investors that its "solutions may be used by customers in a way that is, or that is perceived to be, incompatible with human rights."[63] Another

---

national security, especially given the lack of substitute channels for communication." U.S. WeChat Users All. v. Trump, 488 F. Supp. 3d 912, 928 (N.D. Cal. 2020).

[58] *See* Peter Beaumont & Philip Oltermann, *Israel to Examine Whether Spyware Export Rules Should be Tightened*, GUARDIAN (July 22, 2021, 11:45 AM), https://www.theguardian.com/news/2021/jul/22/israel-examine-spyware-export-rules-should-be-tightened-nso-group-pegasus.

[59] Stephanie Kirchgaessner, Paul Lewis, David Pegg, Sam Cutler, Nina Lakhani, & Michael Safi, *Revealed: Leak Uncovers Global Abuse of Cyber-Surveillance Weapon*, GUARDIAN (July 18, 2021, 12:00 PM https://www.theguardian.com/world/2021/jul/18/revealed-leak-uncovers-global-abuse-of-cyber-surveillance-weapon-nso-group-pegasus).

[60] *Id.*

[61] *See* Christopher Bing & Joseph Menn, *U.S. State Department Phones Hacked With Israeli Company Spyware*, ROUTERS (Dec 4, 2021), https://www.reuters.com/technology/exclusive-us-state-department-phones-hacked-with-israeli-company-spyware-sources-2021-12-03/.

[62] *See Open Letter: Cellebrite Should Not Go Public Without Demonstrating Human Rights Compliance*, ACCESS Now (July 13, 2021), https://www.accessnow.org/cms/assets/uploads/2021/07/CSO_Open-Letter_on_Cellebrite.pdf [https://perma.cc/5TW6-SDSL] (archived Jan. 9, 2022); *See* Avi Asher-Schapiro, *Israeli Surveillance Firm's Nasdaq Plans Challenged by Digital Rights Groups*, REUTERS (July 13, 2021), https://www.reuters.com/article/tech-business-surveillance/israeli-surveillance-firms-nasdaq-plans-challenged-by-digital-rights-groups-idUSL8N2OO5IP.

[63] Cellebrite DI Ltd., Registration Statement, Registration No. 333-256177 (June 29, 2021), at 27.

86 DIGITAL SOVEREIGNTY AS DOUBLE-EDGED SWORD

Israeli "hacking-for-hire" firm, Candiru, has helped government clients spy on "politicians, human rights activists, journalists, academics, embassy workers and political dissidents," at least according to Microsoft.[64] The Israeli company Verint Systems reportedly sold spying tools to Azerbaijan that were used to identify its citizens' sexual orientations through Facebook and sold to Indonesia to collect personal information about LGBT rights activists.[65]

This is hardly a problem of Israeli exporters alone. In 2015, the Italian company Hacking Team was itself hacked, revealing an extensive client list in governments accused of human rights abuses, including governments and security services of Azerbaijan, Kazakhstan, Uzbekistan, Russia, Bahrain, Saudi Arabia, and the United Arab Emirates.[66] The U.S. networking equipment company Sandvine reportedly supplied an Internet-blocking technology to Belarus that was used to block access to websites and repress protests during the 2020 Belarussian elections.[67] Furthermore, NSO's exports themselves implicate the laws of EU member states Bulgaria and Cyprus, as NSO exports its products from those countries as well.[68]

Western commentators rightly point out that Chinese technology companies often sell their technologies to repressive governments across Africa and elsewhere. They sometimes distinguish a liberal Western approach to technology from a repressive Chinese approach.[69] But why use Chinese surveillance technology when one can buy Western technology that

---

[64] Cristin Goodwin, *Fighting Cyberweapons Built by Private Businesses*, MICROSOFT (July 15, 2021), https://blogs.microsoft.com/on-the-issues/2021/07/15/cyberweapons-cybersecurity-sourgum-malware/; *see* Bill Marczak, John Scott-Railton, Kristin Berdan, Bahr Abdul Razzak, & Ron Deibert, *Hooking Candiru: Another Mercenary Spyware Vendor Comes into Focus*, CITIZEN LAB (July 15, 2021), https://citizenlab.ca/2021/07/hooking-candiru-another-mercenary-spyware-vendor-comes-into-focus/.

[65] *See* Jason Murdock, *Israeli Companies Sold Surveillance Tech and Knowledge Used for Persecuting Dissidents, Journalists, LGBT People*, NEWSWEEK (Oct. 19, 2018), https://www.newsweek.com/Isra eli-companies-sell-surveillance-tech-and-knowledge-used-persecuting-1178084 [https://perma.cc/ RV4E-VSTV] (archived Jan. 9, 2022).

[66] *See* Alex Hern, *Hacking Team Hacked: Firm Sold Spying Tools to Repressive Regimes, Documents Claim*, GUARDIAN (July 6, 2015, 7:46 PM), https://www.theguardian.com/technology/2015/jul/06/ hacking-team-hacked-firm-sold-spying-tools-to-repressive-regimes-documents-claim.

[67] *See* Ryan Gallagher, *U.S. Company Faces Backlash After Belarus Uses Its Tech to Block Internet*, BLOOMBERG (Sept. 11, 2020), https://www.bloomberg.com/news/articles/2020-09-11/sandvine-use-to-block-belarus-internet-rankles-staff-lawmakers (subscription required).

[68] *See* AMNESTY INT'L, OPERATING FROM THE SHADOWS: INSIDE NSO GROUP'S CORPORATE STRUCTURE 7 (2021).

[69] *See, e.g.*, U.S. DEP'T OF STATE, THE ELEMENTS OF THE CHINA CHALLENGE 17 (2020) ("Beijing provides digital technology and physical infrastructure to advance the CCP's authoritarian objectives throughout the [Indo-Pacific] region"); ALINA POLYAKOVA & CHRIS MESEROLE, EXPORTING DIGITAL AUTHORITARIANISM 5–6 (2019), https://www.brookings.edu/wp-content/uploads/2019/08/FP_20190826_digital_authoritarianism_polyakova_meserole.pdf.

CONCLUSION 87

will get the job done?[70] And this argument seems to forget that it was Western companies that helped build China's Great Firewall in the first instance.[71]

Israeli law requires exports of such spyware to be approved by its Defense Department, and NSO claims to have received the necessary permits.[72] The NSO spyware scandal reveals the importance of governments regulating not only foreign companies, but also domestic companies, to ensure that these companies do not help infringe human rights elsewhere. A former Cellebrite employee noted that other employees would justify the sales on the ground that "governments could buy the same services from China, therefore better that we sell it to them instead."[73] But this reasoning would allow one to sell the most deadly services in the world, as long as someone else was selling them too. Furthermore, buying surveillance services from a democratic country may draw less scrutiny than buying services from companies in authoritarian states. Finally, the argument ignores the possibility of jointly pressuring foreign governments to stop permitting their companies to sell such services in the global markets.[74]

IV. Conclusion

On May 15, 2000, French plaintiffs accused Internet pioneer Yahoo! of American imperialism because Yahoo.com made Nazi materials accessible to people across the world.[75] Yahoo!'s lawyers responded that to apply French

[70] *Cf.* Maya Wang, *China's Techno-Authoritarianism Has Gone Global*, FOREIGN AFFS. (Apr. 8, 2021), https://www.foreignaffairs.com/articles/china/2021-04-08/chinas-techno-authoritarian ism-has-gone-global [https://perma.cc/8NGR-ESQP] (archived Jan. 15, 2022) (observing that while countries from Ecuador to Kyrgyzstan have "adopted Chinese surveillance technology," "the United States and its tech companies also have a checkered history with the very ideals they claim to uphold.").

[71] According to one report, "China relied on two U.S. companies—Cisco Systems and Juniper Networks—to help carry out its network upgrade, known as "CN2," in 2004. This upgrade significantly increased China's ability to monitor Internet usage. Cisco also sold several thousand routers *(IHT)* used to censor web content, and 'firm's engineers have helped set it to spot 'subversive' keywords in messages.'" Robert McMahon & Isabella Bennett, *U.S. Internet Providers and the 'Great Firewall of China'*, COUNCIL FOREIGN RELS. (Feb. 23, 2011, 7:00 AM), https://www.cfr.org/backgroun der/us-internet-providers-and-great-firewall-china [https://perma.cc/2L7B-G8T7] (archived Jan. 9, 2022).

[72] *See* Defense Export Control Law 5766–2007 (Isr.).

[73] *See* Anonymous, *I Worked at Israeli Phone Hacking Firm Cellebrite. They Lied to Us*, HAARETZ (July 27, 2021), https://www.haaretz.com/israel-news/i-worked-at-israeli-phone-hacking-firm-cel lebrite-they-lied-to-us-1.10041753 [https://perma.cc/AZ3H-5AVT] (archived Jan. 9, 2022).

[74] For a related argument for a national statute backed by an international treaty to regulate information services that operate in repressive jurisdictions, *see* Anupam Chander, *Googling Freedom*, 99 CALIF. L. REV. 1, 36–44 (2011).

[75] *See* Greg Wrenn, *Yahoo! V. LICRA*, 24 COMM. LAW. 5, 5–6 (2006).

law to a site based in the United States more closely resembled French imperialism.[76] The French court carefully tailored its order to only require Yahoo! to desist from providing the prohibited materials within France.[77] Today, countries across the world have adopted the French position to insist that foreign companies comply with local law, at least on matters significant to them.[78] (The French themselves have gone on occasion further to demand global takedowns of information—a radical and alarming assertion of jurisdiction.[79])

A quarter of a century after the birth of the global Internet, neither the libertarian wishes of early Internet pioneers nor the globalist desire for a single global community have prevailed. Instead, there are increasing efforts by the countries of the world to gain control over the Internet. This is understandable. As Andrew Woods observed, "states remain the single greatest source of legitimate rules for different peoples with varied community values and experiences on a diverse planet."[80] States make the law and enforce it, hopefully for our protection. There is at present no international substitute for such protection. Digital sovereignty is simultaneously necessary and scary—necessary to ensure that ordinary laws follow us as we move increasingly online, disciplining the corporations that govern our work, school, and private lives—but scary because regulation of the Internet gives governments even more power to invade broader spheres of our lives. Just as the power wielded by digital corporations must be carefully regulated, so must the power of digital regulators themselves.

---

[76] *See id.* at 6.

[77] *See id.* at 6–7.

[78] This does not mean that a foreign court will necessarily enforce such an order, however. In the Yahoo! case, District Judge Fogel, we believe properly concluded, "Although France has the sovereign right to regulate what speech is permissible in France, this Court may not enforce a foreign order that violates the protections of the United States Constitution by chilling protected speech that occurs simultaneously within our borders." Yahoo!, Inc. v. La Ligue Contre Le Racisme et L'Antisemitisme, 169 F. Supp. 2d 1181, 1192 (N.D. Cal. 2001), *rev'd*, 379 F.3d 1120 (9th Cir. 2004), *on reh'g en banc*, 433 F.3d 1199 (9th Cir. 2006), *rev'd and remanded*, 433 F.3d 1199 (9th Cir. 2006).

[79] Kevin Benish, *Whose Law Governs Your Data?: Takedown Orders and "Territoriality" in Comparative Perspective*, 55 WILLAMETTE L. REV. 599, 615–19 (2019) (describing French application of the right to be forgotten worldwide); *see generally* Jennifer Daskal, *Speech Beyond Borders*, 105 VA. L. REV. 1605 (2019).

[80] Andrew Keane Woods, *Litigating Data Sovereignty*, 128 YALE L.J. 328, 369 (2018).

4

From Data Subjects to Data Sovereigns

Addressing the Limits of Data Privacy in the Digital Era

Anne SY Cheung

I. Introduction

Power is the characteristic content of sovereignty. One can easily think of the state exercising power or sovereignty over its territory and its population free from any interference by outside authorities. Yet, with the emergence of digital transformation and global technical infrastructure of the Internet from the 1990s, it has posed great challenge to the state exercising sovereignty over the digital frontier. A new call for the claim of digital sovereignty has since been opened up.[1] Among the various hardware (infrastructure) and software (codes, protocols) to win over,[2] data is the core and critical content of the digital world. This fight for the control of the digital—power over the Internet domain[3]—has largely become the struggle to control data. To a certain extent, the claim for digital sovereignty is also an assertion for data sovereignty. Chander and Sun observed that while data sovereignty can be seen as a subset of digital sovereignty, the two are so intertwined that it is difficult to disentangle them clearly because control over data is heavily involved in other important issues including data protection, competition, national security, and content regulation.[4] Different from traditional understanding on sovereignty with state occupying the center stage, the current claim for digital sovereignty is affecting everyone.[5] This chapter focuses on

---

[1] Julia Pohle & Thiel Thorsten, *Digital Sovereignty*, 9 INTERNET POL'Y REV. 1 (2020), https://policyreview.info/concepts/digital-sovereignty.

[2] According to Floridi, the fight for the control of the digital ranges from the control of data to infrastructure, software, standards, protocols, processes, hardware, and service. Luciano Floridi, *The Fight for Digital Sovereignty: What It Is, and Why It Matters, Especially for the EU*, 33 PHIL. & TECH. 369, 370–71 (2020).

[3] Anupam Chander & Haochen Sun, *Sovereignty 2.0*, 55(2) VAND. J. TRANSNAT'L L. 283 (2023).

[4] *Id.*

[5] Floridi, *supra* note 2.

Anne SY Cheung, *From Data Subjects to Data Sovereigns* In: *Data Sovereignty*. Edited by: Anupam Chander and Haochen Sun, Oxford University Press. © Oxford University Press 2023. DOI: 10.1093/oso/9780197582794.003.0005

90 FROM DATA SUBJECTS TO DATA SOVEREIGNS

the struggle for data sovereignty so as to highlight the relationship and connection between the stakeholders and data. This connection becomes crucial as illustrated in the later discussion on the COVID-19 crisis. Regardless of the context, the fight has always been about who has control and who can exercise control. Nation-states remain to be the prime player, asserting long-arm jurisdiction over cross-border data flows.[6] Equally important are tech companies playing an essential and strategic role in investing in digital capacity and infrastructure. Meanwhile, there is growing awareness for individuals to retain meaningful control over their personal data, leading to a turn to the concept of self-sovereignty in the digital age.[7] This view asserts that individuals are sovereigns with regard to their personal data, like the nation-states are sovereigns over their territories.

The individual self is supposed to be at the center stage endeavoring to exercise control over one's personal data against surveillance not only by the state, but also against exploitation by commercial giants. For a long while, the self is used to be protected under the orthodox personal data protection framework.[8] Consent should be sought so that individuals can authorize and exercise control over the collection, use, and processing of their personal data, including access, correction, and deletion of data.[9] However, facing a deluge of data enhanced with big data and artificial intelligence (AI) technologies, the ability of individuals to rule over their data has almost vanished. Individuals have been diminished into powerless objects when their identities can be easily discovered even through anonymized data,[10] inferences about them can be drawn by AI technologies,[11] and profiles can be built from their online and offline daily lives without their awareness.[12] As a result, protection based on consent and control by individuals becomes illusory in the use of data-driven technologies.

This chapter asks why the traditional data privacy protection framework is inadequate in the modern age. It points out, first of all, that the current

---

[6] Andrew Keane Woods, *Litigating Data Sovereignty*, 128 YALE LAW J. 328 (2018).

[7] *See* discussion in Part II.

[8] OECD, OECD PRIVACY FRAMEWORK (2013), http://www.oecd.org/sti/ieconomy/oecd_privac y_framework.pdf.

[9] Fred H. Cate & Viktor Mayer-Schönberger, *Notice and Consent in a World of Big Data*, 3 INT. DATA PRIV. L. 67 (2013).

[10] Paul Ohm, *Broken Promises of Privacy: Responding to the Surprising Failure of Anonymization*, UCLA L. REV. 1701 (2010).

[11] Sandra Wachter & Brent Mittelstadt, *A Right to Reasonable Inferences: Re-Thinking Data Protection Law in the Age of Big Data and AI*, 2019 COLUMBIA BUS. L. REV. 494 (2019).

[12] DAVID LYON, SURVEILLANCE AS SOCIAL SORTING: PRIVACY, RISK, AND DIGITAL DISCRIMINATION (2003).

protection that depends on the concept of personal data is unable to guard against the erosion of data privacy in the digital age. Second, protection based on the need to obtain consent under the terms of services gives only a false sense of control and security to the data subjects. Third, individuals can hardly exercise meaningful control over their own data in the fast-evolving data ecosystem. Instead, the author argues that data self-sovereignty, understood as the empowerment of the self to have effective and meaningful control over one's data, should complement the current framework of data privacy protection. The COVID-19 pandemic, which has hit the world since 2020, has accelerated the reflection on the need and strengthened the call for self-sovereignty. Through expanding the scope and means of control, we reclaim sovereignty over our data, and more importantly, our personal beings.

Part II of this chapter first analyzes the meaning of data sovereignty and the emerging concept of data self-sovereignty, with heightened awareness to give individuals greater control over their data. Part III then critiques the current data privacy protection legal framework focusing on the definition of personal data, the requirement of consent, and the principle of control. The current attempt to fight the COVID-19 pandemic by various governments in utilizing location information and AI technology in prediction will be used to illustrate the shortcomings of present data privacy frameworks. The discussion ends in Part IV by looking at how data self-sovereignty is used as an overarching concept to give better coordinated protection to our rights and entitlements over our data against manipulation and exploitation. This includes current attempts to empower individuals to protect and control their data and digital destiny through the concepts of dynamic consent, collective data rights, guardianship by independent watchdogs, information fiduciaries, and data intermediaries.

II. Data Subjects vs. Data Sovereigns

Sovereignty, a loaded term, conjures up considerations of power, influence, and control, and it is often linked to the assertion of jurisdiction by nation-states. In the seemingly borderless world of cyberspace, the challenge for nation-states is to demarcate boundaries for exclusive control and to extend their extraterritorial reach.[13] Data circulating in the digital world become a valuable asset to be captured, controlled, and utilized. Yet, it is not

---

[13] Kristina Irion, *Government Cloud Computing and National Data Sovereignty*, 4 POL'Y INTERNET 40 (2012).

only nation-states that are keen to claim ultimate control. There are multiple candidates joining in the claim of authority over data. In a study by Hummel and others over more than 340 publications on the study of data sovereignty, they found that there are multiple agents involved in this debate, ranging from nation-states, indigenous groups, and corporations to individuals.[14] Indeed, featuring prominently in the study of data sovereignty are nation-states asserting control in cross-border data by extending their territorial long-arm jurisdictions, or by legislating data localization law, and erecting firewalls and shutdowns.[15] The former includes supranational sovereigns like the Eurozone extending its extraterritorial reach through the General Data Protection Regulations,[16] while the latter includes China's commitment to prevent data access by foreign authorities.[17] At the same time, data sovereignty is a pressing concern for indigenous communities to collect and manage their own data.[18] Also, attention has been drawn to growing influence of tech giants, like Google, Facebook, and Amazon as being the real regulators of data processing in the Internet. Frank Pasquale points out that there has been a gradual displacement of juridical power of the state with control by corporate actors, a move from territorial to functional sovereignty in our society.[19] Shoshana Zuboff, in her seminal work on surveillance capitalism, describes the monopoly of corporations over our behavioral data, and almost over our lives, with profiles being created against us and our intimate and personal desires being shaped.[20] Besides centralized state, indigenous groups and corporations claiming sovereignty over data, what remains are the powerless individuals fighting for data self- sovereignty, mostly by patient groups, struggling for ownership of health data against online platforms

---

[14] Patrik Hummel et al., *Data Sovereignty: A Review*, 8 BIG DATA SOC. 1 (2021).

[15] *Id.* at 9. It was reported that by 2019, 45 countries have data localization laws. Akash Kapur, *The Rising Threat of Digital Nationalism*, WALL ST. J. (Nov. 1, 2019), https://www.wsj.com/articles/the-rising-threat-of-digital-nationalism-11572620577.

[16] Regulation (EU) 2016/679 of the European Parliament and of the Council of 27 April 2016 on the Protection of Natural Persons with Regard to the Processing of Personal Data and on the Free Movement of such Data, and Repealing Directive 95/46/EC (General Data Protection Regulation), 2016 O.J. (L119) 1. *See* Christopher Kuner, *Territorial Scope and Data Transfer Rules in the GDPR: Realising the EU's Ambition of Borderless Data Protection* (Univ. of Cambridge Faculty of Law, Research Paper No. 20/2021, 2021), https://ssrn.com/abstract=3827850.

[17] Emmanuel Pernot-Leplay, *China's Approach on Data Privacy Law: A Third Way Between the U.S. and the EU?* 8 PENN ST. J.L. & INT'L AFF. 49 (2020).

[18] MAGGIE WALTER ET AL., INDIGENOUS DATA SOVEREIGNTY AND POLICY (2021).

[19] This includes the areas of room-letting, transportation, and dispute resolution. Frank Pasquale, *From Territorial to Functional Sovereignty: The Case of Amazon*, THE LAW AND POLITICAL ECONOMY PROJECT (Dec. 6, 2017), https://lpeproject.org/blog/from-territorial-to-functional-sovereignty-the-case-of-amazon.

[20] SHOSHANA ZUBOFF, THE AGE OF SURVEILLANCE CAPITALISM (2019).

and pharmaceutical companies;[21] and also by individuals with interest in the use of blockchain technology to protect "self-sovereign identity."[22] Apart from the identification of the range of agents in this debate of data sovereignty, Hummel and others have highlighted the constitutive components of data self-sovereignty as autonomy, control, power, and privacy.[23]

Here, I focus on the "self" and advocate for the recognition of self-sovereignty. After all, it is the self who is the source of data but it is also the self that is most vulnerable and is losing fundamental rights concerning the control and power over the use of data about oneself, be it personal or not.[24] Sovereignty is chosen as the normative reference point as it provides a powerful tool for individuals not only to protect their data privacy, but also other human rights including the right not to be discriminated and not to be manipulated in decision-making. Furthermore, sovereignty enables individuals to claim meaningful and effective control over data infrastructure through themselves or through dedicated third parties to guard their digital destiny.[25]

One may ask what the similarities and differences between data privacy and data self-sovereignty are, and why we need a new concept. Apparently, privacy and sovereignty have much in common. Historically, the regulatory concept of sovereignty has the nation-states claiming absolute power over a domain or a realm of data at its focal point, Now, the same concern is shared by individuals.[26] In their work on information sovereignty, Polčák and Svantesson argue that sovereignty of states and privacy of individuals are equivalent because of the common principles shared between the two.[27] While the nation-states are claiming jurisdiction and non-intervention, and the right to be let alone within their territory, individuals are also asserting legitimate power over their bodies and choices, and effective control over the

---

[21] Xueping Liang et al., *Towards Decentralized Accountability and Self-Sovereignty in Healthcare Systems, in* INFORMATION AND COMMUNICATIONS SECURITY 387 (Sihan Qing et al. eds., 2018).

[22] Self-sovereign identity refers to a system that allows users to control their online identities. JOSEPH CUTLER, J. DAX HANSEN, & CHARLYN HO, SELF-SOVEREIGN IDENTITY AND DISTRIBUTED LEDGER TECHNOLOGY: FRAMING THE LEGAL ISSUES (2018), https://www.perkinscoie.com/images/content/2/1/v3/218495/Perkins-Coie-Self-Sovereign-Identity-and-Distributed-Ledger-Tech.pdf.

[23] Hummel et al., *supra* note 14 , at 3, 13.

[24] Nydia Remolina & Mark Findlay, *The Paths to Digital Self-Determination—A Foundational Theoretical Framework* (SMU Centre for AI & Data Governance, Research Paper No. 03/2021, 2021), https://papers.ssrn.com/abstract=3831726.

[25] RADIM POLČÁK & DAN JERKER B. SVANTESSON, INFORMATION SOVEREIGNTY: DATA PRIVACY, SOVEREIGN POWERS AND THE RULE OF LAW 181 (2017).

[26] *Id.*

[27] *Id.* at 2, 58–61.

use of data so that they can be "left in peace."[28] Individuals are sovereigns with regard to their personal data, like the nation-states are sovereigns over their territory.

Seemingly, to a certain extent, the data privacy protection regime has striven to make individuals data sovereigns, in endowing them the status of "data subjects" and recognizing their rights of control. In his study on international data privacy instruments, Lee Bygrave identifies that a fundamental principle of data privacy laws is that individuals as data subjects should be "able to participate in, and have a measure of influence over, the processing of data on them by others."[29] Furthermore, he further classifies the manifestation of this core principle into three types of rules. The first type aims at making individuals aware of data-processing activities generally.[30] The second type aims at making individuals aware of basic details of the processing of data on themselves, covering the rules on collection of data directly from data subjects, and rules prohibiting processing of personal data without the data subjects' consent.[31] The third type grants individuals the right to gain access to data kept on them by other persons, and the right to object to others' processing of data on themselves.[32] It is this right to object that is linked intrinsically with the notion of consent by which the data subjects signify their agreements to personal data being processed.[33] It is the individuals forming the basic units encompassing rights to give consent to share data with others, and entitlements to have access to data, deletion, or correction of data. In contemporary terms, this principle of empowering the data subjects is translated into the right to information; right to access; rights to rectify, block, and erasure; right to object; right to data portability; rights related to profiling; rights related to automated decision-making; right to an effective remedy; and right to compensation and liability under various international legal instruments.[34]

---

[28] *Id.* at 86–87. The authors consider that right to be let alone refers only to the aspect of leaving people to their selves in the struggle against others, or against themselves. In contrast, the right to be left in peace includes peace between nations, peace within a nation and individual peace.

[29] Lee A. Bygrave, Data Privacy Law: An International Perspective 158 (1st ed. 2014). Bygrave traces this to the "Individual Participation Principle" of the OECD Guideline.

[30] *Id.* at 158.

[31] *Id.* at 158–59.

[32] *Id.* at 159.

[33] *Id.* at 160.

[34] Privacy Int'l, The Keys to Data Protection 52 (2018), https://privacyinternational.org/sites/default/files/2018-09/Data%20Protection%20COMPLETE.pdf.

No doubt, the legal framework aims to give comprehensive protection to individuals, who become the basic units of data subjects with the power to exclude others from one's informational sphere; to protect oneself from misuse of data; to determine when, how, with whom, and to what extent, control over data can be exercised. The right to give consent and raise objections is central. However, as rightly pointed by Bygrave, the exercise of such right depends much on one's *awareness* of the processing and flow of one's personal data. In the age of big data and AI (as will be explained in the next section), it is extremely difficult for one to learn the process and the flow of one's data. Individuals can be denied reasonable control over their personal data or overwhelmed in taking care of their own personal data in the age of big data and artificial intelligence.[35] In other words, data subjects cease to be sovereigns when they are unable to articulate or enforce claims to power about their data when faced with two major challenges. First, they have been "violated outside their conscious attention" when data about them have been used by multiple unknown third parties in the downstream use of data without their knowledge.[36] Second, they have been degraded from data subjects to mere objects of data flows with fast-evolving data-driven technologies. These hollow out one's ability to articulate or attain certain data privacy rights.[37]

With this understanding, data self-sovereignty requires more than just data privacy protection. At one level, data self-sovereignty calls for empowerment of the self. Echoing literature on digital self-determination, it is concerned with restoring control to individuals, and empowering them with the actual ability to govern their data, and to define their identities online and offline.[38] It calls for an expansion on the understanding of personal data to include data and inferences drawn about individuals.[39] While it shares the same concern with data privacy, the focus is on enabling individuals in developing relevant competences needed for meaningful and effective control over their data.[40] The controllability of data flows become the major concern. Individuals should be enabled to restrict and share their data, to control both

---

[35] Ira S. Rubinstein, *Big Data: The End of Privacy or a New Beginning?*, 3 INT'L. DATA PRIVACY L. 74 (2013).

[36] Remolina & Findlay, *supra* note 24.

[37] Patrik Hummel et al., *Sovereignty and Data Sharing*, 1 ITU J.: ICT DISCOVERIES 10 (2018).

[38] & Findlay, *supra* note 24 , at 22.

[39] *Id.* at 29.

[40] Hummel et al., *supra* note 37, at 10. Pascal D. König, *The Place of Conditionality and Individual Responsibility in a "Data-Driven Economy,"* 4 BIG DATA SOC. 205395171774241 (2017).

the input and output of their data.[41] At another level, data self-sovereignty focuses on the social and collective settings in which individuals' claims can be articulated, recognized, and respected.[42] It is about designing a new type of data infrastructure that covers how data are shared and used, allowing individual deliberations to control data input and output, and individuals' destiny.

III. Data Privacy in the Time of Pandemic

In a digital world where power and authority become much more invisible, and controlling every day,[43] data privacy is almost gone. Legal instruments aiming to protect data privacy started out with noble ideas in the 1980s.[44] But as the years went by, we began to realize we are ill equipped to tackle the challenges brought by data-driven technologies. The record is clear enough: individuals can be re-identified through anonymized data, inferences can be drawn by raw data with the use of big data and AI, and new identities and profiles can be built against them without their knowledge. Against this background, consent becomes largely irrelevant. The above-mentioned problems become magnified in the fight against the COVID-19 pandemic.

A. The Challenge of Non-Personalized Data

The conventional data privacy protection regime hinges on the crucial involvement of personal data, defined generally to depend on whether a person is identified or identifiable: that is, whether a substantial connection between the individuals and the data originating in the personal domain of the individuals in question can be found. For instance, under Article 4(2) of the General Data Protection Regulation (GDPR), personal data is defined as "any information relating to a data subject." In turn, data subject is defined under article 4(1) as

---

[41] Hummel et al., *supra* note 37, at 6.

[42] *Id.* at 3.

[43] ZYGMUNT BAUMAN & DAVID LYON, LIQUID SURVEILLANCE: A CONVERSATION (2013).

[44] Graham Greenleaf, *It's Nearly 2020, so What Fate Awaits the 1980 OECD Privacy Guidelines? (A Background Paper for the 2019 OECD Privacy Guidelines Review)*, 159 PRIVACY LAWS & BUS. INT'L REP. 18 (2019), https://papers.ssrn.com/abstract=3405156.

an identified natural person or a natural person who can be identified, directly or indirectly, by means reasonably likely to be used by the controller or by any other natural or legal person, in particular by reference to an identification number, location data, online identifier or to one or more factors specific to the physical, physiological, genetic, mental, economic, cultural or social identity of that person.

In parallel, although there is no uniform privacy law in the United States, personal identifiable information (PII) refers generally to information that identifies a person or to a list of specific types of data that constitute PII.[45] The concept of PII includes "any information" relating to a data subject, whereas the standard of "identifiable" includes any direct or indirect means reasonably likely to be used. And the list of nominative identifiers can include location data and online identifier. For instance, under the California Privacy Act,[46] personal information is defined as information that "identifies, relates to, describes, is reasonably capable of being associated with, or could reasonably be linked (directly or indirectly) with a particular consumer or household."[47] "Identifiability" of individuals remains a core criterion.[48] The primary considerations are to look at what means are available to identify an individual and the extent to which such means are readily available to the data controller in the processing of data.

However, this approach is no longer suitable in the modern world of technologies. As I have explained in an earlier work,[49] it has been a common practice to combine bits of seemingly non-personal information to identify individuals, and to profile them. Arguably, any data emanating from an individual is a form of potential identifier. De-anonymization and re-identification techniques have become so powerful in the 21st century that

[45] Paul Schwartz & Daniel Solove, *The PII Problem: Privacy and a New Concept of Personally Identifiable Information*, N.Y. Univ. L. Rev. 1814 (2011).

[46] Cal. Civ. Code § 1798.199 (Deering 2020). California Privacy Rights Act of 2020 (CPRA), amended the California Consumer Privacy Act (CCPA), which took effect earlier in 2020. The new law is also known as "CCPA 2.0" to indicate it is the combined effect of the CCPA as amended by the CPRA. The CPRA will take effect on January 1, 2023, but will apply to data collected from January 1, 2022, except for the right of access.

[47] Personal information includes but are not limited to real name, alias, postal address, unique personal identifier, online identifier, Internet Protocol address, email address, account name, social security number, driver's license number, license plate number, passport number, or other similar identifiers. *See id.* § 1798.140(v)(1)

[48] Graham Greenleaf, *California's CCPA 2.0: Does the US Finally Have a Data Privacy Act?*, 168 Privacy Laws & Bus. Int'l Rep. 13 (2020), https://papers.ssrn.com/abstract=3793435.

[49] Anne SY Cheung, *Re-personalizing Personal Data in the Cloud, in* Privacy and Legal Issues in Cloud Computing 69 (2015).

98 FROM DATA SUBJECTS TO DATA SOVEREIGNS

one may question whether complete anonymization or retaining the status of being non-identifiable is ever feasible.[50] Personal data can be de-identified into pseudonymous or anonymized data, but the latter can be re-identified.[51] In other words, personal data has a life of its own evolution. For instance, data scientists were able to re-identify 90 percent of more than one million individuals from a set of anonymized credit card transactions.[52] In addition, data-mining technologies allow the combination and cross-referencing of data from different sources, which then easily permits the identification of individuals.[53] Furthermore, data analysts can also draw accurate inferences of someone who is not even a part of an online social network (i.e., inferences from non-membership).[54]

B. From Tracking the Pandemic to Tracking Individuals

The power and perils of data-driven technologies prove to be critical in the fight against COVID-19. The world has been in a public health emergency for more than two years since early 2020.[55] At the time of writing, the number of confirmed cases of COVID-19 worldwide has been more than 340 million, and more than 5.5 million people had died from the disease, affecting 222 countries.[56] In the fight against the pandemic, governments in different countries have taking unprecedented measures to track, trace, and contain the spread of the highly contagious virus in the use of data-driven technologies.[57] Massive amounts of data have been collected and processed

---

[50] Ohm, *supra* note 10.

[51] Boris Lubarsky, *Re-Identification of "Anonymized" Data*, 1 GEO. L. TECH. REV. 202 (2017).

[52] The study used a data set of three months of credit card transactions for 1.1 million users in 10,000 shops. The data set had been anonymized, which did not contain any names, account numbers, or obvious identifiers. It showed that four spatiotemporal points were enough to uniquely re-identify 90 percent of individuals. Yves-Alexandre de Montjoye et al., *Unique in the Shopping Mall: On the Reidentifiability of Credit Card Metadata*, 347 SCIENCE 536 (2015).

[53] Latanya Sweeney, *Weaving Technology and Policy Together to Maintain Confidentiality*, 25 J. LAW. MED. ETHICS 98 (1997). Latanya Sweeney, *Only You, Your Doctor, and Many Others May Know*, TECH. SCI. (Sept. 29, 2015), https://techscience.org/a/2015092903.

[54] Solon Barocas & Helen Nissenbaum, *Big Data's End Run Around Anonymity and Consent*, in PRIVACY, BIG DATA, AND THE PUBLIC GOOD 44 (Julia Lane et al. eds., 2014).

[55] WHO, WHO-CONVENED GLOBAL STUDY OF ORIGINS OF SARS-CoV-2: CHINA PART (2021), https://www.who.int/publications/i/item/who-convened-global-study-of-origins-of-sars-cov-2-china-part.

[56] *WHO Coronavirus (COVID-19) Dashboard*, WHO, https://covid19.who.int (last visited Jan. 24, 2022).

[57] VI HART ET AL., OUTPACING THE VIRUS: DIGITAL RESPONSE TO CONTAINING THE SPREAD OF COVID-19 WHILE MITIGATING PRIVACY RISKS (2020), https://ethics.harvard.edu/files/center-for-ethics/files/white_paper_5_outpacing_the_virus_final.pdf?m=1586179217.

in the pandemic, including geolocation, proximity, social contacts, health and medical history, and biometric data. Inevitably, this raises concerns of privacy infringement.

1. Anonymized Telecommunications Data

One common method in using data technology to fight the pandemic is for governments to collaborate with telecommunications companies in the collection and process of mobile call data. It was reported that at least 27 telecommunications providers in different countries had been sharing mobile call data records with governments in an aggregated and anonymized format.[58] This included Deutsche Telekom from Germany,[59] Vodafone from Lombardy (Italy),[60] and Telco A1 from Austria.[61] Data provided on telephone calls and other telecommunications transactions provide helpful and valuable insights into population movements. The "anonymized" location data showing users' movement can alert authorities to the gathering of crowds, and allow authorities to know whether the population has been following social distancing and quarantine orders. In addition, the public may also benefit from such information. The South Korean government created a publicly available map from cellphone data that identified infected individuals' routes and those likely to be infected by the virus.[62] This enabled people to determine if they had come into contact with someone who had been infected with coronavirus.[63] While anonymized data do not fall within the scope of legal regulation and protection, concerns are raised about privacy violations and state surveillance.[64] For instance, in South Korea, information published promptly on the government's website showing the route, when combined

---

[58] Kareem Fahim et al., *Cellphone Monitoring Is Spreading with the Coronavirus. So Is an Uneasy Tolerance of Surveillance*, WASH. POST (May 2, 2020), https://www.washingtonpost.com/world/cellphone-monitoring-is-spreading-with-the-coronavirus-so-is-an-uneasy-tolerance-of-surveillance/2020/05/02/56f14466-7b55-11ea-a311-adb1344719a9_story.html.

[59] *Tracking and Tracing COVID: Protecting Privacy and Data while Using Apps and Biometrics*, OECD (Apr. 23, 2020), https://www.oecd.org/coronavirus/policy-responses/tracking-and-tracing-covid-protecting-privacy-and-data-while-using-apps-and-biometrics-8f394636.

[60] *Id.*

[61] Foo Yun Chee, *Vodafone, Deutsche Telekom, 6 other Telcos to Help EU Track Virus*, REUTERS (Mar. 25, 2020), https://www.reuters.com/article/us-health-coronavirus-telecoms-eu-idUSKBN21C36G.

[62] Mark Ryan, *In Defence of Digital Contact-Tracing: Human Rights, South Korea and Covid-19*, 16 INT. J. PERVASIVE COMPUT. COMMUN. 383 (2020).

[63] Sangchul Park et al., *Information Technology–Based Tracing Strategy in Response to COVID-19 in South Korea—Privacy Controversies*, 323 J. AMER. MED. ASSOC. 2129 (2020).

[64] *Telecommunications Data and Covid-19*, PRIVACY INT'L, https://privacyinternational.org/examples/telecommunications-data-and-covid-19 (last visited Mar. 9, 2021).

100 FROM DATA SUBJECTS TO DATA SOVEREIGNS

with other non-personal data,[65] had led to "witch hunting," harassment, and bullying when people were connecting the dots to identify individuals.[66]

2. Location Information and Contact Tracing Apps

Likewise, the use of contact tracing technologies raises similar concerns on privacy. Contact tracing is a common strategy used in the time of pandemic to help stop the spread of disease like Ebola virus disease, Middle East respiratory syndrome (MERS), SARS, and many other infections.[67] Typically, it involves speaking with patients who have been confirmed to be carrying a virus or showing symptoms in order to identify anyone who has been in close contact with them.[68] Each of these individuals will then be placed in isolation or quarantine. The traditional method carried out by trained health officials is time consuming. Apart from limitations such as whether the patients could remember their contacts and the availability of trained medical personnel, its effectiveness is dependent on how quickly a disease is spreading. In contrast, digital contact tracing software or mobile apps used in the COVID-19 pandemic, enabled by smartphones, allows effective tracing of individuals and tracking their contacts, resulting in effective slowing down in the spread of the virus in countries like South Korea and Singapore.[69]

Digital contact tracing was so popular that it had been reported that more than 30 governments had deployed contact tracing apps to fight the pandemic.[70] These contact-tracing apps and software typically need to use geographical positioning system (GPS) to collect users' location data, or require the use of Bluetooth-based technology to collect proximity data (physical proximity to other devices, including duration of encounters among users).[71] Data collected are then automatically uploaded onto a central database or

---

[65] Although names of individuals were not reviewed, sex, nationality, age, health status, medical institutions treated, and path and means of transportation of infected persons were disclosed. Park et al., *supra* note 63.

[66] Choe Sang-Hun, *In South Korea, Covid-19 Comes With Another Risk: Online Bullies*, N.Y. TIMES, (Sept. 19, 2020), https://www.nytimes.com/2020/09/19/world/asia/south-korea-covid-19-online-bullying.html; Park et al., *supra* note 63.

[67] Joel Hellewell et al., *Feasibility of Controlling COVID-19 Outbreaks by Isolation of Cases and Contacts*, 8 LANCET GLOB. HEALTH e488 (2020).

[68] HART ET AL., *supra* note 57, at 10.

[69] *Id.* at 11.

[70] Patrick Howell O'Neil et al., *A Flood of Coronavirus Apps are Tracking Us. Now It's Time to Keep Track of Them.*, MIT TECH. REV. (May 7, 2020), https://www.technologyreview.com/2020/05/07/1000961/launching-mittr-covid-tracing-tracker.

[71] GPS based apps collect time-stamps GPS points from individuals all day long. GPS is dependent on a constellation of satellites to give accurate positional information in four dimensions of latitude, longitude, altitude and time. It works best outdoor, providing accurate positioning between 4 and 15

stored locally on a user's phone. For instance, the South Korea's app Corona 100m was an example of centralized model using GPS technology to track location, contact information, and health status. In comparison, Germany opted for a de-centralized Bluetooth model.[72] Less private data are collected in the Bluetooth-based approaches as exact location information from users need not be collected.[73] For instance, Apple and Google jointly introduced Bluetooth-based digital contact tracing apps known as Google-Apple Exposure Notifications (GAEN) that only collected an anonymized, constantly changing ID created by other devices running an app based on the same protocols.[74] Exposure notification data were stored and processed on individuals' devices.[75] A user who tested positive for COVID-19 could enable the authorities to notify other significant contacts without actually identifying them.

Regardless of which models are being adopted, different levels of anonymity can be deployed to collect, store, and share data, and alert users regarding potential infection exposure. Take the Singapore example of the TraceTogether app, which employed Bluetooth technology in tracking individuals under a centralized model.[76] Although encrypted Bluetooth data exchanged was stored in the app or token, a random user ID (a string of numbers and letters) had been generated and linked to the user's contact phone number and identification details, such as one's name when signing up for TraceTogether.[77] All these details were stored in a central server with the government.[78] From this perspective, the data privacy risk for individuals in this Bluetooth technology app is similar to a GPS-based scheme in a centralized model. Since the authorities know the users' phone numbers, they can link this information to other databases that contain information of the users.[79]

---

meters. But it is battery intensive and inconsistent or unavailable indoor. Janice Y Tsai et al., *Location-Sharing Technologies: Privacy Risks and Controls*, 6 J.L. Pol'y Inf. Soc. 34 (2010).

[72] Douglas Rinke & Andreas Busvine, *Germany Flips to Apple-Google Approach on Smartphone Contact Tracing*, Reuters (Apr. 26, 2020), https://www.reuters.com/article/us-health-coronavirus-europe-tech-idUSKCN22807J.

[73] Dong Wang & Fang Liu, *Privacy Risk and Preservation in Contact Tracing of COVID-19*, CHANCE, https://chance.amstat.org/2020/09/contact-tracing-covid-19/ (last visited Jan. 6, 2021).

[74] Apple & Google, *Privacy-Preserving Contact Tracing - Exposure Notification: Frequently Asked Questions*, Apple, https://www.apple.com/covid19/contacttracing (last visited May 31, 2021).

[75] *Id.*

[76] The app does not collect GPS data, or data about a user's Wi-Fi and mobile networks. Kenny Chee, *What Data Does TraceTogether Collect?*, The Straits Times (Jan. 6, 2021), https://www.straitstimes.com/singapore/what-data-does-tracetogether-collect.

[77] *Id.*

[78] *Id.*

[79] Wang & Liu, *supra* note 73.

102 FROM DATA SUBJECTS TO DATA SOVEREIGNS

Despite initial assurance from the Singapore government that data collected would only be used for virus tracking, officials later admitted to Parliament that data would be shared with police for criminal investigation.[80] It is the ability of governments or other data users to find new purposes for shared data and to identify individuals that renders the use of contact tracing apps to be particularly controversial and worrying.

Regardless whether we are referring to GPS or Bluetooth technology, one's location information is being collected and processed.[81] By the term "location information," we refer to any data that places one at a particular location at any given point in time, or at a series of locations over time.[82] This also includes the combination of the above location information with other information about an identifiable individual to create a data picture.[83] Core to location information are the elements of space, time, and content. In particular, it is the descriptive aspect or the type of location that is most important and telling to most of us.[84] Our location, our movements, and our social interactions (e.g., the calls that individuals make) can lead to reconstruction of one's social graph. Summed up by the U..S Supreme Court in Carpenter v. US, frequent and detailed location data open up "an intimate window into a person's life, revealing not only his particular movements but through them his familial, political, professional, religious, and sexual associations."[85] Also, scholars have found that human mobility traces are highly unique.[86] With four spatiotemporal points, 95 percent of individuals in a mobile phone database of 1.5 million people could be identified even from coarse datasets.[87]

---

[80] Andreas Illmer, *Singapore Reveals Covid Privacy Data Available to Police*, BBC News (Jan. 5, 2021), https://www.bbc.com/news/world-asia-55541001.

[81] Location tracking can also be done through Bluetooth beacons though there has not been any reports that Bluetooth-based apps have been used to track users' location during the pandemic. Peta Mitchell, Marcus Foth, & Irina Anastasiu, *Geographies of Locative Apps*, *in* Routledge Handbook of Media Geographies (Paul C. Adams & Barney Warf eds., 2021).

[82] David H. Goetz, *Locating Location Privacy*, 26 Berkeley Tech. L.J. 823 (2011); Teresa Scassa, *Information Privacy in Public Space: Location Data, Data Protection and the Reasonable Expectation of Privacy*, 9 Canadian J. L. & Tech. 193 (2009).

[83] Scassa, *supra* note 82, 193.

[84] Bennett and Crowe explain that location information has three dimensions of being geospatial, civic and descriptive. While geospatial refers to the positioning on the globe through longitude, latitude and altitude, and civic refers to the locational coordinates that are provided as a result of political decisions concerning borders, it is the descriptive aspect that reveals the immediate type of location that one is in or has visited at a certain time. Colin J. Bennett & Lori Crowe, Location-Based Services and the Surveillance of Mobility: An Analysis of Privacy Risks in Canada 33 (2005), http://www.colinbennett.ca/wp-content/uploads/2012/06/OPCREPORTFINAL.pdf.

[85] 565 U. S. 430, 415 (opinion of Sotomayor, J.).

[86] Yves-Alexandre de Montjoye et al., *Unique in the Crowd: The Privacy Bounds of Human Mobility*, 3 Sci. Rep. 1376 (2013).

[87] *Id.*

3. Predictions Based on Data

AI technologies have been proven to be powerful in the fight against the COVID-19 pandemic from the initial stage of detection to latter stages of diagnosis, prediction, monitoring, and prevention.[88] The efficacy of AI system, based on machine learning works by identifying patterns in data, requires large amounts of data being available. Often, it involves collecting and sharing data across sectors. South Korea, which is often praised as a successful example to contain and track the virus, has leveraged AI technology by using, combining, and analyzing location data (stored on or generated by smartphones), credit card transactions, immigration entry information, CCTV footage, medical and prescription records, transit pass records for public transportation, and other personal identification information to trace individuals suspected to be infected.[89] In effect, the large-scale surveillance system has turned tracking of the disease to tracking of individuals. How data are collected and how algorithms are deployed raise heightened data privacy and human rights considerations.[90] Of particular concern is AI power to identify and predict potential carriers of the virus.

Myriad examples around the world show the benefits and risks of AI's prediction prowess in combating the pandemic. In Israel, AI is being used to identify who were more at risk from the virus, to determine the level of treatment that one would get if fallen sick, and to reach the decision of who should be isolated as being high-risk members of the population.[91] Millions of health records (including one's age, BMI, and health conditions dating back 27 years ago) were used to make the predictions.[92] In China, AI is used to predict high risk of mortality among COVID-19 patients in Wuhan.[93] In Canada, AI-enabled contact tracing apps has been developed to track the probability of infection for users based on their movements and encounters.[94] AI can work

---

[88] *Using Artificial Intelligence to Help Combat COVID-19*, OECD (Apr. 23, 2020), https://www.oecd.org/coronavirus/policy-responses/using-artificial-intelligence-to-help-combat-covid-19-ae4c5c21.

[89] Park et al., *supra* note 63.

[90] Carmel Shachar et al., *AI Surveillance during Pandemics: Ethical Implementation Imperatives*, 50 HASTINGS CENT. REP. 18 (2020).

[91] Will Douglas Heaven, *Israel Is Using AI to Flag High-Risk Covid-19 Patients*, MIT TECH. REV. (Apr. 24, 2020), https://www.technologyreview.com/2020/04/24/1000543/israel-ai-prediction-medical-testing-data-high-risk-covid-19-patients.

[92] *Id.*

[93] Ian A. Scott & Enrico W. Coiera, *Can AI Help in the Fight against COVID-19?*, 213 MED. J. AUST. 439 (2020).

[94] COVI, the AI contact tracing app was developed by Mila, a Montreal based technology institute but the app was not adopted by the Canadian Federal Government. Martin Patriquin, *Federal Government Rules Out Adoption of Mila Institute's COVID-19 Contact-tracing App*, THE LOGIC (June 4, 2020),

104 FROM DATA SUBJECTS TO DATA SOVEREIGNS

wonders in controlling the spread of virus, cutting off the route of transmission, protecting vulnerable groups and saving human lives. Yet scholars have warned that AI technology has not reached operational maturity.[95] When AI predictions would have a direct impact on the treatment that one would get, and on the extent of one's freedom that would be curtailed, this sparks legal and ethical concerns beyond data privacy, including issues of transparency, fairness, and due process of decisions. For instance, when healthy individuals are forced to be quarantined based on the prediction that they are high risk carriers, can they challenge the decisions made by AI? Do they have access to judicial review?

The implications for privacy and human rights go beyond the immediate concerns of containing COVID-19. Indeed, location information and social graph data can be sensitive data revealing much of personally identifiable information for social control. While it is indisputable that geolocation technologies serve important functions especially in times of the current global health crisis, their potential to be surveillance and privacy invasive tools should not be overlooked. With big data analytics and AI, location data can be used for social control and monitoring and also for predicting travel and movement patterns.[96] How to balance the protection of fundamental rights and public health requires rigorous scrutiny and deep considerations of legal tests of necessity and proportionality. Questions raised but left unanswered include what type of data are collected and how those data will be used, stored, and shared; and what levels of de-identification and re-identification are involved. Safeguards on auditing for efficacy and misuse, independent supervision of data use, due process, or affected people have yet to be addressed.[97]

---

https://thelogic.co/news/federal-government-rules-out-adoption-of-mila-institutes-covid-19-contact-tracing-app.

[95] Scott & Coiera, *supra* note 93. Will Douglas Heaven, *AI Could Help with the Next Pandemic—but Not With this One*, MIT TECH. REV. (Mar. 12, 2020), https://www.technologyreview.com/2020/03/12/905352/ai-could-help-with-the-next-pandemicbut-not-with-this-one.

[96] Philip Howard & Lisa-Maria Neudert, *AI Can Battle Coronavirus, but Privacy Shouldn't Be a Casualty*, TECHCRUNCH (May 26, 2020), https://techcrunch.com/2020/05/26/ai-can-battle-coronavirus-but-privacy-shouldnt-be-a-casualty.

[97] HART ET AL., *supra* note 57, at 27.

C. The Illusory Promise of Consent

Facing the privacy challenges posed by advancing data-driven technologies, individuals have become helpless data selves being profiled and monitored by authorities. Consent becomes a feeble concept in the face of technologies.[98]

Consent, which is used to be a cardinal doctrine in personal data protection, is premised on the respect for individual autonomy, embodying the principle of self-rule that is free from "controlling interference by others and limitations that prevent meaningful choice."[99] It is enshrined in numerous international treaties, legal guidelines, and codes.[100] Under article 4 of the GDPR, consent means "any freely given, specific, informed and unambiguous indication of the data subject" by a clear affirmative action signifying agreement to the processing of personal data. "Explicit consent" is necessary for the processing of genetic, biometric, and health data. However, consent can be overridden in times of emergency and be rendered illusory in the data ecosystem.

First, in times of emergency like the COVID-19 pandemic, governments, health, and other public or private institutions need to respond quickly, and so there are various grounds of exemptions under the law that waive the requirement of consent. Take the example of GDPR. Although it is often seen as setting a high and stringent standard on data protection, the European Data Protection Board stated clearly that data protection rules including the GDPR do not hinder measures taken in the fight against the pandemic.[101] Article 6(1)(d) of the GDPR allows processing of data without consent from the data subject that is necessary to protect the vital interest of individuals, and to safeguard public interest. The grounds of public interest and the vital interests of the data subject are specifically mentioned in Recital 46 to include monitoring epidemics and their spread. Exceptions also apply to the processing of special categories of data. Article 9(2)(1) of the GDPR, which

---

[98] Debates have also emerged over whether the requirement of notice and consent should be replaced by focusing on the control over the use of data. Cate & Mayer-Schönberger, *supra* note 9.

[99] Tom L. Beauchamp & James F. Childress, Principles of Biomedical Ethics 101 (7th ed. 2012).

[100] For a historical overview, see Benjamin M. Meier, *International Protection of Persons Undergoing Medical Experimentation: Protecting the Right of Informed Consent*, 20 Berkeley J. Int'l. L. 513, 514–33 (2002). For further comparison of global guidelines on consent and informed consent, *see* Zulfiqar A. Bhutta, *Beyond Informed Consent*, 82 Bull. WHO 771 (2004).

[101] European Data Protection Board, Statement on the Processing of Personal Data in the Context of the COVID-19 Outbreak, European Data Protection Board (2020), https://edpb.europa.eu/our-work-tools/our-documents/other-guidance/statement-processing-personal-data-context-covid-19_en.

prohibits processing of biometric and health data without explicit consent, allows exceptions when processing is necessary for reasons of public interest in the area of public health "such as protecting against serious cross-border threats to health." Recital 46 explicitly refers to the control of an epidemic as a ground for derogation from the rule of consent.[102]

Second, scholars have pointed out that in the age of big data analytics, the conventional notice and consent paradigm gives only an illusion of control. This is partly due to the difficulty of navigating terms of service and privacy policies that require individuals to deal with endless and evolving consent materials and datasets, and partly due to the evolving nature of personal data. It is estimated that an average user has more than 150 different online accounts,[103] held by different entities worldwide, which adopt different terms of service and privacy policies. How can a user realistically be able to familiarize with all those different details in order to give informed consent? Helen Nissenbaum characterizes the phenomenon as the "transparency paradox."[104] On the one hand, data privacy principles require the conveying of information to achieve the goals of transparency and informed consent. Yet fine details from terms of services often result in information overload that users seldom read.[105] On the other hand, abbreviated or simplified consent materials may hide important truth on how one's data privacy maybe infringed. Further, as we have discussed in the earlier section, personal data can be anonymized or de-identified, thus evading the rules or data privacy principles and the need to obtain consent from data subjects. Jonathan Obar criticizes the presumption that data subjects can control, manage, and oversee their data and their digital destiny to be an "unattainable ideal" and a "fallacy of data privacy self-management."[106]

---

[102] For further discussion on the position under GDPR, *see* Emanuele Ventrella, *Privacy in Emergency Circumstances: Data Protection and the COVID-19 Pandemic*, 21 ERA FORUM 379 (2020).

[103] *Data Sovereignty in Data Sharing – What Needs to Happen in the Digital Identity Landscape?*, INNOPAY (Nov. 21, 2019), https://www.innopay.com/en/publications/data-sovereignty-data-sharing-what-needs-happen-digital-identity-landscape.

[104] Helen Nissenbaum, *A Contextual Approach to Privacy Online*, 140 DAEDALUS 32, 36 (2011).

[105] According to a Deloitte survey of 2,000 U.S. consumers in 2017, it was found that 91 percent of the respondents consent to terms of service without reading them. Jessica Guynn, *What You Need to Know before Clicking "I Agree" on that Terms of Service Agreement or Privacy Policy*, USA TODAY (Jan. 28, 2020), https://www.usatoday.com/story/tech/2020/01/28/not-reading-the-small-print-is-privacy-policy-fail/4565274002.

[106] Jonathan A. Obar, *Searching for Data Privacy Self-Management: Individual Data Control and Canada's Digital Strategy*, 44 CAN. J. COMMUN. 35, 37 (2019).

IV. Beyond Privacy: From Data Subjects to Data Sovereigns

Current legal instruments on data privacy, which rely heavily on the concept of personal data and a notice and consent regime, have failed to deliver the promise of privacy and autonomy in the digital age. We have seen the "self" being left powerless in countering state requests and corporate intervention. In order to better safeguard our autonomy and rights, we need mechanisms in law and an infrastructure that can give effect to data subjects' sovereignty. To empower the individuals, arguments have been advanced to implement the model of dynamic consent and to recognize collective data rights.

Dynamic consent is an option commonly used in biobanks or medical health research databases.[107] The term used to describe personalized, online consent on secure information technology-based platforms.[108] Participants are allowed to engage in the interactive personalized interface as much or as little as they choose or to alter their consent choices in real time. Consent is seen as a process, as an ongoing interaction between researchers and participants. In this way, participants can have better control about the downstream use of their data, which is over both the input and output of their data.[109] Consent becomes dynamic because it allows participants to interact with the researchers over time, to consent to new projects, and to alter their consent choices in light of any new circumstances.

Scholars praise the model of dynamic consent as providing a "personalised communication interface for interacting with patients, participants and citizens."[110] Apparently, it enables consent to be given to multiple researchers and projects, to open-ended and ongoing research, and to the use of secondary research or downstreaming of data use. Besides, dynamic consent overcomes the problem of locked-in consent confined to one experimental procedure for granting autonomy, choice, and control to individuals. At the same time, researchers can also manage the necessity to re-contact and to seek re-consent from participants much more easily. Individuals are seen as

---

[107] Hummel et al., *supra* note 37. Anne Cheung, *Moving Beyond Consent for Citizen Science in Big Data Health and Medical Research*, 16 NORTHWEST. J. TECHNOL. INTELLECT. PROP. 15 (2018).

[108] Isabelle Budin-Ljøsne et al., *Dynamic Consent: a Potential Solution to Some of the Challenges of Modern Biomedical Research*, 18 BMC MED. ETHICS 4 (2017).

[109] Hummel et al., *supra* note 37.

[110] Kaye et al., *Dynamic Consent: A Patient Interface for Twenty-first Century Research Networks*, 23 EUR. J. HUM. GENETICS 141 (2015).

108 FROM DATA SUBJECTS TO DATA SOVEREIGNS

partners, rather than objects, of research. There is much potential to extend this model beyond the biomedical research contexts.

Another way of empowerment is for individuals to join together for class lawsuits to assert their "collective data rights,"[111] or their right to group privacy.[112] For example, a class action was lodged against Google for its GAEN used for contact tracing which was eventually settled.[113] While the harm results from a violation of privacy rights by tech companies in profiling or targeted advertisement may be relatively small to an individual, it can be profound to all affected individuals as a group, and as citizens.[114] Established categories of groups holding right to group privacy include patient advocacy groups and indigenous people. It has been argued that algorithmically grouped individuals should also have a collective interest in how information describing the group is generated and used.[115] However, for individuals to join together for class lawsuits to assert their collective data rights or group privacy, evidence is required. Often, public bodies play a pivotal role in government investigations in unearthing evidence, which proves to be critical in facilitating class action brought by individuals in subsequent litigation.[116] For example, in the United States, the Federal Trade Commission (FTC) has the power to collect internal documents and interview executives before filing a lawsuit. Individuals can then seek to rely on that evidence revealed to file their lawsuits. It has been reported that more than 10 private lawsuits have been filed after the FTC has successfully sued Google and Facebook.[117]

Other than strengthening the individual self, we also need an infrastructure that enables individuals to overcome the hurdles of inadequate expertise

---

[111] Martin Tisne, *Collective Data Rights can Stop Big Tech from Obliterating Privacy*, MIT TECH. REV. (May 25, 2021), https://www.technologyreview.com/2021/05/25/1025297/collective-data-rights-big-tech-privacy.

[112] Brent Mittelstadt, *From Individual to Group Privacy in Big Data Analytics*, 30 PHIL. & TECH. 475 (2017).

[113] Diaz et al. v. Google LLC., No. 5:21-CV-3080 (N.D. Cal. Apr. 27, 2021), https://www.classaction.org/media/diaz-et-al-v-google-llc.pdf. For settlement order made in October 2022, *see* https://www.docketalarm.com/cases/California_Northern_District_Court/5--21-cv-03080/Diaz_et_al_v._Google_LLC/78/#q=21-cv-03080-NC. The allegation was that Google has exposed GAEN participants' private personal and medical information. The plaintiffs argued that the implementation of GAEN has allowed sensitive contact tracing data to be placed on a device's system logs, thereby providing dozens or even hundreds of third parties access to the log data which can be linked to specific individuals.

[114] Tisne, *supra* note 111.

[115] Mittelstadt, *supra* note 112 , at 476.

[116] David McCabe, *Big Tech's Next Big Problem Could Come From People Like 'Mr. Sweepy,'* N.Y. TIMES (Feb. 16, 2021), https://www.nytimes.com/2021/02/16/technology/google-facebook-private-antitrust.html.

[117] The news report was on anti-competition lawsuits. *Id.*

BEYOND PRIVACY: FROM DATA SUBJECTS TO DATA SOVEREIGNS 109

and resources. One effective way is to delegate specific authority to dedicated regulators. For instance, discussed earlier on how the exposure of location data through a government website had led to online bullying in South Korea, the Korea's National Human Rights Commission condemned the practice as unwarranted in revealing exceedingly detailed information about individuals.[118] Soon after, the Korea Centers for Disease Control and Prevention issued a guideline to municipal and local governments restricting the extent and detail of information that can be disclosed, resulting in a change of government practice.[119] A patient's age, sex, nationality, or workplace is no longer posted on the relevant webpage and information will be deleted from public view after two weeks.[120] Likewise, the Dutch Data Protection Authority recommended against a bill allowing government to force telecom operators to collect and share data as part of the country's pandemic response.[121] Although Korea's National Human Rights Commission, the Dutch Personal Data Authority, and the FTC are encouraging examples of watchdogs with strong bite, much depends on resources, and the extent of independent power that the regulatory agencies have.

Another alternative is to apply an information fiduciary model that has been advocated by Jack Balkin.[122] Classic fiduciaries duties are developed from equity duties of confidentiality, care, and loyalty. Established categories of fiduciaries include lawyers, board directors, and trustees who are required to apply specialized skills or knowledge, which their clients cannot perform for themselves, to act in the best interests of their clients. Fiduciary duty is both power conferring and duty imposing.[123] Balkin argues that in the digital age, many online service providers should be seen as "information fiduciaries" because they hold valuable data that might be used to our disadvantage, and they hold themselves out as experts.[124] In comparison, we are in a position of relative dependence and vulnerability with respect to these tech companies. It is difficult for individuals to verify the tech companies'

---

[118] Park et al., *supra* note 63.

[119] *Id.*

[120] Sang-Hun, *supra* note 66.

[121] Jamie Davies, *Dutch Watchdog Warns against Data Sharing to Combat COVID-19*, TELECOMS (July 3, 2020), https://telecoms.com/505348/dutch-watchdog-warns-against-data-sharing-to-com bat-covid-19.

[122] Jack M. Balkin, *Information Fiduciaries and the First Amendment*, 49 UC DAVIS L. REV. 1183 (2016).

[123] Matthew Harding, *Fiduciary Relationships, Fiduciary Law, and Trust*, *in* RESEARCH HANDBOOK ON FIDUCIARY LAW 61 (D.G. Smith & Andrew S. Gold eds., 2018).

[124] Balkin, *supra* note 122 , at 1222.

110 FROM DATA SUBJECTS TO DATA SOVEREIGNS

representation about data collection, security, and use, to understand what they do with our data, and how we have been monitored.[125] In light of this, fiduciary duties of care and trust will provide a solution that prohibit the tech companies from engaging in digital harms such as manipulation, discrimination and exploitation against us as end users, consumers, and data subjects.[126] However, one major challenge to implementing this model is enforcement of fiduciary obligations—how individual users are supposed to find out when a tech company has violated its fiduciary duties. In the United States, the proposed Data Care Act lays out a framework of care, loyalty, and confidentiality protecting "individual identifying data" against online service providers, with lawsuits actionable by the FTC or state attorneys general.[127] Other than resorting to litigation, scholars have observed that regular investigations and inspections, affirmative duties to disclose data breaches, and notification of other compliance failures are equally important.[128] Safeguard measures like auditing and privacy impact assessment will also be crucial.

In similar vein, the European Commission has proposed the Data Governance Act (DGA) recognizing the role of data intermediaries (article 9).[129] Although "data intermediaries" is not defined under the proposed Act, Recital 23 of the DGA stipulates that data intermediaries should seek to "enhance individual agency and the individuals' control over the data pertaining to them" and assist individuals in exercising their rights under the GDPR.[130] Specifically mentioned under article 9(1)(c) of the GDA is the role of data cooperatives to negotiate terms and conditions for data processing before consent is given by data subjects, assist in making informed choices before consenting to data processing, and allowing for mechanisms to exchange views on data processing purposes and conditions that would best represent

---

[125] *Id.*

[126] Lindsey Barrett, *Confiding in Con Men: U.S. Privacy Law, the GDPR, and Information Fiduciaries*, 42 SEATTLE UNIV. LAW REV. 1057, 1094 (2018).

[127] Data Care Act of 2019, S. 2961, 116th Cong. (2019).

[128] Lina M. Khan & David E. Pozen, *A Skeptical View of Information Fiduciaries*, 133 HARV. L. REV. 497, 526 (2019).

[129] *Proposal for a Regulation of the European Parliament and the Council on European Data Governance (Data Governance Act)*, COM (2020) 767 final (Nov. 25, 2020), https://eur-lex.europa.eu/legal-content/EN/TXT/?uri=CELEX%3A52020PC0767.

[130] This includes managing individuals' consent to data processing, their right of access to their own data, their right to the rectification of inaccurate personal data, their right of erasure or right "to be forgotten," their right to restrict processing and the data portability right, which allows data subjects to move their personal data from one controller to the other.

the interests of data subjects or legal persons.[131] Under article 10 of the DGA, the information intermediaries have to be governed under a competent authority.

The above suggestions are attempts to respect individuals as data self-sovereigns in enabling them to act effectively on their own, or through a system analogous to guardianship, enabling individuals to articulate their rights through an independent party that is resourceful and knowledgeable. The conception of data self-sovereignty is not to replace data privacy principles but to act as a complement to prevailing standards of fair and lawful processing of personal data, data minimization, purpose limitation, data security, transparency, and accountability.[132]

V. Conclusion

Succinctly put by the Korean-born German philosopher Byung-Chul Han, we are no longer subjects but rather projects.[133] This observation has sadly been proven to be most valid in the current fight against the pandemic. Our technology devices have become Trojan horses in encouraging so many of us to accept intrusive monitoring in the name of public health and safety.[134] Instead of profiling the pandemic, individuals have been profiled by state authorities and tech companies in being measured, tracked, predicted, and regulated. Inferences have been drawn on our behavior and predictions have been made about us from the risk level of spreading the disease to our mortality rate. Data privacy, which is premised on principles of personal data, notice, and consent is no longer adequate to protect individuals' rights and autonomy in the digital age. In fact, data privacy protection dependent on the concept of personal data becomes curiously complex in the digital age when anonymized data can be re-identified and any piece of data about us can be a useful puzzle to tell a new narrative about us.

---

[131] Examples of data cooperatives include MIDATA and SALUS COOP for medical research projects. *See* Mahsa Shabani, *The Data Governance Act and the EU's Move towards Facilitating Data Sharing*, 17 MOL. SYST. BIOL. e10229 (2021).

[132] BYGRAVE, *supra* note 29, at 1–2.

[133] BYUNG-CHUL HAN, PSYCHOPOLITICS: NEOLIBERALISM AND NEW TECHNOLOGIES OF POWER 1 (Erik Butler trans., 2017).

[134] Martin French & Torin Monahan, *Dis-ease Surveillance: How Might Surveillance Studies Address COVID-19?*, 18 SURVEILL. SOC. 1, 6 (2020).

As much as we want to protect our data privacy, it is not an easy task for most of us to keep abreast of the data-driven technologies and the increasingly complicated and ever-evolving terms of service provided by online service providers. Being data subjects easily turns us into easy targets for data projects. To reclaim ourselves as data self-sovereigns, we need a governance mechanism and infrastructure that can protect and uphold our rights and autonomy effectively. What is required is an infrastructure that recognizes our voices of informed consent and objection in the process of data about us; uphold our collective data rights; and acknowledge our entitlements through regulatory agencies powerful enough to act on our behalf, and protect our best interests through information fiduciaries or intermediaries that have to comply with duties beyond the data privacy standards. Only in this way that our privacy rights and autonomy can remain, be respected, and become legally and practicably enforceable.

PART II
TECHNOLOGY AND ECONOMIC INSTITUTIONS

5
Digital Sovereignty + Artificial Intelligence

Andrew Keane Woods

I. Introduction

When we think about the impact of new technologies on state sovereignty, we usually focus on the Internet. This makes sense. The ideal of a truly borderless Internet is inherently in tension with territorial boundaries. Those boundaries are a key feature of the state, a delimiter of its power; states police their borders jealously. So we should expect the state to take seriously anything that purports to operate across borders. It is precisely because of this tension that states will seek to assert greater authority over the digital networks that pass through their borders and affect their interests.

The idea of a global Internet—a World Wide Web—is both a technical structure and a political ideal. The technical piece is the fiber networks that reach across state borders where there sit routers that are set to allow information to flow freely in and out of the state. The openness of these digital networks to the outside world is not an inevitability, and as China's experience shows, it is also not necessary for a rich and entrepreneurial domestic digital ecosystem. But most countries around the world have adopted this technical structure. Why? Because they initially adopted the political ideal of a relatively borderless Internet.

That has started to change, with states increasingly taking steps to behave more like China and impose more of a border on the Internet—more of a sense that the Internet in one country should behave according to local customs and rules, and subject to the approval of the local sovereign. States appear likely to assert ever-greater authority over digital networks. The question at this point is largely normative: What are the appropriate limits on state authority over the Internet, and should we worried if those limits make

---

Andrew Keane Woods, *Digital Sovereignty + Artificial Intelligence* In: *Data Sovereignty.* Edited by: Anupam Chander and Haochen Sun, Oxford University Press. © Oxford University Press 2023. DOI: 10.1093/oso/9780197582794.003.0006

the Internet less open and global—that is, if those limits further accelerate the splintering of the Internet? I have argued that greater state authority over the Internet is both inevitable and desirable.[1] Others are deeply worried and continue to pursue a John Perry Barlow-style vision for the Internet where state efforts to replicate borders online are to be resisted.[2] The stakes of this debate have increased dramatically over the years, but the fundamental issues have not.

Does the rise of artificial intelligence (AI)—a radical and influential technology—change the terms of this debate? That is the question that motivates this chapter. There are at least two ways to think about the question. First, we can ask whether the rise of artificial intelligence does or should change the state's power over digital networks. For example, if AI develops in such a way that the logic of its growth is dependent on large accumulations of data, we might imagine that this will have implications for state authority over the digital realm. Or perhaps the causal story runs the other way: Does a state's approach to digital sovereignty have any effects on the development of artificial intelligence? For example, suppose that a state mandates that locally-generated data be stored locally, on servers within the state's territory. Such data localization mandates necessarily mean that there is more data sitting on servers within the territory and, depending on access rules, might mean there is more training data available for the development of AI tools.

These are two distinct sets of hypotheses, but they might be interrelated. For example, suppose that a state has a strong vision of digital sovereignty—meaning that the state develops a coherent industrial policy around digital technologies, imposes tight import and export restrictions, perhaps mandates the local storage of certain kinds of data, and so on. Does this strong form of digital sovereignty redound to the benefit of the state's AI initiatives, both public and private? If so, we would expect that as the successes of these initiatives grow, the state might double down on its digital sovereignty stance. In this scenario, AI and sovereignty create a kind of feedback loop that increases state interest in asserting ever more control

---

[1] Andrew Keane Woods, *Litigating Data Sovereignty*, 128 YALE L.J. 328, 371 (2018).
[2] *See* Mark A. Lemley, *The Splinternet*, 70 DUKE L.J. 1397, 1399 (2021) ("The balkanization of the internet is a bad thing, and we should stop it if we can.").

INTRODUCTION 117

Table 5.1 Russell & Norvig: Four Kinds of AI

	Human Standard	Ideal Standard
Reason Based	*Thinks like a person*	*Thinks rationally*
Behavior Based	*Acts like a person*	*Acts rationally*

over data. Conversely, perhaps weaker forms of digital sovereignty mean fewer controls, less state interference, and greater experimentation and innovation in AI.

The second set of hypotheses relates to how AI's growth might affect the state's stance toward the digital domain. If AI initiatives are used in ways that benefit the state—there are obvious military applications, to pick just one example—then we should expect the state to double down on its digital sovereignty policies. In this way, AI intensifies trends in data sovereignty and might even create feedback loops where the state's policies inform AI growth, and AI growth then fuels state policy, and on and on. But the state could also react to externalities produced by AI in ways that create disincentives. Suppose, for example, that American regulators decide that the untrammeled use of AI-powered algorithms on the country's most popular speech platforms is a national security threat and they regulate the use of those algorithms. This could slow the development of AI tools by social media companies. This might be a good thing or a bad thing—my point is only that regulation will affect AI development and regulation will be informed by the state's broader approach to digital sovereignty.

It is perhaps worth noting that since the inquiry is structured as two questions—"How might A influence B?" and "How might B influence A?"—much will depend on how we define the two key variables in this inquiry, state sovereignty, and artificial intelligence. By "digital sovereignty" (or "data sovereignty"), I mean the state's policy or set of policies toward ensuring national sovereignty online. This includes things like national cybersecurity policy, industrial policy, national law or policy related to data handling and data storage, and much more. Of course, digital sovereignty comes in many flavors, as the chapters in this book illustrate. Rather than articulate a singular definition of digital sovereignty, I will survey three different models for state control over the digital domain.

By "artificial intelligence," I mean the use of computers to make rational decisions that might otherwise have been made by a human. Note that this definition captures all four quadrants of the classic framing by Russell and Norvig: machines that think like humans, machines that act like humans, machines that think rationally, and machines that act rationally.[3]

For the purposes of this chapter, I will use the term AI as each state uses the term. There will be differences between how different national AI policies define the technology, but there is quite a bit of overlap at the core. Each country is concerned, in particular, with large-scale adoption of machine decision-making tools that are sophisticated enough to replace human decision makers. That human substitution will be the focus of this essay.

There are obviously profoundly important questions—much larger moral questions—about the politics of artificial intelligence. For example, it has been hypothesized that artificial intelligence will fundamentally change our political institutions. It has been suggested that artificial intelligence and the logic of data-driven machine decision-making, which is essentially centralized, will benefit autocratic political structures more than democratic political structures.[4] This is an essential question but one that is beyond the scope of this chapter. For the purposes of this book, I focus only on the relationship between digital sovereignty—the states attempt to map sovereignty onto the digital domain—and the rise as computer decision makers.

The focus of this chapter is on establishing a set of considerations—mostly hypotheses for further study—about the relationship between sovereignty and AI. There are so many interesting descriptive questions to establish first before we jump to normative questions. I will resist the urge to say, "state policies like X make AI better" or "state policies like Y make AI worse." Defining "better" in the context of AI is complicated and is the subject of another book.

To keep things manageable—though of course at the cost of comprehensiveness—I look at three different sovereigns: China, the European

---

[3] Peter Norvig & Stewart J. Russell, Artificial Intelligence: A Modern Approach 1–2 (4th ed. 2020).

[4] Yuval Noah Hariri, *Why Technology Favors Tyranny*, The Atlantic (Oct. 2018), https://www. theatlantic.com/magazine/archive/2018/10/yuval-noah-harari-technology-tyranny/568330 ("AI makes it possible to process enormous amounts of information centrally. In fact, it might make centralized systems far more efficient than diffuse systems, because machine learning works better when the machine has more information to analyze.").

Union, and the United States. These are three of the most well-documented visions of digital sovereignty and AI, but they are far from the only models. India and Brazil, for example, are huge countries in the midst of articulating national policies regarding both digital sovereignty and AI. Their exclusion here is necessarily a limitation of the chapter.

The chapter has three parts. First, I explore how digital sovereignty policies might influence the development of AI, paying particular attention to these three sovereigns. Next, I explore the reverse question, how AI and its growth might influence digital sovereignty, paying particular attention to the same three sovereigns. Finally, I sketch some of the variables that seem to be particularly important for understanding the dynamic interaction between digital sovereignty and artificial intelligence.

II. How Digital Sovereignty Might Influence AI

It seems inevitable that a state's politics would influence how AI develops there. But how? Even if policies to control the digital domain will affect the growth of digital technologies like artificial intelligence in general, it is harder to predict precisely how any single aspect of a state's digital sovereignty policies will influence the development of AI. Take privacy rules, for example—an aspect of digital sovereignty where states have varied considerably. On the one hand, suppose that a state insists on strong privacy protections, and this consequently inhibits researchers from collecting or accessing the kind of large datasets needed to train AI systems. Strong digital sovereignty policies—in the form of strict privacy rules—would seem likely to inhibit the growth of AI. Yet the same state might also, as a consequence of its strong privacy regime, have policies in place to ensure that whatever data pools are available to be accessed by local researchers and not simply exploited by foreign corporations. In this case, perhaps strong national privacy rules actually encourage the growth of domestic AI industry, even if they inhibit foreign investment. Both seem plausible. We can expect that a state's strong controls over the digital domain would influence the growth of AI there, but the *direction* of that influence is less clear.

Perhaps it will help to look at how three very different sovereigns are asserting sovereignty online.

120 DIGITAL SOVEREIGNTY + ARTIFICIAL INTELLIGENCE

A. Three Models

1. China

China has a long-standing vision for digital sovereignty—perhaps the most clearly articulated framework in the world—going back over a decade. The Chinese government first outlined its notion of cyber sovereignty in 2010, well before other world powers.[5] In 2017, President Xi released the *International Strategy of Cooperation on Cyberspace*, a fairly comprehensive account of the state's vision for sovereignty online.[6] The general aim is to ensure that the Internet advances, rather than hinders, the broader ambitions of the Chinese government. Specifically, China scholar Adam Segal notes that there are three broad aims:

(a) To maintain tight control over information flows to reduce unrest and ensure the stability of the Chinese Communist Party, at home and abroad;

(b) To develop a strong domestic technology sector to reduce dependence on foreign firms; and

(c) To shape cyberspace in ways that extend Beijing's influence and limit Washington's, including by promoting state-centric controls.

Implicit in these goals is the core idea that the state, not the private sector, should set the rules for the Internet.[7] The Internet is seen as a threat, a potential vehicle to undermine or destabilize the government's primacy. In foreign relations terms, China's sovereigntist vision places a premium on non-interference in other countries' affairs. As the 2017 *International Strategy of Cooperation on Cyberspace* notes:

> Countries should respect each other's right to choose their own path of cyber development, model of cyber regulation and internet public policies,

---

[5] State Council Information Office of the People's Republic of China, *The Internet in China* (June 8, 2010), http://www.china.org.cn/government/whitepaper/node_7093508.htm.

[6] Ministry of Foreign Affairs of the People's Republic of China, *International Strategy of Cooperation on Cyberspace* (Mar. 1, 2017), https://www.fmprc.gov.cn/mfa_eng/wjb_663304/zzjg_663340/jks_665232/kjlc_665236/qtwt_665250/t1442390.shtml.

[7] Adam Segal, *China's Vision for Cyber Sovereignty, in* NBR SPECIAL REPORT 87: AN EMERGING CHINA-CENTRIC ORDER 87 (Nadège Rolland ed., 2020) ("Cyber sovereignty represents a push-back against the attempted universalization of these norms as well as a reassertion of the priority of governments over nonstate actors.").

and participate in international cyberspace governance on an equal footing. No country should pursue cyber hegemony, interfere in other countries' internal affairs, or engage in, condone or support cyber activities that undermine other countries' national security.[8]

Much more could be said about this vision than space allows here, but for now it might be useful to merely note how statist the policy is—how expansive this vision is in terms of state policy over the digital world and how much this vision stops at the Chinese border, leaving other states to emulate it or not as they see fit. Contrast this with the extreme alternative, the American vision for an Internet that is in many senses unregulated, dominated by private American firms, and which the United States openly promoted as a tool to interfere in the domestic affairs of other countries.[9]

2. Europe

When Ursula von der Leyen took the presidency of the European Commission in 2019, she called for Europe to achieve digital sovereignty. For Europe, this has primarily meant establishing and enforcing a massive set of privacy rules on cyberspace—especially on foreign technology firms—to control how and where data is collected, stored, and processed. Digital sovereignty has become something of a buzzword in Brussels, and Europe's increasingly aggressive actions to regulate the Internet are nearly always described in terms of European sovereignty.

The idea is not merely that Europe wants to establish its own rules; it is that Europe wants American firms to know that they may no longer collect data about Europeans and make money in Europe without following European rules. That is, European policies reflect political backlash, at least in part reflecting public outcry about the Snowden revelations. The news that American intelligence agencies were heavily surveilling Europeans,

---

[8] Ministry of Foreign Affairs of the People's Republic of China, *supra* note 6.

[9] *See* EVGENY MOROZOV, THE NET DELUSION (2011) (describing how the Internet and in particular American social media platforms were promoted by the U.S. State Department as a vehicle for democracy that could upend autocratic rule in many countries, and which was indeed received by many of those countries as a dangerous tool that could lead to domestic disruption). Indeed, the Tor browser, which has proved one of the most widespread tools for evading government internet surveillance, was developed by the U.S. government and distributed abroad. *See* Shane Harris & John Hudson, *Not Even the NSA Can Crack the State Dept's Favorite Anonymous Network*, FOREIGN POLICY (Oct. 4, 2013), https://foreignpolicy.com/2013/10/04/not-even-the-nsa-can-crack-the-state-depts-favorite-anonymous-network.

leveraging in some cases the primacy of American technology firms, shocked European sensibilities, even if that surveillance happened with the acquiescence and often at the request of European authorities.[10] Today, nearly 10 years later, Europe's vision for digital sovereignty is primarily about how to control foreign technology firms.

Nothing has come to characterize Europe's aspirations for digital sovereignty better than the General Data Protection Regulation, Europe's singular, sweeping privacy regime that has for better or worse transformed privacy policies around the world. It is celebrated as a success in Europe because it has forced American technology firms to bend to European will. But more importantly it has become, thanks to its first-mover advantage as the earliest and most developed privacy regime, a kind of global standard bearer for privacy regimes being built in Brazil, India, and California, among others.[11]

But there are several other examples of European digital sovereignty, including the *Schrems* decisions at the European Court of Justice, both of which invalidated transatlantic data-sharing arrangements, and the many court battles regarding the right to be forgotten. Each of these has been important in establishing a distinctively European set of policies regarding the Internet. And once again, each of these involved European rule makers imposing rules on American technology companies. If European digital sovereignty is about imposing European rules on cyberspace, it is also at least as much about ensuring that American technology companies may not impose American rules in Europe.

3. United States

For nearly twenty years, the United States emphasized the importance of "internet freedom," a flexible concept that borrows rhetoric from human rights and freedom of speech but that in practice often means freedom from regulation for American technology companies. The United States heavily promoted this concept and funded its advancement around the world. The

---

[10] *See, e.g.*, Laura Poitras, Marcel Rosenbach, Fidelius Schmid, Holger Stark, & Jonathan Stock, *How the NSA Targets Germany and Europe*, DER SPIEGEL (July 1, 2013) (describing how the German BND, the British GCHQ, and the American NSA regularly engage in reciprocal intelligence collection and sharing). *See also German Intelligence Under Fire for NSA Cooperation*, DER SPIEGEL (Apr. 24, 2015) (describing how the German intelligence agencies were aware of and facilitated American spying of Western Europe).

[11] *See, e.g.*, ANU BRADFORD, THE BRUSSELS EFFECT: HOW THE EUROPEAN UNION RULES THE WORLD (2020) (describing the significant effect of European rules and standards on the world, focusing in particular on the influence of the GDPR).

Internet, the United States thought, would perfectly promote U.S. values and undermine un-American values around the world. This global network was also a hugely valuable asset to the American intelligence community. This was true at least for the first 20 years of the Internet's existence. The United States pursued something like non-regulation and non-interference in the digital marketplace, where American technology companies dominated.[12] This was true both at home and abroad. At home, the United States passed laws like the Communications Decency Act, which famously granted service providers huge leeway from responsibility for the content of speech on their platforms. Abroad, the United States urged states not to regulate the Internet, to let service providers (most of which were American) set their own terms of use. The Internet freedom agenda was, in essence, a kind of anti-sovereigntist view of the digital domain.

Unsurprisingly, the Internet freedom agenda was perceived by many countries as a direct threat to state control over the Internet. Indeed, as we have seen many countries conceived of cyber sovereignty or digital sovereignty in direct counterpoise to the United States' efforts to promote an open Internet.

Today, however, the United States looks much more like China did 20 years ago. One of the most notable trends over the last 20 years of American Internet policy is the shift from an hands-off approach to a recognition that the Internet poses many dangers to American stability, safety, and security. If the bipartisan consensus 20 years ago was that the Internet represented a vehicle for entrepreneurship and promoting American values, a new bipartisan consensus has emerged today: the Internet is dangerous and threatens to undermine American democracy if left unregulated. In this sense, American policy makers started out very far from their European and Chinese counterparts, even motivating their different conceptions of digital sovereignty, but they are quickly moving in the direction of Beijing and Brussels.

B. Implications

These are three different political systems and three different approaches to managing digital sovereignty. Which differences in these systems are notable

---

[12] *See* Jack Goldsmith, *The Failure of Internet Freedom*, Knight First Amendment Institute Emerging Threats Paper (2018).

and potentially consequential for the development of new technologies like AI? Here are a few: in China and the European Union, there seems to be a consensus that the state makes the rules for the Internet, whereas in the United States there has been a long-standing presumption that the industry can determine its own rules. Second, in Europe there is extremely careful attention to privacy rules, much more so than the United States or China, though China has recently passed considerable sweeping privacy legislation.[13] Third, there is a sense in which the location of the data matters for European and Chinese authorities, and somewhat less so for the United States, perhaps as a result of the historical fact that so many of the dominant technology firms are American. (When the United States needed data that Microsoft held on Irish servers, the U.S. government made the argument at the Supreme Court—later codified in the CLOUD Act—that the government could access such data regardless of its location.) Fourth, the United States and Europe regularly apply their technology laws and policies abroad—the United States in its Internet Freedom agenda and Europe through its GDPR (General Data Protection Regulation) private regime—while China has done less of this, even going so far as to encourage states around the world to exert more independence from Western technology firms and resist the extraterritorial application of their rules. Fifth and finally, there is agreement in all three sovereigns that digital sovereignty requires strong domestic technology industries.

What do we make of these findings, vis-à-vis the relationship between digital sovereignty and AI? At a minimum, we might hypothesize two possibilities: (1) strong versions of digital sovereignty will positively impact AI development, while weaker forms of digital sovereignty will negatively impact AI development; or conversely (2) strong versions of sovereignty will negatively impact AI development while weaker versions of digital sovereignty are positive for AI development. It is simply too early to tell the direction of the influence, but it is reasonable enough to think that there will be a connection in one direction or the other. The variables listed above should be helpful markers for identifying such a trend in either direction.

Now let's look at the reverse question, how a state's experiences with AI might influence its efforts at digital sovereignty.

---

[13] For a helpful overview of the privacy regimes in China, the United States, and the EU, *see* Anupam Chander, Meaza Abraham, Sandeep Chandy, Yuan Fang, Dayoung Park, & Isabel Yu, *Achieving Privacy*, 74 SMU LAW REV. 607 (2021).

III. How AI Might Influence Digital Sovereignty?

AI is rapidly evolving, but we already have two important sets of data points to study how AI might influence digital sovereignty: (1) official state policies regarding AI and (2) popular reactions to the current use of the technology. Both can tell us something about how states and their polities understand the new technology. A quick survey of three different sovereigns' policies and attitudes toward AI may provide some insight into how AI will shape the state's efforts at establishing sovereign control over the digital realm.

A. Three Models

1. China

The Chinese government outlined its national artificial intelligence policy in a 2017 document, "New Generation Artificial Intelligence Development Plan."[14] The plan notes unequivocally that AI will "profoundly change human society," and that the technology presents a "major strategic opportunity" for China, especially if the country can enjoy "first-mover advantage." The Party clearly sees the strategic importance of AI in its capacity to transform every sphere of society—political, economic, and social—both at home and abroad. It notes that AI will fuel the next wave of economic development and industrial change—both hugely important to China's future. The report outlines how government use of AI can improve education, medical care, environmental monitoring, "judicial services," and more. It is also seen as a way to manage social stability:

> AI technologies can accurately sense, forecast, and provide early warning of major situations for infrastructure facilities and social security operations; grasp group cognition and psychological changes in a timely manner; and take the initiative in decision-making and reactions—which will significantly elevate the capability and level of social governance, playing an irreplaceable role in effectively maintaining social stability.[15]

---

[14] Graham Webster et al., *Full Translation: China's "New Generation Artificial Intelligence Development Plan" (2017)*, New America (Aug. 1, 2017), https://www.newamerica.org/cybersecur ity-initiative/digichina/blog/full-translation-chinas-new-generation-artificial-intelligence-deve lopment-plan-2017.
[15] *Id.*

The Chinese government feels the country is well poised to take advantage of AI, but also that there is "still a gap between China's overall level of development of AI relative to that of developed countries." Closing that gap is essential to the party's economic ambitions because AI is expected to become "the main driving force for China's industrial upgrading and economic transformation."[16] Xi Jinping reiterated the strategic importance of AI at an event the next year, noting the possibility to leapfrog ahead of competitor nations.[17] China is fully embracing AI as a national priority.

Meanwhile, the Chinese public appears to be open to a greater role for AI in society—more so than almost any polity in the world. A survey done in 2020 revealed that only 9 percent of Chinese respondents believe that AI will be mostly harmful, and the vast majority—nearly 60 percent—of Chinese respondents believe it will be mostly helpful.[18] Moreover, there are few examples of national scandals driven by the misuses of AI, unlike the kinds of headlines that regularly appear in the European Union and the United States. As the authors of the 2020 study put it, "Each major misstep in AI will have consequences for public interest in having government agencies involve AI systems in governance."[19] Moreover, the labor force and manufacturing system in China is much younger than those in Europe and the United States, and labor is much less well organized, so automation in manufacturing is perhaps seen as less of a threat to an incumbent base. But labor concerns only partly explain societal anxiety around machine decision makers, so China's relatively optimism about AI must also be due to other things.[20]

2. Europe

In 2021—four years after China rolled out its AI policy—the European Commission released its own policy paper. The report, titled "Proposal for a Regulation Laying Down Harmonized Rules on Artificial Intelligence," addresses many of the risks posed by AI, including discrimination, human

---

[16] *Id.*

[17] Elsa Kania & Rogier Creemers, *Xi Jinping Calls for "Healthy Development" of AI (Translation)*, NEW AMERICA (Nov. 5, 2018), https://www.newamerica.org/cybersecurity-initiative/digichina/blog/xi-jinping-calls-for-healthy-development-of-ai-translation.

[18] LISA-MARIA NEUDERT ET AL., GLOBAL ATTITUDES TOWARDS AI, MACHINE LEARNING & AUTOMATED DECISION MAKING (2020), https://oxcaigg.oii.ox.ac.uk/wp-content/uploads/sites/124/2020/10/GlobalAttitudesTowardsAIMachineLearning2020.pdf.

[19] *Id.*

[20] *See generally* Andrew Keane Woods, *Robophobia*, 93 COLO. L. REV. 51 (2022) (cataloging the many different forms that manifest anxiety about AI).

oversight, privacy, security, and accuracy.[21] It has been described as a "direct challenge to Silicon Valley's common view that law should leave emerging technology alone."[22] The regulation bans artificial intelligence systems then might cause harm. Notably, the regulation pays special attention to "high-risk AI," in domains like medical devices, the administration of justice, law enforcement, and critical infrastructure. And while the regulation pays close attention to the risks of algorithm at discrimination, it has been criticized for not mandating remedial measures like algorithmic impact assessments.[23]

Europe is framing its late AI efforts as a way to "spearhead the development of global norms," similar to how Europe was a privacy norm entrepreneur with the GDPR.[24] The new AI policy seeks to ensure that the European Union remains competitive, while also developing AI rules that are compatible with EU values. As the policy notes: "Only common action at Union level can also protect the Union's digital sovereignty and leverage its tools and regulatory powers to shape global rules and standards." Europe's policy for AI then is an attempt to further its other data sovereignty plans, including rebuking American technology firms' dominance on the continent. But it is also, importantly, a recognition that its earlier data sovereignty programs, including the GDPR, pose limits to its AI ambitions.

That is why Europe has launched an ambitious new known as GAIA-X to create regional data pools for the development of AI—something that is necessary because of Europe's political structure and because of its hulking privacy regime. These shared data resources are seen as a key tool for ensuring continental digital sovereignty and they have obvious applications for artificial intelligence. For example, if artificial intelligence models require training on large datasets, then the GAIA-X program should produce larger datasets for European researchers and firms, which should enable the growth of artificial intelligence technologies. Indeed, GAIA-X now includes a project called

---

[21] *Proposal for a Regulation Laying Down Harmonized Rules on Artificial Intelligence (Artificial Intelligence Act) and Amending Certain Union Legislative Acts*, COM (2021) 206 final (Apr. 21, 2021), https://digital-strategy.ec.europa.eu/en/library/proposal-regulation-laying-down-harmonised-rules-artificial-intelligence.

[22] Mark MacCarthy & Kenneth Propp, *Machines Learn That Brussels Writes the Rules: The EU's New AI Regulation*, LAWFARE (Apr. 28, 2021), https://www.lawfareblog.com/machines-learn-bruss els-writes-rules-eus-new-ai-regulation.

[23] *Id.*

[24] Press Release, European Commission, Europe Fit for the Digital Age: Commission Proposes New Rules and Actions for Excellence and Trust in Artificial Intelligence (Apr. 21, 2021), https://ec.europa.eu/commission/presscorner/detail/en/ip_21_1682.

AI Marketplace, with the express aim of developing artificial intelligence tools and research platforms to make use of the larger European data pool.

Europe's policy is also notable for the emphasis it places on trust—on establishing public confidence in AI systems. This is because many European citizens are especially skeptical of AI. In the same Oxford study that found that 9 percent of Chinese citizens thought AI would be harmful, 43 percent of Europeans reported that AI would be harmful—more than said it would be helpful.[25] Another study done by Pew suggests that Europeans are actually split along country lines, with France showing the highest levels of anxiety about AI around the world, and Spain and Sweden some of the lowest.[26] This suggests again that the huge but loosely tied federal structure of the European Union may pose a problem for efforts at crafting continent-wide rules about a technology where opinions vary considerably by country.

3. United States

The United States, despite its huge technology sector and long history of leading AI research, has focused on AI in a decentralized and ad hoc manner effectively creating a default policy of nonregulation. In late 2020, the Office of Management and Budget issued guidance to federal agencies about the use of AI, in furtherance of an earlier executive order.[27] The document outlines policy considerations that should guide the regulation of AI by different agencies. The focus is on AI use in general, and not on government use of AI. Much like the Chinese and European AI policies, the memo notes the strategic importance of AI: "The deployment of AI holds the promise to improve efficiency, effectiveness, safety, fairness, welfare, transparency, and other economic and social goals, and America's continued status as a global leader in AI development is important to preserving our economic and national security."[28] But very much unlike the Chinese and European policies, the

---

[25] NEUDERT ET AL., *supra* note18.

[26] Courtney Johnson & Alec Tyson, *People Globally Offer Mixed Views of the Impact of Artificial Intelligence, Job Automation on Society*, PEW RESEARCH (Dec. 15, 2020), https://www.pewresearch.org/fact-tank/2020/12/15/people-globally-offer-mixed-views-of-the-impact-of-artificial-intelligence-job-automation-on-society.

[27] Memorandum from Russell T. Vought, Director, Executive Office of the President Office of Management and Budget, to the Head of Executive Departments and Agencies (Nov. 17, 2020), https://www.whitehouse.gov/wp-content/uploads/2020/11/M-21-06.pdf.

[28] *Id.*

U.S. policy explicitly notes the costs of overly burdensome regulations, which could hinder innovation and "undermine America's position as the global leader in AI innovation."[29]

The national policy embraces makeshift, agency-by-agency policymaking and leaves considerable room for state and local authorities. This is a national AI policy that disclaims the need for a unified national AI policy. There is some substantive similarity to the European and Chinese models—concerns about public trust in AI, transparency, fairness, and non-discrimination. But the key difference of the U.S. policy is the emphasis on non-regulation. A significant portion of the policy is dedicated to "non-regulatory approaches to AI," which include pilot programs, experiments, guidance, consensus standards, and voluntary frameworks. The policy suggests that these softer non-regulatory frameworks are appropriate where the benefits of hard regulation would be outweighed by the costs. Ultimately, the U.S. AI policy is more of a statement that the country—regulators, firms—can carry on as it had before.

This non-regulation of AI is consistent with the U.S.' long-standing approach to the digital world more generally, but it does not reflective a population that is optimistic about unregulated AI. As a populace, the United States has some of the highest levels of skepticism and anxiety about AI in the world. The same Oxford study that found only 9 percent of Chinese citizens were worried that AI would be mostly harmful found that 47 percent of North Americans said AI would be "mostly harmful." The Pew study found largely similar results, noting that 44 percent of Americans said the development of AI was a "bad thing." This perception might be especially pronounced in the wake of the public uproar over foreign election interference in the U.S. presidential elections in 2016. Since that event, there has been considerable attention paid to the AI-powered algorithms that drive social media platforms that seem to encourage disinformation or misinformation. Scandals like the misuse of social media algorithms in the 2016 election interference could reflect preexisting anxieties about the harmful impact of AI on society, and they could accelerate them.

[29] *Id.*

B. Implications

It seems likely that AI will amplify several trends in how sovereigns assert control over the digital world. China appears to have the most synergy between its AI ambitions and its long-stated digital sovereignty. As compared to other sovereigns, China has relatively tighter controls over the development and use of new technologies like AI, and relatively fewer obstacles to ensuring that AI is developed and implemented in a way that is consistent with state aims. State-investment in AI tools seems likely to be a boon to well-run authoritarian states.

Things are more complicated in the United States and Europe. Both sovereigns have ambitions for AI that may be in tension with their approach to digital sovereignty. In the United States, the key questions are something like the following: (1) Can an unregulated AI, largely in the hands of powerful private actors, be deployed without rules and in a manner consistent with its democratic ideals? (2) Will popular anxieties about the technology inhibit its growth? (3) Will the lack of meaningful industrial policy inhibit collaboration between the state and private firms?[30]

In Europe, the issues are related but somewhat different. Europe has a much less well-developed AI research and development base. It has much more granular and bureaucratic privacy protections, which could easily be a barrier to building the kinds of data sets needed to train effective AI systems. And Europe has issues that are unique to a super-state, where the EU governing bodies are quasi-sovereign whose rules are often overridden by each individual state. Take, for example, the GDPR's exemption for research. The GDPR is a stringent set of privacy protections that delimit where and when and why and for how long data can be collected and processed. But Article 89(2) creates a carve-out for researchers—including, presumably, those working on AI. The scope of this researcher exemption is dependent on domestic law, so the EU-wide rule has been implemented very differently— and to very different degrees of specificity—across Europe. This will naturally complicate efforts to create Europe-wide data pools for developing and researching AI.

---

[30] The protests at large technology firms over plans to work with the Defense Department suggest as much. *See, e.g.*, Scott Shane & Daisuke Wakabayashi, *"The Busines of War": Google Employees Protest Work for the Pentagon*, N.Y. TIMES (Apr. 5, 2018), https://www.nytimes.com/2018/04/04/technology/google-letter-ceo-pentagon-project.html.

IV. Key Variables

We should expect that sovereigns with aggressive plans for AI will define cyber sovereignty in ways that complement their AI ambitions. It is less clear that a strong commitment to digital sovereignty will likely enhance a country's AI plans. Europe and China have stronger commitments to digital sovereignty and they lag the United States in developing AI, though China is quickly catching up. What other variables might help us understand this dynamic? Here are four. These are the most obvious; they are far from the only relevant factors to understanding the relationship between digital sovereignty and AI. They are a start.

A. Access to Training Data

The size of a country does not necessarily tell you much about its digital capabilities, sophistication, or impact. Small, resource-strapped North Korea has had an outsized impact in offensive cyber operations, for example. Estonia, a tiny country, has had an outsized impact on a range of issues likes cryptocurrencies and digital citizenship. If anything, with cybersecurity we might expect that larger countries would be overall less secure because there is a much larger attack surface. Yet it seems that insofar as AI tools depend on large and representative data sets, countries with access to large data sets will be better situated than countries without such access. Sometimes this will benefit larger countries, which will have a comparative advantage over smaller countries at least vis-à-vis domestic data. This is especially true for large countries with few barriers to data access. As a recent report put it bluntly: "the greater accessibility of big data, which is needed to train smart algorithms, puts China at an important advantage."[31]

But smaller countries can also band together or agree to share data across borders for the development of AI. This is the idea behind Europe's plan to build "data pools" in key sectors that would allow easier access to large aggregations of data that might otherwise—thanks to European privacy rules—be unavailable to AI researchers. The idea of data pools was outlined

---

[31] Mathew Burrows & Julian Mueller-Kaler, Smart Partnerships amid Great Power Competition: AI, China, and the Global Quest for Digital Sovereignty 7 (2021), https://www.atlanticcouncil.org/wp-content/uploads/2021/01/Smart-Partnerships-2021-Report-1.pdf.

in the European Commission's February 19, 2020, data strategy, which noted that "there is not enough data available for innovative re-use, including for the development of artificial intelligence."[32]

To the extent that countries, especially large countries, mandate things like forced data localization, they *might* be in a better position to take advantage of large sets of data for the purposes of training AI. This is dependent on several other things, of course—like the assumption that AI needs large data sets to be trained, which is only true for some kinds of AI—and the idea that data cannot be found elsewhere, outside the state. But it is reasonable enough to think that for machine learning algorithms, and representative national data pools, countries like India will benefit from having more data available to researchers in the country. Smaller countries may be at a disadvantage here.

It is worth noting that the United States does not have the same degree of data localization requirements found in India or China, and yet the *commercial actors* in the United States have access to enormous data sets for training AI systems. This suggests that commercial capacity and the relationship between the state and its commercial actors—in other words, industrial policy—is also an important variable.

B. Industrial Policy

The extent to which a sovereign has a clearly articulated and well-implemented policy for developing domestic industry in AI would seem likely to play a role in the country's success in the field. Yet, the United States is a global leader in AI and at least until 2020 it never had a serious industrial policy around the technology. This can partly be explained by the fact that most of the world's leading technology firms are in the United States, and they all have made significant investments in AI, in some cases many orders of magnitude more than any nation. But there is also now a growing concern that the lack of industrial policy will hinder the further development and use of AI. For example, the leading AI labs are in private hands, and they

---

[32] *Communication from the Commission to the European Parliament, the Council, the European Economic and Social Committee and the Committee of the Regions on a European Strategy for Data,* COM (2020) 66 final (Feb. 19, 2020), https://ec.europa.eu/info/sites/info/files/communication-european-strategy-data-19feb2020_en.pdf.

are reluctant to work with the U.S. military. From the perspective of the government, this is a considerable drawback compared to an arrangement like the relationship the state had with the industrial base in the middle of the 20th century. Or compared to the relationship the Chinese government has with its leading technology firms. If industrial policy requires a state plan, cooperation between the private and public sectors, and public support, then China is uniquely situated to build industrial policy around AI. Europe has announced ambitious steps to create industrial policy around AI, but so far it has done little to advance them. The European AI proposal will face the unique challenges of a decentralized power structure of federated sovereigns. It will also have to carefully manage the tensions between its announced AI ambitions and its long-standing commitment to privacy protections.

C. National Laws and Norms

Each country has its own set of normative priorities and values, and those values inform the way both that state sovereignty is asserted online and how the state treats novel technologies like AI. In general, we might expect that liberal sovereigns, those with a commitment to individual rights including speech rights and privacy rights, will treat AI very differently from more community-oriented societies like China.

For example, in the United States, the deep commitment to unfettered free speech in particular and the libertarian regulatory stance in general have and will continue to create space for innovation by private actors in AI, in ways that will incentivize huge advances in AI but also create the potential for blowback as the public recoils from the use of AI. For example, thanks to the barely there regulation of the collection of data, companies are free to collect huge volumes of user data to train their AI systems. But the unfettered market for AI tools also has the capacity to backfire. (Two recent examples are the AI algorithms that drive social media in ways that enable the spread of disinformation and the use of facial recognition by firms like Clearview AI.) In the event that the public were to recoil at the use of new AI technologies, liberal constitutional commitments may stand in the way of meaningful reform. Even if regulators wanted to do something about the use of AI—regulate deep fakes, prohibit the viral spread of disinformation campaigns during elections, stop firms from scraping facial recognition data—they might be inhibited by the country's strong constitutional commitment to free speech.

In Europe, the commitment to privacy could inhibit the kind of data collection that will be necessary for the development of meaningful AI systems. This could inhibit the development of novel technologies. An Atlantic Council report, summarizing a years-long series of meetings, put it this way: "the systematic collection of data is more difficult for private companies in the West than for China's tech giants."[33] However, it is entirely plausible that Europe's strong privacy policies—and just as importantly the perception of its commitment to privacy—could give the public time to develop confidence and trust in the novel technology. It is simply too early to tell. Additionally, the increasingly aggressive European digital sovereignty initiatives, including demanding the local storage of data, might counterbalance some of this.

Meanwhile AI is likely to develop differently in countries like China with comparatively fewer commitments to individual rights and due process but comparatively greater concern with social stability and collective gains. The barriers to data collection, either in private or public hands, seem relatively low in China. The Communist Party retains considerable control over the private sector and has not hesitated to exercise that control when it feels a private firm is straying too much from party policy, as illustrated by Xi's scuttling of the huge IPO-to-be for technology giant Ant Group, the creator of Alipay. Additionally, the relatively weak judiciary in China will likely mean comparatively little independent oversight of government choices regarding the rollout of these novel technologies.

D. Attitudes toward AI-Powered Machines

How far AI develops in a given place—and how integrated it is in society— might also be a function of the public's embrace of AI. That might seem tautological, but the public reception of the technology and its experiences with the technology will define a set of political constraints that will influence policymakers. As we have seen, public attitudes about machine decision makers are strikingly different in China, where there is mostly optimism and trust, than they are in the United States and Europe where there is mostly anxiety and distrust. Relatedly, Europe and the United States have had huge

---

[33] Burrows & Mueller-Kaler, *supra* note 31, at 7.

public scandals involving perceived misuses of AI, whereas China really hasn't, certainly not to the same degree.

How much trust people place in machines will of course reflect but also drive the policy standards they deploy around the technology. Are self-driving cars—a potentially lifesaving use of AI—deployed for training on public streets in huge numbers when the technology is only marginally better than human drivers, or are they only released when the technology is close to perfect? That is, does society judge machines by the standard of perfection, or does it tolerate mistakes and imperfections the way we judge human actors? Different countries' policy approaches, reflecting different public attitudes, will of course have a huge impact on how AI develops there.

There are a few potential paradoxes here. It might be the case that countries that are lenient about the kinds of stringent requirements placed on AI will see more innovation and will in turn have more advanced AI. Whereas countries that are suspicious of AI or overly restrictive at the outset might not develop the tech quickly and will be left behind. Those that don't embrace machines early will have less say in their development and might consequently find the technology even less suited to their needs than if they had adopted early. And those countries that adopt early and see huge innovation will also have higher numbers of adverse events with the technology that could force the country to reverse course.

Not every country has articulated the same level of openness toward AI. The focus in the United States has been hands off, while the focus in Europe has been on safety, privacy, and trust. In China, meanwhile, the president has personally made it a goal that the country become the global leader in technology. This means, according to President Xi, the government "must promote the deep application of AI in people's daily work, study, and life."[34] He went on to say:

> It is necessary to: strengthen the combination of AI with social governance; develop AI systems suitable for government services and decision-making; strengthen the integration of government information resources and accurate prediction of public requirements; promote the construction of smart cities; promote the deep application of AI in the field of public security; strengthen the use of AI in the ecological field; and improve the level of public services and social governance using AI.[35]

[34] Kania & Creemers, *supra* note 17.
[35] *Id.*

136 DIGITAL SOVEREIGNTY + ARTIFICIAL INTELLIGENCE

This makes China relatively unique in terms of both social attitudes toward machines and government ambition regarding the adoption of the technology in nearly every sphere of life.

V. Conclusion

By now it should be clear that AI and data sovereignty are such expansive concepts that are both early in their development and in such a state of flux that it is hard to draw any definitive conclusions about their impact on each other. It is also clear that there are significant differences between (a) how different sovereigns assert their authority over the digital world and (b) their ambitions and fears for AI. Important research will need to be done to track whether these countries' strategies converge or diverge further in the coming years, and whether AI considerably changes state sovereignty in the digital realm. The four variables identified here are a useful starting point, as they may help to explain how and why a particular country makes the political choices it does regarding AI.

6

Taobao, Federalism, and the Emergence of Law, Chinese Style

Lizhi Liu and Barry R. Weingast[*]

I. Introduction

When a start-up in the West invents a new form of consumer electronics and creates a website from which to sell its products, all national law stands behind it, helping to prevent various forms of fraud, theft, and encroachment on intellectual property. Similarly, disputes that arise between the firm and its customers, suppliers, or competitors are negotiated in a rich legal and commercial environment. Because China lacks a strong legal infrastructure, a similar venture attempting to sell by website is far riskier.[1] The inchoate, variable, and sometimes corrupt nature of the Chinese legal system makes the prevention and resolution of legal problems much harder.[2] Chinese start-ups and small and medium firms that sell products by their own website are considerably more vulnerable than similar ventures in Europe or the United States.

Enter Taobao (which means "searching for treasure"), an online trading platform that hosts over 700 million active traders as of 2020.[3] Created by

[*] The authors gratefully acknowledge helpful comments from Isa Camyar, Anupam Chander, Rouying Chen, Julia Cohen, Kevin Davis, Richard Epstein, Roderick Hill, Stephan Haggard, Haifeng Huang, Hanzhang Liu, Xiao Ma, Jean Oi, Wendell Pritchedtt, Shitong Qiao, Weiyi Shi, Susan Shirk, Haochen Sun, Andrew Walder, Yuhua Wang, Xun (Brian) Wu, Thomas Streinz, Yang Xie, Chenggang Xu, Guanghua Yu, Ming Zeng, Qi Zhang, Xueguang Zhou, and participants at several seminars and conferences. All errors are our own.

[1] *See* SUSAN L. SHIRK, THE POLITICAL LOGIC OF ECONOMIC REFORM IN CHINA 1–7 (1993) (discussing the government's persistent refusal to create legal institutions in China).

[2] *Id.*

[3] *See* ALIBABA HOLDING GRP., LTD., ALIBABA GROUP ANNOUNCES DECEMBER QUARTER 2020 RESULTS (2021), https://www.alibabagroup.com/en/news/press_pdf/p210202.pdf. In this paper, we use "Taobao" to refer to both Taobao.com and its spinoff site, Tmall.com. Alibaba owns both sites and both have nearly identical institutional arrangements. Tmall.com hosts fewer, but larger, businesses and brands because it is the business-to-consumer version of Taobao.com.

Lizhi Liu and Barry R. Weingast, *Taobao, Federalism, and the Emergence of Law, Chinese Style* In: *Data Sovereignty*. Edited by: Anupam Chander and Haochen Sun, Oxford University Press. © Oxford University Press 2023.
DOI: 10.1093/oso/9780197582794.003.0007

Alibaba, Taobao is China's largest online trading platform. At first glance, Taobao's online trading platform appears to be the Chinese version of eBay or Amazon. As with these popular American online trading sites, Taobao serves as an exchange mechanism matching buyers and sellers.[4] We argue, however, that Taobao is far more. It has begun to develop many aspects of market infrastructure that the Chinese government has been unwilling or unable to provide; that is, it has been forced to create law. To clarify, this is not to say that Amazon or eBay have no rules governing exchange, dispute, and fraud. Rather, the underlying legal environment in China compared to Western countries differs so considerably that online trading platforms in China must be far more developed in their legal functions than Western analogs in order to sustain a functioning market. As this legal function of Taobao has become more complex and systematic, the central government appears to have acquiesced in Taobao's assertion of authority to experiment with various components of private law, including, contracts, property rights relevant to the platform, prevention of theft and fraud, and especially the resolution of disputes.[5]

Taobao's efforts to create law address a perennial problem facing most developing countries, including China: How to foster market transactions in the absence of strong formal institutions—in particular, those indispensable to the rule of law? The path for the West, which involved parliaments and independent judiciaries, often proves to be too politically constraining to duplicate in the developing world.[6] The case of China's thriving online market, however, suggests that it has taken a considerably different path from that of the West.

In this chapter, we propose that an alternative approach to establishing legal market infrastructure has emerged in China. We call this approach, "law, Chinese style." We argue that facing tremendous political barriers to establishing legal market infrastructure, the state can effectively transfer a part of the development of law to private actors that are limited in scope. Using as context China's e-commerce market, we observe a private building of legal market infrastructure sponsored by online platforms. We argue that Taobao is not simply an exchange platform, but one in the process of developing a modern private legal system that enforces contracts, resolves disputes

---

[4] *Id.*

[5] *Taobao Various Illegal Deductions Summary*, Taobao, https://www.rule.taobao.com/detail-143.html (last visited Nov. 20, 2017).

[6] *See* Shirk, *supra* note 1, at 333–37.

and prevents fraud. As a private supplier of market legal infrastructure when formal institutions are lacking, Taobao essentially provides a means for creating law, Chinese style.

Understanding Taobao's private legal system also informs how digital sovereignty is built and exercised in China. While many have focused on the direct regulatory powers of the Chinese state, private platforms in fact play a critical role in governing the cyberspace, often under the state's acquiescence or explicit delegation. Even after the year 2020, when the state has ostensibly tightened the control over platforms, the state continues to outsource many legal, social, and political functions to platforms without directly enforcing these functions on its own. Therefore, to fully understand how China exercises its digital sovereignty, it is crucial to examine the collaborations between the Chinese state and private platforms: in particular, how the formal and private legal systems dynamically interact.

The development of law, Chinese style, parallels previous instances where the central government delegated reform authority during the reform period from the early 1980s through the early 1990s.[7] In part, our argument builds on important precedents for the private development of law when economic agents in a range of markets provided private rules and adjudication mechanisms, such as the diamond and cotton industries,[8] cattle ranchers,[9] 19th-century settlers on the American frontier,[10] medieval merchants,[11] pirates,[12] 19th-century American railroads,[13] and stock exchanges.[14]

To expound the argument, we identify a parallel between the law, Chinese style, which we currently observe; and "federalism, Chinese style," which helped create markets in China's early reforms (1980s–1993).[15] We argue that

---

[7] *See infra* Part II.

[8] *See*, e.g., Lisa Bernstein, *Opting Out of the Legal System: Extralegal Contractual Relations in the Diamond Industry*, 21 J. LEGAL STUD. 115, 155–57 (1992).

[9] *See* ROBERT ELLICKSON, ORDER WITHOUT LAW: HOW NEIGHBORS SETTLE DISPUTES 22–28 (1991).

[10] JAMES WILLARD HURST, LAW AND THE CONDITIONS OF FREEDOM IN THE NINETEENTH-CENTURY UNITED STATES 3–12 (1956).

[11] *See*, e.g., AVNER GREIF, INSTITUTIONS AND THE PATH TO THE MODERN ECONOMY: LESSONS FROM MEDIEVAL TRADE 309–12 (2006).

[12] *See* PETER T. LEESON, THE INVISIBLE HOOK: THE HIDDEN ECONOMICS OF PIRATES (2009).

[13] *See*, e.g., ALFRED D. CHANDLER, THE VISIBLE HAND: THE MANAGERIAL REVOLUTION IN AMERICAN BUSINESS 175–88 (1977).

[14] EDWARD PETER STRINGHAM, PRIVATE GOVERNANCE: CREATING ORDER IN ECONOMIC AND SOCIAL LIFE 61–78 (2015).

[15] Gabriella Montinola et al., *Federalism, Chinese Style: The Political Basis for Economic Success in China*, 48 WORLD POL. 50, 52 (1995).

both serve as institutional underpinnings for markets and economic growth in the absence of a strong, public legal system. Both approaches involve the delegation of a limited set of institutional functions from the central government to certain domestic actors: in federalism, Chinese style, the central government delegated reform authority to local governments;[16] and in the present case of law, Chinese style, the central government has in effect offloaded legal functions to platforms. We further suggest that the political logic is consistent for both cases.

In addition to the parallels identified above, both forms of delegation involve the ability to affect the institutional structure of the state. In federalism, Chinese style, provinces gained authority to reform and change policies but also to experiment with institutional features of the state in the form of subnational governments.[17] In law, Chinese style, platforms have asserted authority to affect legal institutions. One of the weak aspects of federalism, Chinese style, has been the lack of the common market condition. The central government has been unable to ensure the mobility of products and factors across provincial borders, and many of the interior provinces have erected internal trade barriers.[18] As a national market, Taobao holds the promise of breaking down internal trade barriers erected by the provinces. Local governments simply lack effective means to regulate market platforms.

This chapter proceeds as follows. In Part I, we discuss the importance of legal infrastructure for the development of markets, and the common political obstacles that prevent developing states from establishing legal infrastructure. Part II discusses federalism, Chinese style, a previous phase of delegation in the early reform period. Part III provides the necessary background on Taobao, its platform operation, and its legal creation. We then, in Part IV, analyze Taobao's effect on the national common market, and on China's institutional structure of economic governance.

---

[16] *Id.* at 61–63.

[17] *Id.* at 79–81.

[18] *See* Montinola et al., *supra* note 17, at 65; Chenggang Xu, *The Fundamental Institutions of China's Reforms and Development*, 49 J. ECON. LITERATURE 1076 (2011).

II. Development and Legal Market Infrastructure

The process of development involves building a set of legal infrastructures to support efficient markets, including commercial law, contract enforcement, and secure property rights.[19]

Law is central to the prevention of fraud; the resolution of disputes; and, generally, to foster agents to act within the rules. Adam Smith, the father of economics and author of the monumental *Wealth of Nations*,[20] recognized the importance of legal underpinnings for markets over two centuries ago. Without law, Smith explained, "men are continually afraid of the violence of their superiors, they frequently bury and conceal a great part of their stock."[21] Smith suggested that to solve this problem, "[l]ittle else is requisite to carry a state to the highest degree of opulence from the lowest barbarism, but peace, easy taxes, and a tolerable administration of justice."[22] But how is a tolerable administration of justice established?

The Western approach to legal development involved legislatures and independent judiciaries, often with jurisdiction over both public and private law.[23] Courts came to protect various citizen rights and are one of many checks against government predation.[24] These institutions—all backed by strong, explicit constitutional foundations—ultimately constrain executive discretion.[25]

But for developing countries, following the Western path of legal development has proven to be remarkably difficult.[26] The main challenge is not the lack of technical knowledge, but a variety of political obstacles that prevent developing countries from providing legal market infrastructure through formal means.[27] For example, Acemoglu and Robinson observe that

---

[19] *See, e.g.*, DARON ACEMOGLU & JAMES A. ROBINSON, WHY NATIONS FAIL: THE ORIGINS OF POWER, PROSPERITY, AND POVERTY (2012).

[20] 1 ADAM SMITH, AN INQUIRY INTO THE NATURE AND CAUSES OF THE WEALTH OF NATIONS (R.H. Campbell et al. eds., Liberty Classics 1981) (1776) [hereinafter SMITH, WEALTH OF NATIONS].

[21] *Id.* at 285.

[22] DUGALD STEWART, *Account of the Life and Writings of Adam Smith, LL.D.*, *in* 7 THE WORKS OF DUGALD STEWART 64 (Hilliard & Brown 1829) (1827).

[23] *See* F.A. HAYEK, THE CONSTITUTION OF LIBERTY 167–75 (1960).

[24] *See* Douglass C. North & Barry R. Weingast, *Constitutions and Commitment: The Evolution of Institutions Governing Public Choice in Seventeenth-Century England*, 49 J. ECON. HIST. 803, 812–14 (1989).

[25] *See* F.A. HAYEK, *supra* note 25, at 212–14.

[26] *See* Barry R. Weingast, *Why Developing Countries Prove So Resistant to the Rule of Law*, *in* GLOBAL PERSPECTIVES ON THE RULE OF LAW 28, 50 (James J. Heckman et al. eds., 2010).

[27] *See id.* at 46–49.

various innovations, including a legal system, are likely to make incumbent political officials worse off (for example, by raising the likelihood they will be replaced). [28]Incumbents are therefore reluctant to foster a legal system that they cannot control.[29]Similarly, Cox, North, and Weingast argue that, in all developing countries, there exist powerful groups with the potential to threaten the regime.[30] Regimes typically buy these groups' cooperation through privileges.[31] An effective legal system typically threatens these groups, and so they will not support it.[32] Therefore, rulers of developing states find it difficult to establish the rule of law necessary to support thriving, competitive markets.[33]

Political obstacles intrinsic to the developing world lead to an undersupply of legal market infrastructure.[34] In the case of China, the Chinese Communist Party's (CCP) steadfast refusal to impose direct constitutional constraints necessary for a legal system has foreclosed the Western route to legal development through an independent court system and the rule of law.[35] The question becomes this: How to foster market growth in the absence of a strong, preexisting, or newly emerging public legal system? China's path to economic development has indicated at least two potential solutions: federalism, Chinese style, which was the philosophy behind China's early reforms in the 1980s and 1990s; and law, Chinese style, the philosophy behind the changes we currently observe.

---

[28] *See* Daron Acemoglu & James A. Robinson, *Economic Backwardness in Political Perspective*, 100 Am. Pol. Sci. Rev. 115, 129 (2006).

[29] *See id.*

[30] *See* Gary W. Cox et al., The Violence Trap: A Political-Economic Approach to the Problems of Development 1–3 (Sept. 2017) (unpublished manuscript) (on file with authors).

[31] *See* Weingast, *supra* note 28, at 50.

[32] *Id.* at 46.

[33] *See id.* at 46–47; Cox et al., *supra* note 32, at 20–21.

[34] This does not mean that developing countries do not have legal systems or would never engage in legal reforms. But due to the political obstacles already mentioned, their legal systems are often underdeveloped.

[35] The Chinese government has long resisted the Western-style rule of law. For example, Zhou Qiang, head of the Supreme People's Court, said, "We should resolutely resist erroneous influence from the West: 'constitutional democracy,' 'separation of powers' and 'independence of the judiciary.' . . . We must make clear our stand and dare to show the sword." Michael Forsythe, *China's Chief Justice Rejects an Independent Judiciary, and Reformers Wince*, N.Y. Times (Jan. 18, 2017), https://www.nytimes.com/2017/01/18/world/asia/china-chief-justice-courts-zhou-qiang.html.

III. Federalism, Chinese Style: Delegation and the Origins of Chinese Political and Economic Reform, 1981–1993

In China's early reforms between the early 1980s and 1993, federalism, Chinese style, provided an institutional underpinning for China's spectacular growth in the absence of a rule-of-law system.[36] China's political system during this period shared much in common with Western federalism, especially that in the 19th-century United States, as the Chinese central government allowed provincial and local governments to have primary control over economic matters within their jurisdictions.

The key of federalism, Chinese style, is a combination of the delegation of reform authority from the central to local governments, high-powered-fiscal incentives for local governments, and the active experimentation by local governments. In the following, we briefly go over each component of federalism, Chinese style.

Perhaps the most significant reform steps taken by the Chinese central government were its delegation of authority from the central to local governments. It did so in a series of steps, the first allowing Guangdong Province the ability to undertake market reform "one step ahead" of other provinces, and then allowing the latter to reform as well.[37] This process of decentralization granted provincial and local governments a wide range of authority within their own jurisdictions to make economic policies.[38] Foreign capital, for example, flowed into businesses and projects that were not controlled by the central government.

Coupled with the delegation of authority from the central to local governments were high-powered-fiscal incentives for local governments to compete with one another. The fiscal system during this period allowed provinces and lower governments to capture a substantial portion of marginal tax revenue generated within their jurisdictions.

> Starting in 1980, China implemented a fiscal revenue-sharing system between any two adjacent levels of governments. Although schemes var[ied] across both regions and time, the basic idea [was] that a lower-level regional

---

[36] *See, e.g.*, Hehui Jin et al., *Regional Decentralization and Fiscal Incentives: Federalism, Chinese Style*, 89 J. PUB. ECON. 1719, 1721–22 (2005).

[37] *See* SHIRK, *supra* note 1, at 166–68.

[38] *See* Montinola et al., *supra* note 20, at 62–63.

144   TAOBAO, FEDERALISM, AND THE EMERGENCE OF LAW

government contract[ed] with the upper-level regional government on the total amount . . . of tax and profit revenue . . . to be remitted for the next several years; the lower-level government ke[pt] the rest [of the tax and profit revenue].[39]

These new fiscal arrangements "induce[d] a strong positive relationship between local revenue and local economic prosperity . . . thus providing local officials with . . . incentive[s] to foster prosperity."[40]

With both significant authority over their jurisdictions and considerable incentives to develop their own economies, local governments adopted political and regulatory policies that were favorable to growth. The competition among jurisdictions for exports and growth encouraged active experimentation within each subnational unit, which facilitated policy innovation from the bottom up. Failed experiments were terminated either by the subnational government or through bankruptcy while successful ones were scaled up and imitated.[41]

The above summary of federalism, Chinese style, suggests the importance of delegation of authority by the central government in its efforts to launch the early stages of economic reform. In this period, local governments, not the central government, undertook the major market-reform effort and engaged in policy experiments on which the modern Chinese economy was built.[42] This strategy of delegating reform authority proved advantageous to the central government for several reasons. First, in the beginning, no one knew the best way to reform, and delegation to provinces and lower governments allowed multiple and independent approaches and experiments.[43] Once reform strategies proved successful, they could be shared with and imitated by other local governments, initially allowing many provinces to adopt a "wait and see" approach.[44] Second, delegation afforded the central government the opportunity of "blame-ducking"—that is, to disassociate itself with failures if the reform experiments did not produce results.[45] A massive failure to

---

[39] *Id.* at 63.

[40] *Id.* at 64.

[41] *Id.* at 73 (showing that price reforms illustrate this kind of policy experimentation).

[42] *See* Montinola et al., *supra* note 20, at 74.

[43] *See* SHIRK, *supra* note 1, at 336 ("Reforms were enacted in a gradual, piecemeal fashion, not according to a comprehensive plan.").

[44] *See id.* at 129 (describing the reformists as being "extremely cautious" and "taking one step forward and looking around before taking another" (internal quotations omitted)).

[45] In China's decentralized system, local officials often bear the blame for violating central spirits and policies.

produce growth would likely have resulted in the reversal of delegation of authority by the central government.[46] Third, since the delegation was limited in scope, the central government was able to reap the economic benefits without losing political grip.[47] The delegated authority focused on economic reform and did not extend to political reform. And provinces did not in effect become new, independent nations, and their continued authority depended on the success of the reforms.

This important precedent helps us to understand the political logic underlying law, Chinese style, which also involves implicit delegation of authority from the central government. In both cases—federalism, Chinese style; and law, Chinese style—delegation allowed non-central government actors to engineer reform. Further, in both cases, the presence of competition—other subnational governments in the early reforms; other platforms in the current era—led these actors to provide institutional infrastructure for markets in the absence of a strong, state-run legal system.

IV. Taobao and Law, Chinese Style

Recently, there has been an additional movement to develop institutional infrastructure for markets. We call this new effort law, Chinese style. Similar to the reform period during the 1980s, law, Chinese style, also depends upon delegation. The difference is that in the present circumstances the central government has allowed specific private actors, rather than provinces, to play a substantial role in the development of market infrastructure, especially legal infrastructure. This development is limited in scope and focuses on e-commerce.

Importantly, law, Chinese style, serves as an alternative route to legal development that is much less politically constraining for the central government than the Western approach, and yet it is still effective to foster market growth. Taobao is one of those private actors that is in the process of developing a modern legal system that enforces contracts, resolves disputes, and prevents fraud. For all of its users, Taobao's system functions in places where Chinese law is inadequate.

---

[46] *See generally* SHIRK, *supra* note 1, at 121 (finding that, in the 1980s, "[p]roblems that were once solved at lower levels" were escalated to higher levels of government.).

[47] *See generally id.* at 117 (describing that "leaders loathe to lose the advantages of delegation" and "do not want to alienate their bureaucratic constituents").

A. Evolution of Law, Chinese Style

Law, Chinese style, had emerged in the context of looming tensions between two primary stances of the Chinese government: (1) an unwavering devotion to economic development and (2) an unremitting refusal to create the institutions typically associated with the rule of law. These two ideas conflict because scholars argue that, to foster long-term economic prosperity, the rule of law is required.[48] The rule of law as part of market infrastructure has come to matter more, especially as China's economy has become more complex and integrated. This is because, first, China has gradually shifted away from a state-led, investment-driven economy. The rule of law helps consolidate a fair business environment for market economy to develop, one with considerably less opportunism. Second, the lack of the rule of law disproportionately hurts the growth of private businesses (small- and medium-sized enterprises in particular),[49] which constitute the main driver of China's economic growth. But as we argued in Part I, the authoritarian government has been unwilling to establish a rule-of-law system, as a strong legal system involves a variety of mechanisms that will inevitably limit the central government's power.

In the absence of a strong public legal system, private actors have begun to provide substitutes. The central government has acquiesced to the authority exercised by private actors to create markets with rule of law. An important feature of the delegation of the development of law, Chinese style, is that the reach of this law is limited in scope to the traditional areas of private law: property; contracting; and, perhaps, torts. The private provision of private law, therefore, allows the central government to foster experiments in law as it relates to the economy while lowering the probability that this form of legal system will challenge the central government in the area of public law, such as citizen rights.

This implicit delegation helps conquer the technical complexities in building a workable legal system. The current delegation parallels the delegation of many reforms earlier in the process of marketization, such as allowing Guangdong Province to reform markets by being "one step ahead," as we discussed in Part II. As with these earlier reforms, the central government's

---

[48] *See, e.g.,* Douglass C. North, Institutions, Institutional Change, and Economic Performance 111 (1990).

[49] Too often these enterprises lack the resources and political ties to advance their interests. *See* Yuen Yuen Ang & Nan Jia, *Perverse Complementarity: Political Connections and the Use of Courts Among Private Firms in China,* 76 J. Pol. 318, 319 (2014).

delegation to create law also allows it to stand above the provision of services, in part, to allow multiple experiments and, in part, so that it is not directly responsible for any failures of the system. Delegation allows the central government to distance itself from any public dissatisfaction that may arise and, if need be, curtail failing experiments. Private actors, on the contrary, bear the risk of failure and buffer the tensions that could have been directed toward the state;[50] but they also reap the profits if the experiments succeed.

Enter Taobao.

B. Taobao Creates a Market

Since its launching in 2003, Taobao has been growing at a stunning rate. By the end of 2020, Taobao (Tmall included) has already hosted more than 700 million active users.[51]

With respect to Gross Merchandise Value (GMV), Taobao currently surpasses Amazon and eBay combined.[52] As of May 2017, Rural Taobao—a rural expansion initiative—has also opened over 30,000 e-commerce service points in remote villages, many of which had no prior access to commercial parcel delivery.[53] These service points afford access to those without online payment methods or who are not Internet savvy.[54]

The most fundamental service Taobao provides is access to a market supported by a private legal system in the process of developing the rule of law.[55] Taobao has the means to create law, Chinese style, because it is a private supplier of legal infrastructure for its market and users when the state-run

---

[50] For example, in 2010, around 300 sellers initiated a physical protest against Taobao. *See Sellers Protest Against Taobao*, PEOPLE'S DAILY ONLINE (July 14, 2010), http://en.people.cn/90001/90778/90860/7065181.html.

[51] Press Release, Alibaba Group, Alibaba Group Announces December Quarter 2020 Results (Feb. 2, 2021), https://www.alibabagroup.com/en/news/press_pdf/p210202.pdf.

[52] *See generally* R. J. HOTTOVY ET AL., MORNINGSTAR EQUITY ANALYST REPORT: ALIBABA GROUP HOLDING LTD (2015), https://invest.firstrade.com/ms/equity_reports/sr/0P00013K81_20151009_RT.pdf (providing data and analyses of Taobao's parent company).

[53] *See Nongcun Taobao Fugai Yichao Sanwan Ge Cun, Fanxiang Chuangye Xian Gun Xueqiu Xiaoying* (农村淘宝覆盖已超3万个村, 返乡创业现滚雪球效应) [*Rural Taobao Has Covered over 30,000 Villages; Snowball Effect of Entrepreneurship Among Return Migrants*], ALI YANJIUYUAN (阿里研究院) [ALI RESEARCH INSTITUTE] (Mar. 21, 2017), http://mp.weixin.qq.com/s/xoYep2mtWml XWUqZWzbLAg (China).

[54] Victor Couture et al., *Connecting the Countryside via E-Commerce: Evidence from China*, 3 AM. ECON. REV.: INSIGHTS 35 (2021).

[55] Lizhi Liu & Barry R. Weingast, Law, Chinese Style: Solving the Authoritarian's Legal Dilemma Through the Private Provision of Law 13 (Aug. 2020) (unpublished manuscript) (on file with authors).

148   TAOBAO, FEDERALISM, AND THE EMERGENCE OF LAW

legal institutions are weak.[56] Of course, to gain the protection of this legal infrastructure, traders must join and trade using Taobao. For its users, Taobao can provide private institutions to enforce contract, resolve disputes, and prevent fraud.[57] Private legal institutions partially explain why platforms dominate e-commerce retailing in China but not in the United States. In the United States, where the strong legal environment makes the substituting effects of platforms less necessary, retailers can sell their goods and services directly through their own websites. But as we noted earlier, the absence of a legal system makes the same approach in China riskier. The demand for Taobao's legal and trading services is bigger in China than it would be in a rule-of-law country.

C. Taobao's Private Legal System

We now draw on our other work[58] to address how Taobao's private legal system works in the absence of strong formal institutions administered by the state. Taobao's private legal system is comprised of institutions that address various types of problems associated with market transactions. In the following section, we focus on how Taobao addresses three major problems intrinsic to trade: (1) contract enforcement, (2) fraud prevention, and (3) dispute resolution.

1. Contract Enforcement through Institutionalized Reputation Mechanisms: The Online Rating System

When trading parties strike a deal, how do they ensure that each party honors the agreed-upon terms? The problem is especially acute when an exchange is a two-step process in which one party to the contract has performed her obligations and awaits the second party to perform his. States in the developed West foster two complementary classes of mechanisms to enforce contracts. The first involves a legal system with the power to sanction individuals for breach of contract. The second involves reputation mechanisms whereby other market participants shy away from doing business with those individuals or firms who develop reputations for fraud, cheating, opportunistic behavior, etc.

---

[56] *Id.*
[57] *See* discussion in Part III.C.
[58] *See* Liu & Weingast, *supra* note 57.

Taobao's online feedback and rating system is at the center of Taobao's attempt to mitigate the assurance problem. As with other online trading systems, such as eBay, Taobao's rating system creates incentives for all trades to maintain a good reputation.[59] But Taobao's system goes well beyond that used by eBay and Amazon. Taobao's rating system consists of two main parts: credit rating (a rating for buyer or seller over the entire past history) and store rating (a rating for sellers).[60] To capture the changing dynamics of service quality, Taobao uses a store rating to complement credit rating for sellers.[61] The store rating is based on three aspects of the seller over the past six months: the accuracy of product description, customer service, and shipping time.[62] In addition to the overall reputation of sellers, buyers can also check all past reviews of each product. Information about the reliability of trading partners is thus central to policing Taobao's market exchange system.

Taobao's fraud prevention program, which we will discuss next, allows users to have access to reliable information that addresses some of the fear inherent in commercial transactions. Further, relevant punishment is enforced through an escrow system embedded in Alipay,[63] which we will discuss.

2. Fraud Prevention through Risk Framework: Big Data, Manual Review, and State Coercion

Fraud must be limited, lest trade stalls. Fraud in online markets includes online payment fraud, account hacks, attempts to manipulate online reviews, and counterfeit products.[64] To help identify fraud, Taobao utilizes big data analytics and manual review to identify suspicious cases.[65] Taobao's system relies on a high volume and variety of information generated by the platform (e.g., user behavioral data, network data, delivery details, and IP addresses). The trove of proprietary data enables Taobao to use big data models to detect suspicious activities and to counter fraud risks. Manual review assists big data analytics. For example, consider how this system would handle online payment fraud. Taobao uses five layers of checks to identify fraud beginning with account check—a process that leverages big data analytics to examine

---

[59] *See id.* at 15.

[60] *See id.*

[61] *See id.* at 16.

[62] *See id.*

[63] *See infra* Part III.C.4.

[64] Jidong Chen et al., *Big Data Based Fraud Risk Management at Alibaba*, 1 J. FIN. & DATA SCI. 1, 2 (2015).

[65] *See id.* at 3–4.

150   TAOBAO, FEDERALISM, AND THE EMERGENCE OF LAW

account information of both the seller and the buyer, including whether these accounts have exhibited suspicious activities—and ending with manual review, if necessary.

After detecting a case of fraud, Taobao can punish fraudulent behavior through online and offline means. Online, Taobao can lower the user's rating, make the fraudulent store unsearchable for a certain period, or, in extreme cases, ban the accounts. A party who deems the judgment to be unfair can appeal to Taobao. Offline, Taobao has cooperated with the state police. For example, to combat counterfeit products fraud at its source, Taobao uses its massive datasets (e.g., shared phone numbers, chat histories, product return and delivery addresses) to track the location of offline warehouses and producers involved in counterfeiting.[66] Taobao has shared this location information with the police and has helped them arrest suspects who produce and sell counterfeits.[67] In 2014 alone, Alibaba's collaboration with the state enforcement agencies in over one thousand counterfeiting cases led to the arrest of four hundred suspects and the shutdown of two hundred brick-and-mortar stores, warehouses, or factories.[68] Although the state apparatus suffers from many liabilities, such that it is slow, cumbersome, and can be highly corrupt, the state can help in punishment of the most egregious traders.

3. Dispute Resolution through Crowdsourcing Justice: User Dispute
   Resolution Center

Dispute resolution is an indispensable aspect of a workable legal system. Every functioning market needs mechanisms to handle disputes. Taobao resolves two types of disputes: (1) disputes between pairs of market participants (e.g., a seller and a buyer or two competitors); and (2) disputes between market participants and Taobao, as embodied in its function as market owners or regulators. When a dispute occurs, the party initiating the case may choose from two channels: (1) asking a designated Taobao employee to adjudicate or (2) using a jury-like panel of public assessors to arbitrate. Launched in 2012, Taobao's User Dispute Resolution Center, which we call a jury-like system, has been crowdsourcing minor, everyday disputes to an online panel

---

[66] Taobao was able to track these producers because it has business connections with its online sellers.

[67] *See* Catherine Shu. *Alibaba Removed 90M Suspicious Listings from Its Sites Before IPO*, TechCrunch (Dec. 23, 2014), https://www.techcrunch.com/2014/12/23/alibaba-listings-purge.

[68] *See id.*

of "jurors."[69] Most of these disputes are of two types: buyer-seller disputes, which often involve contract violations (e.g., complaints about items received that fail to match store descriptions); and platform-seller disputes in which a seller believes that Taobao has unfairly penalized it for violating certain rules.

In the jury system, Taobao chooses 13 public assessors randomly from a pool of nearly two million volunteers as of 2017. Taobao selects these assessors from experienced users who have volunteered to serve. Qualified candidates for the public assessor pool must have high reputations based on Taobao's system of rating. The public assessors' principal responsibility is to review the evidence submitted by disputing parties and then vote within 48 hours. The public assessors decide which party wins by a simple majority vote. This system allows Taobao to address a large and growing number of complaints. As of September 30, 2017, 1,643,852 public assessors have resolved 2,550,802 disputes in total.[70]

Importantly, Taobao has several means of enforcing its decisions from both employee adjudicators and public accessors. Taobao can freeze the payment in dispute, take money from the store deposit (for sellers only), lower the rating of the users involved, or deny the losing party's privileges to use the platform.

4. Supporting Institutions: Payment and Escrow

"Taobao's private legal system . . . relies on several supporting institutions. Although these institutions do not specifically address any of the major issues in trade (i.e., contract, fraud, and dispute), they ensure that platform rules are interconnected, adaptable, and easier to enforce."[71] Alipay, in particular, is an important part of the Taobao system. Alipay works similarly to PayPal, except that Alipay also provides escrow service. Escrow service means that the buyer's payment for each order is held by Alipay until the goods are received, and the funds are released only when both trading parties are satisfied with the transaction.

While Alipay does not enforce contracts on its own, its escrow service enhances Taobao's enforcement capability. Alipay can directly freeze

---

[69] Jim Erickson, *How Taobao Is Crowdsourcing Justice in Online Shopping Disputes*, Alizila (July 17, 2014), http://www.alizila.com/how-taobao-is-crowdsourcing-justice-in-online-shopping-disputes.

[70] *Ali Dazhong Pingshen* (阿里大众评审) [*Alibaba Public Assessors*] (Sept. 30, 2017), http://pan.taobao.com (China).

[71] *See* Liu & Weingast, *supra* note 57, at 20–21.

or deduct from the money that a user has in her account if she violates platform rules. When a dispute over a trade arises, Alipay can freeze the payment in escrow, forcing feuding parties to choose between losing the money or engaging in, and complying with, Taobao's dispute resolution system.[72] Thus, Alipay supports Taobao's legal system because it provides a means of enforcement of decisions and a means of forcing people to operate within the system.

V. Taobao and the Evolution of Federalism, Chinese Style: Recentralization

The preceding parts allow us to draw a parallel between law, Chinese style; and federalism, Chinese style. Both approaches involve delegation of central government authority to particular domestic actors with a limited scope; both serve as institutional bases for markets in a weak-rule-of-law environment; and both induce the domestic actors to experiment with policies and rules that can help foster growth.

Despite the similarities between federalism, Chinese style, and law, Chinese style, the two sets of delegation differ considerably in how they affect the national common market. Taobao has helped foster a common, national market, which did not happen in the initial model of federalism, Chinese style. Earlier reform efforts did not support the national market because the central government was unable or unwilling to ensure the mobility of factors (such as capital and labor) and products across regions.[73] First, federalism was an entirely offline movement. Second, as we will argue in this part, local governments are less able to resist and reverse a common market achieved online than one formed offline. This Taobao-induced process of market integration has political implications. Because Taobao has provided a potential instrument for the center to strengthen its ability to monitor and discipline local powers, it may influence the power balance between the central and local governments in favor of the former.

[72] *Id.*
[73] *See* Montinola et al., *supra* note 20.

A. Decentralization and the Incomplete Common Market

Since its inception, federalism, Chinese style, has lacked a common market because the Chinese national government does not have an effective means to police the internal common market, that is, to ensure the mobility of goods and factors across subnational jurisdictions.[74] The absence "explains in part why many local governments have focused on trade barriers and aggressive antimarket policies within their jurisdiction."[75] Alternatively stated, decentralization of authority creates the incentives and political means for the local governments to erect trade barriers. In the absence of an effective central means to contain local protectionism, many problems occur, including localized corruption and patronage networks and beggar-thy-neighbor policies. This is especially true of interior provinces that have had only limited participation in reform and exports.

The common market condition is difficult to achieve. While the central government retains important personnel control over local governments, local governments can resist a common market through multiple means: for example, (1) by not fully implementing central policies (such as policies in which the local governments are the main enforcers); and (2) by misrepresenting the information about central policy implementation (because, for example, local governments enjoy information advantages over the center).

Federalism in China has not guaranteed a common market. In a decentralized fiscal and economic system, local governments have to compete for scarce capital and labor and for fiscal revenues.[76] In addition, provinces in China have had to compete for business on the international market, as the Chinese economy has long been export driven. These two sources of political and economic competition—among lower jurisdictions and on the international market—have generated the incentives for China's economic growth; but they have also created problems for the rise of a national common market.[77] In the absence of a central authority to ensure factor mobility, decentralization may, in fact, hinder the creation of a common market, putting economies of scale in peril.

---

[74] *See id.* at 55.
[75] *Id.* at 53.
[76] *Id.* at 58.
[77] *Id.* at 59.

B. Taobao and the Formation of a Common Market

While the central government in China has struggled to create and support a national market, Taobao has been able to foster a common market for the exchange of certain products and services. Taobao's system facilitates market integration for three reasons. First, Taobao lowers the entry barrier to the national market, facilitating inter-provincial trade. In particular, it allows small or rural sellers and buyers to participate in the national market, access that they otherwise would not enjoy in the offline setting. This development parallels the access to markets in the mid- and late 19-century United States when mail order catalogs greatly expanded rural citizens' access to consumer goods, and at far lower prices.[78] Second, Taobao has strong vested interests in keeping the platform free of trade and regulatory barriers across regions so as to facilitate market exchange. No matter whether a seller or buyer lives in Beijing or Tibet, she is governed by the same set of platform rules.

As a result, Taobao facilitates the cross-regional mobility of goods and capital. It intensifies national economic competition, and it breaks down monopolies, for example, physical stores benefiting from geographical isolation and internal trade barriers. All of this creates a virtuous circle. The larger market increases the demand for market infrastructure, such as roads, power plants, railway lines, electric power, and so on. The improvement of infrastructure, in turn, facilitates the rise of a national common market.

Local governments have limited means to resist or reverse these advances in the common market achieved by online exchange. First, Taobao's private market infrastructure is independent of those provided—or restrained—by local governments. Taobao's system is largely self-sufficient.[79] Even if local governments want to intervene and regulate the online market, they need to first address a coordination problem among themselves. For example, consider a situation where a seller lives in Beijing, but her factory is in Hebei and she has a dispute on Taobao with a buyer in Guangdong. Which local government should take the lead to address the dispute, and how do they coordinate with the other local governments who may or may not agree with the lead government's decisions? This confusion makes it difficult for provinces to hinder or restrict Taobao.

---

[78] *See* DAVID BLANKE, SOWING THE AMERICAN DREAM: HOW CONSUMER CULTURE TOOK ROOT IN THE RURAL MIDWEST 186 (2000) (describing mail-order catalogs' role in integrating rural consumers into the mass market).

[79] *See supra* Part III.C.

TAOBAO AND THE EVOLUTION OF FEDERALISM   155

Additionally, Taobao creates an information barrier for local governments. Local governments have scant information about the online market,[80] and they do not have sufficient power to bargain for full information against a transcendent platform. For example, if local governments do not know who within their jurisdictions are selling and buying, those transactions are difficult to tax and regulate. This lack of information makes it difficult for local governments to tax and regulate online platforms.

Taobao's market platform therefore seems a potentially important mechanism for improving the common market. Because local governments have great difficulty regulating national market platforms, Taobao and similar platforms provide a means around internal trade barriers. The platforms may, therefore, allow a wide range of products to take advantage of economies of scale that trade barriers had prevented. Further, market exchange on platforms enhances inter-province competition.[81] Local firms, protected under internal trade barriers, often cannot survive competition in a common market.[82]

C. Taobao and Recentralization

As shown above, in its politically and economically decentralized system, China's central government has faced, and continues to face, difficulties in policing the internal common market. But Taobao raises the possibility for the central government to use Taobao as an indirect means to monitor and discipline local governments. Indeed, Taobao and its parent company, Alibaba, have started to collaborate with the central government on a variety of issues, including credit scoring and e-government.[83]

---

[80] Interview with a City Government Official, Suzhou City, Jiangsu Province (Aug. 26, 2014); Interview with a Township Government Official, Shaji Township, Jiangsu Province (Aug. 26, 2014).

[81] *See id.* at 281–82.

[82] *See id.; cf.* Montinola et al., *supra* note 20, at 66.

[83] For collaboration on credit scoring, see *Guojia Fagaiwei Yu Alibaba Gongjian Shangwu Lingyu Chengxin Tixi Jianshe* (国家发改委与阿里巴巴共建商务领域诚信体系建设) [*National Development and Reform Commission Works with Alibaba Jointly to Establish a Credit Rating System in the Commercial Area*], *Zhongguo Jingji Wang* (中国经济网) [CHINA ECONOMIC NET] (Dec. 2, 2016) [hereinafter *National Development and Reform Commission*], http://www.ce.cn/xwzx/gnsz/gdxw/201612/02/t20161202_18347172.shtml (China). For e-government, see Huanqiu Tech, *Chinese Central Government Procurement Platform Uses Alibaba Cloud*, MARBRIDGE DAILY (Mar. 9, 2015), http://www.marbridgeconsulting.com/marbridgedaily/2015-03-10/article/81778/chinese_central_government_procurement_platform_uses_alibaba_cloud.

156   TAOBAO, FEDERALISM, AND THE EMERGENCE OF LAW

Taobao helps strengthen central authority in three ways. First, as a powerful, centralized tool of collecting market information, Taobao can reduce, and even reverse the information disadvantage of the central government, which has limited information about economic activity. In the past, the central government has had to rely on economic data provided by the local governments, but local governments are known for faking economic numbers.[84] Online transaction data, in contrast, can provide a real-time, objective barometer about a region's economic vitality. For example, Alibaba invented Alibaba Shopping Price Index (aSPI), an index based on the price changes of a particular basket of goods and services.[85] The index can be used as an alternative to the central government's consumer price index to reflect real-time inflation and price fluctuations.[86] Increasingly, there will be more data collaboration between Alibaba and the central government, including the establishment of a national credit information-sharing platform.[87]

Second, Taobao helps enforce central policies and provide public goods, including poverty alleviation and rural development. For example, the Rural Taobao Program subsidizes logistics services to rural markets and helps people in poor, rural areas sell agricultural products to urban consumers through sales on Taobao's platform.[88] This initiative was, in part, financially backed by the central government. By 2016, the Ministry of Commerce and the Ministry of Finance offered 200 counties a total of $300 million for expenditures on e-commerce training, warehouses, and other related facilities and services that could advance the project.[89] As the central government continues to rely on positive economic performance for its legitimacy, the prospect of bringing market infrastructure, markets, and jobs to rural areas furthers this government's goals.

Third, as discussed in Part IV.B., Taobao weakens the authority, revenue, and rent creation by local governments by breaking down internal trade

---

[84] *See* Jeremy L. Wallace, *Juking the Stats? Authoritarian Information Problems in China*, 46 BRIT. J. POL. SCI. 11, 12–13 (2016).

[85] *See The Price Changes in Online Shopping in December, 2015*, ALI RES. INST. (Jan. 29, 2016), http://www.aliresearch.com/en/news/detail/id/20807.html.

[86] Tom Orlik, *Inflation Deflated? Evaluating the "Alibaba Index,"* WALL ST. J.: CHINA REAL TIME REP. (May 20, 2013), http://blogs.wsj.com/chinarealtime/2013/05/20/inflation-deflated-evaluating-the-alibaba-index (comparing aSPI with China's official consumer price index).

[87] *See National Development and Reform Commission, supra* note 85.

[88] *See* Julie Makinen, *Chinese E-Commerce Giant Alibaba Connects Rural Residents to Online Shopping*, L.A. TIMES (Apr. 2, 2016), http://www.latimes.com/world/asia/la-fg-china-rural-econ omy-20160403-story.html ("Government officials and Alibaba executives say Rural Taobao jibes neatly with national goals . . .").

[89] *Id.*

CONCLUSION   157

barriers. It therefore has mixed effects on federalism. By bringing national markets to provinces with trade barriers, Taobao strengthens market-preserving federalism by contributing to the common market. Yet it has the opposite effect with respect to the power of the central government vis-à-vis the provinces.

VI. Conclusion

We asked two questions at the outset: (1) What is the scope of Taobao's law creation? and (2) What effects is Taobao likely to have on federalism, Chinese style, and the common market?

Online market platforms, such as Taobao, appear to be changing the politics, economics, and legal infrastructure of China. We argued that Taobao has created far more than an exchange system; it has created a national market platform, including the market infrastructure necessary to sustain markets that the central government has found difficult to provide. We called this phenomenon law, Chinese style.[90]

Law, Chinese style, has emerged because the central government in China has effectively delegated the authority to develop this infrastructure to private parties. This delegation gives the central government several advantages: it provides an institutional basis for markets in a weak-rule-of-law environment; it permits experimentation; and it also allows the central government to distance itself from any failures. We drew connections between these benefits and the advantages that characterize "federalism, Chinese style"— one that existed during the early reform efforts in the 1980s and early 1990s.[91]

But, unlike federalism, Chinese style, this new system of creating a national market through private online platforms seems to tip the power balance toward the central government, rather than the other way around. On the one hand, Taobao holds the potential to circumvent internal trade barriers between provinces by fostering a national online market. While the rise of a national common market is likely to generate substantial economic growth, it has begun to challenge the regulatory power of local governments, as now many problems are no longer localized. On the other hand, the rise of national platforms such as Taobao seems to help reinforce the power of

---

[90] *See supra* Part III.
[91] *See supra* Part IV.

the central government. The central government can use national platforms as centralized tools to collect market information and to enforce central policies.[92]

As Taobao grows, however, it has become a force that can potentially demand concessions from the central government. Were the central government to shut down and expropriate Taobao's assets, it would face 700 million doomed citizens whose interests the government has trampled. Even though Alibaba and Taobao did not seem to credibly challenge the central authority, their growing influence has invited unwanted suspicions from the latter. Since late 2020, the central government has imposed tighter regulations on Alibaba and other large tech companies.

It is important to note that the post-2020 crackdown on tech platforms do not contradict the fact that platforms and the state still work together. The state still outsources various legal, social, and political functions to private platforms rather than directly enforcing these functions on its own. In fact, regulations and collaborations are two sides of the same coin. Facing scrutiny and penalty from the state, the private platforms will work even more closely with the state and align with the state's economic and political vision. Therefore, by imposing tighter regulations on platforms, the state can ensure that platforms' private institutions do not undermine—but help enforce—public institutions. Law, Chinese style continues to operate after 2020, albeit in a slightly different form.

---

[92] *See supra* Part IV.C.

7
Leveling the Playing Field between Sharing Platforms and Industry Incumbents

Good Regulatory Practices?

Shin-yi Peng

I. Introduction: Increasing Regulatory Fragmentation

The fragmentation of global governance in the digital economy is growing. In exercising their regulatory powers, states effectively realize their "digital sovereignty" objectives. Uncertainty surrounding divergent applicable regulations, stemming from disparate value preferences and legal approaches at the national and local levels, prevents the benefits of the digital economy from fully materializing. Indeed, diverse national "behind-the-border measures" are becoming barriers to digital trade. Different domestic requirements and standards have diverted business resources away from more effective allocation and management.[1]

In this context, the regulatory issues of the sharing economy provide a case study for reflection. Sharing platforms and intermediaries directly compete with the "incumbents," the "brick-and mortar" services suppliers, whose business activities have traditionally been governed by highly localized and heavily regulated frameworks.[2] This therefore raises specific regulatory issues regarding how to regulate sharing platforms. A primary question is whether and, if so, to what extent sharing platforms should be subject to

---

[1] *See generally* Beyond-the-Border Policies: Assessing and Addressing Non-Tariff Measures (Joseph Francois & Bernard Hoekman eds., 2019).

[2] *See* Raz Godelnik, *The Sharing Economy Dilemma: The Response of Incumbent Firms to the Rise of The Sharing Economy*, 8 Int'l J. Innovation 176 (2020).

Shin-yi Peng, *Leveling the Playing Field between Sharing Platforms and Industry Incumbents* In: *Data Sovereignty*. Edited by: Anupam Chander and Haochen Sun, Oxford University Press. © Oxford University Press 2023. DOI: 10.1093/oso/9780197582794.003.0008

160   LEVELING THE PLAYING FIELD

the same regulations over market structure (e.g., licensing requirements) and conduct (e.g., minimum quality standards) as their competing "traditional" services suppliers. Is Uber a taxi service? Should the city authority enforce existing taxi regulations over Uber? Is Airbnb a hotel servicer supplier? Should Airbnb hosts be required to obtain a hotel permit? Innovative technologies and novel business models have posed challenges to domestic policies and regulations.

To clarify ambiguities surrounding local regulations, sharing platforms must usually advocate or lobby for regulatory reform on a city-by-city basis. Even when local governments enact tailor-made regulations for sharing platforms, jurisdictions all over the world have taken a diversity of approaches.[3] This chapter explores the question of whether the regulatory cooperation chapters under regional trade agreements (RTAs) can govern local regulations. Given the diverse approaches to questions of housing, taxi services, and other local services among municipalities and other authorities, is it still possible to achieve regulatory coherence among countries? If so, how should international regulatory cooperation align with the desire for national regulatory sovereignty?

II. A Case Study: Regulating the Sharing Economy and Its "Enemies"

A. Innovation: The Sharing Platforms

Now officially listed in the Cambridge Dictionary, the sharing economy is defined as "an economic system that is based on people sharing possessions and services, either for free or for payment, usually using the internet . . ."[4] Often referred to as the "collaborative economy" or the "gig economy,"[5] the sharing economy has been described in several ways, with various emphases.[6] Several official government documents refer to it as a business model in

---

[3] *See generally* Stephen Miller, *First Principles for Regulating the Sharing Economy*, 53 HARV. J. ON LEGIS. 147, 185–195 (2016).

[4] *Sharing economy*, Cambridge DICTIONARY, https://dictionary.cambridge.org/dictionary/engl ish/sharing-economy (last visited September 27, 2021).

[5] *See* World Econ. F., *What Exactly Is the Sharing Economy?*, MEDIUM (Dec. 14, 2017) https://med ium.com/world-economic-forum/what-exactly-is-the-sharing-economy-62dc23ce49d2.

[6] *Id.*

which transactions are "facilitated by collaborative platforms that create an open marketplace for the temporary usage of goods or services . . . often provided by private individuals . . . either for free or for a return."[7] Organisation for Economic Co-operation and Development (OECD) documents describe it as "new marketplaces" that allow services to be provided "on a peer-to-peer shared usage basis."[8]

No matter the deviations in various definitions, the essential element of such an open marketplace is the intermediaries: sharing platforms that connect users and foster transactions.[9] In most cases, sharing platforms facilitate the exchange of goods or services by matching demand and supply. Namely, when individuals make an offer or a request for goods or services, the sharing platform acts as an intermediary between them and facilitates the trading process.[10] From an economic perspective, the sharing economy creates value in many ways. It allows underutilized goods and services to be put to more productive use by providing people an opportunity to use others' assets or properties. At the same time, it cuts transaction costs and expands the scope of trade by facilitating people in their efforts to find traders.[11] Overall, it creates "new" markets in property and labor that were not as practically effective as they had previously been, which brings new supply, and arguably also new demand, into the economy.

There has been explosive growth in sharing economy activities in recent years. Today, there are a great variety of sharing platforms operating in a wide range of sectors.[12] Companies like Uber and Airbnb, among other outstanding examples, connect individuals with others to share resources, time, and services in exchange for a fee. Such an innovation, however, has generated controversy and conflict with existing market operators. At the crux of the matter is the competition brought about by disruptive innovation in the market. How can innovative platforms be regulated in light of their enemies—incumbents in the same sector?

---

[7] *Collaborative Economy*, EUROPEAN COMM'N, https://ec.europa.eu/growth/single-market/servi ces/collaborative-economy_en (last visited May 27, 2021).

[8] OECD, OECD TOURISM TRENDS AND POLICIES 2016, at 89 (2016), https://www.oecd-ilibrary. org/oecd-tourism-trends-and-policies-2016_5jrtcqccl79s.pdf?itemId=%2Fcontent%2Fpublicat ion%2Ftour-2016-en&mimeType=pdf.

[9] *See* WORLD ECON. F., WHITE PAPER ON COLLABORATION IN CITIES: FROM SHARING TO SHARING ECONOMY (2017), http://www3.weforum.org/docs/White_Paper_Collaboration_in_Cities_report_ 2017.pdf.

[10] *Id.* at 7.

[11] Rashmi Dyal-Chand, *Regulating Sharing: The Sharing Economy as an Alternative Capitalist System*, 90 TUL. L. REV. 241, 251–59 (2015).

[12] WORLD ECON. F., *supra* note 9.

162   LEVELING THE PLAYING FIELD

B. Competition: The Incumbents

1. Uber in Taiwan

Uber in Taiwan provides an intriguing case study in this context. The conflict between the Taiwanese government and Uber went back to Uber's entry into the Taiwanese market in 2013. There has been a strong backlash from taxi drivers and taxi companies, claiming that Uber should be subject to "the same regulations" as taxi companies.[13] They were assured that the Uber model was "simply a taxi service under another name," which directly competed with taxi business. Uber's response, however, was that it provides "information services" and thus should not be subject to regulations governing "transportation services."[14]

Relevant authorities, mainly, the Ministry of Transportation and Communications of Taiwan (MOTC), supported taxi drivers' assertion, and pointed out that Uber did not have the proper registration to operate as a taxi service in Taiwan. The government's position was clear: Uber was registered as an "information services provider," but it operates as a "*de facto* taxi dispatcher."[15] Consequently, the government imposed strict restrictions and sanctions on Uber for violations of its business registration through "operating a passenger transport business and evading regulatory requirements." All of the sanctions are aimed at forcing Uber to comply with local taxi rules. Such a position was also supported by a court, which found that Uber's core business was, in fact, "hiring drivers to transport passengers for money; it is a taxi service."[16]

In 2019, the MOTC introduced an "Uber clause" into transportation regulations, which effectively forced Uber to join the "Multi-Purpose Taxi Program," under which Uber must rely on third parties to hold a

---

[13] Eli Lake, *Taiwan's War Against Uber*, BLOOMBERG (Feb. 24, 2017), https://www.bloomberg.com/opinion/articles/2017-02-24/taiwan-s-war-against-uber.

[14] The Professional Drivers' Union of Taiwan stated, "Uber claims itself as a technology service provider, but what it actually does is the same as what taxi companies do in Taiwan, except it does not have to be regulated like us." Lauly Li & Cheng Ting-Fang, *Uber Spat with Taiwan Could Force Exit from Market*, NIKKEI ASIA (Mar. 27, 2019).

[15] The Administrative Decision of MOTC.

[16] The Ruling of the Higher Administrative Court. Since Uber entered the Taiwan market, the company and drivers together have already been fined a total of US $10 million. Uber refused to pay the fines and filed administrative lawsuits. The court, although it agreed with the arguments of the lower courts, ruled that "the penalty would only be legal if it were issued by the Taipei City Government's road authority," as the Directorate General of Highways has no authority over taxi services operating in Taipei. The court waived the fine.

REGULATING SHARING ECONOMY AND ITS "ENEMIES"   163

transportation business license.[17] In other words, unless Uber partnered with local taxi companies, it would not have a way forward in the Taiwan market.[18] At the end of the day, regulators, to a certain degree, deferred to the legacy competitors.

2. Airbnb in Japan

A similar tension took place in Japan in a different context. Under its Hotels and Inns Act, Japan has long implemented a "Minshuku" (rooms in private homes that are offered as a lodging) system. The Act required a minimum size for Minshuku, and the owner was also required to apply for a license. In addition, a person with management responsibility must always be on the premises.[19] Arguably, Airbnb operations were illegal under such a strict scheme.

In 2018, Japan "legalized" home sharing by amending the Japanese Hotels and Inns Act. Pursuant to the new regulation, a "Minpaku" (private temporary lodging) system was introduced.[20] Minpaku hosts have to register their listing with the local authority in order to maintain an active status as a Minpaku. Any host without a license number must cancel all reservations.[21] Before the amendment became effective, Airbnb Inc. had 62,000 listings in Japan, but only 150 Minpaku had been approved by the authority.[22] In this regard, Airbnb was forced to remove nearly 80 percent of its listings without government approval. Airbnb hosts canceled thousands of reservations following the implementation of the new regulation.[23]

The new regulation limits home sharing to 180 days a year and mandates that local governments should impose a stricter cap. In other words, private lodgings are subject to local regulations, which vary from city to city. For example, Minpaku hosts in Kyoto are allowed to operate only during the low

---

[17] Chih Mei Tsai, *As Uber Had Taxi Drivers Take to the Streets, Taiwan's Democracy Is Tested*, COMMONWEALTH MAGAZINE (May 1, 2019), https://english.cw.com.tw/article/article.action?id=2380.

[18] Jeffrey Wu & Evelyn Kao, *Uber Calls for Withdrawal of New Proposal for Rental Car Industry*, CHINA POST (Mar. 8, 2019), https://chinapost.nownews.com/20190308-523316.

[19] Junko Fujita, *Japan's Home-Sharing Offering Evaporate Ahead of New Regulations*, REUTERS (Jan. 8, 2018), https://www.reuters.com/article/us-japan-airbnb-idUKKCN1J40BK.

[20] Dani Deahl, *Airbnb Cancels Bookings Under New Japan Law*, VERGE (Jan. 8, 2018), https://www.theverge.com/2018/6/8/17442230/airbnb-cancels-bookings-under-new-japan-law.

[21] *Id.*

[22] Pavel Alpeyev, *Airbnb Japan Listings Rebound after Home-Sharing Law Freeze*, BLOOMBERG (June 6, 2019), https://www.bloomberg.com/news/articles/2019-06-06/airbnb-listings-in-japan-rebound-after-home-sharing-law-freeze.

[23] *Id.*

164 LEVELING THE PLAYING FIELD

tourism season spanning from mid-January to mid-March.[24] The Japanese government has been "pushing" Airbnb to "respect the legal structure," which, according to Airbnb,[25] is not in line with the guidance the company had previously been given by the Japanese Tourism Agency. As explained by an expert, "[t]he strict rules were designed to protect Japan's hotel industry."[26]

C. Regulation: Dynamic and Divergent Approaches

1. A Level Playing Field?

The identical plots of the stories of Uber in Taiwan and Airbnb in Japan are happening all over the world. The tension is imminent. On the one hand, sharing platforms, which initially operated in a regulation-free zone, directly compete with incumbents, which have traditionally been heavily regulated. As a result, the "brick-and-mortar" incumbents became the "enemies" of innovative services and called for "a level playing field"—fair conditions between competitors.

Indeed, "treating like services alike" and refraining from using regulations as a means of choosing "technological winners" are commonly shared regulatory principles. As revealed by the dispute of Uber in Taiwan, the taxi associations' main argument is that the government should not adopt regulatory regimes that discriminate against different business models. Regulatory regimes should be designed to have a "neutral" effect on services, regardless of their technological differences. In the taxi associations' view, Uber gained unfair advantages simply by bypassing existing taxi regulations.[27] In this regard, the same requirements should be imposed on all suppliers competing in a particular sector, no matter whether the supplier is a "traditional" service supplier or a platform-based new entrant. Unequal and differential regulatory treatment in favor of the latter may mean that the regulators inevitably choose winners.[28]

On the other hand, an innovative market rapidly evolves. Thus, a certain degree of regulatory flexibility is needed in light of the uncertainty surrounding the development of a sharing economy.[29] Any precise and

---

[24] *Id.*

[25] *Id.* Statement of Chris Lehane, the global head of policy and public affairs for Airbnb.

[26] *Id.* Statement of Takayuki Miyajima, a senior economist at Mizuho Research Institute.

[27] Vanessa Katz, *Regulating the Sharing Economy*, 30 BERKELEY TECH. L.J. 1067, 1072–81 (2015).

[28] *See* Shin-yi Peng, *The Rule of Law in Times of Technological Uncertainty: Is International Economic Law Ready for Emerging Supervisory Trends?*, 22 J. INT'L ECON. L. 1, 1–3 (2019).

[29] Anna Butenko et al., *Regulation for Innovativeness or Regulation of Innovation?* 7 LAW INNOVATION & TECH. 52, 66 (2015).

comprehensive regulations related to innovative services may soon "become disconnected from rapidly changing technologies that are its regulatory targets."[30] That said, how can sectoral regulators articulate that the characteristics of certain sharing economy activities are "similar to" or "different from" their offline analogues? Based on this, how can regulators decide whether the two types of services should be required to meet the same standards because of their significant similarities? The answer to these queries will necessarily activate the assessments of sector-specific policy objectives and market conditions in which legacy suppliers and sharing platforms compete.

2. Case-by-Case Basis

It is evident that dynamic (and divergent) approaches have been taken to assess the need for regulation of the sharing economy. A case-by-case assessment, which requires the exercise of a good deal of judgment, would allow regulators or, in the case of litigation, judges to take into account the factual circumstances of a specific sector.

One striking example is the opinion of Judge Richard Posner. He posited that there are sufficient differences between the business models for taxis and ridesharing services such as Uber, which make regulation under varying city ordinances justified.[31] He held that while taxi services are heavily regulated by a City of Chicago ordinance and ridesharing services are much more lightly regulated, such a separation violates neither the property nor the equal-protection rights of taxi drivers.[32] Using an analogy, Judge Posner wrote that many cities and towns require dogs to be licensed but not cats. In his analogy, he articulated the following:

> Suppose the district judge happened to think dogs and cats interchangeable, and on that ground ruled that requiring dogs but not cats to be licensed was a violation of equal protection. The proper response would be that she is entitled to her opinion but not entitled to impose it when the market perceives [. . .] a rational difference between the competing animals that she does not perceive.[33]

---

[30] *Id.*

[31] Ill. Transp. Trade Ass'n, v. City of Chicago, 839 F.3d 594 (7th Cir. 2016). It should be noted that this ruling was appealed to the U.S. Supreme Court but a *writ of certiorari* was not granted. *See* Ill. Transp. Trade Ass'n, v. City of Chicago, 839 F.3d 594 (7th Cir. 2016), *cert. denied*, 137 S. Ct. 1829 (2017).

[32] Arguing before the U.S. Seventh Circuit Court of Appeals, the taxi attorney stressed that Uber is a taxi, and therefore, taxi drivers are entitled to equal protection and equal treatment.

[33] Ill. Transp. Trade Ass'n, v. City of Chicago, 839 F.3d, at 9.

166 LEVELING THE PLAYING FIELD

Posner then concluded that the district judge's belief that taxis and Ubers are interchangeable is similarly "not shared by the entire relevant consumer market."[34] In summary, based on "consumer market perception," there is a rational difference between Uber services and taxi services.

Another interesting example can be seen in the approaches taken by the European Court of Justice (ECJ).[35] The ECJ held that Airbnb and Uber should be treated differently. The ECJ argued that Uber "exercised a decisive influence over the conditions under which transport services are provided," and that therefore Uber service is a "service in the field of transport."[36] In the ECJ's view, Uber's business operation consists of more than an intermediary service. Uber's activities should therefore be regarded as "intermediation services forming an integral part of an overall service," and "the main component of which is a transport service."[37] In this regard, Uber must comply with the domestic regulations of each EU Member State pertaining to "transport services." However, the ECJ stressed that "a similarly decisive influence of Airbnb [...] over the conditions of the accommodation service" could not be identified. The ECJ thus qualified the platform service offered by Airbnb as an "information society service" that is entitled to the benefits of free movement under the EU's E-Commerce Directive.[38]

In the ECJ rulings, the different assessments of the two sharing platforms are primarily attributable to two factors: first, the ability of users to successfully operate without the sharing platform; and second, the ability of the platforms to control transactions. According to the ECJ's assessment, Airbnb's business model is not comparable to the service provided by Uber, in the sense that "Airbnb's intermediation service is in no way indispensable to the provision of accommodation services."[39] In addition, Uber had exercised "decisive influence" over "economically significant aspects of the service," while Airbnb had not.[40]

---

[34] *Id.*

[35] The key legal issue was whether the sharing platforms at issue should be classified as "information society services," which can therefore enjoy the benefits of free movement.

[36] Case C-434/15, Asociación Profesional Elite Taxi v. Uber Systems Spain, SL, 2017 E.C.R. 981 [hereinafter ECJ Ruling on Uber]. Case C-390/18, Airbnb Ireland, 2019 E.C.R. 1112 [hereinafter ECJ Ruling on Airbnb].

[37] ECJ Ruling on Uber, *supra* note **36**.

[38] ECJ Ruling on Airbnb, *supra* note **36**.

[39] *Id.*

[40] *Id.* This chapter was written during a period spanning from January to June of 2021. Note that the EU's Digital Services Act (DSA), that became effective in November 2022, is intended to modernize the EU's E-Commerce Directive.

To conclude, business models for a sharing economy are complex and involve a great number of variables. The regulatory approaches that embrace contingency and flexibility pose risks related to legal uncertainty and regulatory fragmentation. Lessons from the Uber disputes are reflective in nature. Uber has faced a variety of legal battles around the world. Local regulations surrounding Uber are diverse, complex, and scattered, ranging from caps on cruising, number of licenses, obligations on trips, congestion surcharges, driver safety education, and minimum fares to commercial passenger vehicle registration, vehicle inspections, driver accreditation, vehicle standards, and vehicle identification stickers.[41] In some jurisdictions, Uber overcame tough regulatory hurdles after a rough start. In other jurisdictions, Uber still faces a showdown, struggling to give up the battle.[42] Such regulatory fragmentation creates costly and burdensome tasks for sharing platforms. After all, platform service suppliers that operate across borders must meet different standards worldwide due to the lack of regulatory consistency among countries.

Moreover, as shown above, the existing approaches to classifying the commercial nature of a sharing platform are dynamic and pragmatic. Various conclusions can be drawn as to whether a specific sharing platform qualifies as an "information service." The nature of a sharing platform is therefore legally unsettled. In the wake of both the U.S. federal court and the ECJ judgments, it would seem that the answer to the question of how to determine the exact nature of the services provided by sharing platforms depends upon a case-by-case assessment of the characteristics of a particular platform. This, however, begs the question of relevant criteria as well as their hierarchy. That said, the central questions are as follows: How can we combat discretionary abuse in order to prevent regulatory overreach? Can international regulatory cooperation through trade agreements help achieve that objective? How can we apply the "good regulatory practice" principles given the complex issues involved? The remainder of this chapter explores the regulatory cooperation trends at the regional level and identifies the factors affecting good regulatory practices for platform regulations.

---

[41] EUROPEAN PARLIAMENT, THE COLLABORATIVE ECONOMY: SOCIOECONOMIC, REGULATORY AND POLICY ISSUES 22–24 (2017), https://www.europarl.europa.eu/RegData/etudes/IDAN/2017/595 360/IPOL_IDA(2017)595360_EN.pdf.

[42] *Id.* at 23.

III. Regulatory Cooperation on Platform Regulations: Good Regulatory Practices?

A. Regulatory Cooperation Trends in the Regional Trade Agreements

1. The Regulatory Chapters

Governments are increasingly cooperating to coordinate policies "behind the borders" through efforts at the regional or bilateral level.[43] The regulatory cooperation chapters in the RTAs have generated heated debate.[44] In particular, cumulative momentum has emerged in the Regulatory Coherence Chapter under the Comprehensive and Progressive Agreement for Trans-Pacific Partnership (CPTPP),[45] Regulatory Cooperation Chapter under the Comprehensive Economic and Trade Agreement between Canada and the EU (CETA),[46] and also in the Good Regulatory Practices Chapter under the United States-Mexico-Canada Agreement (USMCA).[47] The regulatory chapters under the RTAs are designed to offer promising venues for overcoming regulatory divergence, with a basic assumption that a set of regulatory principles and methodological tools aimed at improving the quality

---

[43] *See generally* Jonathan B. Wiener & Alberto Alemanno, *The Future of International Regulatory Cooperation: TTIP as a Learning Process Toward a Global Policy Laboratory*, 78 LAW & CONTEMP. PROBS. 103, 104 (2015) ; Reeve T. Bull et al., *New Approaches to International Regulatory Cooperation: The Challenge of TTIP, TPP and Mega-Regional Trade Agreements*, 78 LAW & CONTEMP. PROBS. 1, 3 (2015).

[44] *See e.g.*, Rodrigo Polanco, *The Trans-Pacific Partnership Agreement and Regulatory Coherence*, *in* TRADE LIBERALIZATION AND INTERNATIONAL COOPERATION: A LEGAL ANALYSIS OF THE TRANS-PACIFIC PARTNERSHIP AGREEMENT 231, 232–38 (Tania Voon ed., 2013). *See also* Thomas Bollyky, *Regulatory Coherence in the TPP Talks*, *in* THE TRANS-PACIFIC PARTNERSHIP: A QUEST FOR A TWENTY-FIRST CENTURY TRADE AGREEMENT 172 (C.L. Lim et al. eds., 2012).

[45] Comprehensive and Progressive Agreement for Trans-Pacific Partnership, THE MINISTRY OF FOREIGN AFFAIRS AND TRADE OF NEW ZEALAND, https://www.mfat.govt.nz/assets/Trade-agreeme nts/CPTPP/Comprehensive-and-Progressive-Agreement-for-Trans-Pacific-Partnership-CPTPP-English.pdf (last visited July 24, 2021) [hereinafter CPTPP].

[46] Comprehensive Economic and Trade Agreement between Canada, of the One Part, and the European Union and its Member States, of the Other Part, Eur.-Can., Oct. 30, 2016, 2017 O.J. (L11) 23, https://ec.europa.eu/trade/policy/in-focus/ceta/ceta-chapter-by-chapter.

[47] *Agreement between the United States of America, the United Mexican States, and Canada 12/13/19 Text*, OFF. OF THE U.S. TRADE REPRESENTATIVE, https://ustr.gov/trade-agreements/free-trade-agreements/united-states-mexico-canada-agreement/agreement-between (last visited July 24, 2021) [hereinafter USMCA]. More recent examples include Chapter 22 (Good Regulatory Practices and Regulatory Cooperation) of the EU-New Zealand FTA, concluded in 2022, and Chapter 26 (Good Regulatory Practice) of the UK-Australia FTA, concluded in 2021.

of regulations might indeed offer promising governmental actions to bring about substantive regulatory coherence.[48]

Prior to the launch of the CPTPP, the notion of regulatory cooperation/coherence had emerged in conjunction with the initiatives of the OECD and the Asia-Pacific Economic Cooperation (APEC).[49] The OECD "recommendations" set out the importance of "political commitment to regulatory reform" and "good regulation," with the aim of enhancing economic performance and cost-effectiveness through the improvement of regulatory quality.[50] Consistent with the efforts of OECD and APEC,[51] the development of the regulatory chapters under the RTAs in recent years has emphasized regulatory quality, rationality, clarity, and transparency.[52]

As declared by the participating parties, the Regulatory Coherence Chapter under the CPTPP is expected to "promote good regulatory practice principles in the regulatory development process,"[53] and to "eliminate the problem of overlapping and inconsistent regulatory requirements being developed unfairly and without a sound basis."[54] The Regulatory Cooperation Chapter under CETA establishes a Regulatory Cooperation Committee and strengthens cooperation in regulatory development processes, with the expectation that "the differences in regulatory approaches between Canada and the EU will be reduced over time."[55] In a similar vein, although many of the provisions are similar to the CPTPP, the Good Regulatory Practices Chapter under the USMCA contains innovative provisions that go beyond

---

[48] Alberto Alemanno, *Is There a Role for Cost-Benefit Analysis Beyond the Nation-State? Lessons from International Regulatory Co-operation, in* THE GLOBALIZATION OF COST-BENEFIT ANALYSIS IN ENVIRONMENTAL POLICY (Michael A. Livermore & Richard L. Revesz eds., 2013).

[49] Robert Basedow & Céline Fauffmann, *International Trade and Good Regulatory Practices: Assessing the Trade Impacts of Regulation* 10 (OECD, OECD Regulatory Policy Working Papers No. 4, 2016); APEC & OECD, APEC-OECD INTEGRATED CHECKLIST ON REGULATORY REFORM (2005), https://www.oecd.org/regreform/34989455.pdf.

[50] OECD, RECOMMENDATION OF THE COUNCIL ON IMPROVING THE QUALITY OF GOVERNMENT REGULATION (1995), https://legalinstruments.oecd.org/en/instruments/OECD-LEGAL-0278.

[51] OECD, INTERNATIONAL REGULATORY CO-OPERATION: ADDRESSING GLOBAL CHALLENGES 100–05 (2013), https://read.oecd-ilibrary.org/governance/international-regulatory-co-operation_9789264200463-en.

[52] OECD, OECD REGULATORY POLICY OUTLOOK 2018, at 41 (2018), https://www.oecd-ilibrary.org/sites/9789264303072-en/index.html?itemId=/content/publication/9789264303072-en.

[53] OFF. OF THE U.S. TRADE REPRESENTATIVE, REGULATORY COHERENCE, https://ustr.gov/sites/default/files/TPP-Chapter-Summary-Regulatory-Coherence.pdf (last visited May 27, 2021). Note that in January 2017, the United States withdrew from the TPP agreement. The other 11 TPP countries reached the CPTPP agreement in January 2018.

[54] *Id.*

[55] *CETA Summaries*, GOVERNMENT OF CANADA, https://www.international.gc.ca/trade-comme rce/trade-agreements-accords-commerciaux/agr-acc/ceta-aecg/chapter_summary-resume_chapi tre.aspx?lang=eng#a21 (last visited May 27, 2021). *See also* Nanette Neuwahl, *CETA as a Potential Model for (Post-Brexit) UK-EU Relations*, 22 EUR. FOREIGN AFF. REV. 279, 279–301 (2017).

170 LEVELING THE PLAYING FIELD

the CPTPP, including much more "advanced" standards in the areas of "information quality" and "transparency."[56] As defined in the Good Regulatory Practices Chapter, regulatory cooperation means an effort between the Parties "to prevent, reduce, or eliminate unnecessary regulatory differences between jurisdictions" and, in doing so, "to facilitate trade and promote economic growth."[57] The long-term objectives are to "reduce or eliminate unnecessarily burdensome, duplicative, or divergent regulatory requirements."[58]

2. Impact Assessment

The basic assumption of these regulatory chapters is that good regulatory practices are fundamental to effective international cooperation on regulatory issues. Accordingly, these chapters, and in particular, those under the CPTPP and the USMCA, set forth specific obligations with respect to "good regulatory practices," such as promoting information quality, procedural transparency, clear and plain regulatory language, early planning and retrospective review of regulations, central and internal coordination, and engagement with interested persons.[59]

Under both the CPTPP and the USMCA, core to good regulatory practices is the need to conduct an impact assessment when developing regulations. Article 28.11 of the USMCA delineates the procedures and considerations under which a regulatory impact assessment should be conducted.[60] The impact assessment requires an examination of the need for a regulatory

---

[56] USMCA, *supra* note 47., art. 28.5 (Information Quality); *Id.* art. 28.9 (Transparent Development of Regulations).

[57] *Id.* art. 28.1 (Definitions).

[58] *Id.*

[59] *See e.g.*, USMCA, *supra* note 47, art. 28.4 (Internal Coordination); *Id.* art. 28.6 (Early Planning); *Id.* art. 28.8 (Use of Plain Language); *Id.* art. 18.13 (Retrospective Review). *See also* CPTPP, *supra* note 45, art. 25.8 (Engagement with Interested Persons).

[60] USMCA, *supra* note 47, art. 28.11 (Regulatory Impact Assessment)

1. The Parties recognize that regulatory impact assessment is a tool to assist regulatory authorities in assessing the need for and potential impacts of regulations they are preparing. Each Party should encourage the use of regulatory impact assessments in appropriate circumstances when developing proposed regulations that have anticipated costs or impacts exceeding certain thresholds established by the Party.

2. Each Party shall maintain procedures that promote the consideration of the following when conducting a regulatory impact assessment:

   (a) the need for a proposed regulation, including a description of the nature and significance of the problem it is intended to address;

   (b) feasible and appropriate regulatory and non-regulatory alternatives that would address the need identified in subparagraph (a), including the alternative of not regulating;

   (c) benefits and costs of the selected and other feasible alternatives, including the relevant impacts (such as economic, social, environmental, public health, and

proposal, feasible alternatives, the benefits and costs of the alternatives, and the grounds for the selected alternative. Such an assessment is an analytical tool to ensure "welfare maximization"[61] that guides the regulators regarding whether to, as well as how to, achieve public objectives. Through a systemic approach that critically assesses the impact of the proposed regulations and non-regulatory alternatives,[62] the procedure is designed to facilitate a careful balance of public interests and ensure that regulations are adopted and implemented in an efficient and effective manner.[63] Methodologically, during stage three, an ex ante policy evaluation tool measuring the benefits and costs of the alternatives—or a cost-benefit analysis—is applied. In simplified terms, this refers to a determination regarding whether or not "the sum of all benefits of regulation, including both market and non-market, exceeds the sum of all costs."[64] Although in theory a variety of analytical tools can be employed to conduct an impact assessment,[65] a cost-benefit analysis has been commonly used by governments to both formulate and assess regulatory policy.[66]

A full application of the cost-benefit analysis or, more generally, the regulatory impact assessment requires data and information regarding the design and implementation of regulation. In this regard, Article 25.2 of the CPTPP stresses the importance of considering input from interested persons in the development of regulatory measures. Article 25.5 further indicates

> safety effects) as well as risks and distributional effects over time, recognizing that some costs and benefits are difficult to quantify and monetize, and
> (d) the grounds for concluding that the selected alternative is preferable.
>
> 3. Each Party should consider whether a proposed regulation may have significant adverse economic effects on a substantial number of small enterprises. If so, the Party should consider potential steps to minimize those adverse economic impacts, while allowing the Party to fulfill its objectives.

[61] Rex Deighton-Smith et al., *Promoting Inclusive Growth through Better Regulation: The Role of Regulatory Impact Assessment* 8 (OECD, OECD Regulatory Policy Working Papers No. 3, 2016), https://www.oecd-ilibrary.org/docserver/5jm3tqwqp1vj-en.pdf?expires=1627091596&id=id&accname=guest&checksum=874478F6DC66DD3693D6D4AA21C5AFEB.

[62] Basedow & Fauffmann, *supra* note 49. BERNARD HOEKMAN ET AL., REGULATORY SPILLOVERS AND THE TRADING SYSTEM: FROM COHERENCE TO COOPERATION 2–3 (2015), http://e15initiative.org/wp-content/uploads/2015/04/E15-Regulatory-OP-Hoekman-and-Mavroidis-FINAL.pdf.

[63] Alemanno, *supra* note 48.

[64] *Id.*

[65] Anne C.M. Meuwese & Stijn van Voorst, *Regulatory Impact Assessment in Legal Studies*, in HANDBOOK OF REGULATORY IMPACT ASSESSMENT 21–32 (Claire A. Dunlop & Claudio M. Radaelli eds., 2016). Heng Wang, *The Future of Deep Free Trade Agreements: The Convergence of TPP (and CPTPP) and CETA?*, 53 J. WORLD TRADE 317, 317–42 (2019).

[66] Susan Rose-Ackerman, *Putting Cost-Benefit Analysis in Its Place: Rethinking Regulatory Review*, 65 U. MIAMI L. REV. 335 (2011).

172   LEVELING THE PLAYING FIELD

that regulatory agencies should rely on "the best reasonably obtainable existing information," which includes relevant "scientific, technical, economic or other information," when conducting an impact assessment. Article 28.5 of the USMCA also imposes a high standard on "information quality," which requires the Parties to "use sound statistical methodologies before drawing generalized conclusions concerning the impact of the regulation," and to "avoid unnecessary duplication and otherwise minimize unnecessary burdens on those being surveyed." Article 28.9 of the USMCA further requires the Parties to allow interested persons to submit any comments and other input electronically.

Let's now turn to the question this chapter previously raised as to whether good regulatory practices and regulatory cooperation in trade agreements can help converge the fragmented legal approaches to the sharing economy. When faced with the question of whether or not to regulate particular sharing economy activities, how can regulators systematically evaluate the design and implementation of relevant regulations? How can we identify the problems of sharing platforms and their drivers to evaluate the need for intervention, to assess policy options and their underlying rationales, and, therefore, to "choose the best regulatory option"?

B. Good Regulatory Practices for Platform Regulations?

1. Local Values

The proliferation of sharing economy activities and the entry of new business models into the market provide a strong case study on the limitations of the application of good regulatory practices for platform regulations. Indeed, domestic platform regulations differ from country to country. Even under the shared premise that regulators recognize the need to "level the playing field," some jurisdictions achieve regulatory parity by "regulating up," while others achieve parity by "deregulating down."[67] To illustrate, some jurisdictions maintain that the objectives pursued in existing regulation remain valid, both in relation to traditionally operating service suppliers and the sharing economy. On the other end of the spectrum, some jurisdictions, spurred by the entry of sharing platforms into the market, reflected on the requirements

---

[67] Jessica Leight, *Public Choice: A Critical Reassessment, in* GOVERNMENT AND MARKETS TOWARD A NEW THEORY OF REGULATION 230–31 (Edward Balleisen et al. eds., 2010).

of the old regulations and decided to "level the playing field" by deregulating those requirements imposed on incumbents.[68] Given this regulatory divergence, can "good regulatory practices" ensure a converged policy direction that better balances the interests of the sharing economy and its enemies?

The answer might not be straightforward. It should first be noted that in some cases, the applicable coverage of the obligations of good regulatory practices is rather limited.[69] Under the CPTPP, the "covered regulatory measures" found in the Regulatory Coherence Chapter are limited to the regulatory measures determined by each Party.[70] In other words, each Party to the CPTPP has the right to decide to what extent its domestic regulation should be subject to the obligations of good regulatory practices under the trade agreement. Unlike the CPTPP, Article 28.1 of the USMCA explicitly limits the scope of "regulation" under the Good Regulatory Practices Chapter to the "measure of general application adopted, issued, or maintained by a regulatory authority with which compliance is mandatory." Annex 28-A of the USMCA further excludes certain national measures from coverage under the chapter, including "general statements of policy or guidance that do not prescribe legally enforceable requirements." Most importantly, "regulatory authority" is defined under the chapter as an administrative authority or agency at the Party's "central level of government" that develops, proposes, or adopts a regulation. As most sharing economy activities are arguably subject to city or municipal regulations, USMCA Parties can simply claim that they fall outside the scope of the Good Regulatory Practices Chapter.[71]

Moreover, rationales for and against regulatory intervention in a sharing economy are complex. Depending on sectoral characteristics, regulatory intervention is usually driven by complex policy objectives, ranging from public safety, public health, and tax revenue to fairness. When introducing the regulatory impact assessment, measurement is problematic, because not every public policy objective involved can be measured precisely,[72] leaving more judgment calls regarding how to "quantify" costs and benefits, as well

---

[68] World Econ. F., *supra* note 9.

[69] *See* Shin-yi Peng, *Lessons from the TPP Regulatory Coherence Chapter: The Laws Governing Unsolicited Commercial Electronic Messages as a Case Study, in* GOVERNING SCIENCE AND TECHNOLOGY UNDER THE INTERNATIONAL ECONOMIC ORDER: REGULATORY DIVERGENCE AND CONVERGENCE IN THE AGE OF MEGA-REGIONALS 64 (Shin-yi Peng et al. eds., 2018).

[70] CPTPP, *supra* note **45.**, art. 25.1 (Definitions).

[71] USMCA, *supra* note **47.**, annex 28-A.

[72] Cass R. Sunstein, *Cost-Benefit Analysis and Arbitrariness Review,* 41 HARV. ENVIR. L. REV. 1, 28 (2017).

174 LEVELING THE PLAYING FIELD

as how to "weight" them against each other.[73] In other words, when quantification is not possible, regulators have the discretion to proceed as they consider fit.[74] Therefore, assessing and choosing among alternative policy options is not based entirely on the character of the services, but, rather, on a given society's value preference.[75] As commentators have aptly pointed out, the regulatory impact assessment might become a mere justification for the regulator's choices rather than serving as a tool to improve regulatory quality.[76] When the underlying issues are complicated and controversial, as in the present case, a regulatory impact assessment may "serve as a mechanism for promoting agency decisions rather than scrutinizing them."[77] Local value preferences may play an important role in the process of a cost-benefit analysis.[78] After all, when local knowledge and community values are included, the "problems identified" have a more subjective character, reflecting local values. Variations in local value preferences have resulted in regulatory divergence among countries, which cannot be overcome simply by a methodological tool for regulatory assessment.[79]

Furthermore, and perhaps more significantly, the fact that the regulator applied the regulatory impact assessment in its decision-making process may not lead to the conclusion that the selected alternative is the less trade restrictive measure. Regulators tend to limit their analysis to the impact experienced within domestic borders.[80] The negative effect of regulatory divergence across borders is therefore usually beyond the reach of such measurements. In other words, a cost-benefit analysis generally does not include extterritorial impacts.[81] How a fragmented regulatory framework would have affected a global-scale platform is most likely an issue that was omitted by national regulators in past practices. In short, a cost-benefit

---

[73] *Id.*

[74] *Id.* at 2.

[75] European Parliament, *supra* note 41.

[76] OECD, Policy Brief: Improving the Quality of Regulations (2009), https://www.oecd.org/regreform/regulatory-policy/Policy%20Brief%20-%20Improving%20the%20Quality%20of%20Regulations.pdf; Stuart Shapiro, *The Triumph of Regulatory Politics: Benefit–Cost Analysis and Political Salience*, 6 Regulation & Governance 189–206 (2012).

[77] Wendy E. Wagner, *The CAIR RIA: Advocacy Dressed Up as Policy Analysis*, in Reforming Regulatory Impact Analysis 57 (2009).

[78] Rose-Ackerman, *supra* note 66, at 335; Shapiro, *supra* note 76, at 189.

[79] *Id.*

[80] Alemanno, *supra* note 48.

[81] *Id. See also* Elizabeth Sheargold & Andrew Mitchell, *The TPP and Good Regulatory Practices: An Opportunity for Regulatory Coherence to Promote Regulatory Autonomy?*, 15 World Trade Rev. 587, 587–612 (2016).

analysis is generally, as put by Alemanno, "extra-territorially blind."[82] There are limits as to how far an impact assessment can extend beyond national borders.[83]

2. Regulatory Capture

The danger of regulatory capture may also weaken the effectiveness of good regulatory practices in addressing the problem of regulatory fragmentation. Wide and equal access among stakeholders is an important element of good regulatory practices. Theoretically speaking, active participation among global platforms may contribute to regulatory convergence. More specifically, an open and more inclusive regulatory process might reduce the emerging gap between jurisdictions and their regulatory impact, which would in turn facilitate regulatory convergence. In practice, allowing key stakeholders to jointly shape policy may also serve as a counterbalance—effectively offsetting either an overestimation of benefits or an underestimation of costs.[84] After all, regulators need data and information from relevant private actors.[85] Transparency and stakeholder participation allow for input from interested groups and, at the same time, enable regulators to access empirical data necessary for regulatory assessment.[86]

In the context of a sharing economy and its enemies, however, in most cases the legacy incumbents have long established connections with local governments.[87] They are well-organized interest groups that have been actively lobbying local governments to press their case. The reality is that platform-based disruptive innovation erodes the market share of traditional service suppliers. When the latter claims that the same old requirements should be imposed on all suppliers competing in a particular sector, sectoral regulators face the challenge of assessing the characteristics of certain sharing-economy activities so as to decide whether they are sufficiently similar to their off-line analogues. The quality of regulation cannot be ensured if the problem of regulatory capture emerges. When taxi companies seek

---

[82] Alemanno labeled it as "extra-territorially blind." Alemanno, *supra* note 48. *See also* Alberto Alemanno, *Courts and Regulatory Impact Assessment, in* HANDBOOK OF REGULATORY IMPACT ASSESSMENT 137 (Claire A. Dunlop & Claudio M. Radaelli eds., 2016).

[83] Basedow & Fauffmann, *supra* note 49.

[84] BRONWEN MORGAN ET AL., AN INTRODUCTION TO LAW AND REGULATION: TEXT AND MATERIAL 61–62 (2007).

[85] *Id.* at 61.

[86] Polanco, *supra* note , at 253.

[87] John O. McGinnis, *The Sharing Economy as an Equalizing Economy*, 94 NOTRE DAME L. REV. 329 (2018).

176 LEVELING THE PLAYING FIELD

protectionist measures from local governments to prevent their markets from being disrupted by sharing platforms,[88] regulators may fall victim to regulatory capture, as demonstrated by the case of Uber in Taiwan.

By its very nature, stakeholder participation in the regulation of sharing economy represents a battle between incumbents and innovation. In this sense, industry capture of regulators might be an inevitable risk. Interest groups, both industry incumbents and platform-based new entrants, have strong incentive to become active players in the process of regulation design. Engagement with interested persons may have significant value to policy makers. However, at the same time, such engagement raises the risk that policymakers will be dominated by well-organized and locally connected incumbents and will in turn respond to the one-sided demands.[89]

IV. Conclusion: Regulatory Cooperation and Sovereignty

At the outset of this chapter, the author raised questions regarding whether regulatory cooperation could possibly reduce the diversity of municipal approaches to questions of housing, taxi services, and other local services, as well as how the obligations of good regulatory practices under trade agreements may help to govern local regulations. Business models of sharing economies involve a great number of variables. The approach to classifying a sharing platform is dynamic, and the nature of a sharing platform is uncertain, which depends upon a case-by-case assessment of the characteristics of a particular platform. The case study on the sharing economy illustrates that regulatory approaches pose the specific risk of regulatory fragmentation through embracing contingency. However, good regulatory practices and regulatory cooperation in trade agreements might not contribute much, if at all, to the harmonization of fragmented legal approaches to a sharing economy.

First, local regulations, which are the most controversial area due to competition between sharing platforms and local incumbents, may be largely beyond the scope of international trade obligations surrounding

---

[88] FED. TRADE COMM'N, THE "SHARING" ECONOMY: ISSUES FACING PLATFORMS, PARTICIPANTS & REGULATORS (2016), https://www.ftc.gov/system/files/documents/reports/sharing-economy-iss ues-facing-platforms-participants-regulators-federal-trade-commission-staff/p151200_ftc_staff_re port_on_the_sharing_economy.pdf.

[89] Richard B. Stewart, *Remedying Disregard in Global Regulatory Governance: Accountability, Participation, and Responsiveness*, 108 AM. J. INT'L L. 211 (2014).

good regulatory practices. Second, variations in local value preferences have resulted in regulatory divergence among countries, which cannot be converged merely by an assessment tool. Third, in general, a cost-benefit analysis does not consider extraterritorial impacts. Consequently, national regulators are likely to fail in generating a full evaluation that includes the negative impact of a globally fragmented regulatory framework on platforms. Finally, the risk of regulators being captured by local voices further complicates the process of stakeholder participation in the regulation of sharing platforms.

Additionally, regulatory cooperation among platform regulations is a particularly salient regulatory problem because such cooperation inherently conflicts with the desire for "digital sovereignty," which is the digital dimension of a nation's strategic autonomy.[90] The potential erosion of regulatory sovereignty would further render international regulatory cooperation even more difficult. Arguably, regulatory divergence represents a manifestation of democratic legitimacy.[91] That said, the issue of international regulatory cooperation surrounding platform regulations is not exclusively an international economic law issue but is also a matter of digital sovereignty. Any further cooperative regulatory efforts may face constraints associated with digital sovereignty.[92]

Trade negotiators must rethink the role of good regulatory practice obligations in the context of digital platform regulations. Although international regulatory cooperation remains a valuable tool, this chapter demonstrates its limitations. Pressing digital regulatory fragmentation problems do not fit well into the paradigm of good regulatory practices. More specifically, a regulatory impact assessment, while an effective tool for "conventional" policy issues, might not translate itself into an appropriate methodology for digital policy with significant global impact.[93] Such an assessment is methodologically underequipped to address the digital context. Trade negotiators should re-examine how to most effectively reduce regulatory divergence, as well as how to best engage in international regulatory cooperation in the formulation of platform regulations.[94]

[90] LOKKE MOEREL & PAUL TIMMERS, REFLECTIONS ON DIGITAL SOVEREIGNTY (2021), https://eucyberdirect.eu/wp-content/uploads/2021/01/rif_timmersmoerel-final-for-publication.pdf. *See also* Anupam Chander & Uyên P. Lê, *Data Nationalism*, 64 EMORY L.J. 677 (2015).

[91] Anne Meuwese, *Constitutional Aspects of Regulatory Coherence in TTIP: An EU Perspective*, 78 LAW & CONTEMP. PROBS. 153 (2015).

[92] *Id.*

[93] Rose-Ackerman, *supra* note **66.**, at 335.

[94] *Id.*

8

The Emergence of Financial Data Governance and the Challenge of Financial Data Sovereignty

Giuliano G. Castellano, Ēriks K. Selga and Douglas W. Arner

I. Introduction

The essence of the Fourth Industrial Revolution is digital transformation. The "digitalization of everything" combines two interrelated processes. First, a process of digitization transforms analog information into digital form.[1] Second, datafication is converting every aspect of modern life into digital data that is gathered and analyzed through a range of rapidly evolving technologies and methods, including increasingly artificial intelligence (AI).[2] Digital transformation continues as communications, computing, processing, and data storage technologies become ever more available and powerful, connecting billions of people and their interactions across the world.[3] The COVID19 crisis accelerated the process, triggering unprecedented creation, collection, aggregation, and dissemination of—and most crucially—dependence on data.[4]

Data is thus a strategic priority. Like other strategic assets—land, energy, food, water, capital[5]—governments are seeking to assert sovereign control in

---

[1] On digitization, *see* VIKTOR MAYER-SCHONBERGER & KENNETH CUKIER, BIG DATA 78 (2013).

[2] On datafication, *see* Ulises A. Mejias & Nick Couldry, *Datafication*, 8 INTERNET POL'Y REV. (2019).

[3] See Ross P. Buckley et al., *Regulating Artificial Intelligence in Finance: Putting the Human in the Loop*, 43 SYDNEY L.J. (2021).

[4] Especially in in the context of digital communications, interactions, payments, commerce, and finance, see DOUGLAS W. ARNER ET AL., DIGITAL FINANCE, COVID-19 AND EXISTENTIAL SUSTAINABILITY CRISES: SETTING THE AGENDA FOR THE 2020S, No. 1 (2021).

[5] As indicated by *The Economist* in 2017: "[t]he world's most valuable resource is no longer oil, but data." *Data Is Giving Rise to a New Economy*, ECONOMIST (May 6, 2017), https://www.economist.com/briefing/2017/05/06/data-is-giving-rise-to-a-new-economy.

Giuliano G. Castellano, Ēriks K. Selga and and Douglas W. Arner, *The Emergence of Financial Data Governance and the Challenge of Financial Data Sovereignty* In: *Data Sovereignty*. Edited by: Anupam Chander and Haochen Sun, Oxford University Press. © Oxford University Press 2023. DOI: 10.1093/oso/9780197582794.003.0009

an emerging era of multipolar geopolitical competition. Through the implementation of new data-specific policies and regulation, general data governance frameworks are emerging, defining a new set of rights and obligations for stakeholders such as data generators and owners. As analyzed elsewhere, the general data governance styles of the largest economies—the EU, United States, People's Republic of China—are colliding, threatening the paradigm of free transnational data flows and fragmenting the global economy.[6]

Finance is also highly dependent on data and its transnational movement. Since the invention of the telegraph in the 19th century, finance has grown into perhaps the most globalized and digitized but also regulated sector of the modern economy.[7] Underlying this digital transformation, the financial sector has undergone a process of dematerialization of financial assets and processes over the past 50 years, transforming financial products and information into digital data.[8] Hence, financial entities, consumers, and regulators routinely share data (in digital form) to provide their services and maintain the stability and integrity of the financial system. This dependence of finance on data flows in an environment of growing autonomous data regulation rules raises complex questions regarding how data governance and financial regulation interact and what the implication is for a digitally globalized financial system.

This chapter thus seeks to address the challenges of datafication of finance and financial data sovereignty. Section II considers the datafication of finance. Section III considers the intersection of data, finance, and data governance, highlighting both emerging general data governance styles. Section IV highlights the intersection of financial data regulation and personal data regulation, in the context of the evolution of a range of Open Banking strategies, focusing on personal financial data. Section V presents four emerging financial data governance strategies, exemplified by the United States, EU, China, and India, seeking to bring together finance and its regulation with their evolving domestic data governance regimes. Section VI elaborates how the

---

[6] Douglas W. Arner et al., *The Transnational Data Governance Problem*, 37 BERKELEY TECHNOL. L.J. 623 (2022). (Discussing the various regulatory and policy clashes taking place that are inhibiting free transnational data movement).

[7] Douglas W. Arner et al., *The Evolution of Fintech: A New Post-Crisis Paradigm*, 47 GEO. J. INT'L L. 1271 (2015) (presenting a framework for the globalization of financial transactions enabled by financial technology).

[8] Dematerialization is a central phenomenon in finance, propelling financial globalization as noted by Campbell Jones, *The World of Finance*, 44 DIACRITICS 30 (2016); and financial innovation, as indicated by Patrice Baubeau, *Dematerialization and the Cashless Society: A Look Backward, a Look Sideward, in* THE BOOK OF PAYMENTS 85 (Bernardo Batiz-Lazo & Leonidas Efthymiou eds., 2016).

180   FINANCIAL DATA GOVERNANCE AND DATA SOVEREIGNTY

result of differences in these strategies combined with prudential objectives are converging toward territorialization via data localization. We then address this growing challenge of fragmentation in Section VII by outlining how the well-developed transnational regulatory frameworks in finance offer an opportunity to develop technological solutions and approaches that may in fact support both the objectives of financial and data regulation.

II. The Datafication of Finance

Finance is inextricably linked to the acquisition, analysis, and processing of massive volumes of diverse forms of information, today mostly in digital form. Capital markets can be conceptualized as networks of social relationships, where participants send signals about the quality and quantity of different financial products, thus determining their prices. More broadly, financial information, intended as data concerning transactions of businesses and individuals, is the core fuel of modern financial systems. Financial information underlies both the Efficient Capital Markets hypothesis as well as financial regulatory requirements for information disclosure, access, and quality. In addition to investors in stock markets who rely on analysis of information to make investment and trading decisions, lenders, for instance, estimate the creditworthiness of potential borrowers through a variety of financial information, such as repayment history, credit card transactions, income statements, and asset information. A wide range of proprietary but also shared sources such as credit rating agencies, credit bureaus, and increasingly a range of Big Data and alternative data sources compound such sources of data, exemplified in the rise of FinTech and BigTech credit.

Finance, technology, and law are co-developmental, paralleling and interacting with the evolution of past and modern civilization.[9] Since the invention of paper in China (2,000 years ago) until the late 1970s, finance was an industry based on paper: paper ledgers, paper certificates, paper money (in addition to coins).[10] With electrification, the diffusion of electronic storage and computing power, finance evolved into a digital industry, where financial

---

[9] Finance can be traced back to ancient Sumer, whereby grain and ingots of copper and silver were used as payment. Financial transactions were codified in the Babylonian Code of Hammurabi circa 1800 B.C. For more, *see* George Levy, *A Brief History of Finance, in* COMPUTATIONAL FINANCE USING C AND C# 275 (2016).

[10] *Id.*

instruments (such as stocks and other securities) are dematerialized, and financial information is digital.

In this context, the law evolves and interacts with the technology underpinning finance. As financial assets, such as securities, are dematerialized and, thus, exist and are held electronically in depository systems, legal rules have had to adapt. The legal status, the evidentiary nature, and the enforceability of electronic transactions must correspond to the needs of market participants and function at least as well as those attributed to paper-based transactions. While most of the legal issues concerned with the emergence of electronic financial activities have been debated, and to a large extent addressed, since the second half of the 20th century,[11] new challenges have emerged as the processes of dematerialization ushered a more profound, and ongoing, transformation. These have been clearest over the past decade with the emergence of new technologies in finance, in particular new forms of digital assets.

To unlock the potential of digital finance, regulatory policies have been focusing increasingly on facilitating the circulation of data, within and across financial industries. In addition to traditional focuses on standardization and regulatory sharing, a notable new example is offered by Open Banking initiatives, whereby payment and banking service providers should ensure that authorized third parties can have access to customer and payment accounts information. While complying with this core objective, however, financial institutions and jurisdictions can adopt a variety of approaches, selecting the level of openness, the type of services, and how to integrate their offerings with the business model of other players. The result is a financial system where financial data becomes a resource to expand the reach of financial services and a commodity that should be integrated to new financial services.

Financial data is a broad but distinct form of data. It includes traditional banking data, transactions history, and other information typically tied to individual accounts and users. Such data is used for various purposes, including for the assessment of various risks—based on models calculating the probability of repayment—and for the pricing of different services. It also refers to data about financial markets and products, such as stock prices and accounting data about firms and governments. In a similar vein, the data

---

[11] For an early discussion of the challenges posed by the dematerializations of financial transactions and assets, *see* CHRIS REED, ELECTRONIC FINANCE LAW (1991).

gathered by financial institutions is routinely used for regulatory purposes: financial institutions are required to gather data to detect suspicious activities in fight against money laundering and financing of terrorism, and market, client, statistical, and transaction data are used determine the level of protection against various prudential risks, including credit risk, market risk, and operational risk.[12]

Financial data thus pertains to a variety of classes of data. It includes non-personal data used by financial services and their clients to send instructions for payments transnationally, or to report to regulators, or interact with clients. It also comprises personal data with information tied to any individual account, transaction, or other sensitive information.

The breadth and depth of financial data, as well as the critical character of the financial sector itself to jurisdictions makes its regulation a priority. The challenge is that regulating financial data requires coordinating several policy aims concurrently. For instance, financial data must be sufficiently pliable to support its use by the financial services industry, while affording sufficient protection to the growing amounts of personal and public data.

III. Financial Data Governance and General Data Governance

Financial data governance encompasses a variety of rules and principles that can be grouped into three categories.[13] The first category of components comprises regulatory regimes designed to govern the production, acquisition, use and circulation of financial data. These rules are core aspects of traditional regulatory policies aimed at ensuring market efficiency, consumer and investor protection, financial stability, and market integrity. Such rules cover most aspects of finance and have had to continually evolve as a result of technological evolution and digitalization, including industry, regulatory, and customer data. The second category comprises broader data governance styles. These styles are autonomous sets of rules and principles designed at the domestic level to extend sovereign control over data, data flows, and

---

[12] For discussions exemplifying regulatory reporting requirements for financial data, *see* Abdullahi Usman Bello & Jackie Harvey, *From a Risk-Based to an Uncertainty-Based Approach to Anti-Money Laundering Compliance*, 30 Secur. J. 24 (2017); Patrik Alamaki & Daniel Broby, The Effectiveness of Regulatory Reporting by Banking Institutions (2019).

[13] Douglas W. Arner et al., *Financial Data Governance*, 74 Hastings L.J. 235 (2023) (Introducing the notion of "financial data governance").

infrastructure. These emerged initially in the context of personal data but are now being extended more broadly for a range of reasons including national security, competitiveness, and developmental objectives. The third category encompasses a range of emerging regulatory initiatives, strategies, and models for digital finance, such as Open Banking policies focusing on personal financial data, which have been developed to address challenges and opportunities of the digital transformation of financial sectors. The coming together of a diverse range of traditional and novel regulatory regimes that are (directly or indirectly) concerned with financial data and the datafication of finance are evolving into a new governance framework for digital finance.

A. Regulating Financial Data

The regulatory framework for financial data is a manifestation of both the increased centrality of data in modern society and the digitization and datafication of finance. Hence, regulation affects financial data through two intertwined dynamics.

The first dynamic that defines the regulatory perimeter for financial data stems from the digitization of finance. Financial regulation has adapted to ensure that the risks related to the growing reliance on digital information, financial assets, and related infrastructures are properly addressed. The gathering, processing, management, and use of financial information in digital form has, thus, become central to financial regulatory policies concerned with the solvency of financial institutions, the stability and the integrity of the financial system at large. Hence, regulatory regimes concerned with the digitization of finance have evolved around prudential regulation, conduct of business rules (with particular attention to AML requirements), and supervisory initiatives.

In respect to prudential policies, strong attention has been given to the risks emerging from the growing integration of digital systems in financial activities. Technological failures, cyber-attacks, legal actions, and regulatory sanctions related to the mistreatment of data are forms of operational risk that may compromise the solvency of financial institutions. As data and technology are inextricably related to finance, new international standards have been elaborated to ensure that technology-related operational risks are properly addressed. In particular, the Basel Committee on Banking Supervision (BCBS) has launched an epochal overhaul of the rules that banks must

184 FINANCIAL DATA GOVERNANCE AND DATA SOVEREIGNTY

implement vis-à-vis the assessment and management of data and technology risk: TechRisk. The result is an increased level of capital requirements to ensure enough loss absorbing capacity against operational risk and the implementation of a principle-based approach to strengthen operational resilience within banks.[14]

Lastly, financial data is becoming the direct corollary of broader regulatory reporting requirements and supervisory action. Regulators are requiring banking data to be machine readable to enable supervisory automation processes and more granular data aggregation capabilities.[15] Many regulatory initiatives enacted after the 2008 Global Financial Crisis require financial institutions to report a large set of data on individual operations, such as security-by-security, and loan-by-loan reporting.[16] Regulatory and supervisory technology (RegTech/SupTech) models are requiring financial data to be structured so that regulators have direct access via automatically packaged business data (data-input approach), through collecting business data directly from bank systems (data-pull approach), through analyzing operational bank data at will (real-time access), or other formats. These RegTech/SupTech instruments are not only expanding the micro-prudential supervisory capacity but enabling the aggregation of vast data pools for machine learning and AI solutions used for risk management.

Second, as data is treated as a strategic resource and governance expands its reach domestically and internationally,[17] regulatory regimes concerned with the treatment of financial information naturally intersect and interact with general data policies. In fact, financial data encompasses myriad classes and types of data that, while used for financial purposes, may also fall squarely into the general category (or categories) of data, particularly personal data. The holders and processors of financial data are thus being

---

[14] Capital requirements for operational risks are enshrined in the Consolidated Basel Framework; with the new rules the ability of banks to use own estimations to assess capital requirements is limited; see Consolidated Basel Framework (Basel Committee on Banking Supervision ed., Comprehensive version ed. 2019). In addition, with the last revision of the Principles for Operational Resilience, the BCBS issued an updated guidance on operational risk to include information and communication technology risks, including cybersecurity, but also to require the sound structuring of data, especially in regard to third-party service providers; see Revisions to the Principles for the Sound Management of Operational Risk (Basel Committee on Banking Supervision ed., Comprehensive version ed. 2021) at 7.

[15] Financial Stability Board, The Use of Supervisory and Regulatory Technology by Authorities and Regulated Institutions (2020).

[16] Toronto Center, FinTech, RegTech and SupTech: What They Mean for Financial Supervision (2017).

[17] Especially, and increasingly in regard to critical infrastructure, and critical functions like national security, financial markets, or transportation. See Arner et al., supra note 6.

increasingly directly or indirectly regulated by general data governance rules in force in any given jurisdiction. These general regimes typically establish different rights concerned with the alienability, circulation, or management of personal financial data. However, at the same time financial data—both personal and non-personal—are also the object of specific regulatory initiatives, stemming from sector-specific needs and concerns.

B. The Evolution of Data Governance Styles

In the past 30 years, economic globalization has been supported by a common approach to data. Originating from a U.S.-led conception, the digital world developed as a permission-less, open, and liberal space, as evidenced by the Internet. Here, individuals, corporate entities, state actors, and international organizations converged in a global network of networks.[18] Upon these premises, market-like mechanisms gathered and exchanged data that, in turn, became the primary commodity in the digital space. As the links between digital and physical worlds multiplied, owing to the development of new technologies and to the expansion of infrastructural capabilities, a data economy developed and expanded beyond the digital perimeter. From daily tasks personal and professional capacities of individuals to critical societal functions, such as payment and healthcare systems, societal dependence on data has become ubiquitous.

As data becomes a strategic asset, nation-states have begun to assert sovereignty over the digital world, both domestically and internationally. Legal and regulatory frameworks are being developed to define rights and obligations for data generators and holders.[19] Competition policies have been triggered to curb data abuse by dominant incumbent firms.[20] New rules

[18] The Internet has been described a burgeoning "Network of Networks" that enables interaction between many different domains. *See* Sara Helen Wilford et al., *The Digital Network of Networks: Regulatory Risk and Policy Challenges of Vaccine Passports*, 12 EUROPEAN J. OF RISK REGULATION 393 (2021); WILLIAM H. DUTTON, MULTISTAKEHOLDER INTERNET GOVERNANCE? (2015).

[19] Rights and obligations for data stakeholders extends across many policy domains. *See generally* Rene Abraham, Johannes Schneider, & Jan vom Brocke, *Data Governance: A Conceptual Framework, Structured Review, and Research Agenda*, 49 INTERNATIONAL J. OF INFO. MGMT. 424–38 (2019).

[20] For instance, the FTC recently filed a complaint against Facebook in an ongoing federal antitrust case, alleging that Facebook resorted to illegal buy-or-develop schemes to maintain market dominance. See Federal Trade Commission, *FTC Alleges Facebook Resorted to Illegal Buy-or-Bury Scheme to Crush Competition After String of Failed Attempts to Innovate*, FEDERAL TRADE COMMISSION, https://www.ftc.gov/news-events/press-releases/2021/08/ftc-alleges-facebook-resorted-illegal-buy-or-bury-scheme-crush (last visited Aug. 22, 2021)

to assert control over internal and external data flows and related infrastructure are being enacted.[21] At the heart of these initiatives lies the urge for state actors to assert their sovereignty over data.[22] The result is the emergence of an increasingly fragmented global data governance framework.

Taken together, the domestic efforts to reign the digital world define specific patterns. As argued elsewhere, such patterns create specific data governance styles.[23]

Crucially, data governance styles manifest in the cardinal direction taken to regulate data, data flows, and digital infrastructures within and outside domestic borders. When applied to the three major world economies and primary standard-setters—notably, China, the EU, and the United States— the domestic trajectories for data governance emerge starkly. Starting from the United States, it is clear that a market-based style and a laissez-faire regulatory approach to data and technology have nurtured the rise of the Internet and its current paradigm: globalized, permission-less, and supportive of free trade.[24]

Largely in response to the dominance of American players in the global digital economy, the EU, first; and China, more recently, have developed their own digital strategies. In the EU, the governance style is right-based at it establishes protections for the gathering, the use, and the circulation of personal data of EU citizens, while spurring the emergence of a digital economy within the European Single Market.[25] A more centralized governance style is emerging in China, where a state-based approach treat data and data flow as part of broader policies, ranging from national security and infrastructural autonomy to general socioeconomic goals of improving the quality of life of Chinese citizens.[26] The analysis of data governance styles can be extended to other jurisdictions. For example, India is a jurisdiction where

---

[21] These interventions cover a variety of areas of law and are related to asserting control for the purposes of privacy, competition, socioeconomic development, and other reasons. For more, *see* Arner et al., *infra* note 36.

[22] OECD, THE PATH TO BECOMING A DATA-DRIVEN PUBLIC SECTOR (2019); UN SECRETARY-GENERAL, DATA STRATEGY OF THE SECRETARY-GENERAL FOR ACTION BY EVERYONE, EVERYWHERE WITH INSIGHT, IMPACT AND INTEGRITY, 2020–22 (2020)

[23] The locution has been first coined in Arner et al., *supra* note 6.

[24] *Id.*

[25] Brett Aho & Roberta Duffield, *Beyond Surveillance Capitalism: Privacy, Regulation and Big Data in Europe and China*, 49 ECON. & SOC'Y 187 (2020)

[26] FAZHI ZHENGFU JIANSHE SHISHI GANGYAO (2021–2025) (法治政府建设实施纲要 (2021– 2025年)) [Implementation Outline for the Construction of a Government Under the Rule of Law (2021–2025)] (promulgated by Central Comm. CCP & St. Council, Aug. 11, 2021), http://xinhuanet. com/2021-08/11/c_1127752490.htm (China).

data governance focuses on a rights-based approach, while also embracing utilizing data policy as the main vehicle for the delivery of public goods and services.

Each data governance style connects and interacts with the strategies to regulate financial data and digital finance in various manners. In particular, as financial data encompasses a variety of different classes of general data, from personal to non-personal information, the emergence of data governance styles necessarily intersects with rules and principles designed to regulate financial data and its related ecosystem. More broadly, as data is the object of financial transactions, data governance styles represent a major influence as the financial data governance strategies are developed. Depending on whether a given data governance style promotes or inhibits the digitization and datafication of finance, financial data governance will result in complementarities or exceptionalisms. This connection is particularly evident in the context of Open Banking initiatives, as they presuppose the circulation of data within a given jurisdiction.

IV. Open Banking

Financial data is thus impacted directly by both financial regulation and also by general data governance styles. In an increasing range of aspects, frictions, overlaps, and conflicts are emerging in the relationships between the two regulatory regimes both within and across different jurisdictions.

For instance, unlike the EU, which has had a formal legal framework for personal data since 1995,[27] the United States has not had a general legislative framework governing personal data but rather a complex series of federal and state legislation and case law. California adopted the first comprehensive state data protection legislation in 2018, the California Consumer Privacy Act (CCPA), which entered into force in 2020.[28] However, the United States has developed legislation in a number of specific areas, including finance. The most significant are the Fair Credit Reporting Act enacted in 1970[29] and

---

[27] European Data Protection Supervisor, *The History of the General Data Protection Regulation*, https://edps.europa.eu/data-protection/data-protection/legislation/history-general-data-pro tection-regulation_en (last visited Feb. 9, 2022) (describing the development of data protection in the EU).

[28] Ch. 55, 2018 Cal. Stat. 1807 (codified as amended at CAL. CIV. CODE §§ 1798.100-.199.100 (2020).

[29] Pub. L. No. 91-508, tit. VI, 84 Stat. 1114, 1127-36 (1970) (codified as amended at 15 U.S.C.Hi 1681-1681x (2018)).

amended by the Fair and Accurate Credit Transactions Act of 2003[30] and the Gramm-Leach-Bliley Act[31] and its creation of the Consumer Financial Protection Bureau (CFPB)[32] specifically addressing consumer financial data. Absent a general data protection framework, these can be seen as sector specific elements of the U.S. general data governance style, albeit ones provide for a sectorally specific set of rules and that may in fact eventually form the basis of a broader set of rules governing personal data in the United States.

In contrast, while the EU has long had a general framework for personal data protection, prior to 2018, this had a limited impact in the context of financial data, personal or otherwise. This however changed with the implementation of both PSD2 and GDPR in 2018.[33] PSD2 (adopted in 2015) provides a framework for Open Banking while GDPR (adopted in 2016) provides a comprehensive framework for personal data protection. Together they are central to both the EU's general data governance style and also its financial data governance strategy.

Open Banking parallels and interacts with the general data governance style but also is emerging as a separate yet related strategy, with the EU as first mover and the leading proponent of a mandatory legislative approach, reflecting and extending its more general data governance style. In the EU, PSD2 (which predates GDPR) establishes a framework that promotes the emergence of novel payment-service providers, through a licensing structure that requires banks to provide access to a client's payment account to third parties on the basis of their consent.[34] Banks have to comply with a system of rules that facilitate the transferability of data, by developing APIs that meet a minimum set of functional standards.[35] PSD2 however only mandates sharing by banks, an aspect for which is has been criticized.[36]

---

[30] Fair and Accurate Credit Transaction Act of 2003, Pub. L. No. 108-159, 117 Stat. 1952 (codified at 15 U.S.C. § 1681 (2006))

[31] Pub. L. No. 106-102, 113 Stat. 1338 (1999) (codified as amended in sections of 12 U.S.C. and 15 U.S.C.).

[32] Jolina C. Cuaresma, *Commissioning the Consumer Financial Protection Bureau*, 31 Loy. Consumer L. Rev. 426 (2018–2019) (discussing the unique leadership and accountability structure of the Consumer Financial Protection Bureau).

[33] Douglas W. Arner et al, *The Future of Data-Driven Finance and RegTech: Lessons from EU Big Bang II*, 25 Stan. J.L. Bus. & Fin. 245 (2020) (2019)

[34] Michael R. King & Richard W. Nesbitt, The Technological Revolution in Financial Services: How Banks, FinTechs, and Customers Win Together 143 (2020).

[35] See EU General Data Protection Regulation (GDPR): Regulation (EU) 2016/679 of the European Parliament and of the Council of 27 April 2016 on the protection of natural persons in regard to the processing of personal data and on the free movement of such data, and repealing Directive 95/46/EC (General Data Protection Regulation), OJ 2016 L119/1.

[36] Douglas W. Arner et al., *Open Banking, Open Data and Open Finance: Lessons from the European Union*, in Linda Jeng (ed), Open Banking (2022)

The Open Banking movement has now spread globally, albeit in a range of differing forms. To unlock the potential of the digital economy, jurisdictions are pursuing a range of Open Banking variants.

At the most basic level, Open Banking enables consumer generated data to be transferred (data portability) or accessed by third parties. Approaches can range from legislatively mandated (as in the EU) to industry-led voluntary systems (as in the United States), with a range of roles for regulators in between.[37] In mandatory systems like the EU, Australia and United Kingdom, core granular provisions have been adopted, mandating financial institutions to grant third-party access to their data, regulating access through APIs, and establishing standardization of digital ID for users. The comparison with different rules offers a useful illustration of how policymakers in different jurisdictions understand and promote Open Banking: Open Banking in one jurisdiction can be very different from Open Banking in another, particularly in the context of its level of legal basis and its interaction with general data governance styles.

Data portability lies at the heart of Open Banking strategies; key variances lie in the degree of portability required. For instance, while U.S. federal law does not require information portability (and thus is the basis of a voluntary Open Banking strategy in the United States and one which so far has largely been ineffectual as a result of industry recalcitrance despite outward enthusiasm), the California Consumer Protection Act grants users a right to receive their personal information in a useable readable format for easy transmission from their data holder.[38] The EU GDPR provides a similar right, highlighting that the copy of a user's data should be in a commonly used and machine-readable format. Both regimes establish a requirement for data holders to initially classify and compartmentalize personal data and to be able to divide it from the rest of their data.

The approach adopted to Open Banking in any given jurisdiction is an important proxy to gauge the trajectory being adopted for financial data governance. In general terms, Open Banking policies are typically concerned with regulating the relationships with (i) financial data holders, such as banks and other financial institutions; (ii) processors, such as technology-focused and

---

[37] *See generally Id.*
[38] Ch. 55, 2018 Cal. Stat. 1807 (codified as amended at CAL. CIV. CODE §§ 1798.100-.199.100 (2020)).

190   FINANCIAL DATA GOVERNANCE AND DATA SOVEREIGNTY

FinTech firms; and (iii) users mostly represented by individuals and small business.[39]

These actors can be further divided into a set of subcategories. Data processors can be divided into those that can aggregate user-generated data but cannot use (or that cannot have access to such data), and payment service initiators that can perform transactions on behalf of customers. These relationships can take a variety of archetypal forms. Aggregators are typically banks and other financial institutions that combine services from third-party providers to enhance their offerings or provide new services. Financial institutions can also be "distributors," acting as service providers for a third-party processor that manages client interface. Other entities can offer data orchestration services, for instance, by bringing together data from multiple sources into a marketplace. The result is a data ecosystem that can be harnessed to promote more advanced and inclusive financial services.

Along with the EU, the United Kingdom and Australia[40] are typically seen as strongest example of legislatively mandated Open Banking strategies while the United States is usually seen as a (so far largely ineffectual) example of an industry led voluntary Open Banking strategy. The EU in fact is moving beyond Open Banking toward Open Finance and eventually Open Data, reflecting the parallel evolution of its general data governance style, as is Australia. In between these extremes lie a range of models, usually characterized by the level of regulatory guidance and involvement, with Singapore and Hong Kong both being characterized by active regulatory encouragement and standard-setting but absent legislative mandates. Singapore, in particular, has been very active in building infrastructure and implementing regulatory encouragement as the basis of its Open Banking strategy, suggesting the regulator-led approach as a third major form.

China is also developing its own variant of Open Banking. In China, much of the consumer-authorized financial data access takes place through private platforms. However, there are no laws expressly requiring consumer consent-based data sharing or financial portability. The Chinese government issued recommended rules on standard API specifications for commercial banks in 2020. These standards require banks to establish internal,

---

[39] These are the core stakeholders in the open banking cycle, and consist of entities that generate, process, and hold data; see Yan Carrière-Swallow et al., *India's Approach to Open Banking: Some Implications for Financial Inclusion*, No. WP/21/52 (2021)

[40] Ross P. Buckley et al., *Australia's Data-Sharing Regime: Six Lessons for the World*, 33 King's Law Journal 61 (2022).

enterprise, and external APIs, instead of just focusing on bank-to-customer interactions. The 2018 guidelines for data governance set out detailed architectural structures for the data management of financial institutions.[41] A more recent set of interim provisions stipulate minimum consent and as well as requiring that consent is requested if giving access to third parties.[42] It is emerging as a mandatory system albeit with data as a common resource rather than one controlled by individuals or financial institutions.

Likewise, India is developing yet another Open Banking strategy, one based on individual control of data (as in the EU, United Kingdom and Australia) but with its use facilitated via a system of aggregation via licensed data aggregators:[43] In India, Open Banking follows a data aggregator model. Firms licensed by the Reserve Bank of India act as fiduciaries, collecting customer's financial data and sharing it with their consent to third parties.[44] Following the objectives of financial inclusion and facilitating financial competition in the market, account aggregators are a public good that ensures a level playing field, precluding the accrual and appropriation of data management costs by individual institutions while allowing reciprocal data sharing. Through aggregate banking, the goal is to extend the India Stack from payments into credit, personal finance, wealth management, and insurance.

Thus, Open Banking is emerging in a variety of jurisdictional strategies, each designed to maximize the benefits of personal financial data, bridging financial regulation and general data governance styles and often modifying both.

V. Financial Data Governance Strategies

General data governance styles interact with financial regulation in the financial data governance model of any given jurisdiction. The main footprint left by each data governance style onto the financial data governance model pertains to the attribution of different degrees of control over data to one

---

[41] China Banking and Insurance Regulatory Commission issued the "Guidelines for Data Governance of Banking Financial Institutions," available at http://gdjr.gd.gov.cn/gdjr/jrzx/jryw/cont ent/post_2870321.html

[42] Interim Provisions on the Protection and Management of Personal Information of Mobile Internet Applications, available at http://www.cac.gov.cn/2021-04/26/c_1621018189707703.htm

[43] Shri Rao, Remarks by Shri M. Rajeshwar Rao, Deputy Governor, Speech at Reserve Bank of India (Apr. 14, 2021) (2021)

[44] Nandan Nilekani, *Data to the People: India's Inclusive Internet*, 97 FOREIGN AFF. 19 (2018).

category of the societal actors populating the data ecosystem. The control over data, in general, and financial data, more specifically, is attributed by prioritizing (i) market dynamics, where data holders, such as business organizations and financial institutions, are key players; (ii) the interests of individuals, intended primarily as the data generators; or (iii) the public interests, representing the collectivity organized by state actors and public entities.

Through this prism, we identify three archetypical data governance models, based on which group of social actors is prioritized. These archetypes extend to financial data governance. In particular, the different levels of control attributed to societal actors over data influences the regulation of financial data and intersects with Open Banking policies. These three models are analyzed next.

A. Property-Based: United States

Central to a financial data governance model that is market orientated is the notion that data is an asset that can be produced, priced, and exchanged. Essentially, data is addressed as property that is freely alienable. Regulatory interventions are limited and intended to promote confidence in the market while protecting the integrity and stability of the financial system. Access to and transfer of data are contractual matters, left to the free negotiation between parties. Property rights over data concerning accounts, payments, and transactions are retained by the financial institutions. Data generators, however, may be granted a right to data portability and can request third-party access.

This approach is epitomized by the general style adopted in the United States, where the market-based approach has favored the emergence of a diverse FinTech ecosystem. FinTech firms have and continue to obtain data without the involvement of other banks via credential-based access or "screen-scraping." Screen scraping is the use of software to read the user data inputs and outputs in their bank without drawing on the data from the bank's servers—it is a process that can be completed without the participation of a customer's bank. Though there is consensus that direct access to data via APIs is superior to screen scraping in way of security, reliability, and user control—there is no binding regulatory input on how to address the issues of informed consumer consent, the scope

FINANCIAL DATA GOVERNANCE STRATEGIES   193

and duration of access, as well as the allocation of liability in case of data loss or misuse.

The lead in establishing standards for Open Banking products and services is taken by the industry. The Clearing House—a banking association responsible for core payments system infrastructure in the United States[45]— has proposed a Model Agreement standard created for data sharing between financial service providers. The aim is to transition from screen scraping to APIs. A more technical set of standards has been established by the Financial Data Exchange—a cross-section of banks, data aggregators, and technology companies created in 2018. These standards create an interoperable API for user-permissioned financial data sharing with over 600 financial data elements currently available, including banking, tax, insurance, and investment data.[46]

While the United States may be seen as the clearest example of the ideal of a market-based model for financial data governance, in reality financial regulation in the United States—as highlighted above—has long addressed consumer protection in the context of financial data. Therefore, the United States can be seen as the leading example of a market-based based model for general data governance; however, in the context of financial data governance, it has developed a range of personal and other financial data rules designed to support market efficiency, consumer protection, and financial stability.

B. Rights-Based: European Union

An individual rights-based model for financial data governance prioritizes the control of individuals over market dynamics. Data is treated more as a right of individuals rather than as freely alienable property. The gathering, use, and transfer of data are regulated through statutory rights that canvas contractual negotiation and limit transferability of data ownership and the control over data. Separation of personal and non-personal data is generally

---

[45] The Clearing House is owned by the largest banks of the United States and has a daily clearing and settlement volume of two trillion U.S. dollars. *See* The Clearing House, *Our History*, https://www. theclearinghouse.org/about/history (last visited Jan. 9, 2022)

[46] Financial Data Exchange, *Home*, FINANCIAL DATA EXCHANGE, https://financialdataexchange. org/FDX/Home/FDX/Default.aspx?hkey=bd839735-ebf5-426a-91f9-8334cbae1438 (last visited Jan. 9, 2022); Oana Ifrim, *The State of Open Banking and Open Finance in the US and Canada – Interview with FDX (Part 1)*, THE PAYPERS, https://thepaypers.com/interviews/the-state-of-open-banking-and-open-finance-in-the-us-and-canada-interview-with-fdx-part-1--1253761 (last visited Jan. 9, 2022).

194 FINANCIAL DATA GOVERNANCE AND DATA SOVEREIGNTY

key, as more restrictions are applied to the former category encompassing information that are deemed sensitive. Non-personal data is generally treated as alienable property.

This model is epitomized by the approach adopted in the EU. The general data governance framework of the Union has evolved around three core priorities: (i) a focus on individual rights and privacy; (ii) the prevention of data concentration in the hands of a handful of dominant firms; and more recently (iii) the promotion of sufficient technological capacity to promote the growth of the internal market. Starting with a series of data protection and privacy directives primarily focused on protecting consumers (EU citizens), the data governance framework expanded in scope and influence.[47] Most recently, both GDPR and PSD2 adopted a series of measures granting ownership and control of data to individuals.[48] The trajectory is posed to be maintained and reinforced with the EU-wide digital ID regime via the eIDAS regulation, which establishes a framework for digital access to cross-border public and private services in the internal market.

In this context, different regulatory regimes apply to non-personal and personal data. Non-personal data is generally alienable and can circulate freely.[49] Domestic authorities must be able to retain access to certain data even if located in different Member States and data holders must implement measures to facilitate data portability procedures between service providers.[50] A different regime applies to personal data, which are inalienable from the individual they pertain to and regardless of any contractual agreement.[51] GDPR allows personal data to be exported, subject to the official recognition from the European Commission that the regulatory framework of the receiving (non-EU) jurisdiction ensures basic protection that are

---

[47] Thomas Streinz, *The Evolution of European Data Law*, No. ID 3762971 (2021) (presenting an overview of the burgeoning EU data governance framework).

[48] See Article 36 of Directive (EU) 2015/2366 of the European Parliament and of the Council of 25 November 2015 on Payment Services in the Internal Market, Amending Directives 2002/65/EC, 2009/1 1O/EC and 2013/36/EU and Regulation (EU) No 1093/2010, and Repealing 2007/64/EC, 2015 O.J. (L 337) 35, known as PSD2.

[49] Article 4 of Regulation 2018/1807 prohibits "data localization requirements" thus requiring free flow of data in the EU. See Regulation (EU) 2018/1807 on a framework for the free flow of non-personal data in the EU [2018] OJ L303/59.

[50] Article 5 of Regulation 2018/1807 presents competent authorities with the right to "request, or obtain, access to data for the performance of their official duties . . ." and such requests can in practice require real-time access, and data localization. Article 6 encourages the development of "principles of transparency and interoperability" to facilitate switching service providers and the porting of data.

[51] See EU General Data Protection Regulation (GDPR): Regulation (EU) 2016/679 of the European Parliament and of the Council of 27 April 2016 on the protection of natural persons in regard to the processing of personal data and on the free movement of such data, and repealing Directive 95/46/EC (General Data Protection Regulation), OJ 2016 L119/1.

deemed equal to those applied in the EU.[52] Furthermore, Member States can enact data localization measures, in the context of health, financial services, or other sectors.[53]

The allocation of control over data to individuals is a pillar of this system. In open banking strategy, individuals maintain control over their data, as financial institutions can share them with authorized third parties only if requested by customers.[54] Yet, financial institutions must ensure that the transfer of data can occur in a systematized fashion and in compliance with a set of minimum requirements.[55]

Built on this framework, the 2020 EU Digital Finance Strategy aims to create a digital Single Market to boost the scalability and competition between financial service providers.[56] This strategy includes enabling EU-wide interoperable use of digital identities to allow easier on-boarding, suitability assessments, and the "re-use" of on-boarding for other purposes beyond financial services. This data space will be centered on a new EU digital finance platform that enables industry and supervisory authorities to interact online, offering e-licensing procedures on the basis of the expanded on-boarding regimes and data exchange.[57] One of the key strategies of the 2020 EU DFS is moving from "Open Banking" of PSD2 and GDPR to "Open Finance" in which all financial data must be freely transferable to third parties and eventually under the new EU Digital Strategy, moving to "Open Data," in which data are fully under individual control with the necessary standards and infrastructure to enable use.

---

[52] *Id.*

[53] *Id. See* Nigel Cory et al., Principles and Policies for "Data Free Flow With Trust" (2019) (highlighting the limits of data protection under the GDPR); Nigel Cory, *Cross-Border Data Flows: Where Are the Barriers, and What Do They Cost?* (2017) (highlighting the transaction costs of data protection regimes).

[54] Article 64 of PSD2 expressly requires authorization of payment transactions to be considered only if the "payer has given consent to execute the payment transaction." *See supra* note 48.

[55] Articles 65–72 set out a variety of rules on the procedural aspects of, for example, initiating a payment on behalf of a client via a third-party service provider. *See id.*

[56] *Communication from the Commission to the European Parliament, the Council, the European Economic and Social Committee and the Committee of the Regions on a European Strategy for Data,* COM (2020) 66 final (Feb. 19, 2020), https://ec.europa.eu/info/sites/info/files/communication-european-strategy-data-19feb2020_en.pdf; Reiner Schulze & Dirk Staudenmayer, EU Digital Law: Article-by-Article Commentary (2020); Despoina Anagnostopoulou, *The EU Digital Single Market and the Platform Economy, in* Economic Growth in the European Union 43 (Christos Nikas ed., 2020); Luís Cabral et al., The EU Digital Markets Act: A Report from a Panel of Economic Experts (2021), https://publications.jrc.ec.europa.eu/repository/bitstream/JRC122910/jrc122910_external_study_report_-_the_eu_digital_markets_acts.pdf.

[57] Cabral et al., *supra* note 56.

C. Shared Resource: China

In jurisdictions adopting a shared-resource model, data is considered as a shared resource that is managed and controlled by public entities in a centralized fashion. While market dynamics are still present, and encouraged, private accumulation of power over data is limited primarily through direct public interventions. Protections are established for data generators (individuals) through the establishment of minimum rights. Yet, the ultimate control over data, and related flows and infrastructures, is left to public authorities.

China is most emblematic case of a jurisdiction that is implementing a public-focused model. Characterized by a state-centric structure, the emergence of an internal market for data occurs having in view the interest of the collectivity. Following the overarching developmental goal, enshrined in the notion of Common Prosperity,[58] data governance policy pursues a two-fold objective. First, the recent emergence of a data governance framework is intended to pursue stability for social, economic, and financial purposes, while maintaining national security. Second, data policies aim at bolstering and supporting the competitive dynamics to promote innovation, through the development of an internal digital market.[59]

This twofold objective results in public-private relationships that evolved in a co-dependent manner. While prior to 2020, data was largely treated in a way that was functionally similar to the U.S. approach, whereby a small number of large firms gathered and traded data on consumer behavior, the central control to curb excessive accumulation of power in private hands became more dominant with a series of legislative and policy interventions.[60] Furthermore, over the past decade, the domestic market was largely protected from foreign competition. This combination of factors led to the development of national champions, such as Alibaba, Weibo, Baidu, and QQ as well as technical mechanisms to block data inflows and outflows. In fact, the existence of indigenous incumbent firms led to develop institutional

---

[58] The "Common Prosperity" agenda was set in various official announcements. In particular, see CCCPC (Central Committee of the Communist Party of China) and SCC (State Council of China), 2021, "14th Five-Year Plan (2021–2025) for National Economic and Social Development and the Long-Range Objectives through the Year 2035."

[59] Rogier Creemers, *China's Conception of Cyber Sovereignty*, in GOVERNING CYBERSPACE: BEHAVIOR, POWER, AND DIPLOMACY 107 (D. Broeders & Bibi van den Berg eds., 2020).

[60] Together, the 2017 Cybersecurity law, 2021 Data Security Law, and 2021 Personal Information Protection Law limit private company dominance of data.

capacity for the central government to monitor a vast amount of data.[61] As a result, data flows and access have been more easily governed and deployed as a part of a general strategy to achieve overarching policy goals, such as socio-economic stability, innovation, and growth. Ultimately, the data circulating in mainland China amount to almost a third of global movements.[62]

In the past years, a "cyber sovereignty" framework has been developed and gradually enacted to promote innovation under a state-centric framework. The central pillars of this framework are three fundamental laws: the 2017 Cybersecurity law, 2021 Data Security Law, and 2021 Personal Information Protection Law (PIPL). The overall approach is reflected in a new State Council policy framework enacted in August 2021.[63] While control over data under the emerging system follows an individual-based model, similar to the one deployed in the EU—whereby personal data are inalienable and non-personal data can be freely disposed—ultimate control over data belongs to the central government. Not only does the government have access to data, it also mandates data collection and analysis in both the public and private sector, with a focus on enhancing the Social Credit Score as a central mechanism for monitoring. Moreover, although the government allows un-inhibited flows internally, data can only leave or enter China with express government permission.[64]

This state-based data governance style extends to a shared banking paradigm and in fact has been implemented most directly in this context, with a series of regulatory interventions triggered by concerns about Ant Financial leading to a related series of regulatory changes specifically targeting Ant in some cases, addressing the financial sector more generally in others, and in some addressing data and cybersecurity requirements more generally. Financial data is treated as a public resource, under the control of the

---

[61] China blocks access to 10 of the top 25 top global websites creating a parallel Internet for domestically dominant platform to flourish, *see* Sebastian Hermes et al., *Breeding Grounds of Digital Platforms: Exploring the Sources of American Platform Domination, China's Platform Self-Sufficiency, and Europe's Platform Gap*, ECIS (2020) (discussing the access dynamic between online platforms around the world).

[62] Aho and Duffield, *supra* note 25; Wei Yin, *A Comparison of the US and EU Regulatory Responses to China's state Capitalism: Implication, Issue and Direction*, 19 ASIA EUR. J. 1–25 (2021) (discussing the size of China's state-centric form of capitalism).

[63] Implementation Outline for the Construction of a Government under the Rule of Law (2021–2025), issued by the Central Committee of the Communist Party of China and the State Council, Aug. 11, 2021. Available at http://www.xinhuanet.com/2021-08/11/c_1127752490.htm.

[64] Angela Huyue Zhang, *Agility Over Stability: China's Great Reversal in Regulating the Platform Economy*, University of Hong Kong Faculty of Law Research Paper No. 2021/36 (2021) (highlighting China's expanding regulatory oversight via antitrust, financial, and data regulation).

central government. The largest Chinese digital platforms and BigTechs are entrusted to gather data that feed into the users' social credit score and other credit, commercial and financial scoring systems, both public and proprietary. For this purpose data generated from dispute resolution cases, contract fulfillment, and other financial activities contribute to determine these various credit scores.[65] WeChat—an omnichannel platform with 1 billion active users owned by Tencent—feeds the information back to the Chinese government to build personalized emotional, behavioral, and physiological data and add to user health portfolios.[66] Similarly, the Chinese authorities have provided express lists of essential and nonessential data that financial service providers can request from users.[67] More profoundly, with a recent regulatory intervention, the People's Bank of China together with other financial supervisory authorities, ordered 13 of the largest technology firms to unbundle and restructure their business in order to separate the Internet-based activities from financial activities; to the undertake the latter type of activities a license is required.[68] As a result, financial services developed to support the data economy are brought squarely within the financial regulation perimeter to "break [the] information monopoly" and "enhance the sense of social responsibility."[69]

Thus, China is taking a very different avenue to the United States or EU, although all three are seeking to address similar concerns around financial stability, consumer protection, national security, competitiveness, and innovation.

---

[65] Lizhi Liu & Barry R. Weingast, *Taobao, Federalism, and the Emergence of Law, Chinese Style*, 102 MINN. L. REV. 1563 (2017).

[66] Michael Paulsen & Jesper Tække, *Acting with and against Big Data in School and Society: The Big Democratic Questions of Big Data*, 5 J. COMM. & MEDIA STUD. 15 (2020); Lizhi Liu, *The Rise of Data Politics: Digital China and the World*, 56 STUD. COMP. INT'L DEV. 45 (2021). Quan Li et al., *A Framework for Big Data Governance to Advance RHINs: A Case Study of China*, 7 IEEE ACCESS 50330 (2019); Lulu Yilun Chen, *China Considers Creating State-Backed Company to Oversee Tech Data*, BLOOMBERG (Mar. 24, 2021), https://www.bloomberg.com/news/articles/2021-03-24/china-is-said-to-mull-state-backed-company-to-oversee-tech-data.

[67] *China to Rein in Mobile Apps' Collection of Personal Data, Technology*, BUS. TIMES (Mar. 22, 2021), https://www.businesstimes.com.sg/technology/china-to-rein-in-mobile-apps-collection-of-personal-data.

[68] THE PEOPLE'S BANK OF CHINA, FINANCIAL REGULATORS HAVE JOINT REGULATORY TALK WITH INTERNET PLATFORM ENTERPRISES ENGAGED IN FINANCIAL BUSINESSES (2021) (the 13 firms include Tencent, Du Xiaoman Financial, JD Finance, ByteDance, Meituan Finance, DiDi Finance, Lufax, Airstar Digital Technology, 360 DigiTech, Sina Finance, Suning Finance, Gome Finance and Ctrip Finance.).

[69] *Id.*

D. Hybrid Models

Jurisdictions can be categorized depending on whether they prioritize market dynamics, individual rights, or public interests, resulting in archetypical models. In existing jurisdictional contexts, although different domestic approaches are epitomizing such archetypes, a balance between the interests of different categories of actors always occurs. This is to say that "pure" market-based, individual-based, and public-focused models for financial data governance do not exist. Each real-world model is, to a different extent, the result of a balance, where stronger priority is given more prominently to one of the three main constituencies. When the resulting model does not have a distinct prioritization, hybrid archetypes emerge. In particular, financial regulatory objectives interplay with general data governance objectives, resulting in novel combinations of financial data governance approaches.

As an example, India is emerging as a key leader in strategically harnessing the potential of the digitization and datafication of finance.

The Indian data governance approach reflects a hybrid model that prioritizes the allocation of control to individuals and the state. At the heart of this model is the need to increase financial and public services inclusion through digitalization, combined with a rights-based systems for data and combined with a general market framework.[70]

Over the past 10 years, India has introduced the multilayered digital infrastructure known as the "India Stack." India Stack is a strategy designed to put in place infrastructure to enable wider development, innovation, and digitalization across India. It consists of a range of APIs, open standards, and infrastructure standards that enable access to a broad range of services digitally for Indian citizens.[71] Since 2011, over 90 percent of the Indian population has received a digital identity, and more than half of the identity holders have linked bank accounts to it.[72]

India Stack consists of four layers of infrastructure and standards. The digital identity layer, known as Aadhaar, links individuals to a unique identity number tied to their biometric identifiers—a photograph, fingerprints, iris scans, and demographic information. The second layer consists of the

---

[70] NANDAN NILEKANI, IMAGINING INDIA: THE IDEA OF A RENEWED NATION 140–52 (1st American ed. 2009) (arguing for IT infrastructure as one of the main enablers of the Indian economic growth)

[71] Carrière-Swallow et al., *supra* note 39 (describing the development of the India Stack and noting the upcoming "consent layer" as a further enabler of financial data governance).

[72] *Id.*

Unified Payments Interface (UPI), an API-based interoperable payments interface that can be used by banks and vendors to send money between financial service providers.[73] The third layer is the digitization of documentation and verification, allowing public and private sector participants to authenticate users and perform electronic Know-Your-Client procedures.[74] The last layer is the consent layer, which enables the active management of an individual's data through regulated intermediaries. The government has established, for instance, a voluntary standard consent-providing template that enterprises must use to replace opaque and unclear terms and conditions.[75]

The general financial inclusion ethos dovetails with the objective of promoting competition within the domestic financial sector.[76] The Indian financial landscape is dominated by state-owned banks, holding almost two-thirds of total banking assets.[77] By increasing ease of access to financial services—especially in cashless format—competition within its banking sector is expected to increase.[78]

The resulting hybrid model reflects a strong concentration of control over data infrastructure for broader economic, financial, and developmental purposes. Yet, the powers of state actors are curtailed within the Indian constitutional framework and India's approach to personal data embodied in a bill expected to be enacted in the near future.[79] In this regard, the Supreme Court decided that Aadhaar identities can be required to receive welfare benefits,[80] while also finding that mandatory linking of Aadhaar accounts is generally unconstitutional with limited exceptions.[81] Banks, for example, are not allowed to deny service if the customer has no linked Aadhaar number.[82]

This general trend is reflected also in India's Open Banking strategy, based on account aggregators, whereby financial institutions are mandated to collect data and shared them with a third party. In this context, financial

---

[73] NILEKANI, *supra* note 70.

[74] Carrière-Swallow et al., *supra* note 39.

[75] NILEKANI, *supra* note 70.

[76] RESERVE BANK OF INDIA, NATIONAL STRATEGY FOR FINANCIAL INCLUSION (2019).

[77] *Id.*

[78] Carrière-Swallow et al., *supra* note 39.

[79] Alpha law, *Update on Data Protection Law*, https://www.mondaq.com/india/privacy-protection/1146570/update-on-data-protection-law (last visited Feb. 12, 2022).

[80] Utkash Anand, *4-1 Verdict: Supreme Court Dismisses Pleas Seeking Aadhaar Ruling Review*, HINDUSTAN TIMES, https://www.hindustantimes.com/india-news/41-verdict-supreme-court-dismisses-pleas-seeking-aadhaar-ruling-review-101611189869910.html (last visited Jan. 10, 2022).

[81] Ananya Bhattacharya Anand Nupur, *Aadhaar Is Voluntary—but Millions of Indians Are Already Trapped*, QUARTZ, https://qz.com/india/1351263/supreme-court-verdict-how-indias-aadhaar-id-became-mandatory/ (last visited Jan. 10, 2022).

[82] *Id.*

institutions act as fiduciaries to source data,[83] but they may not access, store, or further sell the acquired data.[84] Account Aggregators authenticate subjects using their Aadhaar ID and map the ID to the available documents in the third layer of the India Stack, gaining access and retrieving the subject's financial assets, liabilities, or cash flows.[85] Through these systems, they enable broader financial service origination, underwriting, disbursement, and payments.[86]

Through Account Aggregators, India is seeking to provide an interoperable data standard. The operational framework extends data sharing to more classes of data than other jurisdictions, lending availability to any data held in the India Stack. The broader aggregate banking approach is also not limited to the relationship between financial services providers and natural persons—the India Stack data is used also by and for legal persons, with no categorical distinction. However, there is no expectation to extend the notion of data aggregators to other areas like search and social media businesses.[87]

India's model can thus be seen as a hybrid approach to financial data governance and one that seeks to provide technological infrastructure to enable the aggregation and use of rights-based data while constraining the dominance of private sector platforms (whether banks or BigTech firms).

These emerging financial data governance models depict an international landscape that is increasingly localized particularly for personal financial data. Reflecting the trend observed in the context of general data governance styles, fragmentation is steering the global data governance framework away from the traditional market-led approach that has underpinned the re-emergence of global finance in tandem with digitization since the 1970s. This trend is particularly evident in the context of financial data that are categorized as "personal" under domestic laws but are also increasingly impacting other forms of financial data.

---

[83] Account aggregators are defined under Section 3 of the Reserve Bank of India Act. For a comment, see Directions regarding Registration and Operations of NBFC—Account Aggregators under section 45-IA of the Reserve Bank of India Act, 1934.

[84] *Id.*

[85] *Id.*

[86] Jame DiBiasio, *What Is the India Stack? Nandan Nilekani Explains*, DIGITAL FINANCE (Jul. 28, 2020), https://www.digfingroup.com/what-is-india-stack/.

[87] Carrière-Swallow et al., *supra* note 39.

VI. Financial Data Sovereignty: Localization vs. Globalization

The intersection between data, finance, law and regulation is not always harmonious. Financial data governance engenders potential conflicts between its core components. Finance is one of the most highly regulated industries, with complex networks of rules addressing financial stability, market integrity, market efficiency, and consumer protection.[88] A dense soft-law architecture ensures a minimum level of international coordination, with overarching policy objectives set by the Group of 20 and standards set by transnational regulatory bodies, such as the BCBS and the FSB. While the regulatory framework for financial data and the emergence of Open Banking initiatives tend to coexist cohesively with financial regulatory policies, the expansion of domestic data governance styles aimed at asserting jurisdictional sovereignty over data, their flows, and infrastructure creates new—at times incongruous—regulatory challenges.

A. Regulatory Fragmentation

In the context of financial data governance, coordination failures can take place at two different levels. At the first level, conflicts pertain to the policy objectives of financial and data regulation.[89] This is to say that at least one of the policy aims of data regulation, such as cybersecurity or privacy of individuals,[90] is at odds (or largely incompatible) with one or more of the policy objectives of financial regulation, such as financial stability, market fairness, and consumer protection or efficiency.[91] The second level of

---

[88] Douglas W. Arner, Financial Stability, Economic Growth, and the Role of Law (2007).

[89] Policy aims formulate the ordering criteria and shape the development of each law branch. These policy aims may be extrapolated from a range of diverse sources including statutes, regulatory principles, or case law. *See* Giuliano G. Castellano and Andrea Tosato, *Commercial Law Intersections*, Hastings L.J. (2021).

[90] In the United States, the right to privacy has been enshrined in the Privacy Act, which stringently regulates how the U.S. government collects data about individuals. See 5 U.S.C. § 552a; In the EU, the respect for private and family life and protection of personal data are a fundamental right enshrined in the European Charter of Fundamental Rights, see Charter of Fundamental Rights of the European Union, Dec. 18, 2000, 2000 O.J.(C364) 1.

[91] This is considered a multi-core CLI coordination failure—one which is characterized by gaps or incongruences that stem from tension between the core spheres of two or more of the converging legal branches. *See* Castellano & Tosato, *supra* note 89.

conflictual relationships comprises contrasts that, while not involving policy objectives, result in incongruencies between dispositive rules and principles,[92] such as those establishing the non-alienability of personal data, or "operative prepositions,"[93] like the rules regulating APIs or the format and modes in which customers data must be collected.[94]

An example of a coordination failure of the first level involves the frictions between privacy objectives, prudential rules, and efficiency and transparency of payment systems. In cash payments, there is an innate element of full privacy, owing to the inherent anonymity of cash-based transactions. However, such a degree of anonymity, which is a rich ground for money laundering activities, is not a feature of DLT payments.[95] In the context of central bank digital currencies (CBDCs), while anonymity (at least vis-à-vis regulators and enforcement authorities) is not an option, the protection of privacy is critical in many societal contexts.[96] As a public good, privacy is important to ensure a variety of outcomes, from preventing data-based price discrimination, to ensure democratic functions.[97] For this reason, different forms of privacy measures have been considered, including regulatory techniques like government access based solely on issuance of a warrant, or cryptographic methods that automate pseudo-anonymization. Nonetheless, each option requires a compromise, or a trade-off, between policy objectives.[98] A prioritization of privacy objectives will necessarily result in a subordination of financial regulation policies, aiming at ensuring the integrity, fairness, and efficiency of financial markets. In a similar vein, the sole pursuit of financial regulation policies would imply a way to lessen privacy protections. In the context of CBDCs, this is likely to result in a range of different structures reflecting differing balances of societal objectives.

---

[92] This is considered a "coordination failure" characterized by gaps or incongruencies stemming from tensions between different aspects of multiple branches of law. *See* Castellano & Tosato, *supra* note 89 at 1022.

[93] Operative propositions are defined as the rules that "govern their subject matter with a high level of determinacy" and they are typically establishing key technical elements. *See* Castellano & Tosato, *supra* note 89 at 1045.

[94] For example, PSD2 requires the European Banking Authority to develop regulatory technical standards setting technical requirements to be used by payment service providers. *See supra* note 48 Art 98.

[95] Rodney J. Garratt & Maarten RC Van Oordt, *Privacy as a Public Good: A Case for Electronic Cash*, 129 J. OF POLITICAL ECONOMY 2157 (2021).

[96] Ellie Rennie & Stacey Steele, *Privacy and Emergency Payments in a Pandemic: How to Think about Privacy and a Central Bank Digital Currency*, 3 LAW, TECHNOLOGY AND HUMANS 6 (2021).

[97] Bilyana Petkova, *Privacy as Europe's First Amendment*, 25 EUROPEAN L.J. 140 (2019).

[98] Trade-offs require a prioritization of the policy aims of one branch over those of another. *See* Castellano & Tosato, *supra* note 89 at 1036.

However, it is AML that exemplifies the coordination challenge between data governance (data privacy and use) and financial regulation (financial integrity) dispositive rules most directly. AML rules seeks to minimize the criminal and terrorist use of the financial system and are thus based on identifying the identity of those seeking to access the financial system and the origin of their funds. It seeks to ensure that assets enter the economy licitly, under legal ownership. As such, AML regulation generally consists of numerous compliance rules for financial service provides but also establishes a growing list of predicate crimes and legal instruments to allow supervisors and law enforcement to detect, prevent, and otherwise combat money-laundering activity. Access to, and accumulation and analysis of financial and other forms of data is central to achieving the goals of both sides of the AML regime, yet this access is being restricted with increasing frequency by data privacy rules.

The international regulatory framework for AML focuses on the role of intermediaries (particularly financial intermediaries such as banks) and law enforcement agencies in collecting data to ensure compliance. AML measures by financial institutions are managed via a risk-based assessment (RBA) framework, as set by the main international AML standard-setting body—the Financial Action Task Force. Under the RBA, each financial services provider must create risk profiles for their clients, products, correspondent banks, and other parts of the financial service supply chain. These profiles feed off data that the bank must collect through its own sources, from B2B services, its own affiliates, public, or other sources. Law enforcement and financial intelligence agencies will likewise develop similar profiles.

An issue with dispositive rules and AML has emerged particularly in the context of Open Banking rules, most dramatically in the EU. Open Banking is a function of retail consumer ownership and/or control of their financial data. This ownership and/or control entails classifying an array of types of information, including creditworthiness, customer preferences, but also transaction histories. In the EU, PSD2—which mandates the Open Banking regime—provides a level of data protection for personal data, with an exception for processing personal data by obliged entities when "necessary to safeguard the prevention, investigation and detection of payment fraud."[99] However, a later law, GDPR, establishes a higher level of data protection that, while providing similar exceptions applies them particularly to processing

---

[99] Art. 94.

personal data in "criminal cases," not collection.[100] In 2019, the European Data Protection Service (EDPS) requested the cease of operations of FIU. net—a core tool for the exchange of financial intelligence between Member States operated by Europol—due to a lack of status as criminals.[101] In early 2021, a similar conflict led the EDPS to require Europol to delete huge databases on individuals with no criminal status. Through these direct conflicts in approach, AML supervisors lost access to data to undertake their functions and share with regulated entities to construct in pursuit of their own obligations.

Thus, both from the standpoint of the industry seeking to comply with conflicting requirements of data regulation and financial regulation as well as from the standpoint of conflicting regulatory objectives resulting in suboptimal results, there is a need for a process of cross-consideration of objectives and contents in the context of data governance. It is no longer possible for a siloed approach as had evolved in the EU in the context of personal and financial data rules.[102] Financial data governance must seek to balance competing regulatory objectives.

This is also a pressing issue as both financial data governance and general data governance have extraterritorial reach to to gain sovereignty over data and data flow beyond jurisdictional border. The result is an increase compartementalization of data.

B. Territorialization and Data Localization

The second set of challenges to the paradigm of global financial flows regards the growing tendency of data territorialization. Data territorialization is the demarcation of digital space. It involves asserting digital sovereignty via rules for data mobility, ownership, alienability, and other factors. Through the

---

[100] Art. 2 (2)(c).

[101] Foivi Mouzakiti, *Cooperation between Financial Intelligence Units in the European Union: Stuck in the Middle between the General Data Protection Regulation and the Police Data Protection Directive*, 11 New J. of European Criminal Law 351 (2020). See also the recent discussion over a Judgment of the Court of Justice of the European in *WM and Sovim SA* to revoke public access to ultimate beneficial owner registries, highlighting the substantial risk the balancing adds to financial integrity. Mathias Siems, *Privacy vs shareholder transparency: did the ECJ decision in WM and Sovim SA impair the global fight against money laundering?*, 60 *Common Market Law Review* (2023) no. 4, 1137-1157

[102] See Emilios Avgouleas & Alexandris Seratakis, *Governing the Digital Finance Value Chain in the EU: MIFID II, the Digital Package, and the Large Gaps between*, European Co. & Financial L. Rev. (2021).

process of territorialization, jurisdictions seek to protect and maximize the value of domestic data in the context of their wider data governance strategy. These purposes can range from the establishment of national ID regimes for financial inclusion purposes, like India's Aadhar system; data localization requirements for certain types of data, as China requires for domestic and foreign companies in a range of sectors; or even the imposition of extraterritorial data rules, required for personal data under the GDPR. Financial data is also impacted by this process but also by its own objectives, particularly financial stability but also national security and competitiveness.

Unlike many other forms of data, financial data is—until recently—a partial exception to general trends of data territorialization. To allow access to international markets, and fulfill the derivative goal of financial stability, and the functioning of the economy itself, certain financial data are expressly free to traverse jurisdictions. This is best exemplified by the special status financial data receive in bilateral trade agreements, using those enacted by the United States, EU, and China as examples.

An example of the territorialization of financial data is Open Banking. Open Banking, by mandating certain technical levels of interoperability from banks, via data portability or API standards, integrates client financial data into a broader—usually domestic—data system.

More significantly, reflecting a trend away from the branch model and toward separately incorporated, capitalized, and regulated subsidiarity requirements in the aftermath of the 2008 Global Financial Crisis, similar trends toward "ring-fencing" and localization of regulatory, customer and risk management data of regulated financial institutions have emerged. In this context, an increasing range of financial regulators around the world are requiring not only customer data but also regulatory and risk management data locally or, at the least, ensure immediate and unconditional access of such data to regulators. With the digitalization of finance and the fact that an increasing range of financial businesses are not only digital but in fact digitally native, this is posing a significant challenge to the dominant operating paradigm of the global digital financial services industry: free flow of data enabling centralized control, use and analysis in pursuit of business objectives, risk management needs, and regulatory requirements.

These data localization requirements are being driven by financial stability concerns (the need for regulators to access data in order to meet their mandates as well as to safeguard core systems of financial institutions and infrastructure, a major concern for over 20 years as a result of 9/11 and Y2K), by national security concerns (particularly relating to cybersecurity but also increasingly geopolitical), and by competitiveness concerns (maximizing the benefits of financial data in the context of an overall financial data governance strategy, increasingly in tandem with a wider general data governance approach).

The question emerging from financial data localization trends—resulting from a range of prudential, national security, and competitiveness concerns—is their significance. From the standpoint of the financial industry, such data localization requirements—particularly when the extraterritorial reach of one jurisdiction for data for instance in the context of a globally systemically important financial institution (G-SIFI) conflicts with localization requirements of another—are an impossible burden and one that will undermine both the benefits of cross-border finance as well as its regulation and risk management.

However, we argue that they are also problematic from the standpoint of the overall objectives of global financial stability, market integrity and consumer protection.

VII. The Data Sovereignty Challenge

Will financial data territorialization, localization, and competition fundamentally challenge financial globalization? Or will data gaps and regulatory arbitrage as a result of financial data localization sow the seeds of the next financial crisis? We suggest that data localization will remain the status quo of financial data for a variety of reasons. It is critical to the fulfillment of policy objectives, it often lacks interoperability with the financial data of other regimes, and the variety of licensing frameworks ensure that even the same entity may be generating different data in different jurisdictions.

Unlike transnational data governance,[103] global finance has a very well-developed framework for international cooperation and coordination. This framework provides a mechanism for cooperation in areas relating to transnational financial data. Existing mechanisms support standardization of

---

[103] Arner et al., *supra* note 6; Institute of International Finance, *Strategic Framework for Digital Economic Cooperation* (2021) (arguing for the need of a new permanent structure to help guide international digital economic cooperation); VIKRAM HAKSAR CARRIERRE-SWALLOW, YAN, GIDDINGS, ANDREW, ISLAM, EMRAN, KAO, KATHLEEN, KOPP, EMANUEL, QUIROS ROMERO, & GABRIEL, TOWARD A GLOBAL APPROACH TO DATA IN THE DIGITAL AGE (2021) (presenting a case for global data policy frameworks).

208 FINANCIAL DATA GOVERNANCE AND DATA SOVEREIGNTY

disclosure and reporting requirements (essentially the framework for many forms of financial data creation and assurance) as well as cooperation in cross-border enforcement in both market conduct and market integrity, with well-developed cross-border cooperation and information sharing in the contexts of payments, banking, and securities.

As financial data harmonization increases, an expansion of current disclosure requirements due diligence rules is required. Necessarily, this will result in a more assertive utilization of RegTech and SupTech solutions that are capable of drawing on more timely data, and combining data from a variety of sources to build prudential models about traditional and novel financial services.[104] These systems will increasingly depend on the coordination of several foundational infrastructures (like telecommunications), along with digital and financial infrastructures (like mobile data services, data repositories, and payment and settlement services) to facilitate the collection of data from new sources.

More profoundly, a stronger institutional framework at the international level might be needed. A key risk is that the fragmentation, in various guises,[105] will fracture the existing international financial architecture. The global financial architecture has continued to function more effectively than most other aspects of international cooperation and institutions owing to its continuous evolution. In general, as we have argued elsewhere, for areas beyond finance, a Digital Stability Board similar to the Financial Stability Board would provide an important cooperative mechanism going forward.[106]

Looking forward, important areas where shared interests are likely to support further financial data governance cooperation and harmonization include cybersecurity and other forms of TechRisk, and sustainability.

Perhaps the greatest opportunities, however, lie in new technologies.

---

[104] GLOBAL FINANCIAL INNOVATION NETWORK, REGTECH & SUPTECH WORKSTREAM UPDATE (2021), https://static1.squarespace.com/static/5db7cdf53d173c0e010e8f68/t/601d7c09cbd7bc325 5b685bf/1612545036876/GFIN_RegTech_SupTech_Workstream_Update+-+Final.pdf; Ioannis Anagnostopoulos, *Fintech and Regtech: Impact on Regulators and Banks*, 100 J. ECON. & BUS. 7 (2018).

[105] Mark Austen, *Addressing Fragmentation in Asian Markets: Data Localisation – GFMA's Data Privacy, Security and Mobility Principles* (2019); ASIFMA, *Addressing Market Fragmentation through the Policymaking Lifecycle* (2020) (presenting emerging examples of market fragmentation tied to sustainable finance, data privacy, AML compliance, and operational resilience).

[106] Arner et al., *supra* note 6; Institute of International Finance, *Strategic Framework for Digital Economic Cooperation* (2021) (arguing for the need of a new permanent structure to help guide international digital economic cooperation); VIKRAM HAKSAR CARRIERRE-SWALLOW, YAN, GIDDINGS, ANDREW, ISLAM, EMRAN, KAO, KATHLEEN, KOPP, EMANUEL, QUIROS ROMERO, & GABRIEL, TOWARD A GLOBAL APPROACH TO DATA IN THE DIGITAL AGE (2021) (presenting a case for global data policy frameworks).

THE DATA SOVEREIGNTY CHALLENGE   209

In addition to the harmonization and a reinforced architectural framework supporting financial data governance, the financial sector is uniquely placed to develop technological solutions to the challenges of data localization and territorialization. Different technological systems have been developed.[107] All systems originate from the genesis format.[108] Under this model, the data collector has exclusive control over collected data.[109] However, there is an increasing range of variants being offered.

Jurisdictions could agree on pockets of rules for how and what data can be transferred and through which channels. A variety of technologies are already available to help secure such messages, from blockchain applications; to security-by-design solutions that can help guarantee security of transmissions medium; to AI that can rapidly analyze the content of transmitted data. SWIFT, or other systems of payments messaging, or credit card messaging could adopt such a system, for example. The data from local banks could transmit to a central standardized unit that automatically would process whether and where the data is allowed to route through in accordance with agreement by jurisdictions, similarly to how Qualified Trust Service Providers under the EU PSD2 regime certify digital ID certificates by pinging back to domestic authorities. These kinds of pockets will be vital for critical functions like cybersecurity, market integrity, and increasingly—sustainable financing, via technical, trust, and identification requirements for data transfers.

Concurrently, the private sector could facilitate the adoption of new technologies that would lessen regulatory tensions. These technologies use new techniques to reach the outcomes necessary for offering their products and services, without needing to interfere with or even directly access the data of other entities with or across jurisdictions. Federated data systems that divide bundles of data across many different systems can ensure that no party has a data monopoly,[110] whereby cloud data centers can ensure that it is always accessible though cloud infrastructure does raise separate financial stability, national security, and competitiveness issues of its own.[111] Through

---

[107] Bruno Carballa Smichowski, *Alternative Data Governance Models: Moving Beyond One-Size-Fits-All Solutions*, 54 INTERECONOMICS 222 (2019).

[108] *Id.*

[109] *Id.*

[110] World Economic Forum, *Federated Data Systems: Balancing Innovation and Trust in the Use of Sensitive Data* (2019) (discussing federated approaches to sensitive data in healthcare).

[111] See Financial Stability Board, *Third-Party Dependencies in Cloud Services Considerations on Financial Stability Implications* (2019); Financial Stability Board, *Regulatory and Supervisory Issues Relating to Outsourcing and Third-Party Relationships: Discussion Paper* (2020) (presenting benefits and risks of third-party reliance).

210 FINANCIAL DATA GOVERNANCE AND DATA SOVEREIGNTY

federated data analytics, banks and supervisors may not need to access the data of other parties at all, instead only requesting that they run the necessary portion of data analytics locally. Lastly, zero knowledge proof protocols enable secure responses from federated or decentralized data system without any access to or knowledge of the underlying data.[112] From the standpoint of infrastructure for financial data, blockchain and other decentralized structures therefore offer potential approaches, in particular from the standpoint of networking various data sources and enabling proprietary analytics but require a change in mindset about the nature and use of financial data.[113]

This change in mindset, technology, and policy approach would mean evolving from the dominant paradigm of financial data centralization to one focused on federated storage and analytics. We argue that, in fact, such a transition would not only be the best way to address the challenges of fragmentation of financial data governance but also to achieve the broader objectives of financial stability, market integrity, consumer protection, and market efficiency. More than any other, the financial services industry and its regulators are well-placed to make this transition, necessary as part of the ongoing datafication of finance and its regulation.

---

[112] *See* Teresa Alameda, *Zero Knowledge Proof: How to Maintain Privacy in a Data-Based World*, NEWS BBVA (Sept. 11, 2019), https://www.bbva.com/en/zero-knowledge-proof-how-to-maintain-privacy-in-a-data-based-world/; Nihal R. Goawravaram, *Zero Knowledge Proofs and Applications to Financial Regulation* (2018) (introducing how zero knowledge proofs can be used in finance via a variety of examples, mostly tied to disclosing information without showing financial holdings).

[113] Douglas W. Arner et al., *The Identity Challenge in Finance: From Analogue Identity to Digitized Identification to Digital KYC Utilities*, 20 EUROPEAN BUSINESS ORGANIZATION LAW REVIEW 55 (2019).

PART III
TRADE REGULATION

9

Data Sovereignty and Trade Agreements

Three Digital Kingdoms

Henry Gao[*]

Sovereignty is, paradoxically, one of the most important yet misunderstood terms in international law. This is especially true in the international trade law area, where sovereignty and international obligations are often pitted against each other when countries try to enforce binding legal obligations through compulsory dispute settlement systems. This led to the Great 1994 Sovereignty Debate in 1994,[1] when the World Trade Organization (WTO) was coming into being. Some 20 years later, it became a hot issue again when the U.S. administration led by President Trump tried to cite sovereignty as the justification for many of its WTO-inconsistent measures, especially those ostensibly grounded on "national security." Due to space constraints, this chapter does not unpack the many challenges posed to international trade law by sovereignty. Instead, it focuses on an emerging area: data regulation in trade agreements, which best illustrates the conflict between international trade regulation and sovereignty in the digital era.

The chapter starts with an in-depth analysis of the elusive concept of data sovereignty, by trying to blend the classical definitions of canonical authors with the unique features of the data economy. It then conducts an empirical examination on the current approaches to data sovereignty in trade agreements by the three leading players, that is, the United States, China, and the EU. While noting the divergent approaches taken by the three, the chapter also concludes with observations on possible future convergence of the three approaches.

---

[*] This research/project is supported by the National Research Foundation, Singapore, under its Emerging Areas Research Projects (EARP) Funding Initiative. Any opinions, findings, and conclusions or recommendations expressed in this material are those of the author(s) and do not reflect the views of National Research Foundation, Singapore.

[1] John H. Jackson, *The Great 1994 Sovereignty Debate: United States Acceptance and Implementation of the Uruguay Round Results*, 36 COLUM. J. TRANSNAT'L L. 157, 182 (1997).

Henry Gao, *Data Sovereignty and Trade Agreements* In: *Data Sovereignty*. Edited by: Anupam Chander and Haochen Sun, Oxford University Press. © Oxford University Press 2023. DOI: 10.1093/oso/9780197582794.003.0010

I. Data Sovereignty

Sovereignty is one of the most fundamental concepts in modern international law. At the same time, however, it is also one of the most "controversial"[2] concepts with a "long and troubled history."[3] Despite their disagreements on the exact meaning of the term, most international lawyers seem to agree that sovereignty has a "well established" status as either a "highly ambiguous"[4] or "notoriously amorphous" concept.[5] Indeed, the concept is so contested that even many leading international lawyers deem it better to just give up the term, which, called the "S word"[6] by Louis Henkin, is "a mistake, an illegitimate offspring"[7] that is "largely unnecessary and better avoided."[8]

Nonetheless, I am still of the view that we should try to fathom the meaning of sovereignty, as it is "one of those powerful words which has its own existence as an active force within social consciousness" that can not only "represent reality," but also "play a leading part in creating and transforming reality."[9] This is most evident in the repeated reference to sovereignty by national governments in various settings even in the digital age. Thus, without pinning down its meaning, it would not be possible to understand some of the key contentions and approaches in data governance and trade regulation.

In this regard, I will start with classical authors. While the concept of sovereignty has long been used in Europe, Jean Boden is commonly accepted as the "father" of the modern usage of the concept "sovereignty"[10] as he engaged in "the first systematic discussion of the nature" of the concept.[11] In his book *Les six Livres de la Republique*, Bodin defines sovereignty as "the absolute & perpetual power in a Republic."[12] This definition focuses on the internal

---

[2] *See* LASSA OPPENHEIM, 1 INTERNATIONAL LAW – A TREATISE 103 (1905) ("There exists perhaps no conception the meaning of which is more controversial than that of sovereignty.").

[3] JAMES R. CRAWFORD, THE CREATION OF STATES IN INTERNATIONAL LAW 26 (1st ed. 1979).

[4] Hent Kalmo & Quentin Skinner, *Introduction: A Concept in Fragments*, in SOVEREIGNTY IN FRAGMENTS: THE PAST, PRESENT AND FUTURE OF A CONTESTED CONCEPT 4 (Hent Kalmo & Quentin Skinner eds., 2010).

[5] Andrew Keane Woods, *Litigating Data Sovereignty*, 128 YALE L.J. 328, 360 (2018).

[6] Louis Henkin, *That "S" Word: Sovereignty, and Globalization, and Human Rights, Et Cetera*, 68 FORDHAM L. REV. 1 (1999).

[7] *Id.* at 2.

[8] Louis Henkin, INTERNATIONAL LAW: POLITICS AND VALUES 9–10 (1995).

[9] STÉPHANE BEAULAC, THE POWER OF LANGUAGE IN THE MAKING OF INTERNATIONAL LAW: THE WORD SOVEREIGNTY IN BODIN AND VATTEL AND THE MYTH OF WESTPHALIA 1 (2004).

[10] *See id.* at 101 (citing Jacques Maritain, *The Concept of Sovereignty*, in IN DEFENSE OF SOVEREIGNTY 41, 43 (Wladyslaw J. Stankiewicz ed., 1969)).

[11] CHARLES E. MERRIAM, HISTORY OF THE THEORY OF SOVEREIGNTY SINCE ROUSSEAU 13 (1900); JEAN BODIN, LES SIX LIVRES DE LA REPUBLIQUE [SIX BOOKS OF THE COMMONWEALTH] 84 (1576).

[12] BODIN, *supra* note 11, 122 ("La SOUVERAINETÉ est la puissance absolue & perpétuelle d'une République").

DATA SOVEREIGNTY   215

paradigm of the domestic pyramid of power by placing sovereignty as "the most supreme power in the hierarchical organizational structure of society, that is, the highest unified power—as opposed to a subordinate decentralized one—free from any temporal authority."[13]

While this definition does provide a good explanation of sovereignty in the domestic context, it might run into difficulty at the international level, where all states are regarded as equal sovereigns in principle, yet in reality countries do differ in their relative powers depending on their military or economic might. The solution to this problem was provided by Emer de Vattel, who transposed the concept of sovereignty from the national level onto the international plane.[14] In contrast to the internal paradigm of Rodin, Vattel shifted to the external dimension by defining sovereignty as the "exclusivity of power without," that is, "a political body which is the sole representative of the people externally and which is not submitted to any foreign state or to any higher law externally."[15] By focusing on such "incorporated independent authority," Vattel provided the foundation for the discourse on sovereignty under international law, which is based on the fundamental notion of states as independent actors.

It is easy to see where Bodin and Vattel differ, in that the former defines sovereignty vis-à-vis its subjects while the latter places sovereignty in the context of external powers, be they foreign states or international law. Despite their differences, both of these definitions focus on the "general norm"[16] or the "routine" situations.[17] In reality, however, the power of sovereignty is often manifested in decisions concerning "borderline cases" or the "exceptions."[18] This led Carl Schmitt to propose a new definition of sovereignty by stating, at the very beginning of his *Four Chapters on the Concept of Sovereignty*, that "[s]overeign is he who decides on the exception."[19] As illustrated in later discussions in this chapter, the focus on exceptions is also fitting to discussions on data sovereignty, which often needs to wrestle

---

[13] BEAULAC, *supra* note 9, at 122 (citing DOMINIQUE CARREAU, DROIT INTERNATIONAL 15 (7th ed. 2001)).

[14] BEAULAC, *supra* note 9, at 137 (citing E. JOUANNET, EMER DE VATTEL ET L'ÉMERGENCE DOCTRINALE DU DROIT INTERNATIONAL CLASSIQUE 404 [1998]).

[15] *Id.* at 137.

[16] CARL SCHMITT, POLITICAL THEOLOGY: FOUR CHAPTERS ON THE CONCEPT OF SOVEREIGNTY 6 (2008).

[17] *Id.* at 5.

[18] *Id.*

[19] *Id.*

with issues such as exceptions to the general rules on data flow and location of data.

The discussions above reveal a common theme among the definitions by classical authors: power. This is explicit in Bodin ("highest power") and Vattel ("underived power"), and implicit in Schmitt ("exceptional power").[20] Now fast forward to the digital age, where technology giants pose serious competition to the national governments in terms of the powers they possess. In this sense, digital firms could be said to have powers rivaling that of traditional sovereigns. This led Lawrence Lessig to extend the concept of sovereignty by equating it with "control."[21] He developed two models of sovereignty depending on who has the control. The first model of "citizen-sovereignties" deal with institutions such as universities, social clubs, and churches, which "give consumers control over the rules that will govern them."[22] On the other hand, in the model of "merchant-sovereignties" the rules are imposed by the merchants and not chosen by the consumers.[23] These rules are imposed on a "take it or leave it" basis and the only choice consumers can make is whether to go to McDonald's or Burger King. But unlike the switching of your lunch spots in the physical space, which is virtually costless, it can be rather costly to try to switch communities in the cyberspace, as "you must give up everything in a move from one cyber-community to another," which explains the power of digital giants in cyberspace.[24]

Despite the lack of a precise and commonly agreed-upon definition, sovereignty is still regarded as one of the most indispensable concepts in international law. The same, however, cannot be said of the concept of data sovereignty. To start with, the concept has been dismissed by many as just an oxymoron, because data by its nature transcends borders but sovereignty traditionally has been understood to be confined to within borders. Further complications would arise when data is generated, processed, stored, and disseminated in different jurisdictions, as it has become commonplace in the cyberspace these days. Thus, it has been rather difficult to provide a satisfactory definition of data sovereignty, with earlier attempts focusing either on the ethical dimension of the ownership and control of the data by the individual[25] or the technical dimension of "the coupling of stored data

---

[20] *Id.* at 11.

[21] LAWRENCE LESSIG, CODE VERSION 2.0 283 (2006).

[22] *Id.* at 287.

[23] *Id.* at 286–87.

[24] *Id.* at 290.

[25] Ai Thanh Ho, *Towards a Privacy-enhanced Social Networking Site* 50 (Apr. 2012) (Ph.D. dissertation, Université de Montréal), https://papyrus.bib.umontreal.ca/xmlui/bitstream/handle/1866/

authenticity and geographical location in the cloud."[26] After reviewing 602 papers discussing sovereignty in the digital context, a comprehensive survey on the usage of the concept in academic literature classifies six different means to address data sovereignty.[27] However, the survey concludes that "data sovereignty" is typically employed to refer "in some way to meaningful control, ownership, and other claims to data or data infrastructures."[28] Such emphasis on control and power is consistent with the classical concepts of sovereignty discussed earlier.

As illustrated by the foregoing discussion, defining data sovereignty has been an endeavor fraught with difficulties. However, as the focus of this chapter is on data sovereignty in the context of trade agreements, it is not really necessary to try to come up with a general definition of data sovereignty. To paraphrase the famous remark made by Bill Clinton when he tried to persuade the U.S. Congress to grant Permanent Normal Trade Status to the China ahead of China's accession to the WTO in 2000, defining data sovereignty in general would be like "trying to nail jello to the wall."[29] Here, however, we merely need to decide what happens when jello hits the wall, that is, the applicable rules when the concept of data sovereignty somehow interacts with the rules under trade agreements.

By narrowing the scope of our inquiry, we can tentatively define data sovereignty in the context of trade agreements as follows: the highest independent power over data trade, which can define rules and exceptions, especially regarding first, border measures such as the cross-border transfer of data; and second, domestic regulations such as data localization requirements. This definition takes into account the key elements of the different variants mentioned earlier, that is, power, independence and exception. It also situates

---

8581/Ho_Ai_2012_these.pdf;jsessionid=8C6B63BC38E30AC76436C22468476E60?sequence=4 (discussing the "data sovereignty principle", i.e., "the data related to an individual belongs to him and that he should stay in control of how these data are used and for which purpose.").

[26] *See* Zachary N.J. Peterson et al., *A Position Paper on Data Sovereignty: The Importance of Geolocating Data in the Cloud, in* Proceedings of the 3rd USENIX Conference on Hot Topics in Cloud Computing 1, https://www.usenix.org/legacy/events/hotcloud11/tech/final_files/Peterson.pdf (using data sovereignty to describe the notion of "establishing data location at a granularity sufficient for placing it within the borders of a particular nation-state.").

[27] Patrik Hummel et al., *Data Sovereignty: A Review*, 8 Big Data & Soc'y 1 (2021).

[28] *Id.* at 12.

[29] Bill Clinton, President, U.S., Speech on China Trade Bill at the Paul H. Nitze School of Advanced International Studies of the Johns Hopkins University (Mar. 9, 2000), https://www.iatp.org/sites/default/files/Full_Text_of_Clintons_Speech_on_China_Trade_Bi.htm.

218 DATA SOVEREIGNTY AND TRADE AGREEMENTS

the concept in the unique context of data trade, with the cross-border fungibility of data as a key feature.

II. Data Sovereignty and Trade Agreements

When it comes to data governance, there are three main groups of players: the individual, which provides the raw data, and uses the processed data; the firm, which processes the raw inputs from the consumer, and usually controls such data; and the state, which monitors and regulates the data use by the first two groups. Their different interests often result in conflicting priorities, with the individual advocating privacy protection, the firm promoting unhindered data flow, while the state focusing on the security implications.

The clashes between the three groups often result in various restrictive measures, with the most common type being restrictions on cross-border data flow in the name of the protection of individual privacy or national security.[30] More recently, however, data localization requirements have also become popular, with the following as main variations:[31]

(1) Local commercial presence or residency requirements: The origin for such requirements can be traced back to the General Agreement on Trade in Services (GATS), where service providers are often required to have a local commercial presence before they can provide a service. While such requirements could potentially affect all service sectors, e-commerce is especially vulnerable as it is often detached from traditional brick-and-mortar establishments.

(2) Local infrastructure requirements: These include both hardware requirements for service providers to use computing facilities located in the host territory and software requirements to use computer processing and/or storage services located in such territory.

(3) Local content requirements. Depending on the *modus operandi* of the local content requirements, this obligation can be further divided into two categories. One is granting preferences or advantages to goods

[30] MARK WU, DIGITAL TRADE-RELATED PROVISIONS IN REGIONAL TRADE AGREEMENTS: EXISTING MODELS AND LESSONS FOR THE MULTILATERAL TRADE SYSTEM 22–23 (2017), http://e15initiative. org/publications/digital-trade-related-provisions-in-regional-trade-agreements-existing-models-and-lessons-for-the-multilateral-trade-system.

[31] Henry Gao, *Digital or Trade? The Contrasting Approaches of China and US to Digital Trade*, 21 J. INT'L ECON. L. 297, 303–04 (2018).

or electronically transmitted contents produced in a territory, or to local computing facilities or computer processing or storage services supplied locally. The other is requiring foreign service suppliers to purchase or use local goods or electronically transmitted contents.

(4) Local technology requirements. This can also be broken down into two types of obligations. The first is the requirement for foreign service suppliers to transfer technologies as a condition of providing a service. This is often tied to the requirement to have a local partner. The other is the requirement for foreign service suppliers to purchase or use local technologies.

While data flow restrictions and data localization requirements are both barriers to e-commerce, it is important to note the differences between the two. Data flow restrictions curb cross-border transfer of data. They normally target the outflow, but can also affect the inflow, such as banning access to certain foreign websites due to its contents. As such restrictions uniformly affect both domestic and foreign firms alike, they are more akin to a most-favored nation (MFN) treatment type of restriction. While such constraints make it more difficult for firms to move data around, they could reduce data breach risks for individuals and regulatory costs for states. On the other hand, data localization requirements tend to affect mostly foreign firms so they can be viewed more as a National Treatment issue. Such requirements obviously would increase costs for foreign firms, but they could also increase risks of personal data breach and even regulatory costs for states due to the duplication of data on both local and offshore servers.[32] Given the different ways MFN and national treatment obligations under trade agreements are structured, a proper understanding of the differences between the two restrictions can help inform regulatory approaches and negotiations in trade agreements.

At the same time, notwithstanding their differences, it is also important to keep in mind that both types of restrictions could have major implications for international trade, especially given the growing importance of data to trade in general. Moreover, due to their binding natures, trade agreements have also become the forum of choice for regulating data issues at the international level.

---

[32] *See* Anupam Chander & Uyên P. Lê, *Data Nationalism*, 64 EMORY L.J. 677, 719–21 (2015).

220 DATA SOVEREIGNTY AND TRADE AGREEMENTS

Table 9.1 Three Data sovereignty Models

	Free Flow of Data	Prohibition on Data Localization	Data Sovereignty Regime
US	Yes	Yes	Firm Sovereignty
China	No	No	State Sovereignty
EU	Yes, but	Yes, but	Individual Sovereignty

While all countries would agree that there is a need to strike a balance between the clashing interests of different stakeholders, their approaches often differ in practice. Some jurisdictions prioritize the need to safeguard the privacy of users. A good example in this regard is the General Data Protection Regulation ("GDPR") of the EU, which recognizes "[t]he protection of natural persons in relation to the processing of personal data" as "a fundamental right."[33] On the other hand, some jurisdictions put the commercial interests of firms first. In the United States, this is reflected in the 1996 Telecommunication Act, which notes that it is "the policy of the United States . . . to preserve . . . free market . . . unfettered by Federal or State regulation."[34] In contrast, national security concerns are often cited to justify restrictions on cross-border data flow, albeit in varying degrees in different countries. A recent example is China's 2017 Cyber Security Law, which imposes several restrictions aiming to "safeguard cyber security, protect cyberspace sovereignty and national security."[35]

These differences in the domestic regulatory frameworks of these countries are also reflected in their trade agreements, which in turn reveals their different approaches to data sovereignty. Using the twin provisions of free flow of data and prohibition of data localization requirements as proxies, we can group the major approaches to data sovereignty and trade agreements into the following three models, with each represented by a major trader.

---

[33] Regulation (EU) 2016/679 of the European Parliament and of the Council of 27 April 2016 on the Protection of Natural Persons with Regard to the Processing of Personal Data and on the Free Movement of such Data, and Repealing Directive 95/46/EC (General Data Protection Regulation), Recital 1, 2016 O.J. (L119) 1 [hereinafter GDPR].

[34] Telecommunication Act of 1996 § 509(b)(2), 47 U.S.C. § 230(b)(2).

[35] Wangluo Anquan Fa (网络安全法) [Cyber Security Law] (promulgated by the Standing Comm. Nat'l People's Cong., Nov. 7, 2016, effective June 1, 2017), art. 1 (China) [hereinafter PRC Cyber Security Law].

III. United States: The Firm Sovereignty Model

As the world's largest economy and until recently, the largest trader, the United States is a highly competitive exporter in both agricultural and industrial goods and services. Thus, the United States has been very aggressive in promoting free trade and dismantling trade barriers in its trade agreements. This approach is also carried over into the digital age, with the U.S. trade agreements pioneering the inclusion of digital trade issues with an expansive set of obligations.

A. Firm Sovereignty

In particular, two provisions have become the *sine qua non* in the digital trade chapters in U.S. trade agreements, with the recently concluded United States-Mexico-Canada Agreement ("USMCA") as the leading example:

First is the guarantee on free cross-border flow of data by stating that "no Party shall prohibit or restrict the cross-border transfer of information, including personal information, by electronic means";[36] and

Second is the prohibition of data localization requirements by stipulating that "no Party shall require a covered person to use or locate computing facilities in that Party's territory as a condition for conducting business in that territory."[37]

These two provisions provide strong protection of the interests of the firm, which deem the restrictions on cross border flow of data and various localization requirements as obstacles to their ability to conduct businesses across national boundaries. Applying the concept of sovereignty mentioned earlier, the U.S. approach essentially puts the sovereignty into the hands of business firms, so that they have the control of both border measures and domestic regulations.

As we can see from the experiences of China and the EU below, two of the most frequent reasons used by governments to regulate data are protection of privacy or national security. In both of these areas, however, the United States has taken different approaches in its trade agreements.

---

[36] United States-Mexico-Canada Agreement, Can.-Mex.-U.S., art. 19.11, Nov. 30, 2018, 134 Stat. 11 (2020) [hereinafter USMCA].

[37] *Id.* art. 19.12.

222 DATA SOVEREIGNTY AND TRADE AGREEMENTS

B. Privacy as a Consumer Right

On privacy protection, the U.S. trade agreements only require parties to adopt their own legal framework for data protection, which could take many different legal approaches including "comprehensive privacy, personal information or personal data protection laws, sector-specific laws covering privacy, or laws that provide for the enforcement of voluntary undertakings by enterprises relating to privacy."[38] This is very different from the EU approach, which requires its trade partners to adopt GDPR-equivalent clauses. While the U.S. agreements also calls for Parties to "take into account principles and guidelines of relevant international bodies,"[39] the examples only include "the APEC Privacy Framework and the OECD Recommendation of the Council concerning Guidelines governing the Protection of Privacy and Transborder Flows of Personal Data (2013)," which are regarded as providing only minimum levels of data protection or "1st generation" data privacy standards.[40] Moreover, rather than enhancing privacy protection for consumers, the U.S. trade agreements seem to be more concerned with making sure that the commercial interests of the firms are not adversely affected by over-restrictive privacy regimes. Take, for example, the clause on personal information protection under the USMCA, which include a total of six paragraphs. Only one of these contains substantive obligations to adopt or maintain legal framework on personal information protection,[41] while three are aimed at minimizing the regulatory burden for business firms. The first among the three calls the Parties to ensure that "any restrictions on cross-border flows of personal information are necessary and proportionate to the risks presented,"[42] which are apparently modeled after the necessity test and proportionality principle under the WTO. The second requires the Parties to "endeavor to adopt non-discriminatory practices in protecting users of digital trade from personal information protection violations occurring within its jurisdiction," which also draws from the non-discrimination principle of the WTO, especially the national treatment obligation. Lastly, while the

---

[38] *Id.* at n.4.

[39] *Id.* art. 19.8.2.

[40] GRAHAM GREENLEAF, THE UN SHOULD ADOPT DATA PROTECTION CONVENTION 108 AS A GLOBAL RREATY: SUBMISSION ON 'THE RIGHT TO PRIVACY IN THE DIGITAL AGE' TO THE UN HIGH COMMISSION FOR HUMAN RIGHTS, TO THE HUMAN RIGHTS COUNCIL, AND TO THE SPECIAL RAPPORTEUR ON THE RIGHT TO PRIVACY 1 (2018), https://www.ohchr.org/Documents/Issues/Dig italAge/ReportPrivacyinDigitalAge/GrahamGreenleafAMProfessorLawUNSWAustralia.pdf.

[41] USMCA, *supra* note 36, art. 19.8.2.

[42] *Id.* art. 19.8.3.

agreement recognizes the divergent legal approaches the Parties might take on personal information protection, it also encourages the Parties to develop "mechanisms to promote compatibility between these different regimes." Again, trade lawyers would recognize in these provisions vestiges of WTO rules on mutual recognition, harmonization, and equivalence under the various WTO agreements.

C. Security as a Business Risk

On security, the U.S. trade agreements focus on "threats to cybersecurity undermine confidence in digital trade," that is, "malicious intrusions or dissemination of malicious code that affect electronic networks."[43] Put differently, the U.S. approach mainly addresses cybersecurity risks facing the private firm, which is quite different from the Chinese approach that focuses on perceived threats to national security. At the same time, the U.S. approach also tries to minimize disruptions to the operations of firms, by calling Parties to adopt "risk-based approaches that rely on consensus-based standards and risk management best practices to identify and protect against cybersecurity risks."[44] The risk-based approach is apparently carried over from the regulatory framework under the WTO, especially under the Agreements on Technical Barriers to Trade (TBT) and Sanitary and Phytosanitary Measures (SPS). By placing restrictions on the regulatory measures that might be adopted by governments, such an approach provides better protection for the firms' interests. Similarly, the reference to "consensus-based standards" also reflects prevailing practices in the United States, which has been codified in the the Cybersecurity Enhancement Act of 2014.[45] The Act calls for the National Institute for Standards and Technology under the Commerce Department to "facilitate and support the development of a voluntary, consensus-based, industry-led set of standards, guidelines, best practices, methodologies, procedures, and processes to cost-effectively reduce cyber risks to critical infrastructure."[46] Under the Act, the U.S. cybersecurity standards are developed as a public-private partnership between the government and the business sector, which serves to reduce the cybersecurity

---

[43] *Id.* art. 19.15.
[44] *Id.*
[45] Cybersecurity Enhancement Act of 2014, Pub. L. No. 113-274, 128 Stat. 2971 (2014).
[46] *Id.* § 101.

224 DATA SOVEREIGNTY AND TRADE AGREEMENTS

risks for the firms rather than advancing the national security goals of the government.

D. Trade Agreements

Many other provisions in the USMCA are also designed to facilitate the development of digital trade. This is done by either removing regulatory barriers, such as the provision on non-discriminatory treatment of digital products; or providing an enabling framework for digital trade such as the provisions on domestic electronic transaction legal framework; recognition of the legal validity of electronic signatures or electronic authentication methods; the acceptance of electronic documents as the legal equivalent of their paper versions; and open government data. The most interesting provision, though, is the provision on principles on access to and use of the Internet for digital trade.[47] This clause is mainly designed to deal with the risks that market players that own or control key infrastructures could abuse their power by unreasonably denying their business users access to their infrastructures, making it impossible for these users to conduct e-commerce activities. To address this problem, the agreements provide consumers (including business users) with the freedom of access to and use of the Internet for e-commerce, subject only to network management and network safety restrictions. This provision apparently grew out of the net neutrality principle from the domestic telecom regulatory framework within the United States. In a way, it provides digital giants with reverse control over the telecom and Internet services providers in the countries they are operating, shielding the former from being held hostage by the network throttling practices often found in many countries.

As the main proponent of the pluri-lateral Trade in Services Agreement (TISA) negotiations, the United States also proposed similar provisions in the draft TISA agreement. Most of these can be found in the e-commerce chapter, where the United States called for provisions that guarantee service suppliers the freedom to transfer information across countries for the conduct of its business; freedom for network users to access and use services and applications of their choice online, and to connect their choice of devices; prohibition of data localization requirements as a condition of supplying a

---

[47] USMCA, *supra* note 36, art. 19.10.

service or investing; and prohibition of discrimination against electronic authentication and electronic signatures. In addition, the horizontal provisions also include prohibitions on a host of localization requirements as mentioned earlier. While they apply to all service sectors, they would be of particular relevance to e-commerce due to the nature of the sector.

IV. China: The State Sovereignty Model

A. Data Sovereignty

For China, the key to data regulation is data security, which has now been elevated to the level of national security and national sovereignty. Such a regulatory approach, which I dubbed "data regulation with Chinese characteristics" in another paper,[48] is the result of an evolution spanning 25 years. This evolving approach closely traces the development of the Internet sector in China. When the Internet first started as a novelty that was confined to the ranks of tech-savvy geeks, the regulations focused on computer and Internet hardware, by requiring all Internet connections to go through official gateways sanctioned by the Chinese government. As the Internet gradually expanded to the masses with the proliferation of software and social media catered to popular uses, the government moved on to regulate the software and started to demand that software used for Internet access must be sanctioned by the government. As the cyberspace became an indispensable part of everyday life and began to permeate every sector from socializing, shopping to entertainment and education, the government shifted the focus to the regulation of content and now data, which is the essence of cyberspace that powers everything, especially with the rise of big data and artificial intelligence. Moreover, data regulation has now been elevated to the level of national security with the introduction of Cyber Security Law in 2016. The agency that is responsible for content regulation, the CAC (Cyberspace Administration of China), has also evolved into the super-agency that is almost synonymous with data regulation in China. The CAC has no responsibility in promoting the growth of the sector. Instead, its only responsibility is making sure that the cyberspace is secure and nothing unexpected would

---

[48] Henry S. Gao, *Data Regulation with Chinese Characteristics, in* BIG DATA AND GLOBAL TRADE LAW 245 (Mira Burri ed., 2021).

226 DATA SOVEREIGNTY AND TRADE AGREEMENTS

pop up. It is this single-minded pursuit of security that has led to such draconian policies as Internet blockage, filtering and other restrictions on the free flow of data, forced data localization requirements, and the transfer of source code. As the Internet is becoming more complicated and omnipotent, we can only expect Internet and data regulations in China to become more sophisticated and omnipresent.

B. Trade Agreements

At the international level, China has traditionally taken a cautious approach to data regulation in trade agreements. Until very recently, it has not even included e-commerce chapters in its RTAs (regional trade agreements). This only changed with its FTAs (free trade agreements) with Korea and Australia, which were both signed in 2015. Nonetheless, the provisions in these two FTAs remain rather modest, as they mainly address trade facilitation related issues, such as moratorium on customs duties on electronic transmission, recognition of electronic authentication and electronic signature, protection of personal information in e-commerce, paperless trading, domestic legal frameworks governing electronic transactions, and the need to provide consumers using electronic commerce level of protection equivalent to traditional forms of commerce.

A major breakthrough was made in the Regional Comprehensive Economic Partnership (RCEP) Agreement, which China signed along with other 14 countries in the region in November 2020. Under the Chapter on E-commerce, China like all other RCEP Members agreed to not "require a covered person to use or locate computing facilities in that Party's territory as a condition for conducting business in that Party's territory,"[49] or "prevent cross-border transfer of information by electronic means where such activity is for the conduct of the business of a covered person."[50]

Of course, merely agreeing to the twin provisions on data flow and data localization does not mean that China now embraces the U.S. model. Instead, both provisions are still overshadowed by national security concerns. First of all, both provisions allow Members to adopt "any measure that it considers necessary for the protection of its essential security interests." Moreover,

---

[49] Regional Comprehensive Economic Partnership art. 12.14, Nov. 15, 2020, https://rcepsec.org/legal-text [hereinafter RCEP].
[50] *Id.* art. 12.15.

they also explicitly state that such security measures "shall not be disputed by other Parties," which means that the securities measures will be largely self-judging. Finally, as the whole chapter on e-commerce is carved out from the normal dispute settlement procedure under the RCEP, any such security measure will not be subject to legal challenge.

Another exception to these two obligations is "any measure . . . that [the implementing Party] considers necessary to achieve a legitimate public policy objective." Note here the necessity test is not the objective one as found under the general exceptions clause under GATT Art. XX, but what the Party taking such measure "considers necessary," which is only found under the security exceptions clause under GATT Art. XXI. The subjective nature of the necessity test here is further confirmed by the footnotes to the two provisions, which explicitly "affirm that the necessity behind the implementation of such legitimate public policy shall be decided by the implementing Party."

C. Personal Information Protection

What then, could such "legitimate public policy objective" entail? Like most other countries in the world, this could include laws for the protection of privacy or personal information. Yet, the Chinese approach to privacy protection also comes with its own limitations. To start, privacy is a rather new concept in Chinese law, and there was no privacy protection law until 2009, when privacy was first recognized as a civil right under the Tort Liability Law. This was duly incorporated into China's new Civil Code enacted in 2020, which has a separate chapter on privacy and personal information protection as part of the volume on personality rights.[51] According to Art. 1035 of the new Civil Code, the processing of personal information shall be based on the consent of the data subject, "except if there are different requirements under laws or administrative regulations." In China, there are many laws that do not require the consent of the data subject. For example, under Art. 25 of China's Electronic Commerce Law, government agencies may require e-commerce operators to provide e-commerce transaction data, which includes the personal information of the consumers. Similarly, by requiring government agencies in charge of cyber security monitoring and management and their

---

[51] Minfa Dian (民法典) [Civil Code] (promulgated by the Nat'l People's Cong., May 28, 2020, effective Jan. 1, 2021), v.4, ch.6 (China).

228 DATA SOVEREIGNTY AND TRADE AGREEMENTS

staff to keep confidential any personal or privacy information they obtain in the discharge of their duty, Art. 45 of the Cyber Security Law also indirectly confirms that such agencies do have access to personal information of netizens without their consent. This approach is also adopted by China's new Personal Information Protection Law, which confirms that data processors might not need to obtain the consent of the data subject when necessary for discharging official duty and responsibility.[52] Moreover, in cases specified by the relevant laws or administrative regulations, the data subject would not even be made aware that his/her data is being processed.[53] The same exception also applies in cases where the notification or obtaining the consent of the data subject would impede the discharge of official duty by the relevant state organs.[54] Even if the data subject later becomes aware of the occurrence of such data processing activities, he/she would be denied the right to review or copy such personal information, which is normally available to data subjects.[55]

To sum up, the Chinese framework for personal information protection provides extensive exemptions for the government to collect personal information, either directly or through personal information processors. This probably explains why China until this day has yet to participate in the APEC CBPR (Cross-Border Privacy Rules),[56] as the CBPR Program Requirements includes some potentially awkward questions such as "how the collected personal information may be shared, used or disclosed as compelled by law," which neither the companies nor the Chinese government might be ready to answer.

D. "Important Data" and "Core Data"

Despite the gaps in China's personal information protection framework, at least an argument could be made that it is common to have personal information protections laws as exceptions to the twin provisions on data flow and

---

[52] Geren Xinxi Baohu Fa (个人信息保护法) [Personal Information Protection Law of the People's Republic of China] (promulgated by the Standing Comm. Nat'l People's Cong., Aug. 20, 2021), art. 13.3 (China).

[53] *Id.* art. 18.

[54] *Id.* art. 35.

[55] *Id.* art. 45.

[56] *What Is the Cross-Border Privacy Rules System?*, APEC, https://www.apec.org/About-Us/About-APEC/Fact-Sheets/What-is-the-Cross-Border-Privacy-Rules-System (last visited July 24, 2021).

data localization. However, the exceptions under the Chinese data regulation regime covers not only personal data but also "important data," a highly important concept that is poorly defined.

The concept of "important data" was first introduced in the Cyber Security Law, which requires "operators of critical information infrastructure" to locally store not only personal information but also "important data" collected and generated in their operations within China.[57] If they need to send such data abroad due to business necessity, they have to first undergo security assessment by the authorities.[58] Thus, the local storage requirement and restriction on cross-border data flow applies to "important data" collected and generated by operators of "critical information infrastructure," which is defined in Article 31 of the law as infrastructure in "important industries and fields such as public communications and information services, energy, transport, water conservancy, finance, public services and e-government affairs," as well as such "that will result in serious damage to state security, the national economy and the people's livelihood and public interest if it is destroyed, loses functions or encounters data leakage." Such a broad definition could potentially capture everything and is not really helpful nor does it give much guidance, which is why the same Article also directs the State Council to develop the "specific scope of critical information infrastructure."

In 2016, the CAC issued the National Network Security Inspection Operation Manual[59] and the Guide on the Determination of Critical Information Infrastructure,[60] which clarified the scope of critical information infrastructure by grouping them into three categories: (1) websites, which includes websites of government and party organizations, enterprises and public institutions, and news media; (2) platforms, which include Internet service platforms for instant messaging, online shopping, online payment, search engines, emails, online forum, maps, and audio video; and (3) production operations, which include office and business systems, industrial control systems, big data centers, cloud computing, and TV broadcasting systems.

---

[57] PRC Cyber Security Law, *supra* note 35, art. 37.

[58] *Id.*

[59] Guojia Wangluo Anquan Jiancha Caozuo Zhinan (国家网络安全检查操作指南) [National Network Security Inspection Operation Manual] (promulgated by the Central Leading Group on Cyber Security and Informatisation General Office, Network Security Coordination Bureau, June 1, 2016) (China).

[60] Guanjian Xinxi Jichu Sheshi Queding Zhinan (Shixing) (关键信息基础设施确定指南(试行)) [Guide on the Determination of Critical Information Infrastructure (Trial)] (promulgated by the Cyberspace Administration of China, July 2016) (China).

230 DATA SOVEREIGNTY AND TRADE AGREEMENTS

The CAC also laid down three steps in determining the critical information infrastructure, which starts with the identification of the critical operation, then continues with the determination of the information system or industrial control system supporting such a critical operation, and concludes with the final determination based on the level of the critical operations' reliance on such systems and possible damages resulting from security breaches in these systems. More specifically, they listed 11 sectors, which include energy, finance, transportation, hydraulic, medical, environmental protection, industrial manufacturing, utilities, telecom and Internet, radio and TV, and government agencies. The detailed criteria are both quantitative and qualitative. For example, on the one hand, critical information infrastructure includes websites with daily visitor counts of more than one million people and platforms with more than ten million registered users or more than one million daily active users, or daily transaction value of 10 million RMB. On the other hand, even those that do not meet the quantitative criterion could be deemed to be critical information infrastructure, if there are risks of security breaches that would lead to leakage of lots of sensitive information about firms or enterprises, or leakage of fundamental national data on geology, population, and resources; or seriously harming the image of the government or social order or national security. The potentially wide reach of the criteria was well illustrated by the case of the BGI Group, the largest genomics organization in the world, which was fined by the Ministry of Science and Technology in October 2018 for exporting certain human genome information abroad via the Internet without authorization.[61] Given the nature of their business, the BGI case could fall under the category of "leakage of fundamental national data on . . . population," as mentioned earlier.

In addition to the vague concept of "important data," the newly enacted Data Security Law adds another concept of "national core data," which is defined as "data related to national security, the lifeline of the national economy, people's livelihood and major public interests" and will be subject to "a more stringent management system."[62] It is likely that the scope of the new category of "national core data" will be narrower than "important data," but it is unclear how much narrower it will be. Moreover, as mentioned above, the

---

[61] An Shujun (安数君), *Shuju Chujing Ruhe "Anjian"* (数据出境如何"安检") [*How to Conduct "Safety Check" for Exporting Data*], Zнiнu (知乎) (May 11, 2019), https://zhuanlan.zhihu.com/p/65413452.

[62] Shuju Anquan Fa (数据安全法) [Data Security Law of the People's Republic of China] (promulgated by the Standing Comm. Nat'l People's Cong., Jun. 10, 2021), art. 21 (China).

restrictive rules on data flow and data localization only applies to "important data" collected and generated by operators of "critical information infrastructure" as per the Cyber Security Law. It is unclear, however, whether the stricter restrictions on "national core data" will be similarly limited to operators of "critical information infrastructure." A plausible or even compelling argument could be made to argue that due to its utmost importance, the restrictions on "national core data" would apply to all data processors or even private individuals, even if they do not qualify as operators of "critical information infrastructure."

V. EU: The Individual Sovereignty Model

A. The GDPR

Unlike the United States and China, which focus respectively on the firm and the state, the EU has, as its main concern, the privacy of the individual. This started with the Data Protection Directive in 1995, which prohibits the transfer of personal data to non-EU countries unless they have privacy protection standards deemed adequate.[63] The Directive was replaced[64] by the GPDR in 2018.

Despite its name, which suggests a broader reach, the GDPR applies only to personal data, which is defined as "any information relating to an identified or identifiable natural person ('data subject')."[65] It regulates the behaviors of the data controller and processor, which are respectively defined as the one who "determines the purposes and means of the processing of personal data"[66] and "processes personal data on behalf of the controller."[67] Under the GDPR, the processing of personal data is only allowed with the "explicit"[68] consent of the data subject and a few other specifically enumerated reasons,[69]

---

[63] Directive 95/46/EC of the European Parliament and of the Council of 24 October 1995 on the Protection of Individuals with Regard to the Processing of Personal Data and on the Free Movement of Such Data, O.J. 1995 (L281) 31.

[64] *See* Susan A. Aaronson & Patrick Leblond, *Another Digital Divide: The Rise of Data Realms and its Implications for the WTO*, 21 J. INT'L ECON. L. 245, 260 (2018).

[65] GDPR, *supra* note 33, art. 4.1.

[66] *Id.* art. 4.7.

[67] *Id.* art. 4.8.

[68] *Id.* art. 49.1(a).

[69] *Id.* art. 6.1. *See also* Aaditya Mattoo & Joshua P. Meltzer, *International Data Flows and Privacy: The Conflict and its Resolution*, 21 J. INT'L ECON. L. 769, 774 (2018).

232 DATA SOVEREIGNTY AND TRADE AGREEMENTS

pursuant to a set of principles that specifies the scope and manner of such processing.[70] Transfer of personal data to third countries is only allowed on the basis of an adequacy decision[71] or appropriate safeguards.[72]

B. Digital Sovereignty

Since its introduction, the GDPR has become the gold standard of privacy protection in the world. Encouraged by its success, top EU officials started to advocate "technological sovereignty" for the EU.[73] "Technological sovereignty" is a concept closely linked with "digital sovereignty,"[74] which was elaborated in the European Commission's "Communication on a European Strategy for Data" unveiled in February 2020.[75] As many commentators pointed out, the EU's new data strategy is designed to "counter the strong position of US and Chinese digital companies in the European market"[76] and remedy "the key European disadvantage" of "the lack of significant European digital corporations with global influence."[77] The new data strategy aims to create "a single European data space" so that "by 2030, the EU's share of the data economy—data stored, processed, and put to valuable use in Europe— at least corresponds to its economic weight, not by *fiat* but by choice."[78]

---

[70] GDPR, *supra* note 33, art. 5.1. *See also* Mattoo & Meltzer, *supra* note 69, at 774.

[71] GDPR, *supra* note 33, art. 45.

[72] *Id.* art. 46.

[73] Frances Burwell & Kenneth Propp, *The European Union and the Search for Digital Sovereignty: Building "Fortress Europe" or Preparing for a New World?*, ATLANTIC COUNCIL (June 22, 2020), https://www.atlanticcouncil.org/in-depth-research-reports/issue-brief/the-european-union-and-the-search-for-digital-sovereignty. For the statement by EU President Ursula von der Leyen, *see* Mark Scott, *What's Driving Europe's New Aggressive Stance on Tech*, POLITICO (Oct. 28, 2019), https://www.politico.com/news/2019/10/28/europe-technology-silicon-valley-059988. For the statement by incoming EU commissioner for the internal market Thierry Breton, *see* THIERRY BRETON, ANSWER TO THE EUROPEAN PARLIAMENT – QUESTIONNAIRE TO THE COMMISSIONER-DESIGNATE THIERRY BRETON (2019), https://ec.europa.eu/commission/commissioners/sites/comm-cwt2019/files/commissioner_ep_hearings/answers-ep-questionnaire-breton.pdf.

[74] For the distinction between the two, *see* Burwell & Propp, *supra* note 73, at 1.

[75] *Communication from the Commission to the European Parliament, the Council, the European Economic and Social Committee and the Committee of the Regions on a European Strategy for Data*, at 9, COM (2020) 66 final (Feb. 19, 2020), https://ec.europa.eu/info/sites/info/files/communication-european-strategy-data-19feb2020_en.pdf [hereinafter *A European Strategy for Data*].

[76] Burwell & Propp, *supra* note 73, at 2.

[77] Jeremy Shapiro, *Introduction: Europe's Digital Sovereignty*, *in* EUROPE'S DIGITAL SOVEREIGNTY: FROM RULEMAKER TO SUPERPOWER IN THE AGE OF US-CHINA RIVALRY 6, 11 (2020), https://ecfr.eu/wp-content/uploads/europe_digital_sovereignty_rulemaker_superpower_age_us_china_rivalry.pdf.

[78] *A European Strategy for Data*, *supra* note 75, at 4.

For the EU, the quest for digital sovereignty started out as a defensive move to fend off the encroachment into EU cyberspace by big firms from the United States, as well as the big government from China. By combining the powers of its huge market and regulatory apparatus, the EU is trying to reclaim digital sovereignty from not only the other countries, but more importantly, the digital giants.

The EU's data strategy can be seen as part of its broader plan of establishing its own "strategic autonomy."[79] The concept started as an idea of the French, when they published their 1994 white paper on defense.[80] Gradually, however, it was accepted by all of the big three EU Member States: Germany, France, and Italy.[81] The concept was adopted by the EU in 2016 when it unveiled its Global Strategy, which was supposed to "nurtures the ambition of strategic autonomy" for the EU.[82] With Trump's election as U.S. president and Brexit, the concept started to take off among the governments of EU Member States.[83] While there was some ambiguity on the exact content of the concept, the bigger EU Member States typically perceive it as referring to decision-making autonomy.[84] This is recently confirmed by the new trade strategy paper issued in February 2021, where the EU further refined it as a concept of "open strategic autonomy," which emphasizes "the EU's ability to make its own choices and shape the world around it through leadership and engagement, reflecting its strategic interests and values,"[85] with a priority area being the EU's digital agenda.[86]

---

[79] See Henry Gao, *The EU-China Comprehensive Agreement on Investment: Strategic Opportunity Meets Strategic Autonomy* 1–23, https://doi.org/10.1007/16517_2021_1 (last visited Feb 12, 2022).

[80] Jean-Marie Guehenno, Livre Blanc Sur La défense Et La sécurité Nationale [White Paper on Defense and National Security] (1994), http://www.livreblancdefenseetsecurite.gouv.fr/pdf/le-livre-blanc-sur-la-defense-1994.pdf.

[81] Ulrike Franke & Tara Varma, Independence Play: Europe's Pursuit of Strategic Autonomy 6 (2019), https://ecfr.eu/wp-content/uploads/Independence-play-Europes-pursuit-of-strategic-autonomy.pdf.

[82] European Union, Shared Vision, Common Action: A Stronger Europe. A Global Strategy for the European Union's Foreign and Security Policy (2016), https://eeas.europa.eu/archives/docs/top_stories/pdf/eugs_review_web.pdf.

[83] Franke & Varma, *supra* note 81, at 7.

[84] *Id.* at 10–11.

[85] *Communication from the Commission to the European Parliament, the Council, the European Economic and Social Committee and the Committee of the Regions on Trade Policy Review – An Open, Sustainable and Assertive Trade Policy*, at 4, COM (2021) 66 final, https://trade.ec.europa.eu/doclib/html/159438.htm.

[86] *Id.* at 16.

234 DATA SOVEREIGNTY AND TRADE AGREEMENTS

C. Data Flow and Localization

On data flow, the EU takes a bifurcated approach. Non-personal data are supposed to flow freely pursuant to the EU's Framework for the Free Flow of Non-personal Data,[87] while the cross-border flow of personal data is subject to the stringent requirements under the GDPR, despite the explicit recognition under the GDPR that "[f]lows of personal data to and from countries outside the Union and international organisations are necessary for the expansion of international trade and international cooperation."[88] Due to its high compliance costs,[89] the GDPR has proven to be "challenging especially for the small and medium sized enterprises (SMEs)."[90] To stay away from potential legal challenges, many U.S. websites blocked access to EU customers before the GDPR went into effect[91] and remained unavailable in the EU months after.[92]

In addition to its negative impact on cross-border data flow, the GDPR also creates the pressure toward data localization, especially after the decision of the Court of Justice of the European Union in Data Protection Commissioner v. Facebook Ireland, Maximillian Schrems (Schrems II).[93] However, as Chander has eloquently argued, data localization not only will not "solve the policy objectives identified in Schrems II," but also creates "its own policy problems."[94] The data localization requirements for non-personal data are banned by the EU's Framework for the Free Flow of Non-personal Data, which mandates EU Member States to repeal their data localization laws by May 30, 2021. In contrast, however, the GDPR does not include such

---

[87] Regulation (EU) 2018/1807 of the European Parliament and of the Council of 14 November 2018 on a Framework for the Free Flow of Non-Personal Data in the European Union, 2018 O.J. (L303) 59.

[88] GDPR, *supra* note 33, recital 101.

[89] Luke Irwin, *How Much Does GDPR Compliance Cost in 2021?*, IT GOVERNANCE BLOG EN (June 10, 2021), https://www.itgovernance.eu/blog/en/how-much-does-gdpr-compliance-cost-in-2020.

[90] *Communication from the Commission to the European Parliament and the Council Data Protection as a Pillar of Citizens' Empowerment and the EU's Approach to the Digital Transition – Two Years of Application of the General Data Protection Regulation*, at 9, COM (2020) 264 final (June 24, 2020), https://eur-lex.europa.eu/legal-content/EN/TXT/PDF/?uri=CELEX:52020DC0264&from=EN.

[91] Sam Schechner & Natalia Drozdiak, *U.S. Websites Go Dark in Europe as GDPR Data Rules Kick In*, WALL ST. J. (May 25, 2018), https://www.wsj.com/articles/u-s-websites-go-dark-in-europe-as-gdpr-data-rules-kick-in-1527242038.

[92] Jeff South, *More Than 1,000 U.S. News Sites Are Still Unavailable in Europe, Two Months After GDPR Took Effect*, NIEMANLAB (Aug. 7, 2018), https://www.niemanlab.org/2018/08/more-than-1000-u-s-news-sites-are-still-unavailable-in-europe-two-months-after-gdpr-took-effect.

[93] Case C-311/18, Data Prot. Comm'r v. Facebook Ir. Ltd. and Maximillian Schrems, ECLI:EU:C:2020:559 (July 16, 2020).

[94] Anupam Chander, *Is Data Localization a Solution for Schrems II?*, 23 J. INT'L ECON. L. 771, 778–84 (2020).

a prohibition. On the contrary, data localization requirements for personal data are quite common among EU countries,[95] with most covering special categories of sensitive data like health-related personal data or financial services data.[96] On the latter point, it is worth noting that the EU approach again diverges from the current U.S. approach. When the United States negotiated the Trans-Pacific Partnership, it carved out the entire financial services sector from the scope of its e-commerce chapter, including prohibition of data localization requirements.[97] In the new USMCA, however, the United States explicitly brought the financial services sector under the ban by stating that data localization should not be required "so long as the Party's financial regulatory authorities, for regulatory and supervisory purposes, have immediate, direct, complete, and ongoing access to information processed or stored on computing facilities that the covered person uses or locates outside the Party's territory."[98] It would be interesting to see whether the EU shifts closer to the U.S. approach in the future.

D. Trade Agreements

In its RTAs, the EU has not been able to include substantive language on data issues until recently. This was due to the internal differences between the two director-generals (DGs) with overlapping jurisdictions on the issue, that is, DG-Trade, which favors free trade for the sector; and DG-Justice, which has concerns over personal information protection.[99] Thus, notwithstanding its strong interest in privacy protection, the EU positions in its existing FTAs have been rather modest, which usually requires Parties to adopt their own laws for personal data protection to help maintain consumer trust and confidence in electronic commerce.[100] In February 2018, the two DGs were finally able to reach a compromise position, which includes on the

---

[95] Frances G. Burwell, and Kenneth Propp, *The European Union and the Search for Digital Sovereignty: Building 'Fortress Europe' or Preparing for a New World?* Research Reports (June, 2020), Washington, DC: Atlantic Council, at 9.

[96] Nigel Cory, Cross-Border Data Flows: Where Are the Barriers, and What Do They Cost 20–31 (2017), http://www2.itif.org/2017-cross-border-data-flows.pdf?_ga=2.63382255.130 6428313.1587045825-1501175350.15870 45825.

[97] Trans-Pacific Partnership art. 14.1, Feb. 4, 2016, https://ustr.gov/trade-agreements/free-trade-agreements/trans-pacific-partnership/tpp-full-text.

[98] USMCA, *supra* note 36, art. 17.18.2.

[99] Aaronson & Leblond, *supra* note 64, at 261.

[100] *Id.*

236 DATA SOVEREIGNTY AND TRADE AGREEMENTS

one hand horizontal clauses on free flow of all data and ban on localization requirements, while one the other hand, affirms the EU's right to regulate in the sector by making clear that it shall not be subject to investor-state arbitration.[101] Despite this development, the EU still seems to prefer handling data flow issues through bilateral "adequacy" recognitions, which so far has only been granted to a dozen countries.[102] In many of its latest FTAs, data flow issues were left out in the main text, with a separate adequacy decision adopted. This is, for example, the case of its Economic Partnership Agreement (EPA) with Japan, where the adequacy decision[103] was adopted separately from the EPA, which does not include commitments on free flow of data.[104] While its recent FTA with Vietnam lacks not only provisions on data flow and localization but also any plan for an adequacy decision.

VI. Why the Differences?

The diverging approaches among the three major players are not randomly chosen. Instead, they reflect deeper differences in their respective commercial interests and regulatory approaches within each jurisdiction.

First, the global e-commerce market is largely dominated by China and the United States. Among the ten biggest digital trade firms in the world, six are American and four are Chinese.[105] Of course, this does not necessarily mean that they must share the same position. Upon closer examination, one can see that the U.S. firms on the list tend to be pure digital service firms. Firms like Facebook, Google, and Netflix do not sell physical products but only provide digitalized services such as online search, social network, or content services. In contrast, two of the top three Chinese firms—Alibaba and

---

[101] *Id.* at 262.

[102] So far, the EU has granted adequacy recognitions to Andorra, Argentina, Canada (commercial organizations), Faroe Islands, Guernsey, Israel, Isle of Man, Japan, Jersey, New Zealand, Switzerland, and Uruguay. *See* Adequacy Decisions, EUR. COMM'N, https://ec.europa.eu/info/law/law-topic/data-protection/international-dimension-data-protection/adequacy-decisions_en (last visited July 24, 2021).

[103] Press Release, Eur. Comm'n, European Commission Adopts Adequacy Decision on Japan, Creating the World's Largest Area of Safe Data Flows (Jan. 23, 2019), https://ec.europa.eu/commiss ion/presscorner/detail/en/IP_19_421.

[104] According to art. 8.81 of the EPA, "[t]he Parties shall reassess within three years of the date of entry into force of this Agreement the need for inclusion of provisions on the free flow of data into this Agreement."

[105] *List of Largest Internet Companies*, WIKIPEDIA, https://en.wikipedia.org/wiki/List_of_largest_Internet_companies (last visited Feb. 20, 2020).

JD.com—sell mainly physical goods. This is why the United States focuses on the "digital" side while China focuses on the traditional "trade" side when it comes to digital trade, as I argued in another paper.[106]

One may argue that China also has giant pure digital firms like Baidu and Tencent, which are often referred to, respectively, as the Google and the Facebook of China. However, because they serve almost exclusively the domestic Chinese market and most of their facilities and operations are based in China, they do not share the demands for free cross-border data flow like their U.S. counterparts, which have data centers in strategic locations around the world.

As for the EU, with no major players in the game, their restrictive privacy rules could be viewed as a form of "digital protectionism"[107] to fend off the invasions of American and Chinese firms into Europe.

The second influence is their different domestic regulatory approaches. In the United States, the development of the sector has long benefited from its "permissive legal framework,"[108] which aims to minimize government regulation on the Internet and relies heavily on self-regulation in the sector. Such policy is even codified in the law, with the Telecommunication Act of 1996 explicitly stating that it is "the policy of the United States . . . to preserve the vibrant and competitive free market that presently exists for the Internet and other interactive computer services, unfettered by Federal or State regulation."[109] Therefore, it is no surprise that the United States wishes to push for deregulation and the free flow of information at the international level, a long-standing policy that can be traced back to the Framework for Global Electronic Commerce announced by the Clinton administration in 1997.[110] At the same time, the United States does not have a comprehensive privacy protection framework. Instead, it relies on a patchwork of sector-specific laws,[111] which provides privacy protection for consumers of a variety of sectors such as credit reports and video rental. This is further complemented by case-by-case enforcement actions by the Federal Trade Commission, and self-regulation by firms themselves. This explains why, in its RTAs, the

---

[106] Henry Gao, *Digital or Trade? The Contrasting Approaches of China and US to Digital Trade*, 21 J. INT'L ECON. L. 297 (2018).

[107] Susan A. Aaronson, *What Are We Talking about When We Talk about Digital Protectionism?*, 18 WORLD TRADE REV. 541 (2019).

[108] ANUPAM CHANDER, THE ELECTRONIC SILK ROAD: HOW THE WEB BINDS THE WORLD TOGETHER IN COMMERCE 57 (2013).

[109] Telecommunication Act of 1996, § 509(b)(2), 47 U.S.C. § 230(b)(2).

[110] Aaronson & Leblond, *supra* note 64, at 254.

[111] CHANDER, *supra* note 108, at 57–58.

238 DATA SOVEREIGNTY AND TRADE AGREEMENTS

United States does not mandate uniform rules on personal information protection but allows members to adopt their own domestic laws.

On the other hand, in China, the Internet has always been subject to heavy government regulations, which not only dictate the hardware one must use to connect to international networks, but also the content that may be transmitted online.[112] Many foreign websites are either filtered or blocked in China, which confirms China's cautious position on free flow of data. Moreover, in 2016, China also adopted the Cyber Security Law, which requires the operators of critical information infrastructure to store locally personal information they collected or generated in China. This is at odds with the U.S. demand to prohibit data localization requirements. Privacy protection is also weak in China, as it was only incorporated into the Chinese legal system in 2009, along with extensive exemptions for the government.

The EU, in contrast, has a long tradition of human rights protection, partly in response to the atrocities of the Second World War.[113] Coupled with the absence of major digital players wielding significant market power and the lack of a strong central government with overriding security concerns, this translates into a strong emphasis on privacy in the digital sphere. Moreover, the EU is also able to transcend the narrow mercantilist confines of the United States[114] and recognize privacy as not only a consumer right but also a fundamental human right that is recognized in several fundamental EU instruments[115] and the constitution of many Member States.[116] Such a refreshing perspective is probably the biggest contribution made by the EU to digital trade issues.

VII. Conclusion

Trade agreements are complicated. Data sovereignty issues are even more so. This chapter provides a modest attempt to offer some clarity to these issues

---

[112] For an overview of Chinese data regulation, *see* Gao, *supra* note 48.

[113] Mattoo & Meltzer, *supra* note 69, at 771 (citing James Q. Whitman, *The Two Western Cultures of Privacy: Dignity Versus Liberty*, 113 YALE L.J. 1151 (2004)).

[114] *See* Paul M. Schwartz & Karl-Nikolaus Peifer, *Transatlantic Data Privacy Law*, 106 GEO. L.J. 115, 132–37 (2017).

[115] *See, e.g.*, Charter of Fundamental Rights of the European Union art. 8, Dec. 18, 2000, 2000 O.J. (C 364) 1; Convention for the Protection of Human Rights and Fundamental Freedoms art. 8, Nov. 4, 1950, 312 U.N.T.S. 222.

[116] These includes Germany, Greece, Hungary, Poland, and Spain. *See* Mattoo & Meltzer, *supra* note 69, at 772.

CONCLUSION   239

with an in-depth discussion of the data sovereignty models of the three major players. The discussions herein should provide some help in understanding the approaches of most other countries in the world as well because, as illustrated by Ferracane and Marel in their recent comprehensive survey, countries around the world broadly fit in one of the three models discussed here.[117]

At the same time, we should not be disheartened by the wide divergences among the three approaches. Such differences might prove to be short-lived as countries are learning from each other's experiences. For example, with its recent ban on TikTok and WeChat, the United States seems to be taking a leaf out of China's playbook. At the same time, by accepting obligations on free flow of data and prohibitions on data localization requirements, China seems to be edging closer to the U.S. position. Just like the three kingdoms in Chinese history, which were ultimately united into one, hopefully, the three digital kingdoms studied in this chapter can also, through trade agreements,[118] forge their divergent approaches to data sovereignty into one, at least in the cyberspace.

[117] Martina Francesca Ferracane & Erik van der Marel, *Regulating Personal Data: Data Models and Digital Services Trade* (World Bank, Policy Research Working Paper No. 9596, 2021), https://openkn owledge.worldbank.org/bitstream/handle/10986/35308/Regulating-Personal-Data-Data-Models-and-Digital-Services-Trade.pdf.

[118] *See, e.g.,* Douglas W. Arner, Giuliano Castellano, & Ēriks Selga, *The Transnational Data Governance Problem* (Aug. 27, 2021). BERKELEY TECHNOLOGY LAW JOURNAL, Forthcoming, University of Hong Kong Faculty of Law Research Paper No. 2021/039, Available at SSRN: https://ssrn.com/abstract=3912487 or http://dx.doi.org/10.2139/ssrn.3912487.

10

Data Governance and Digital Trade in India

Losing Sight of the Forest for the Trees?

Neha Mishra[*]

I. Introduction

The preferred approach to governing data and digital infrastructure in a country is ever so often reflected in its digital trade policies. While certain countries have advocated the urgent need to safeguard policy space in international trade agreements to regulate data-driven sectors,[1] others have supported free and open data-driven innovation realized through digital trade liberalization.[2] These two conflicting narratives are often characterized as a tussle between data sovereignty and Internet openness.[3] In reality, most countries do not make a binary choice between data sovereignty and Internet openness but adopt a more nuanced framework. This chapter explores the interlinkages between India's complex and unique data governance approach and its reluctance toward negotiating digital trade rules in trade treaties,

---

[*] I thank the organizers, Anupam Chander and Haochen Sun, as well as participants of the Data Sovereignty along the Digital Silk Road Conference, especially Thomas Streinz, for their excellent feedback on previous drafts. I also thank Prannv Dhawan and Ishit Patel for their helpful research assistance

[1] Amiti Sen, *India, South Africa Oppose Plurilateral Initiative for E-commerce at WTO*, THE HINDU BUSINESS LINE (Mar. 6, 2021), https://www.thehindubusinessline.com/economy/policy/india-south-africa-oppose-plurilateral-initiative-for-ecommerce-at-wto/article34004906.ece.

[2] *U.S. Statement at the Meeting of the WTO Joint Statement Initiative on E-Commerce*, Mar 6, 2019, https://geneva.usmission.gov/2019/03/06/u-s-statement-at-the-meeting-of-the-wto-joint-statement-initiative-on-e-commerce/ (last visited Apr 12, 2021); *Australia, Japan and Singapore Welcome Good Progress in WTO Electronic Commerce Negotiations*, Jan. 24, 2020, https://www.meti.go.jp/press/2019/01/20200124004/20200124004-2.pdf (last visited Apr. 12, 2021).

[3] Stanislav Budnitsky & Lianrui Jia, *Branding Internet Sovereignty: Digital Media and the Chinese–Russian Cyberalliance*, 21 EUR. J. CULTURAL STUDIES 594, 597 (2018).

Neha Mishra, *Data Governance and Digital Trade in India* In: *Data Sovereignty*. Edited by: Anupam Chander and Haochen Sun, Oxford University Press. © Oxford University Press 2023. DOI: 10.1093/oso/9780197582794.003.0011

especially pertaining to data localization and cross-border data flows. It then focuses on the ramifications of the tenuous relationship between data governance and digital trade in India, and its role as a champion of developing country interests in digital trade.

India stands at a critical juncture. It is one of the fastest growing e-commerce markets in the world,[4] and often estimated to be the largest data consumer in the world.[5] Cross-border data flows to and from India increased 22,000 times between 2001 and 2019, making it among the fastest growing data markets globally.[6] Several programs of the Indian government including the Digital India Initiative,[7] Smart Cities Mission,[8] #AIforAll Strategy,[9] and India Enterprise Architecture[10] boast of India's immense digital potential. Simultaneously, India has systematically started developing its own brand of data governance modeled predominantly on government custodianship of people's data.

India's data governance approach combines highly prescriptive and all-encompassing Internet/data laws and regulations with policies facilitating ringfencing of data inside borders. In adopting this approach, the government has promised that the data of Indians will be solely used for the economic development of India and its peoples, although the economic (or social) benefits flowing to the individual remain somewhat obscure. Critics argue that the Indian brand of data governance concentrates power in the government to conduct unchecked surveillance and provides it unbridled power to discriminate against minorities.[11] While acknowledging the

---

[4] Avinash Tiwary, *Indian E-commerce Market Estimated to Top $100bn by 2024*, NIKKEI ASIA (Sept. 2, 2020), https://asia.nikkei.com/Business/36Kr-KrASIA/Indian-e-commerce-market-estima ted-to-top-100bn-by-2024.

[5] *Digital India*, MCKINSEY GLOBAL INSTITUTE, https://www.mckinsey.com/~/media/McKin sey/Business%20Functions/McKinsey%20Digital/Our%20Insights/Digital%20India%20Technol ogy%20to%20transform%20a%20connected%20nation/MGI-Digital-India-Report-April-2019.pdf (last visited Apr. 12, 2021).

[6] Toro Tsunamishima, *China Rises as World's Data Superpower as Internet Fractures*, NIKKEI ASIA (Nov. 24, 2020), https://asia.nikkei.com/Spotlight/Century-of-Data/China-rises-as-world-s-data-superpower-as-internet-fractures (last visited Apr. 13, 2021).

[7] DIGITAL INDIA, https://www.digitalindia.gov.in/di-initiatives (last visited Apr. 13, 2021).

[8] GOVERNMENT OF INDIA, SMART CITY, https://smartcities.gov.in/ (last visited Apr. 13, 2021).

[9] NITI AAYOG, NATIONAL STRATEGY ON ARTIFICIAL INTELLIGENCE, http://niti.gov.in/national-strategy-artificial-intelligence (last visited Apr. 13, 2021).

[10] INDIA ENTERPRISE ARCHITECTURE, https://negd.gov.in/india-enterprise-architecture (last visited Apr. 13, 2021).

[11] Amba Kak, *"The Global South Is Everywhere, but Also Always Somewhere": National Policy Narratives and AI Justice* (AIES '20, Feb. 7–8, 2020), https://dl.acm.org/doi/10.1145/3375627.3375 859; Pallavi Bedi, *Does the Personal Data Protection Bill, 2019, Protect Citizens' Privacy From Government Surveillance?*, MEDIANAMA (Jan. 29, 2020), https://www.medianama.com/2020/01/223-pdp-bill-2019-government-surveillance/; Anirudh Burman, *Will India's Proposed Data Protection Law Protect Privacy and Promote Growth?* (CARNEGIE INDIA, Mar. 2020) https://carnegieendowm ent.org/files/Burman_Data_Privacy.pdf; Arindrajit Basu & Justin Sherman, Key Global Takeaways

importance of civil liberties, including the realization of individual economic freedom, this chapter focuses on the economic dimension, that is, the impact of data governance on the digital economy in India.

The Indian brand of data governance remains understudied compared to China, EU, and the United States, although comparisons to these models are common. This chapter argues that India's data governance approach is informed by multiple domestic narratives and is thus more than a mimicry of the Chinese or EU model. Further, the chapter argues that India's vision of data governance reinforces and strengthens its reticent stance in various trade negotiations on electronic commerce issues, particularly at the WTO. Thus, unlike the EU, United States and even China, India has been steadfast in its hostile position toward negotiating comprehensive electronic commerce rules at the WTO. Other developing countries may be swayed by the Indian approach; however, India's position must be viewed with extreme caution, especially in smaller economies without comparable market size or resources.[12]

Section II sets out the multiple narratives and frameworks on data governance in India, providing a high-level perspective outlining the key ideas, policy goals and institutions, and discussing various examples of how several proposed rules and policies impact stakeholders in the domestic digital economy. Section III then draws connections between India's domestic data governance framework and its (non-committal) position in various trade fora in relation to digital trade and cross-border data flows. Section IV concludes that India's domestic framework on data governance is aligned with its foreign digital trade policy, but their combined impact on various sections of the domestic digital economy is unclear and under-evaluated. Additionally, India's staunch refusal to participate in digital trade negotiations at the WTO may invite geopolitical backlash from its trading partners (present and future), thereby harming its economic interests in the long run. Indian policymakers must therefore better balance nationalist interests with the underlying realities of the digital economy.

---

from India's Revised Personal Data Protection Bill, LAWFARE (Jan. 23, 2021), https://www.lawfareblog.com/key-global-takeaways-indias-revised-personal-data-protection-bill.

[12] Neha Mishra, *Background Paper for the UNCTAD Digital Economy Report* (Dec. 2020) (on file with author).

II. Data Governance in India: Multiple Narratives, Multiple Frameworks

This section evaluates the key ideas and policy goals on data governance in India, and how they are affected through a complex governance framework. Based on this assessment, this section finds that India's data governance framework is not purely protectionist or even mercantilist; it reflects the government's ambition to vest absolute power in itself to achieve several policy goals, not only economic self-sufficiency, or domestic growth. In doing so, the government has chosen an ideal of digital development that is politically appealing to the majority (for instance, by coloring the policies with patriotic undertones) and caters to the interests of the most powerful domestic industry lobbies. Although some proposed laws and policies make occasional references to individual digital empowerment and trust, these objectives usually appear secondary to clearly defined national interests.

A. Underlying Ideas of Data Governance

1. Paradoxical Treatment of Data

Many proposed policy instruments in India view "data" from a predominantly economic lens, that is, as an asset or capital over which the government must have absolute control.[13] For instance, in the Draft E-Commerce Policy (currently under revision), data is compared to natural resources such as oil, over which the government must assert its sovereign rights.[14] In this narrative, the government is accorded the role of a 'custodian' or 'trustee' to ensure that the economic benefits of data accrue to India and Indians.[15] The underlying notion is that an open, market-driven framework cannot generate equitable and fair benefits for Indians and, thus, the government must step in as a data trustee to facilitate fair value sharing[16] and preventing market failures.[17] While government custodianship can be a proxy for individual

---

[13] E.g., Department for Promotion of Industry and Internal Trade ("DIPP"), Draft National e-Commerce Policy, at 6, 12 (2019); Ministry of Electronics and Information Technology ("MEITY"), Report by the Committee of Experts on Non-Personal Data Protection Framework (Dec. 16, 2020); NITI Aayog, Data Empowerment and Protection Architecture (Aug. 2020), https://niti.gov.in/sites/default/files/2020-09/DEPA-Book_0.pdf.

[14] DIPP, *supra* note 13, at 8.

[15] *See generally* MEITY, *supra* note 13.

[16] E.g., MEITY, National Open Digital Ecosystems: Consultation Whitepaper (2020).

[17] DIPP, *supra* note 13, at 9.

244 DATA GOVERNANCE AND DIGITAL TRADE IN INDIA

empowerment, the proposed policies, as discussed in various sections below, vest governmental control over data without adequate safeguards to protect user interests and/or ensure equitable distribution of resources.

Given the recognition of informational privacy as a fundamental right in the landmark *Puttaswamy* judgment,[18] and the strong impetus for data protection in India,[19] the formulation of data as an economic asset of which the government is the trustee is paradoxical. For instance, in the report on the policy framework for non-personal data ("NPD Framework"), large amounts of public, private, and community data are presumed to be convertible to anonymized datasets, which in turn can "unlock" value for the domestic digital economy.[20] In contrast, discussions around the social risks of data-driven technologies, including ethical issues and safeguards necessary for the use of AI in public functions, is relatively scarce and cursory.[21]

2. Government as a Market Architect

Another distinguishing feature of the Indian data governance model is that the government itself is seen as a keen market architect instead of acting only as a reactive guardian of public interests. For instance, the Digital India initiative aims to maximize the commercial value of data collected from the public, for example, by combining IoT data with public/community datasets to generate new opportunities for economic entities. The government's role as a market architect is strengthened by its exclusive control over biometric data of over a billion Indians under the Aadhar Programme. As Hicks argues, these datasets are an important component of State-driven capitalism (or what she calls "Digital ID Capitalism"), which the government can commercialize to facilitate delivery of digital services by domestic private sector players.[22] Ironically, the Digital Personal Data Protection ("PDP") Bill 2023[23] also provides a free rein to the government to notify that certain companies including startups, are exempted from specific requirements of notice and

---

[18] *Justice K. S. Puttaswamy (Retd.) and Anr. vs Union Of India And Ors*, (2017) 10 SCC 1.

[19] MEITY, COMMITTEE OF EXPERTS UNDER THE CHAIRMANSHIP OF JUSTICE B.N. SRIKRISHNA, A FREE AND FAIR DIGITAL ECONOMY (Jul. 27, 2018).

[20] *See generally* MEITY, *supra* note 13.

[21] Kak, *supra* note 11. *See, e.g.*, MEITY, REPORT OF COMMITTEE D ON CYBERSECURITY, SAFETY, LEGAL AND ETHICAL ISSUES (Dec. 4, 2019).

[22] *See generally* Jacqueline Hicks, *Digital ID Capitalism: How Emerging Economies Are Re-inventing Digital Capitalism*, 26 CONTEMP. POL. 330 (2020).

[23] The Digital Personal Data Protection Bill ("PDP Bill"), Bill no. 113 of 2023.

procedures regarding obtaining user consent,[24] potentially sidelining privacy concerns.

3. Fighting Digital Colonialism

In several public dialogues, the Indian government often presents its data governance framework as being necessary to counter "data colonialism," that is, the abuse and misuse of data by foreign companies, including appropriating all profits from India.[25] As a data custodian, the government intends to counter the excesses of data colonialism and instead equitably distribute the benefits of the data-driven economy. For instance, the government purports to adopt measures that maintain a level playing field in India,[26] and create "home-grown alternate, cheaper, and efficient digital services,"[27] in what the government believes is a "win-win" situation.[28] Similarly, the Indian government previously imposed taxes targeting foreign e-commerce businesses and online advertising platforms, especially impacting U.S.-based companies.[29] The Indian government also envisages reliance on data localization for inhibiting the unilateral flow of data and underlying profits to foreign companies without any economic returns to India.[30]

B. Policy Goals in Data Governance Instruments

Many legal and policy instruments on data governance in India contain clear policy goals, including protection of privacy; promoting digital innovation; facilitating digital inclusion and development; and ensuring greater security. This section provides explanations of these varied policy goals and their implementation design.

---

[24] PDP Bill 2023, s. 17(3). Notably, the Indian government has deliberated upon several iterations of the data protection bill in the last few years.

[25] Vishnu Makhijani, *Data Colonisation: The New Looming Danger* THE OUTLOOK INDIA (June 27, 2019), https://www.outlookindia.com/newsscroll/data-colonisation-the-new-looming-danger/1562930 (last visited Apr. 12, 2021).

[26] DIPP, *supra* note 13, at 4.

[27] *Id.*

[28] *Id.*, at 13.

[29] Section IIIA.

[30] E.g., MEITY, *supra* note 13, Appendix 2.

1. Privacy, Cybersecurity, and Trust

Various facets of individual privacy are addressed in the PDP Bill (currently tabled before the Lok Sabha). The PDP Bill imposes various obligations on entities collecting 'digital' personal data (or "data fiduciaries") or entities processing digital personal data on behalf of data fiduciaries ("data processors") to protect the rights of individuals to protect their personal data and to ensure that personal data is processed lawfully.[31] Other policy instruments also focus on empowering users to control their data meaningfully,[32] including the risks of algorithmic manipulation by the private sector and the need for explainable AI.[33] However, many of these individual rights are subject to broad exemptions reserved for the central government and its agencies.[34]

In addition to privacy protection, some policy documents refer to cybersecurity, although the focus is neither as comprehensive nor systematic, despite the record number of cybersecurity breaches in India.[35] For instance, the Draft Electronic Commerce Policy recommends that the government must incentivize development of secure domestic standards for devices that store, process, and access data of Indians.[36] India has not yet developed a comprehensive cybersecurity law or strategy and the existing domestic framework sets out nominal requirements for data/cybersecurity. For instance, companies are required to adopt "reasonable security practices" in handling personal data,[37] a relatively low threshold. Similarly, domestic laws do not require companies operating in India to strictly follow international cybersecurity standards.[38]

2. Digital Inclusion, Development, and Innovation

Through various policy frameworks, the Indian government has set out a clear policy objective: the use of data in India must serve the interests of its

---

[31] PDP Bill 2023, Preamble.

[32] DIPP, *supra* note 13, at 6; NITI Aayog, *supra* note 13.

[33] MEITY, *supra* note 21; Saritha Rai, *Amazon, Google Face Tough Rules in India's E-Commerce Draft*, BLOOMBERG INDIA (July 4, 2020), https://www.bloomberg.com/news/articles/2020-07-04/amazon-google-face-tough-rules-in-india-s-e-commerce-draft (last visited Apr. 13, 201).

[34] Section IIC1.

[35] Neeraj Chauhan, *Almost 300% Rise in Cyber-attacks in India in 2020, Gov't Tells Parliament*, THE HINDUSTAN TIMES (Mar. 23, 2021), https://www.hindustantimes.com/india-news/almost-300-rise-in-cyber-attacks-in-india-in-2020-govt-tells-parliament-101616496416988.html (last visited Apr. 12, 2021).

[36] DIPP, *supra* note 13, at 12.

[37] Information Technology Act, S. 43A.

[38] Utsav Mittal, *A New Framework for a Secure Digital India* (ORF Issue Brief No. 422, OBSERVER RESEARCH FOUNDATION, Nov. 2020).

citizens, including facilitating domestic e-commerce industries and fostering domestic research and development for creation of digital products suited to the needs of Indian people.[39] Calls for data localization in various regulations (as discussed below) also echo the need to create opportunities for digital inclusion and development including creating local jobs[40] and market opportunities for domestic industries,[41] promoting high-value domestic digital products,[42] and developing India's data infrastructure.[43] The focus on realizing maximum economic value from the use of non-personal data also advances the government's domestic development agenda. A related policy goal is creating opportunities for innovation by digital start-ups.[44] In addition to the NPD Framework that promises to revolutionize the home-grown data-driven industry, the government has facilitated regulatory sandboxes to facilitate growth of fintech apps.[45] A 2019 iteration of the PDP Bill also incorporated a provision facilitating sandbox for AI/ML technologies, which is absent in later versions of the Bill.[46] Nonetheless, as discussed earlier, the bill provides some degree of flexibility for the government to exempt notified companies inter alia from specific requirements of notice and other compliance requirements.

3. National Security

India's data governance framework also reflects some ambition to achieve national security. For instance, this rationale is reflected in the ban on purportedly malicious foreign applications and technologies from China,[47] as well as greater scrutiny of suspicious foreign investments (potentially, affecting digital investments by Chinese companies in India).[48] Similarly, broad exemptions are available under various domestic laws for the government to monitor or intercept any data for national security purposes,

---

[39] DIPP, *supra* note 13, at 4.

[40] *Id.* at 16.

[41] *Id.* at 9.

[42] *Id.* at 15.

[43] *Id.* at 18; MEITY, DRAFT DATA CENTRE POLICY (2020).

[44] MEITY, *supra* note 13; DIPP, *supra* note 13, at 4.

[45] RESERVE BANK OF INDIA (RBI), RBI NOTIFICATION ON STORAGE OF PAYMENT SYSTEMS DATA (INDIA), RBI/2017-18/153, DPSS.CO.OD No.2785/06.08.005/2017-2018 (Apr. 6, 2018).

[46] The Personal Data Protection Bill ("PDP Bill"), Bill no. 373 of 2019, s.40.

[47] Press Information Bureau, https://pib.gov.in/PressReleseDetailm.aspx?PRID=1635206 (last visited Apr. 13, 2021).

[48] MINISTRY OF COMMERCE AND INDUSTRY (INDIA), PRESS NOTE No 3 (2020 Series).

including under the PDP Bill where it can exempt any government agency from the requirements for "the sovereignty and integrity of India," "the security of the state," or to maintain "public order."[49] Further, the PDP Bill contains stringent requirements obligating data fiduciaries to process data "for the performance by the State or any of its instrumentalities of any function
. . . in the interest of sovereignty and integrity of India or security of the State".[50] In 2014 (post-Snowden), the National Security Council had also suggested that all data of Indians must be routed through India.[51] Press reports from 2020 also indicated that a new body could be set up to safeguard national security in cross-border flows of "potentially commercial data pertaining to defence, medical records, biological records, cartographic data, as well as genome mapping, without authorization."[52]

4. Regulatory Control

Some provisions regulating data flows in domestic laws are intended to facilitate regulatory control over data and data infrastructure for regulatory monitoring purposes. For instance, payment system providers are required to store data locally for the regulator to "have unfettered supervisory access to data stored with these system providers as also with their service providers/intermediaries/third party vendors and other entities in the payment ecosystem."[53] Similarly, as per press reports, the revised e-commerce policy envisages mechanisms for ensuring regulatory access to e-commerce data.[54] Although not explicitly mentioned in any policy document, India's desire to increase control over its domestic data infrastructure could also be linked to its increasingly stringent online censorship practices[55] and Internet shutdowns.[56]

---

[49] PDP Bill 2023, s. 17(2)(a).

[50] PDP Bill 2023, s. 7(c).

[51] Rishab Bailey and Smriti Parsheera, *Data Localisation in India: Questioning the Means and Ends* 7 (NIPFP, 2018), https://macrofinance.nipfp.org.in/PDF/BP2018_Data-localisation-in-India.pdf.

[52] Aditi Agarwal, *India's New Draft E-Commerce Policy Focuses On Data, Competition, Counterfeiting, Consumer Protection*, MEDIANAMA (July 3, 2020), https://www.medianama.com/2020/07/223-second-draft-ecommerce-policy-india/.

[53] RBI, *supra* note 45.

[54] Agarwal, *supra* note 52.

[55] Devdatta Mukhopadhay, *Internet Censorship in India: Peeking Under the Hood*, THE GNI BLOG (Dec. 1, 2020), https://medium.com/global-network-initiative-collection/internet-censorship-in-india-peeking-under-the-hood-b09cecabbbe7 (last visited Apr. 12, 2021).

[56] STATISTA, https://www.statista.com/statistics/1095035/india-number-of-internet-shutdowns/ (last visited Apr. 13, 2021).

C. The "Data Governance Complex" in India

The section outlines the complexity of the data governance framework in India, focusing on the diversity of laws, regulations, policies, and institutions in the data governance space. Ultimately, the Indian "data governance complex" is not a straightforward exercise in mercantilism. It is deeply interconnected with the government's quest for data sovereignty and its ambition to establish itself as a predominant architect of the domestic digital market. This section also identifies the misalignment of various economic incentives in the regulatory framework and the high degree of legal uncertainty generated by the data governance complex, raising concerns whether it is best suited for India's needs.

1. Complexity of Regulatory and Legal Tools

The manner in which the "data governance complex" in India establishes governmental control over data is highly nuanced. Emerging regulatory frameworks on data are all-encompassing; covering different types of data such as personal data, non-personal data, community data, public data, private data; and further categorizing data based on sensitivity and imposing varied obligations on private entities that collect and process data using different categories such as data fiduciaries and data processors,[57] significant data fiduciaries,[58] and data businesses.[59] Data uses are dynamic; thus, the determination of whether data is public or private, or personal or non-personal, sensitive or not sensitive, is usually contextual. However, different legal obligations apply to different types of data, resulting in a dense and unpredictable governance framework for data-driven businesses and Internet users in India.

The PDP Bill provides many tools to establish governmental control over personal data. For instance, if a data fiduciary (including a governmental body) collect personal data for "any subsidy, benefit, service, certificate, licence or permit", where such consent was previously obtained, then the same constitutes "legitimate use" of personal data under the Bill.[60] This provision has a very broad application, given the extensive amount of personal data collected by the Indian government across several routine governmental

---

[57] PDP Bill 2023, s. 2(i) and s. 2(k).
[58] PDP Bill 2023, s. 2(z).
[59] MEITY, *supra* note 13, at ¶ 6.
[60] PDP Bill 2023, s. 7(b).

processes. Similarly, the PDP Bill allows the government to exempt itself and its instrumentalities from complying with the prescribed obligations in the interest of "sovereignty and integrity of India," "public order," "security of the State," "friendly relations with foreign States," or preventing incitement to any cognizable offenses in relation to them.[61] The government also has significant degree of control over the appointment of the proposed Data Protection Board ("DPB") including through an usually short duration of two years.[62] Although the DPB is constituted as an independent body on paper,[63] several concerns remain whether it can function independent of government control. For instance, through the DPB, the government could potentially exercise control over significant data fiduciaries as they have additional obligations including appointing a local Data Protection Officer and data auditor[64] and conducting periodic data protection impact assessment.[65] Further, the Bill provides discretion to the government to notify any social media company as a significant data fiduciary based on different considerations such as volume and sensitivity of data, security, public order, and sovereignty considerations, and risks to electoral democracy.[66]

The Indian government has also proposed a highly ambitious NPD Framework in 2020 to facilitate sharing of non-personal data in India such as between government and businesses, and among businesses. Under this framework, a new body called the Non-Personal Data Protection Authority ("NDPA") was proposed to be established to oversee sharing of non-personal data. This framework is much broader in scope than the framework on the flow of non-personal data proposed in the EU under the Data Governance Act.[67] Although the proposed policy framework is ambitious, it is not without flaws. In particular, issues of conceptualization of different categories of non-personal data, allocation of economic incentives among stakeholders in the digital economy, and safeguards for group privacy protection appear contentious and troubling.

First, the distinction between personal and non-personal data remains a moving target under the NPD Framework proposed in 2020 because any data

---

[61] PDP Bill 2023, s.17(2).
[62] PDP Bill 2023, s. 20(2).
[63] PDP Bill 2023, s. 28(1).
[64] PDP Bill 2023, s. 10(2)(a) and (b).
[65] PDP Bill 2023, s. 10(2)(c).
[66] PDP Bill 2023, s. 10(1).
[67] With regard to the Data Governance Act, see Thomas Streinz, *The Evolution of European Data Law* (Jan. 2021) (on file with author).

that becomes identifiable (for instance, with new data analytics tools) falls under the purview of the PDP Bill and not the NDP framework. It remains unclear how the proposed NDPA would make a determination in practice regarding the anonymization of data.[68] Second, Data Trustees (either public agencies or not-for-profit organizations) have been proposed to create, maintain, and facilitate sharing of high-value datasets while protecting community interests. But there is no clear accountability mechanism applicable to these entities beyond a general "duty of care" to an undefined "community."[69] Although identification of groups in anonymized datasets has become easier with new technologies, group privacy concerns remain mostly unaddressed in this framework. For instance, entities operating on India Stack (the open government API) could conceivably identify and discriminate against specific groups. Third, the policy does not identify the possible winners and losers resulting from a mandatory framework requiring private entities to share metadata and parts of their high-value datasets with the government or other competitors. These datasets are developed with significant resources and the direct incentive (other than it being mandated by law and incurring a "nominal" fee)[70] to share such data remains unclear, especially for start-ups that expend a significant portion of their resources to develop their datasets.

2. Data Localization as a Regulatory Tool

The most prominent measure adopted by the Indian government to manifest several of its data governance policy goals is data localization. Data localization requirements apply to data collected in various sectors such as data collected using public funds,[71] subscriber information collected by broadcasting companies,[72] electronic books of accounts,[73] electronic payments,[74] and policyholder information collected by insurance companies.[75] Further, the current version of the PDP Bill does not provide clear guidelines on cross-border personal data transfers.[76] Instead, it broadly allows the government to

---

[68] See MEITY, *supra* note 13, Appendix 3 (Identifies prevalent anonymisation technologies but does not evaluate their technological effectiveness c).

[69] MEITY, *supra* note 13, at ¶ 7.7.

[70] *Id., at* ¶ 7.7, 8.5.

[71] DEPARTMENT OF SCIENCE AND TECHNOLOGY (INDIA), NATIONAL DATA SHARING AND ACCESSIBILITY POLICY (Feb. 9, 2014).

[72] MINISTRY OF COMMERCE AND INDUSTRY, CONSOLIDATED FDI POLICY 2017 (India).

[73] Companies (Accounts) Rules, 2014, Rule 3(5).

[74] RBI, *supra* note 45.

[75] IRDAI (Outsourcing of Activities by Indian Insurers) Regulations 2017 (India), Rule 18.

[76] PDP Bill 2023, s 16(1).

notify the jurisdictions to which personal data cannot be transferred by data fiduciaries or processors.[77] However, there is no clarity regarding the factors that would be considered in arriving at this finding. The Bill also clarifies that any existing domestic law containing restrictions on transborder transfer of personal data will not be a contravention of this new law.[78]

The Indian government has previously envisaged imposing transborder transfer restrictions on data collected from IoT devices, e-commerce platforms, and social media.[79] Under the NPD Framework, any anonymized data derived from critical or sensitive personal data is also proposed to be subject to the same localization requirements as under the PDP Bill.[80]

While the current government narrative on data localization in India is often supportive, this debate has evolved over the years. For instance, the Justice AP Shah Committee Report in 2012 had identified the value of an accountability-based data protection framework for India.[81] Even a 2019 report from the Ministry of Electronics and Information Technology ("MEITY") had identified the importance of cross-border data flows and, in that regard, recommended against over-regulating data collection and instead supported interoperable frameworks for data transfer such as the Cross Border Privacy Rules of the APEC.[82] The current version of the PDP Bill does not provide specific requirements for data localization, although previous iterations were replete with such provisions. Nonetheless, as discussed above, the government safeguards its discretion to restrict data flows outside the country in the current PDP Bill both by prescribing new notifications and by implementing existing restrictive measures.

The narrative on data localization continues to shift across the world for both legitimate policy and protectionist reasons, and India is no exception. The views regarding the economic and legal impact of data localization vary significantly across stakeholders. For instance, certain industry stakeholders and think tanks have argued that data localization could hamper development of innovative start-ups and have a negative impact on digital services exports in the coming years.[83] In contrast, certain dominant industry players

[77] *Id.*
[78] PDP Bill 2023, s. 16(2).
[79] DIPP, *supra* note 13, at 16.
[80] MEITY, *supra* note 13, at ¶ 8.15.
[81] Planning Commission, Report of the Expert of Groups on Privacy (Oct. 16, 2012).
[82] MEITY, *supra* note 21.
[83] E.g., CUTS International, *Data Localisation India's Double-Edged Sword* (2020) (As per this report, digital services may fall by 10–19% depending on the restrictiveness of data flows); Rajat

such as Reliance and Paytm welcomed India's broad data localization mandate as a tool to fight data colonialism and ensure greater data security.[84] Chinese companies such as Alibaba also supported data localization as they had huge investments in data centers in India.[85] Some experts also think that data localization is necessary to increase the competitiveness of India's domestic digital industries.[86] The various policy documents circulated by the government, however, do not explore the complexities of this discussion by examining stakeholder consensus and/or policy evidence, and instead based largely on prevailing political sentiment.

3. Complexity of the Institutional Framework

The other critical component of the data governance complex in India is its institutional diversity. Several government agencies manage different (and sometimes overlapping) areas of data governance. As indicated earlier, the government has proposed setting up a PDB to oversee implementation of the PDP Bill, and NDPA to oversee the implementation the policy framework on non-personal data in India. Additionally, the NPD Framework proposes the creation of Data Trustees to manage sharing of non-personal data and protecting community interests. The government has also proposed setting up Consent Managers to verify consent management practices of data fiduciaries,[87] and data auditors to oversee data management practices of significant data fiduciaries.[88] The Draft E-Commerce Policy proposes setting up an e-commerce regulator, whose functions would include enforcing data

---

Kathuria et al, *Economic Impact of Cross-Border Data Flows* (INTERNET AND MOBILE ASSOCIATION OF INDIA AND ICRIER, 2019).

[84] Press Trust of India, *Data Localisation Critical for Security of India's Payment Systems: Paytm*, THE ECONOMIC TIMES (Apr. 30, 2018), https://retail.economictimes.indiatimes.com/news/e-comme rce/e-tailing/data-localisation-critical-for-security-of-indias-payment-systems-paytm/63973894 (last visited Apr. 12, 2021); Press Trust of India, *Mukesh Ambani Says 'Data Colonisation' as Bad as Physical Colonisation*, THE ECONOMIC TIMES (Dec. 19, 2018), https://economictimes.indiatimes. com/news/company/corporate-trends/mukesh-ambani-says-data-colonisation-as-bad-as-physi cal-colonisation/articleshow/67164810.cms?from=mdr (last visited Apr. 13, 2021); Parminder Jeet Singh, *Bringing Data Under the Rule of Law*, THE HINDU (Sept. 20, 2018), https://www.thehindu. com/opinion/op-ed/bringing-data-under-the-rule-of-law/article24988755.ece (last visited Apr. 13, 2021).

[85] Mugdha Variyar, *Alibaba Backs Data Localization in India*, THE ECONOMIC TIMES (Sept. 20, 2018), https://economictimes.indiatimes.com/small-biz/startups/newsbuzz/alibaba-backs-data-localisation-in-india/articleshow/65869841.cms?from=mdr (last visited Apr. 13, 2021).

[86] E.g., Rashmi Banga, *Is India Digitally Prepared for International Trade?* (Discussion Paper # 235, RESEARCH AND INFORMATION SYSTEMS FOR DEVELOPING COUNTRIES, Nov. 2018).

[87] NITI Aayog, *supra* note 13. PDP Bill 2023, s. 2(g).

[88] PDP Bill 2023, s.10 (2)(b).

localization and other regulations in the e-commerce sector. Additionally, existing bodies such as the Competition Commission of India ("CCI") facilitate competition in the domestic digital market.

Various ministries/agencies are involved in different aspects of data governance including the MEITY, the Ministry of Commerce and Industry, NITI Aayog, and various sectoral regulators such as the Research Bank of India (payments and fintech) and Telecommunications Regulatory Authority of India. Although different government agencies and ministries can coordinate their functions to adopt a whole-of-government approach to data governance,[89] it remains unclear how this will occur in practice in India, and the role of the central government in managing it. Certain institutional conflicts are already visible. For instance, a committee was set up in 2020 to resolve differences between the MEITY and NITI Aayog regarding allocation of responsibilities for AI regulation.[90] Concerns have also been raised regarding the conflict between CCI's mandate to safeguard competition in the domestic market and the NDPA's role to facilitate sharing of non-personal data, including among domestic competitors.[91]

4. Demystifying the Indian Data Governance Complex

India's foray into data governance is recent but rapid and drastic. This means these new institutions will face a steep learning curve and acute capacity constraints. Further, being a developing country, India has relatively much weaker state capacity compared to its Western counterparts and more experienced and centralized regulators such as China. Some experts argue that overloading fledgling institutions with too many functions can destroy state capacity even before creating it.[92] Anecdotal experience suggests that India has only been partially successful in implementing data localization in the e-payments sector.[93] A similar argument can be made regarding the implementation of the PDP Bill, which is prescriptive and would require extensive

---

[89] MEITY, *supra* note 13, at ¶7.12.

[90] Surabhi Agarwal, *MeitY to Implement AI Mission, While Niti Aayog Will Help in Planning*, The Economic Times (Dec. 25, 2020), https://economictimes.indiatimes.com/tech/tech-bytes/meity-to-implement-ai-mission-while-niti-aayog-will-help-in-planning/articleshow/79950502.cms?from=mdr (last visited Apr. 13, 2021).

[91] Hemangini Dadwal & Aakash Narula, *Mandatory Sharing Of Non-Personal Data At Odds With Competition Law*, Bloomberg Quint (Sept. 22, 2020), https://www.bloombergquint.com/opinion/mandatory-sharing-of-non-personal-data-at-odds-with-competition-law (last visited Apr. 13, 2021).

[92] Matt Andrews et al., Building State Capability: Evidence, Analysis, Action 54 (2017).

[93] CUTS International, *Aatmanirbhar Bharat & Cross Border Data Flows*, YouTube (Jul. 20, 2020) https://www.youtube.com/watch?v=c20hCEWyKZI (comments of Gulshan Rai).

state capacity and regulatory experience for meaningful enforcement. In practice, enforcement could be ineffective, thereby defeating the purpose of the legislation. Coupled with the various concerns regarding the independence of these government agencies and weak accountability mechanisms, the institutional complex of data governance appears complicated, burdensome, and even counterproductive.

India's data governance framework is peculiar to its complex political economy. It is not solely targeted at protecting domestic players, although developing data champions is definitely an important part of India's economic agenda. For instance, Jio Platforms (owned by Reliance and touted as India's first super-app) is likely to be a clear winner from India's restrictive data governance approach, emerging as a leader in e-commerce, online entertainment, digital payments, and suite of other digital services. But another important aspect of this framework is concentration of economic power in the government and commercialization of data collected by government agencies.[94] Further, the government shares a close relationship with certain powerful private companies, resulting in a somewhat impenetrable relationship.[95] The foundation of this close relationship is the government depending on the private sector for intimate surveillance of citizens, and the private sector depending on the public digital infrastructure. These aspects distinguish the Indian model from the EU, although comparisons are drawn due to GDPR-like provisions in the PDP Bill. For instance, several policy choices made in the PDP Bill and the NPD Framework may not be as successful in empowering individuals to make free economic (or political) choices regarding their data.[96] Further, certain exemptions grant unhindered discretion to the government to facilitate the use of data for both governmental functions and commercial purposes.[97]

The economic repercussions of the government engaging in data accumulation in the same manner as private companies is little understood. Can this lead to greater consumer welfare? Are such markets competitive? What are the chances of a politicized relationship between the government and powerful domestic lobbies? Some reports have identified the close links

---

[94] Hicks, *supra* note 22; Srinath Lakshmanan, *What Ails India's Data Economy*, 55 ECON. & POL. WKLY. https://www.epw.in/node/157032/pdf (2020).

[95] MK Venu, *Reliance Jio: A New Test of Cronyism for the Modi Government*, THE WIRE (Aug. 11, 2016), https://thewire.in/economy/reliance-v-india-tela-new-test-of-cronyism-for-modi-government (last visited Apr. 12, 2021).

[96] Basu & Sherman, *supra* note 11.

[97] *See, e.g.*, PDP Bill 2023, s. 16(2)-(5).

between the entities that developed Aadhar and now building digital start-ups supported by India Stack.[98] At its core, the data governance complex in India facilitates "nationalization" of all data and data infrastructure;[99] ultimately, the government dictates who can "unlock" the benefits of the data-driven economy and how.

III. Data Governance and Influences on Digital Trade Policies in India

India's dissonance with the WTO in different areas of trade regulation is well-known and also prominently visible in the realm of digital trade, where its foreign trade policies reinforce domestic policy preferences/goals in data governance. This section explains the close nexus of data governance and digital trade in India, and the possible consequences of India's opposition to digital trade dialogues and negotiations at the WTO, G20, RCEP, and elsewhere. This antagonistic stance has significant political and economic costs for India and the world. While regulatory autonomy is undoubtedly important in regulating the digital sector, it is less clear why ringfencing the domestic digital economy will serve India's regulatory or economic interests. In particular, the closed-door approach to WTO digital trade negotiations may not only mean that India cannot voice its (much needed) opinion in shaping global digital trade rules, but also that an evident gap will continue to exist in the rules being developed in international trade institutions.

A. The Nexus of Data Governance and Digital Trade

The Indian government has proactively opposed several international negotiations on digital trade and cross-border data flows. For instance, it opposed extending the WTO moratorium on customs duties on electronic transmissions, arguing that developing countries will lose revenue from

---

[98] Hicks, *supra* note 22, at 343. *See also* Neelina MS, *From Aadhaar to Aarogya Setu, Vidhi's Questionable Role in Technology-related Policy making*, THE CARAVAN MAGAZINE (Aug. 20, 2020) https://caravanmagazine.in/technology/vidhi-aadhaar-aarogya-setu-arghya-sengupta-privacy-think-tank (last visited Apr. 12, 2021).

[99] Nikhil Pahwa, *India Must Avoid Nationalisation of Data*, MEDIANAMA (July 25, 2020) https://www.medianama.com/2020/07/223-non-personal-data-nationalisation/ (last visited Apr. 12, 2021).

tariffs as more products become digitalized.[100] It refused to endorse the proposal on "Data Free Flow with Trust" proposed at the G20,[101] despite its close political relationship with Japan (who advanced this proposal). Similarly, India has steadfastly refused to participate in the WTO Joint Statement Initiative on Electronic Commerce.[102] Other than few examples such as the *India—Singapore Comprehensive Economic Cooperation Agreement*,[103] and some recent treaties such as *India – UAE Comprehensive Economic Partnership Agreement*, India is not a party to trade treaties containing dedicated electronic commerce provisions. These treaties however do not contain extensive commitments in the e-commerce chapters. India also refused to sign the *Regional Comprehensive Economic Partnership Agreement*, which contained provisions on data localization and cross-border data flows.[104]

India has traditionally not resorted to extensive restrictions on imports of foreign digital technologies and services in the same way as China or Russia, although such measures have recently increased.[105] This may have been due to India's negligible commitments under the *General Agreement on Trade in Services* ("GATS"), especially in sectors such as computer and related services. Therefore, many measures intended to regulate the data-driven sectors in India may not necessarily implicate India's international trade obligations.

However, India banned several foreign digital services from China (to date, 267 Chinese apps remain banned in India). As per the Indian government, these apps are "malicious" as "the[se companies] . . . engaged in activities . . . prejudicial to sovereignty and integrity of India, defence of India, security of state and public order."[106] This measure is unlikely to violate India's WTO law obligations,[107] although some experts argue that the

---

[100] E.g., Work Programme on Electronic Commerce, The E-Commerce Moratorium: Scope and Impact, WTO Doc WT/GC/W/798 (Mar. 10, 2020).

[101] *Press Trust of India, India Not in a Position to Accept Concept of Data Free Flow with Trust: Piyush Goyal*, Financial Express (Sept. 22, 2020), https://www.financialexpress.com/economy/india-not-in-a-position-toaccept-concept-of-data-free-flow-with-trust-piyush-goyal/2089478/(last   visited Apr. 13, 2021).

[102] WTO General Council, The Legal Status of 'Joint Statement Initiatives and their Negotiated Outcomes, WTO Doc WT/GC/W/819 (Feb. 19, 2021).

[103] Chapter 10 contains provisions on digital supply of services, digital products, and exceptions.

[104] Kanksshi Agarwal, *Did Data and E-Commerce Issues Also Influence India's RCEP Exit?*, The Wire (Nov. 14, 2019), https://thewire.in/economy/india-rcep (last visited Apr. 13, 2021).

[105] *See, e.g.,* Rhea Mogul, *India Restricts Laptop, PC Import to Boost Local Manufacturing* CNN (Aug. 3, 2023), https://edition.cnn.com/2023/08/03/tech/india-restrict-import-laptops-intl-hnk/index.html (last visited Aug. 6, 2023)

[106] Press Information Bureau, https://pib.gov.in/PressReleseDetailm.aspx?PRID=1635206 (last visited Apr. 13, 2021).

[107] But see ANI, *China Opposes India's Decision to Continue Chinese Apps Ban, Says It Violates WTO Rules*, The Times of India (Jan. 27, 2021), https://timesofindia.indiatimes.com/india/

ban is inconsistent with *India–China BIT*.[108] The Chinese government has also raised concerns regarding the incompatibility of Make in India and Digital India Initiative with the principles of WTO law.[109] In 2020, India also imposed prior government approval requirements for foreign investments from countries sharing borders with India (primarily targeting Chinese investments and affecting the digital sector)[110] to prevent "opportunistic" takeovers and acquisitions.[111] The government has also imposed taxes on foreign companies: a 2 percent equalization levy on non-resident e-commerce firms, and 6 percent equalization levy on online advertising services provided by non-resident service providers. Expectedly, the above measures faced stiff opposition from China and the United States respectively on the basis that they are likely to violate nondiscrimination obligations in international trade law.[112]

B. Digital Trade Policies Reinforce the Data Governance Complex

Data governance policies can implicate obligations contained in international trade agreements. India's stance on digital trade negotiations is intended to protect its autonomy to regulate data in the "public interest" and ensure that the government can achieve its domestic digital development and data governance goals without being encumbered by its trade obligations. Whether these two outcomes will be achieved in practice remains uncertain. The policies of the Indian government do not rigorously

china-opposes-indias-decision-to-continue-chinese-apps-ban-says-it-violates-wto-rules/articles how/80480454.cms (last visited Apr. 13, 2021).

[108] Particularly for breach of fair and equitable treatment (art. 3(2)). *See* Prabhash Ranjan, *Chinese Investments Enjoy Treaty Protection. Beijing Can Drag New Delhi to Tribunals*, THE PRINT (July 4, 2020), https://theprint.in/opinion/chinese-investments-enjoy-treaty-protection-beijing-can-drag-new-delhi-to-tribunals/453880/ (last visited Apr. 13, 2021).

[109] Asit Ranjan Mishra, *China Rakes Up India's Ban on Apps, FDI Curbs at WTO*, HINDUSTAN TIMES (Mar. 9. 2021), https://www.hindustantimes.com/business/china-rakes-up-india-s-ban-on-apps-fdi-curbs-at-wto-101615249429431.html (last visited Apr. 13, 2021).

[110] Ananth Krishnan, *Following the Money: China Inc's Growing Stake in India-China Relations*, BROOKINGS (Mar. 30, 2020), https://www.brookings.edu/research/following-the-money-china-incs-growing-stake-in-india-china-relations/ (last visited Apr. 13, 2021).

[111] MINISTRY OF COMMERCE AND INDUSTRY, *supra* note 47.

[112] USTR, REPORT ON INDIA'S DIGITAL SERVICES TAX (Jan. 6, 2021); Hindu Bureau, *China Says India's FDI Eestrictions against WTO Eules, G-20 Xonsensus*, THE HINDU BUSINESS LINE (Apr. 20, 2020), https://www.thehindubusinessline.com/news/china-says-indias-fdi-restrictions-against-wto-rules-g-20-consensus/article31386992.ece (last visited Apr. 13, 2021).

account for the economic costs of India's refusal to integrate with the global digital trade framework, for instance, the costs of limiting participation of foreign companies in the data-driven economy through prescriptive laws and policies, or the geopolitical repercussions of India's non-participation in digital trade negotiations.

The first reason why India's digital trade policies reinforce the data governance complex is because they enhance the ability of the government to implement stringent data governance-related laws and regulations. For instance, depending on the sectors affected, data localization provisions may breach obligations contained in GATS and the available exceptions only apply to a defined list of policy objectives under WTO law. However, by not committing to digital trade treaties, the government can freely adopt data localization laws or other restrictive requirements to regulate data flows for various policy reasons.[113]

Further, international trade law can be an impediment to grant preferential treatment to domestic digital products and services, for example, under Make in India or Aatmanirbhar Bharat. The increasingly stringent Internet regulation in India for the purposes of online censorship, regulation of social media intermediaries, and state-driven surveillance for security/public order remain largely unrestrained, if India does not commit to further digital trade liberalization. For instance, in past WTO disputes, measures regulating online gambling and online publications were found to be inconsistent with WTO rules.[114]

The second reason why India's digital trade policies appear to be aligned with its data governance policies is because they are both intended to support domestic digital development by reallocating data resources to domestic companies and boosting the growth of the domestic digital industry. For instance, local players such as Paytm, Phone Pe, and Reliance have not only openly expressed support for data localization, but also argued that the government should adopt a broader definition of critical personal data (e.g., include financial data) to preserve public interest.[115] At the same time, several SMEs in India have opposed various policies pertaining to data localization,

---

[113] DIPP, *supra* note 13, 10. The Indian government, however, may be rightly concerned about the difficulty of data access for law enforcement or other legitimate regulatory purposes. In this regard, India is not an isolated example.

[114] Appellate Body Report, *United States—Measures Affecting the Cross-Border Supply of Gambling and Betting Services*, WTO Doc. WT/DS285/AB/R (adopted May 22, 2007); Appellate Body Report, *China—Measures Affecting Trading Rights and Distribution Services for Certain Publications and Audiovisual Entertainment Products*, ¶ 306, WTO Doc. WT/DS363/AB/R (adopted Jan. 19, 2010).

[115] Press Trust of India, *Data Localisation Critical for Security of India's Payment Systems: Paytm*, THE ECONOMIC TIMES (Apr. 30, 2018), https://retail.economictimes.indiatimes.com/news/e-comme

the highly prescriptive requirements in different iterations of the PDP Bill, and the mandatory data sharing envisaged under the NPD Framework.[116] Several of the prescriptive requirements under the GDPR have had an adverse impact on domestic competition in the EU, especially reducing competitive pressure from maverick firms.[117] Given that the PDP Bill imposes GDPR-like compliance requirements on Indian businesses, domestic market competition may be affected in a similarly adverse manner. Further, although regulatory sandboxes have been proposed in some regulations to encourage local innovation,[118] they are onerous to comply with, and unlikely to benefit most small companies in India especially in light of strict data localization laws.

India's trade policymakers, however, often do not take these diverse perspectives into account, including the possible impact on digital services exports due to data flow restrictions. Further, consumer interests are not of foremost importance in domestic policy circles. For instance, some experts argue that consumer groups may be adversely affected too with higher prices and lower quality, at least in the short run, and the long-term impact is also uncertain.[119]

Finally, as a developing country with limited regulatory capacity, the Indian government must conduct a thorough analysis of the regulatory costs and benefits of a highly complex data governance framework.[120] First, setting up a multitude of data governance institutions will consume significant public resources. It may take several years before these institutions can enforce such a complex framework effectively. In the meanwhile, powerful domestic companies are likely to reinforce their market position, while small start-ups and entrepreneurs may exit the market due to compliance costs and legal and regulatory uncertainties.[121] Thus, the government must consider if less restrictive and less prescriptive routes are available to preserve regulatory

---

rce/e-tailing/data-localisation-critical-for-security-of-indias-payment-systems-paytm/63973894 (last visited Apr. 12, 2021).

[116] Shreya Nandi, *MSMEs, Start-Ups Oppose Policy on Non-Personal Data*, MINT (Sep. 25, 2020), https://www.livemint.com/companies/start-ups/majority-msmes-oppose-proposed-non-personal-data-policy-in-current-form-survey-11600875486689.html; Kathuria et al, *supra* note 83.

[117] Michal S. Gal and Oshrit Gav, *The Competitive Effects of the GDPR*, 16 J. COMPETITION L. & ECO. 349–51 (2020).

[118] E.g., RBI, ENABLING FRAMEWORK FOR REGULATORY SANDBOX (Dec. 16, 2020).

[119] Sai Rakshith Potluri et al, *Effects of Data Localization on Digital Trade: An Agent-based Modelling Approach*, 44 TELECOMM. POL'Y 1020–22 (2020).

[120] Mishra, *supra* note 12.

[121] Burman, *supra* note 11.

interests (e.g., to ensure access to data for regulators or to protect privacy of individuals).[122] Second, although India continues to be an attractive destination for investment in the digital sector, adopting data governance laws without adequate safeguards for state surveillance could reduce investor confidence and trust in the digital sector in India. Third, the proposed policies on data governance do not clearly identify how the incentives and benefits from the public data infrastructure will be re-allocated among various market players. For instance, as discussed earlier, the NDP Framework fails to provide clear economic incentives, especially, for private sector SMEs and start-ups, to participate, despite requiring mandatory sharing of chunks of their non-personal data with the data trustees/government.

C. India in the Global Digital Trade Framework

The discussions above suggest that the current approach in India in data governance and digital trade is largely nationalist and parochial, that is, primarily catered to building domestic data champions and increasing government control as a data custodian. Although the government has occasionally indicated an ambition to be a dominant digital player in the developing world, there is no comprehensive or systematic plan. For instance, the NITI Aayog has set out that India must aim to be an "AI Garage" for 40 percent of the world.[123] This is based on the reasoning that any AI solutions developed in India are scalable in other developing countries especially in health, agriculture, education, and payments. India nurtures an ambition to be a 'technology-provider of choice' and a leader in offering AI as a Service in developing countries.[124] Some other policy documents ambiguously suggest that India's data governance policies will benefit India and benefit the world.[125] However, there is no meticulous assessment of how Indian companies will expand their market access to these foreign markets and compete with established Chinese and U.S. companies, especially in the absence of trade agreements.

The dichotomy between domestic digital development and global integration in India is undesirable and counterproductive. Being a leader in the

---

[122] See examples discussed in Bailey and Parsheera, *supra* note 49.
[123] NITI Aayog, *supra* note 9, at 18.
[124] *Id.*
[125] MEITY, *supra* note 13, at ¶ 3.4.

developing world, India has the potential to offer a model of data governance that enhances individual growth and empowerment while ensuring meaningful integration of developing countries into the global digital economy. For instance, most Electronic Commerce Chapters in FTAs contain weak development-oriented provisions such as regulatory assistance to LDCs, providing support to entrepreneurs in developing countries, and international cooperation to foster digital inclusion in the global economy. Similarly, international dialogues on global governance often do not take into account viewpoints of developing countries regarding the costs of enforcing data protection laws, development of standards for data governance, and costs of participating in interoperable data transfer schemes.[126] Instead of acting as a catalyzing force in bringing such issues to the forefront, India seems to be following a short-sighted approach that may benefit some big domestic players and increase governmental power but is likely to harm long-term interests of its consumers and small businesses, who lie at the heart of its economy. In fact, if several countries adopt this mindset, the future will see greater "divergent data nationalism," widening the global digital divide and reducing trust in the digital ecosystem.[127]

India's stance to not participate in global digital trade discussions has geopolitical costs. India's ambition to move up the global value chain from being a backdoor processing center for developed countries to becoming a digital service/AI provider of choice for developing countries is premised on countries remaining open to engage in digital trade with India. By sidelining negotiations on digital trade, India loses an opportunity to secure future market access. This may include developed country markets where India's software providers have traditionally enjoyed a competitive advantage and, developing countries, where Indian-made digital products and services are likely to be competitive in the future. Finally, a data governance culture that leans toward concentrating power in the government is likely to be viewed with suspicion (as has been the case with Chinese and Russian digital technologies in international markets), making India-made digital technologies less attractive, and potentially hindering both exports and foreign investments in the digital sector.

---

[126] *See generally* Anupam Chander et al, COSTS OF COMPLIANCE AND ENFORCEMENT OF DATA PROTECTION REGULATION, BACKGROUND PAPER FOR WORLD DEVELOPMENT REPORT 2021 (Mar. 2021).

[127] GOVERNMENT OFFICE FOR SCIENCE (U.K.), EVIDENCE AND SCENARIOS FOR GLOBAL DATA SYSTEMS (2020).

IV. Conclusion

The Indian vision of data governance and preferences for a shielded data economy strongly influences India's non-committal position in global digital trade negotiations. However, this position comes with several uncertainties, including a geopolitical backlash by India's trading partners; stifling innovation by domestic start-ups and entrepreneurs; prejudicing market access of Indian companies to other economies; and a lost opportunity for India to advocate robust development-oriented rules in digital trade agreements. Alongside these factors, the rapid adoption of prescriptive regulations and highly complex institutions of data governance in India, the inexperience of these bodies, and the lack of sufficient stakeholder analysis in formulating policies, raise several questions regarding the impact of India's data governance model on the digital economy.

As India marches forward in developing its digital trade and data governance framework, policymakers must pay heed to the underlying socioeconomic realities within the country, the likely inequities in the distribution of "economic value" from data-driven sectors, and the latent potential of Indian tech entrepreneurs to succeed in the global digital trade market. Ultimately, India needs to balance nationalist preferences on data governance with the various opportunities that meaningful integration with the global digital economy could offer to its citizens.

Making policy choices in data governance is not easy, especially for a diverse and dynamic economy like India. To not lose sight of the forest for the trees, India must shift from focusing on exerting absolute government control over data and protecting narrow industry interests to facilitating trust and security in digital trade, including reducing business uncertainties; as well as providing avenues to smaller digital-driven businesses and consumers to integrate in the global digital value chain by seeking opportunities for meaningful international/regional cooperation and integration in digital trade and data governance.

11

Creating Data Flow Rules
through Preferential Trade Agreements

Mira Burri

I. Introduction

The critical importance of data for all economic sectors seems nowadays almost uncontested. Beyond the somewhat flawed mantra of data being the "new oil,"[1] many studies point to the vast potential of data as an enabler of more efficient business operations, highly innovative solutions, and better policy choices in all areas of societal life.[2] It is noteworthy that this transformative capacity refers not only to "digital native" areas, such as search or social networking, but also to "brick-and-mortar," physical businesses, such as those in manufacturing or logistics.[3] The COVID-19 pandemic has further augmented the value of digital transactions and the significance of data-driven platforms.[4] Emerging technologies, like Artificial Intelligence (AI), which are thought to be in many senses a game changer,[5] are also highly dependent on data inputs.[6] Therefore, solutions in the domain of data governance can in many aspects condition the future of the data-driven economy.

---

[1] *The World's Most Valuable Resource Is No Longer Oil, But Data*, Economist (May 6, 2017), https://www.economist.com/leaders/2017/05/06/the-worlds-most-valuable-resource-is-no-lon ger-oil-but-data.

[2] *See, e.g.*, James Manyika et al., *Big Data: The Next Frontier for Innovation, Competition, and Productivity*, McKinsey & Co. (May 1, 2011), https://www.mckinsey.com/business-functions/mckin sey-digital/our-insights/big-data-the-next-frontier-for-innovation; Viktor Mayer-Schönberger & Kenneth Cukier, Big Data: A Revolution That Will Transform How We Live, Work, and Think (2013).

[3] Manyika et al., *supra* note 2.

[4] *See, e.g., E-Commerce, Trade and the Covid-19 Pandemic: Information Note*, World Trade Org. (May 4, 2020), https://www.wto.org/english/tratop_e/covid19_e/ecommerce_report_e.pdf.

[5] *See, e.g.*, Jacques Bughin et al., *Notes from the AI Frontier: Modeling The Impact of AI on the World Economy*, McKinsey & Co. (Sept. 4, 2018), https://www.mckinsey.com/featured-insights/artificial-intelligence/notes-from-the-ai-frontier-modeling-the-impact-of-ai-on-the-world-economy.

[6] Kristina Irion & Josephine Williams, Prospective Policy Study on Artificial Intelligence and EU Trade Policy (2019), https://www.uva.nl/binaries/content/assets/uva/

Mira Burri, *Creating Data Flow Rules through Preferential Trade Agreements* In: *Data Sovereignty.* Edited by: Anupam Chander and Haochen Sun, Oxford University Press. © Oxford University Press 2023. DOI: 10.1093/oso/9780197582794.003.0012

At the same time, as it has been well documented, the increased dependence on data has brought about a set of new concerns. The impact of data collection and use upon privacy has been particularly widely acknowledged by scholars and policymakers, as well as felt by users of digital products and services in everyday life. Such risks have been augmented in the era of Big Data,[7] which presents certain distinct challenges to the protection of personal data and by extension to the protection of privacy.[8] Governments have responded to these concerns in a variety of ways. In terms of external safeguards, states have sought new ways to assert control over data—in particular by prescribing diverse measures that "localize" the data, its storage or suppliers, so as to keep it within the state's sovereign space.[9] This kind of erecting barriers to data flows, however, does affect trade and may endanger the realization of an innovative data economy,[10] even in a domestic context.[11] In terms of internal safeguards, the preoccupation of the perceived perils of Big Data has triggered the reform of data protection laws around the world, perhaps best exemplified by the efforts of the European Union (EU) to set particularly high standards of protection through the adoption of the 2016 General Data Protection Regulation (GDPR).[12] The reform initiatives are, however, not coherent, as they reflect societies' understandings of constitutional values, relationships between citizens and the state, and the role of the

---

en/press-office/ivir_artificial-intelligence-and-eu-trade-policy.pdf; Anupam Chander, *Artificial Intelligence and Trade*, *in* BIG DATA AND GLOBAL TRADE LAW 115 (Mira Burri ed., 2021).

[7] For an introduction on Big Data applications and review of the relevant literature, *see* Mira Burri, *Understanding the Implications of Big Data and Big Data Analytics for Competition Law: An Attempt for a Primer*, *in* NEW DEVELOPMENTS IN COMPETITION BEHAVIOURAL LAW AND ECONOMICS 241 (Klaus Mathis & Avishalom Tor eds., 2019).

[8] *See, e.g.*, Omer Tene & Jules Polonetsky, *Big Data for All: Privacy and User Control in the Age of Analytics*, 11 Nw. J. TECH. & INTELL. PROP. 239 (2013); Urs Gasser, *Recoding Privacy Law: Reflections on the Future Relationship among Law, Technology, and Privacy*, 130 HARV. L. REV. 61 (2016); Sheri B. Pan, *Get to Know Me: Protecting Privacy and Autonomy under Big Data's Penetrating Gaze*, 30 HARV. J.L. & TECH. 239 (2016).

[9] *See* Anupam Chander & Uyên P. Lê, *Data Nationalism*, 64 EMORY L.J. 677 (2015).

[10] Digital Trade in the US and Global Economies, Part 1, Inv. No. 332–531, USITC Pub. 4415 (July 2013); Digital Trade in the US and Global Economies, Part 2, Inv. No. 332–540, USITC Pub. 4485 (Aug. 2014).

[11] *See, e.g.*, Martina F. Ferracane, *The Costs of Data Protectionism*, *in* BIG DATA AND GLOBAL TRADE LAW 63 (Mira Burri ed., 2021); Richard D. Taylor, *"Data Localization": The Internet in the Balance*, 44 TELECOMM. POL'Y 102003 (2020).

[12] Regulation (EU) 2016/679 of the European Parliament and of the Council of 27 April 2016 on the Protection of Natural Persons with Regard to the Processing of Personal Data and on the Free Movement of such Data, and Repealing Directive 95/46/EC (General Data Protection Regulation), 2016 O.J. (L 119) 1 [hereinafter GDPR].

266 CREATING DATA FLOW RULES THROUGH PTAS

market, to name but a few.[13] The striking divergences, both in the perceptions and the regulation of privacy protection across nations, and the fundamental differences between the human rights approach of the EU and the more market-based, non-interventionist approach of the United States,[14] have also meant that conventional forms of international cooperation and an agreement on shared standards of data protection have become highly unlikely.[15]

Against this backdrop of a complex and contentious regulatory environment, data and cross-border data flows, in particular, have become one of the relatively new topics in global trade law discussions. With the stalemate at the multilateral forum of the World Trade Organization (WTO)[16] and despite the current reinvigoration of the e-commerce negotiations,[17] new rule-making has occurred predominantly in preferential trade venues.[18] This chapter aims to shed light on the rules created in preferential trade agreements (PTAs), their evolution over time, and the positioning of the main stakeholders—the EU and the United States. The mapping of the new data governance regime in trade agreements, however, should not be contained to these major players. Therefore, the chapter also seeks to provide a more comprehensive mapping of data-related norms, found in other agreements, to help better understand the big picture of the regulatory framework for digital trade, as well as to highlight trends in rule diffusion and their potential implications.[19]

---

[13] See, e.g., Anupam Chander et al., *Catalyzing Privacy Law*, 105 MINN. L. REV. 1733 (2021); Fernanda G. Nicola & Oreste Pollicino, *The Balkanization of Data Privacy Regulation*, 123 W. VA. L. REV. 61 (2020); Mira Burri, *Interfacing Privacy and Trade*, 53 CASE W. RES. J. INT'L L. 35 (2021); Anupam Chander & Paul M. Schwartz, *Privacy and/or Trade*, 90 U. CHI. L. REV. 49 (2023).

[14] See, e.g., James Q. Whitman, *The Two Western Cultures of Privacy: Dignity versus Liberty*, 113 YALE L.J. 1151 (2004); Paul M. Schwartz & Daniel J. Solove, *Reconciling Personal Information in the United States and European Union*, 102 CALIF. L. REV. 877 (2014); Chander & Schwartz, *supra* note 14.

[15] See, e.g., Nicola & Pollicino, *supra* note 13.

[16] For details, see, e.g., Mira Burri, *The Governance of Data and Data Flows in Trade Agreements: The Pitfalls of Legal Adaptation*, 51 U.C. DAVIS L. REV. 65 (2017) [hereinafter Burri, *The Governance of Data and Data Flows in Trade Agreements*]; Mira Burri, *The International Economic Law Framework for Digital Trade*, 135 ZEITSCHRIFT FÜR SCHWEIZERISCHES RECHT 10 (2015).

[17] World Trade Org., *Joint Statement on Electronic Commerce*, WTO Doc. WT/L/1056 (Jan. 25, 2019). For details, see Mira Burri, *Towards a New Treaty on Digital Trade*, 55 J. WORLD TRADE 71 (2021); Mira Burri, *A WTO Agreement on Electronic Commerce: An Enquiry into its Legal Substance and Viability*, 53 GEO. WASH. INT'L L. REV. 565 (2023).

[18] Burri, *The Governance of Data and Data Flows in Trade Agreements: The Pitfalls of Legal Adaptation*, *supra* note 16; Burri, *The International Economic Law Framework for Digital Trade*, *supra* note 16; WORLD TRADE ORG., WORLD TRADE REPORT 2018: THE FUTURE OF WORLD TRADE: HOW DIGITAL TECHNOLOGIES ARE TRANSFORMING GLOBAL COMMERCE (2018), https://www.wto.org/english/res_e/publications_e/world_trade_report18_e.pdf.

[19] The information stems from our own dataset *TAPED*: Trade Agreement Provisions on Electronic Commerce and Data. The TAPED dataset is available to all to use and further develop under the creative commons (attribution, non-commercial, share-alike) license at the University of Lucerne website (https://www.unilu.ch/taped). See Mira Burri & Rodrigo Polanco, *Digital Trade Provisions in Preferential Trade Agreements: Introducing a New Dataset*, 23 J. INT'L ECON. L. 187 (2020).

II. Digital Trade Provisions in PTAs

A. Developments over Time

From the 384 PTAs agreed upon between 2000 and 2022, more than half of the PTAs have provisions related to digital trade. The largest number of provisions is found in e-commerce and intellectual property (IP) chapters; overall, the provisions remain however highly heterogeneous, addressing an array of different issues ranging from customs duties and paperless trading to personal data protection and cybersecurity. The depth of the commitments and the extent of their binding nature can also vary significantly. Tracing the digital trade provisions along a chronological line, it is evident that the inclusion of provisions in PTAs referring explicitly to electronic commerce started early on (with the 2000 Free Trade Agreement (FTA) between Jordan and the United States[20]) but recent years mark a significant increase of rule-making in the area of digital trade. As of September 2021, specific provisions applicable to e-commerce can be found in 167 PTAs, mostly in dedicated chapters (109). Among the PTAs with digital trade provisions, it is evident that the number of provisions and the level of their detail have also increased significantly over the years. Meanwhile, the United States–Mexico–Canada Agreement (USMCA) with its "Digital Trade" chapter is the most comprehensive with 19 articles comprising 3,206 words. The newer dedicated digital trade agreements go well beyond—the U.S.–Japan Digital Trade Agreement (DTA) has 22 articles and 5,346 words; and the Digital Economy Partnership Agreement (DEPA) between Chile, Singapore, and New Zealand contains 65 articles and 10,887 words.

B. Overview of Data-Related Rules in PTAs

Beyond the unsettled debate on defining "digital trade,"[21] one can speak of the relevance of trade rules for data and data flows for at least three

---

[20] US-Jordan FTA, art. 7. Almost at the same time, New Zealand and Singapore agreed upon the Closer Economic Partnership Agreement (CEPA), including an article on paperless trading. Two years later, the Australia-Singapore FTA (SAFTA), concluded on February 17, 2003, was the first PTA to have a dedicated chapter on e-commerce.

[21] *See, e.g.*, WORLD TRADE ORG., *supra* note 18. *See also* Mira Burri & Anupam Chander, *What Are Digital Trade and Digital Trade Law?*, 117 AJIL UNBOUND 99 (2023), https://doi:10.1017/aju.2023.14.

268 CREATING DATA FLOW RULES THROUGH PTAS

Table 11.1. Overview of Data-Related Provisions in FTAs (2000–2022)[*]

	Provisions on data flows in e-commerce chapters and DEAs	Provisions on data localization
Soft commitments	23	2
Hard commitments	22	33
Total	45	35

[*]For all data, *see* the TAPED dataset at https://www.unilu.ch/taped. For details, *see* Mira Burri, *Data Flows and Global Trade Law, in* BIG DATA AND GLOBAL TRADE LAW 11 (Mira Burri ed., 2021).

reasons—because (1) they condition the cross-border flow of data by regulating trade in goods and services as well as the protection of intellectual property; (2) they may install certain beyond the border rules that demand changes in domestic regulation—for example, with regard to procedures with electronic signatures or data protection; and (3) trade law can limit the policy space that regulators have at home—that is, calibrate their data sovereignty.[22] In addition to this generic framework, whose rules are found both in WTO law and in the WTO-plus preferential treaties, the last decade has witnessed the emergence of entirely new rules that explicitly regulate data flows. Specific data-related provisions[23] are a relatively new phenomenon and can be found primarily in dedicated e-commerce chapters and only in a handful of agreements (see Table 11.1). The rules refer to both the free cross-border flow of data and to banning or limiting data localization requirements. The next sections focus on these provisions, as well as look at the norms regarding data protection, which may condition the free data flow commitments.

1. Rules on Data Flows

It is fair to note at the outset that thus far no common definition of data flows exists, despite the widespread rhetoric around the term and its frequent use in reports and studies.[24] Nonetheless, although there are variations in treaty language, there seems to be a tendency for a broad definition of data flows

---

[22] *See* in this sense Mira Burri, *The Regulation of Data Flows in Trade Agreements*, 48 GEO. J. INT'L L. 408 (2017); Francesca Casalini & Javier López González, *Trade and Cross-Border Data Flows* (OECD, Trade Policy Papers No. 220, 2019).

[23] Provisions on the cross-border flow of data can, however, be also found in chapters, dealing with discrete services sectors, where data flows are inherent to the very definition of those services—this is particularly valid for the telecommunications and the financial services sectors.

[24] *See* Casalini & González, *supra* note 22.

(1) where there are bits of information (data) as part of the provision of a service or a product and (2) where this data crosses borders, although the data flows do not neatly coincide with one commercial transaction and the provision of certain service may relate to multiple flows of data.[25] So far, there also has not been a distinction between different types of data—for instance, between personal and non-personal data, personal or company data or machine-to-machine data.[26] However, personal information is commonly included explicitly in the data-related provisions in PTAs,[27] which may lead to clashes with domestic data protection regimes.

If one looks at the evolution of data flow provisions in PTAs, there has been a major transformation in treaty language over the years. Non-binding provisions on data flows appeared quite early. Already in the 2000 Jordan–US FTA, the Joint Statement on Electronic Commerce highlighted the "need to continue the free flow of information," although no explicit provision in this regard was included. The first agreement having such a provision is the 2006 Taiwan–Nicaragua FTA, where as part of the cooperation activities, the Parties affirmed the importance of working "to maintain cross-border flows of information as an essential element to promote a dynamic environment for electronic commerce."[28] A stronger commitment can be found in the 2007 South Korea–U.S. FTA, where the Parties stated that they "*shall endeavor* to refrain from imposing or maintaining unnecessary barriers to electronic information flows across borders."[29]

---

[25] Casalini & González, *id.* As the OECD further clarifies: 'the actual flow of data reflects individual firm choices: accessing the OECD library from Paris, for instance, actually means contacting a server in the United States (the OECD uses a U.S.-based company for its web services). *Id.* at 1. Moreover, with the cloud, data can live in many places at once, with files and copies residing in servers around the world.'

[26] For instance, Sen classifies data into personal data referring to data related to individuals; company data referring to data flowing between corporations; business data referring to digitized content such as software and audiovisual content; and social data referring to behavioural patterns determined using personal data, *see* Nivedita Sen, *Understanding the Role of the WTO in International Data Flows: Taking the Liberalization or the Regulatory Autonomy Path?*, 21 J. INT'L ECON. L. 323, 343–46 (2018). Aaronson and Leblond categorize data into personal data, public data, confidential business data, machine-to-machine data and metadata, although they do not specifically define each of these terms. *See* Susan Ariel Aaronson & Patrick Leblond, *Another Digital Divide: The Rise of Data Realms and Its Implications for the WTO*, 21 J. INT'L ECON. L. 245 (2018). The OECD has also tried to break the data into different categories. *See* OECD, DATA IN THE DIGITAL AGE (Mar. 2019), https://www.oecd.org/going-digital/data-in-the-digital-age.pdf.

[27] It is typically defined as "any information, including data, about an identified or identifiable natural person." *See, e.g.*, USMCA, art. 19.1.

[28] Nicaragua-Taiwan FTA, art. 14.05(c). A similar wording is used in the 2008 Canada–Peru FTA, 2010 Hong Kong–New Zealand FTA, 2011 Korea–Peru FTA, 2011 Central America–Mexico FTA, 2013 Colombia–Costa Rica FTA, 2013 Canada-Honduras FTA, 2014 Canada-Korea FTA, and the 2015 Japan–Mongolia FTA.

[29] Korea-US FTA, art. 15.8 (emphasis added).

270 CREATING DATA FLOW RULES THROUGH PTAS

The first agreement having a binding provision on cross-border information flows is the 2014 Mexico–Panama FTA.[30] A much more detailed provision in this regard is found in the 2015 amended version of the Pacific Alliance Additional Protocol (PAAP),[31] which was modeled along the negotiated text of the 2016 Trans-Pacific Partnership Agreement (TPP). The TPP text has since then influenced all subsequent agreements having data flows provisions, such as notably the CPTPP and the USMCA[32]—both endorsing a strong protection of the free flow of data, as discussed in more detail below.

2. Data Localization

Recent PTAs have also started to include provisions on data localization, by either banning or limiting requirements of data localization or data use. An important difference with the data flows provisions is that almost all such provisions are binding.[33] The first agreement with a ban on data localization is the 2015 Japan–Mongolia FTA.[34] Later the same year, the 2015 amended PAAP, and as strongly influenced by the parallel TPP negotiations, included a similar provision on the use and location of computer facilities.[35] In 2016, the TPP included a clear ban on localization, which was then replicated in the CPTPP and the USMCA. The diffusion of these norms is clearly discernible also in subsequent PTAs: among others, the 2016 Chile–Uruguay FTA[36] and the 2016 Updated SAFTA,[37] which closely follow the CPTPP template.[38]

---

[30] Mexico-Panama FTA, art. 14.10 states that each Party 'shall allow its persons and the persons of the other Party to transmit electronic information, from and to its territory, when required by said person, in accordance with the applicable legislation on the protection of personal data and taking into consideration international practices.'

[31] PAAP, art. 13.11 (2015).

[32] Such as the 2016 Chile-Uruguay FTA (art. 8.10), the 2016 Updated Singapore-Australia Free Trade Agreement (Chapter 14, art. 13), the 2017 Argentina-Chile FTA (art. 11.6), the 2018 Singapore-Sri Lanka FTA (art. 9.9), the 2018 Australia-Peru FTA (art. 13.11), the 2018 Brazil-Chile FTA (art. 10.12) and the 2019 Australia-Indonesia FTA (art. 13.11).

[33] See Table 11.1. One of the few provisions on data localization that are not directly binding is found in the 2017 Argentina-Chile FTA, where the Parties merely recognize the importance of not requiring a person of the other Party to use or locate the computer facilities in the territory of that Party, as a condition for conducting business in that territory and pledge to exchange good practices and current regulatory frameworks regarding servers' location. See Argentina-Chile FTA, art. 11.7.

[34] Article 9.10 Japan-Mongolia FTA stipulates that neither Party shall require a service supplier of the other Party, an investor of the other Party, or an investment of an investor of the other Party in the area of the former Party, to use or locate computing facilities in that area as a condition for conducting its business.

[35] PAAP, art. 13.11 bis (2015).

[36] Chile-Uruguay FTA, art. 8.11.

[37] SAFTA, ch. 14, art. 15.

[38] Some variations can be found in the 2019 Australia-Indonesia FTA, where a Party may promptly renew a measure in existence at the date of entry into force of the Agreement or amend such a measure to make it less trade restrictive, at any time (art. 13.12(2)). Additionally, the Australia-Indonesia FTA

DIGITAL TRADE PROVISIONS IN PTAS   271

Table 11.2. Overview of Privacy-Related provisions in PTAs

Total number of provisions	120
Soft commitments	94
Hard commitments	26

3. Privacy and Data Protection

So far, 120 PTAs include binding and non-binding provisions on "data protection" (see Table 11.2). Yet, the way data is protected varies considerably due to the very different positions of the major actors and the inherent tensions between the regulatory goals of data innovation and data protection.[39]

Earlier agreements dealing with privacy issues consist of non-binding declarations. The 2000 Jordan–US FTA Joint Statement on Electronic Commerce, for instance, merely declares it necessary to ensure the effective protection of privacy regarding to the process of personal data on global information networks; yet it also states that the means for privacy protection should be flexible and Parties should encourage the private sector to develop and implement enforcement mechanisms, such as guidelines and verification and recourse methodologies, recommending the OECD Privacy Guidelines as an appropriate basis for policy development.[40] Similarly, the 2001 Canada–Costa Rica FTA includes a provision on privacy as part of the Joint Statement on Global Electronic Commerce, with both Parties agreeing to share information on the functioning of their respective data protection regimes.[41] Later agreements include cooperation activities on enhancing the security of personal data in order to improve the level of protection of

---

stipulates that nothing in the agreement shall prevent a Party from adopting or maintaining any measure that it considers necessary for the protection of its essential security interests (art. 13.12(3) (b)). A second variation is found in the 2018 Singapore-Sri Lanka FTA, the 2018 Australia-Peru FTA and the 2018 Brazil-Chile FTA, which slightly deviate from the CPTPP, as there is no least restrictive measure requirement mentioned. *See* Singapore-Sri Lanka FTA, art. 9.10; Australia-Peru FTA, art. 13.12; Brazil-Chile FTA, art. 10.13.

[39] *See, e.g.,* Whitman, *supra* note 14; Schwartz & Solove, *supra* note 14; Chander & Scwartz, *supra* note 14; Burri, *supra* note 13.

[40] U.S.-Jordan Joint Statement on Electronic Commerce, June 7, 2000, art. II, http://www.sice.oas. org/Trade/us-jrd/St.Ecomm.pdf.

[41] Canada-Costa Rica Joint Statement on Global Electronic Commerce, Mar. 1, 2021, http://www. sice.oas.org/trade/cancr/English/e-comme.asp.

272 CREATING DATA FLOW RULES THROUGH PTAS

privacy in electronic communications and avoid obstacles to trade that requires transfer of personal data.[42]

PTAs now increasingly deal with personal data protection with reference to the adoption of domestic standards. While some merely recognize the importance or the benefits of protecting personal information online,[43] in several treaties parties specifically commit to adopt or maintain legislation or regulations that protect the personal data or privacy of users,[44] in relation to the processing and dissemination of data,[45] which may also include administrative measures,[46] or the adoption of nondiscriminatory practices.[47] Few agreements include qualifications of this commitment, in the sense that each Party shall take measures it deems appropriate and necessary considering the differences in existing systems for personal data protection,[48] that such measures shall be developed insofar as possible,[49] or that the Parties have the right to define or regulate their own levels of protection of personal data in pursuit or furtherance of public policy objectives, and shall not be required to disclose confidential or sensitive information.[50] Some PTAs add that in the development of online personal data protection standards, each Party shall

---

[42] These activities include sharing information and experiences on regulations, laws and programs on data protection or the overall domestic regime for the protection of personal information; technical assistance in the form of exchange of information and experts; research and training activities; the establishment of joint programs and projects; maintaining a dialogue; holding consultations on matters of data protection; or in general, other cooperation mechanisms to ensure the protection of personal data.

[43] Australia-Indonesia FTA, art. 13.7(1); Brazil-Chile FTA, arts. 10.2(5)(f), 10.8.1; EU-Japan EPA, art. 8.78(3); Central America-Korea FTA, art. 14.5(1); Canada-Honduras FTA, art. 16.2(2)(e).

[44] Australia-Indonesia FTA, art. 13.7(2); Brazil-Chile FTA, art. 10.8.2; USMCA, art. 19.8(1)-(2); Australia-Peru FTA, art. 13.8(1)-(2); Singapore-Sri Lanka FTA, art. 9.7(1)-(2); Argentina-Chile FTA, art. 11.5(1)-(2); CETA, art. 16.4; Australia-Singapore FTA, Ch. 14, art. 9.1-2 (2016); Chile-Uruguay FTA, art. 8.7(1)-(2); CPTPP, art. 14.8(1)-(2); Singapore-Turkey FTA, art. 9.7(1)-(2); China-Korea FTA, art. 13.5; EAEU-Vietnam FTA, art. 13.5; Korea-Vietnam FTA, art. 10.6(1); Japan-Mongolia FTA, art. 9.6(3); Australia-Japan FTA, art. 13.8(1); Australia-Korea FTA, art. 15.8; Mexico-Panama FTA, art. 14.8; PAAP, art. 13.8(1); Colombia-Panama FTA, art. 19.6; New Zealand-Taiwan FTA, ch. 9, art. 2(d)(i); Colombia-Korea FTA, art. 12.3; Chile-China FTA, art. 55 (2018); Australia-Malaysia FTA, art. 15.8(1); Canada-Colombia FTA, art. 1506.1.

[45] Central America-EFTA, annex II, art. 1(c)(i); EFTA-GCC FTA, annex XVI, article 1(c)(i); EFTA-Colombia FTA, annex I, art. 1(c)(i); EFTA-Peru FTA, annex I, art. 1(c)(i).

[46] Colombia-Costa Rica FTA, art. 16.6(1); Korea-Peru FTA, art. 14.7; Hong Kong-New Zealand FTA, ch. 10, art. 2.1(f); ASEAN-Australia-New Zealand FTA, ch. 10, art. 7.1-2; Australia-Chile FTA, art. 16.8; Canada-Peru FTA, art. 1507.

[47] Australia-Indonesia FTA, art. 13.6(3); Brazil-Chile FTA, art. 10.8(3); USMCA, art. 19.8(4); Australia-Peru FTA, art. 13.8(3); Australia-Chile FTA, art. 11.5(3); Australia-Singapore FTA, ch. 14, art. 9.3 (2016); CPTPP, art. 14.8(3).

[48] Australia-China FTA, art. 12.8(1); Chile-Thailand FTA, art. 11.7(1)(j); Australia-Singapore FTA, ch. 14, art. 7.1 (2003).

[49] Colombia-Israel FTA, annex-B, art. 3.

[50] EU-Japan EPA, arts. 18.1(2)(h), 18.16(7).

take into account the existing international standards,[51] as well as criteria or guidelines of relevant international organizations or bodies[52]—such as the APEC Privacy Framework and/or the OECD Guidelines on Transborder Flows of Personal Data (2013);[53] or to accord a high level of protection compatible with the highest international standards in order to ensure the confidence of e-commerce users.[54] In a handful of treaties, the Parties commit themselves to publishing information on the personal data protection they provide to users of e-commerce,[55] including how individuals can pursue remedies and how businesses can comply with any legal requirements.[56] Certain agreements place special emphasis on the transfer of personal data, stipulating that it shall only take place if necessary for the implementation, by the competent authorities, of agreements concluded between the Parties,[57] or that the countries need to have an adequate level of safeguards for the protection of personal data.[58] Some treaties add that the Parties will encourage the use of encryption or security mechanisms for the personal information of the users, and their dissociation or anonymization, in cases where said data is provided to third parties.[59]

PTA Parties have also employed more binding options to protect personal information online. A first option is to consider the protection of the privacy of individuals in relation to the processing and dissemination of personal data and the protection of confidentiality of individual records as an exception in specific chapters of the agreement—such as for trade

---

[51] EU-Singapore FTA, art. 8.57(4); Argentina-Chile FTA, art. 11.5(1-2); Chile-Uruguay FTA, art. 8.7(2).

[52] Australia-Indonesia FTA, art. 13.7(3); Australia-Peru FTA, art. 13.8(2); CETA, art. 16.4; Australia-Singapore FTA, ch. 14, art. 9.2 (2016); CPTPP, art. 14.8(2); Australia-China FTA, art. 12.8(2); Korea-Vietnam FTA, art. 10.6(2); Australia-Japan FTA, art. 13.8(2); EU-Ukraine AA, art. 139.2; EU-Georgia AA, art. 127.2; Australia-Korea FTA, art. 15.8; Mexico-Panama FTA, art. 14.8; Chile-Thailand FTA, art. 11.7(j); Colombia-Panama FTA, art. 19.6; Colombia-Costa Rica FTA, art. 16.6(1); Colombia-Korea FTA, arts. 12.1(2), 12.3; EU-Central America FTA, art. 201.2; Australia-Malaysia FTA, art. 15.8(2); ASEAN-Australia-New Zealand FTA, Ch. 10, art. 7.3; Australia-Chile FTA, art. 16.8; New Zealand-Thailand FTA, art. 10.5; Australia-Thailand FTA, art. 1106; Australia-Singapore FTA, ch. 14, art. 7.2 (2003).

[53] USMCA, art. 19.8(2).

[54] Armenia-EU CEPA, art. 197.2; Colombia-EU-Peru FTA, art. 162.2; Chile-EC AA, Chile-EC AA 119.2; CARIFORUM-EC EPA, art. 202.

[55] Brazil-Chile FTA, art. 10.8(4).

[56] USMCA, art. 19.8(5); Australia-Peru FTA, art. 13.8(4); Singapore-Sri Lanka FTA, art. 9.7(3); Australia-Singapore FTA, ch. 14, art. 9.4 (2016); Chile-Uruguay FTA, art. 8.7(3); CPTPP, art. 14.8(4); Singapore-Turkey FTA, art. 9.7(3).

[57] EU-Moldova AA, art. 13.2.

[58] Korea-Vietnam FTA, art. 10.6(2).

[59] Brazil-Chile FTA, art. 10.8(6); Argentina-Chile FTA, art. 11.5(6); Chile-Uruguay FTA, art. 8.7(5).

274 CREATING DATA FLOW RULES THROUGH PTAS

in services,[60] investment or establishment,[61] movement of persons,[62] telecommunications,[63] and financial services.[64] Certain agreements, mostly EU-led, have dedicated chapters on protection of personal data, including the principles of purpose limitation, data quality and proportionality, transparency, security, right to access, rectification and opposition, restrictions on onward transfers, and protection of sensitive data, as well as provisions on enforcement mechanisms, coherence with international commitments and cooperation between the Parties in order to ensure an adequate level of protection of personal data.[65] The 2018 USMCA was the first U.S.-led PTA to include such a provision that recognizes key principles of data protection.[66]

A second option lets countries adopt appropriate measures to ensure privacy protection while allowing the free movement of data, establishing a criterion of "equivalence." This has been largely the EU approach and to that end, Parties also commit to inform each other of their applicable rules and negotiate reciprocal, general, or specific agreements.[67] A third, but less used option, leaves the development of rules on data protection to a treaty body.

---

[60] Japan-Singapore FTA, art. 69.1(c).

[61] Chile-EC AA, art. 135.1(e)(ii); Japan-Singapore FTA, art. 83.1(c)(ii).

[62] Japan-Singapore FTA, art. 95.1(c)(ii).

[63] USMCA, art. 18.3(4); EU-Japan EPA, art. 8.44(4); Australia-Peru FTA, art. 12.4(4); Singapore-Sri Lanka FTA, art. 8.3(4); Argentina-Chile FTA, art. 10.3(4); Australia-Singapore FTA, art. 10.3(4) (2016); Singapore-Turkey FTA, art. 8.3(5); Japan-Mongolia FTA, annex 5, art. 3; Korea-Peru FTA, art. 13.3(4); Panama-US FTA, art. 13.2(4); Japan-Switzerland FTA, annex VI, art. IX(a); Nicaragua-Taiwan FTA, art. 13.02(4); Korea-Singapore FTA, art. 11.3(4); Morocco-US FTA, art. 13.2(4)(b); Chile-US FTA, art. 13.2(4).

[64] USMCA, annex 17-A; EU-Japan EPA, art. 8.63; EU-Vietnam FTA, art. 8.45; EU-Singapore FTA, art. 8.54(2); Australia-Peru FTA, art. 10.21; Armenia-EU CEPA, art. 185; CETA, art. 13.15(4); Australia-Singapore FTA, annex 9-B (2016); CPTPP, annex 11-B; Singapore-Turkey FTA, art. 10.12; Japan-Mongolia FTA, annex 4, art. 11; EU-Ukraine AA, art. 129.2; EU-Georgia AA, art. 118.2; ASEAN-Australia-New Zealand FTA, ch. 10, Annex on Financial Services, art. 7.2; Japan-Switzerland FTA, annex VI, art. VIII; EFTA-Colombia FTA, annex XVI—financial services, art. 8; EU-Moldova AA, art. 245; Chile-EU AA, art. 135.1(e)(ii).

[65] Cameroon-EC Interim EPA, ch. 6, arts. 61–65; CARIFORUM-EC EPA, ch. 6, arts. 197–201. Other agreements merely recognize principles for the collection, processing and storage of personal data such as: prior consent, legitimacy, purpose, proportionality, quality, safety, responsibility and information, but without developing this in detail: Argentina-Chile FTA, art. 11.2(5)(f) n.1; Chile-Uruguay FTA, art. 8.2(5)(f) n.3.

[66] USMCA, art. 19.8(3); *see also* below Section A.II.

[67] EU-Singapore FTA, art. 8.54(2); EU-Singapore FTA, Understanding 3—Additional Customs-Related Provisions, arts. 9.2, 11.1; EU-Ghana EPA, Protocol on Mutual Administrative Assistance on Custom Matters, art. 10; Bosnia and Herzegovina-EC SAA, Protocol 5 on Mutual Administrative Assistance on Custom Matters, art. 10.2; Algeria-EU Euro-Med Association Agreement, art. 45 & Protocol No. 7.

III. Different PTA Templates for Digital Trade Governance

As evident from the above overview, the regulatory environment for data flows has been shaped by PTAs. The United States has played a key role in this process and has sought to endorse liberal rules in implementation of its "Digital Agenda."[68] The emergent regulatory template on digital issues is not however limited to U.S. agreements but has diffused and can be found in other PTAs, as evident from the above overview. Despite the fact there are still great variations in treaty language, certain distinct templates have been developed in recent years—one such template is shaped along the TPP model and now endorsed in the CPTPP and a number of subsequent agreements. The other and more recent model for digital trade has been promoted by the EU. The next sections look first at the CPTPP and its variations under the USMCA, the DTA, and the DEPA; then the new EU template and the Regional Comprehensive Economic Partnership (RCEP) are explored.

A. The U.S. Template

1. The Comprehensive and Progressive Agreement for Transpacific Partnership

The Comprehensive and Progressive Agreement for Transpacific Partnership (CPTPP) was agreed upon in 2017 between 11 countries in the Pacific Rim[69] and entered into force on December 30, 2018. Beyond the overall economic impact of the CPTPP, its chapter on e-commerce created the most comprehensive template in the landscape of PTAs and included several new features. Despite the fact that the United States dropped out of the agreement with the start of the Trump administration, the chapter still reflects U.S. efforts to secure obligations on digital trade and is a verbatim reiteration of the TPP chapter.

---

[68] *See* Sacha Wunsch-Vincent, *The Digital Trade Agenda of the US: Parallel Tracks of Bilateral, Regional and Multilateral Liberalization*, 58 AUSSENWIRTSCHAFT 7 (2003). The agreements reached since 2002 with Australia, Bahrain, Chile, Morocco, Oman, Peru, Singapore, the Central American countries, Panama, Colombia, and South Korea, all contain critical WTO-plus (going above the WTO commitments) and WTO-extra (addressing issues not covered by the WTO) provisions in the broader field of digital trade.

[69] Australia, Brunei, Canada, Chile, Japan, Malaysia, Mexico, New Zealand, Peru, Singapore, and Vietnam.

Particularly interesting for this chapter's discussion are the provisions found in the CPTPP e-commerce chapter that tackle the emergent issues of the data economy, previously unaddressed under the WTO framework. Most importantly, the CPTPP explicitly seeks to restrict the use of data protectionist measures. Article 14.13(2) prohibits the parties from requiring a "covered person to use or locate computing facilities in that Party's territory as a condition for conducting business in that territory." The soft language from U.S.–South Korea FTA on free data flows is now also framed as a hard rule: "[e]ach Party *shall* allow the cross-border transfer of information by electronic means, including personal information, when this activity is for the conduct of the business of a covered person."[70] The rule has a broad scope and most data transferred over the Internet is likely to be covered, although the word "for" may suggest the need for some causality between the flow of data and the business of the covered person; the explicit of personal data is also noteworthy.

Measures restricting digital flows or implementing localization requirements are permitted only if they do not amount to "arbitrary or unjustifiable discrimination or a disguised restriction on trade" and do not "impose restrictions on transfers of information greater than are required to achieve the objective."[71] These nondiscriminatory conditions are similar to the strict test formulated by Article XIV of the GATS and Article XX of the GATT 1994—a test that is aimed at balancing trade and non-trade interests by "excusing" certain violations (but is also extremely hard to pass, as we know from existing WTO jurisprudence).[72] The CPTPP test differs from the WTO norms in one significant element: while there is a list of public policy objectives in GATT and GATS, the CPTPP provides no such enumeration and speaks merely of a "legitimate public policy objective."[73] This permits more regulatory autonomy for the CPTPP signatories but may lead to legal uncertainty. Further, it should be noted that the ban on localization measures is softened in regard to financial services and institutions.[74] An annex to the "Financial Services" chapter has a separate data transfer requirement,

---

[70] CPTPP, art. 14.11(2) (emphasis added).

[71] *Id.* art. 14.11(3).

[72] *See, e.g.,* Henrik Andersen, *Protection of Non-Trade Values in WTO Appellate Body Jurisprudence: Exceptions, Economic Arguments, and Eluding Questions,* 18 J. Int'l Econ. L. 383 (2015).

[73] CPTPP, art. 14.11(3).

[74] For the definition of "a covered person," *see id.* art. 14.1, which excludes a "financial institution" and a "cross-border financial service supplier."

whereby certain restrictions on data flows may apply for the protection of privacy or confidentiality of individual records, or for prudential reasons.[75] Government procurement is also excluded.[76] Both exclusions are typical for all PTAs.

Another novel issue that the CPTPP addresses deals with source code. Pursuant to Article 14.17, a CPTPP Member may not require the transfer of, or access to, source code of software owned by a person of another Party as a condition for the import, distribution, sale or use of such software, or of products containing such software, in its territory. The prohibition applies only to mass-market software or products containing such software.[77] This means that tailor-made products are excluded, as well as software used for critical infrastructure and those in commercially negotiated contracts.[78] This provision aims to protect software companies and address their concerns about loss of intellectual property, in particular trade secrets protection, or cracks in the security of their proprietary code; it may also be interpreted as a reaction to China's demands to access to source code from software producers selling in its market.

Overall, these provisions illustrate an interesting development because it is evident that they do not simply entail a clarification of existing bans on discrimination, nor do they merely set higher standards, as is commonly anticipated from trade agreements. Rather, they shape the regulatory space domestically. An important rule in this regard is in the area of privacy and data protection. Article 14.8(2) requires every CPTPP party to "adopt or maintain a legal framework that provides for the protection of the personal information of the users of electronic commerce." Yet, there are no standards or benchmarks for the legal framework specified, except for a general requirement that CPTPP parties "take into account principles or guidelines of relevant international bodies."[79] A footnote provides some clarification in saying that ". . . a Party may comply with the obligation in this paragraph by adopting or maintaining measures such as a comprehensive privacy, personal information or personal data protection laws, sector-specific laws covering

---

[75] The provision reads, "Each Party shall allow a financial institution of another Party to transfer information in electronic or other form, into and out of its territory, for data processing if such processing is required in the institution's ordinary course of business."

[76] CPTPP, art. 14.8(3).

[77] *Id.* art. 14.17(2).

[78] *Id.*

[79] *Id.* art. 14.8(2).

278 CREATING DATA FLOW RULES THROUGH PTAS

privacy, or laws that provide for the enforcement of voluntary undertakings by enterprises relating to privacy."[80]

Parties are also invited to promote compatibility between their data protection regimes, by essentially treating lower standards as equivalent.[81] The goal of these norms can be interpreted as a prioritization of trade over privacy rights. This has been pushed by the United States during the TPP negotiations, as the United States subscribes to relatively weak and patchy protection of privacy. Timewise, this push came also at the phase, when the United States was wary that it could lose the privilege of transatlantic data transfer, as a consequence of the judgment of the Court of Justice of European Union (CJEU) that struck down the EU–U.S. Safe Harbor Agreement,[82] which in hindsight had been a legitimate concern considering the 2020 follow-up decision of *Schrems II*.[83]

Next to the data protection norms, the CPTPP includes also provisions on consumer protection[84] and spam control.[85] These are, however, fairly weak. The same is true for the newly introduced rules on cybersecurity. Article 14.16 CPTPP is non-binding and identifies a limited scope of activities for cooperation, in situations of "malicious intrusions" or "dissemination of malicious code" and capacity-building of governmental bodies dealing with cybersecurity incidents.

2. The United States–Mexico–Canada Agreement and the United States–Japan Digital Trade Agreement

The renegotiated NAFTA, which is now referred to as the "United States–Mexico–Canada Agreement" (USMCA), has a comprehensive e-commerce chapter that is now also properly titled "Digital Trade. "The chapter follows all critical lines of the CPTPP and goes beyond it. In particular, the USMCA

---

[80] *Id.* art. 14.8(2) n. 6.

[81] *Id.* art. 14.8(5).

[82] Case C-362/14, Maximillian Schrems v. Data Prot. Comm'r, EU:C:2015:650 (Oct. 6, 2015). Maximillian Schrems is an Austrian citizen, who filed a suit against the Irish supervisory authority, after it rejected his complaint over Facebook's practice of storing user data in the United States. The plaintiff claimed that his data was not adequately protected in light of the NSA revelations and this, despite the existing agreement between the EU and the United States—the so-called safe harbor scheme.

[83] The later EU-U.S. "privacy shield" arrangement, which replaced the Safe Harbor, was also rendered invalid by a recent judgment: Case C-311/18, Data Prot. Comm'r v. Facebook Ireland Ltd., Maximillian Schrems, ECLI:EU:C:2020:559 (July 16, 2020). A new Transatlantic Data Privacy Framework is currently under negotiation.

[84] CPTPP art. 14.17.

[85] *Id.* art. 14.14.

adheres to the CPTPP model with regard to data issues and ensures the free flow of data through a clear ban on data localization[86] and incorporates a hard rule on free information flows.[87] Article 19.11 specifies further that parties can adopt or maintain a measure inconsistent with the free flow of data provision, if this is necessary to achieve a legitimate public policy objective, provided that there is no arbitrary or unjustifiable discrimination nor a disguised restriction on trade; and the restrictions on transfers of information are not greater than necessary to achieve the objective.[88]

Beyond these similarities, the USMCA introduces some novelties. The first one is that the USMCA departs from the standard U.S. approach and signals abiding to some data protection principles and guidelines of relevant international bodies. After recognizing "the economic and social benefits of protecting the personal information of users of digital trade and the contribution that this makes to enhancing consumer confidence in digital trade,"[89] Article 19.8 USMCA requires from the parties to "adopt or maintain a legal framework that provides for the protection of the personal information of the users of digital trade. In the development of its legal framework for the protection of personal information, each Party should take into account principles and guidelines of relevant international bodies, such as the APEC Privacy Framework and the OECD Recommendation of the Council concerning Guidelines governing the Protection of Privacy and Transborder Flows of Personal Data (2013)."[90] The parties also recognize key principles of data protection, which include limitation on collection, choice, data quality, purpose specification, use limitation, security safeguards, transparency, individual participation, and accountability[91] and aim to provide remedies for any violations.[92] This is a key development because the USMCA may go beyond what the United States may have in its national laws on data protection and also reflects some of the principles the EU has advocated for in the

---

[86] USMCA, art. 19.12.

[87] *Id.* art 19.11.

[88] *Id.* art. 19.11(2). There is a footnote attached, which clarifies: A measure does not meet the conditions of this paragraph if it accords different treatment to data transfers solely on the basis that they are cross-border in a manner that modifies the conditions of competition to the detriment of service suppliers of another Party. The footnote does not appear in the CPTPP treaty text.

[89] *Id.* art 19.8(1).

[90] *Id.* art. 19.8(2). A footnote clarifies further that "For greater certainty, a Party may comply with the obligation in this paragraph by adopting or maintaining measures such as comprehensive privacy, personal information or personal data protection laws, sector-specific laws covering privacy, or laws that provide for the enforcement of voluntary undertakings by enterprises relating to privacy".

[91] *Id.* art. 19.8(3).

[92] *Id.* art. 19.8(4)-(5).

domain of personal data protection. One may wonder whether this is a development caused by the so-called Brussels effect, whereby the EU "exports" its own domestic standards and renders them globally applicable,[93] or whether we are seeing a shift in U.S. privacy protection regimes.[94]

Three further novelties of the USMCA may be mentioned. The first refers to the inclusion of "algorithms," the meaning of which is "a defined sequence of steps, taken to solve a problem or obtain a result"[95] and has become part of the ban on requirements for the transfer or access to source code in Article 19.16. The second novum refers to the recognition of "interactive computer services" as particularly vital to the growth of digital trade. Parties pledge in this sense not to "adopt or maintain measures that treat a supplier or user of an interactive computer service as an information content provider in determining liability for harms related to information stored, processed, transmitted, distributed, or made available by the service, except to the extent the supplier or user has, in whole or in part, created, or developed the information."[96] This provision is important, as it seeks to clarify the liability of intermediaries and delineate it from the liability of host providers with regard to IP rights' infringement.[97] It also secures the application of Section 230 of the U.S. Communications Decency Act,[98] which insulates platforms from liability but has been recently under attack in many jurisdictions in the face of fake news and other negative developments related to platforms' power.[99] While the safe harbor is very much to the benefit of U.S. tech companies, it has stirred controversies in the United States as well,[100] with

---

[93] ANU BRADFORD, THE BRUSSELS EFFECT: HOW THE EUROPEAN UNION RULES THE WORLD (2020).

[94] See Chander et al., supra note 13; Chander & Schwartz, supra note 14.

[95] USMCA, art. 19.1.

[96] Id. art. 19.17(2). Annex 19-A creates specific rules with the regard to the application of art. 19.17 for Mexico, in essence postponing its implementation for three years.

[97] On intermediaries' liability, see, e.g., Sonia S. Katyal, Filtering, Piracy, Surveillance and Disobedience, 103 COLUM. J.L. & ARTS 401 (2009); Urs Gasser & Wolfgang Schulz, Governance of Online Intermediaries: Observations from a Series of National Case Studies (Berkman Ctr. for Internet & Soc'y, Research Publication No. 2015-5, 2015), http://ssrn.com/abstract=2566364.

[98] Section 230 reads: "No provider or user of an interactive computer service shall be treated as the publisher or speaker of any information provided by another information content provider" and in essence protects online intermediaries that host or republish speech.

[99] See, e.g., Lauren Feine, Big Tech's Favorite Law Is under Fire, CNBC (Feb. 19, 2020), https://www.cnbc.com/2020/02/19/what-is-section-230-and-why-do-some-people-want-to-change-it.html.

[100] For literature review, see, e.g., Mira Burri, Fake News in Times of Pandemic and Beyond: An Enquiry into the Rationales for Regulating Information Platforms, in LAW AND ECONOMICS OF THE CORONAVIRUS CRISIS (Klaus Mathis & Avishalom Tor, eds. 2022). See also the two recent Supreme Court cases Gonzalez v. Google LLC, 598 U. S. ____ (2023) and Twitter Inc. v. Taamneh, 598 U. S. ____ (2023).

DIFFERENT PTA TEMPLATES FOR DIGITAL TRADE GOVERNANCE 281

Nancy Pelosi arguing against its inclusion.[101] It remains to be seen whether future U.S. trade deals, struck under the Biden administration, will also include this limited platform's liability.

The third and rather liberal commitment of the USMCA parties regards open government data. This is truly innovative and very relevant in the domain of domestic regimes for data governance. In Article 19.18, the parties recognize that facilitating public access to and use of government information fosters economic and social development, competitiveness, and innovation. "To the extent that a Party chooses to make government information, including data, available to the public, it shall endeavor to ensure that the information is in a machine-readable and open format and can be searched, retrieved, used, reused, and redistributed."[102] There is in addition an endeavor to cooperate, so as to "expand access to and use of government information, including data, that the Party has made public, with a view to enhancing and generating business opportunities, especially for small and medium-sized enterprises."[103]

The U.S. approach toward digital trade issues has been confirmed also by the recent U.S.–Japan Digital Trade Agreement (DTA), signed on October 7, 2019, alongside the U.S.–Japan Trade Agreement.[104] The United States–Japan DTA arguably replicates almost all provisions of the USMCA and the CPTPP.[105] It incorporates the new USMCA rules on open government data,[106] source code,[107] and interactive computer services[108] but notably covering also financial and insurance services as part of the scope of agreement, thereby rendering its impact much broader. A new provision has been added

---

[101] *See, e.g.*, Brian Fung & Haley Byrd, *Nancy Pelosi Wants to Scrap Legal Protections for Big Tech in New Trade Agreement*, CNN (Dec. 5, 2019), https://edition.cnn.com/2019/12/05/tech/pelosi-big-tech-legal-protections/index.html. *See also* Han-Wei Liu, *Exporting the First Amendment Through Trade: The Global "Constitutional Moment" for Online Platform Liability*, 53 GEO. WASH. INT'L L. REV. 1 (2022).

[102] USMCA, art. 19.18(2).

[103] *Id.* art. 19.8(3).

[104] For the text of the agreements, *see* Agreement between the United States of America and Japan Concerning Digital Trade, U.S.-Japan, Oct. 7, 2019, https://ustr.gov/sites/default/files/files/agreements/japan/Agreement_between_the_United_States_and_Japan_concerning_Digital_Trade.pdf.

[105] Art. 7: Customs Duties; art. 8: Non-Discriminatory Treatment of Digital Products; art. 9: Domestic Electronic Transactions Framework; art. 10: Electronic Authentication and Electronic Signatures; art. 14: Online Consumer Protection; art. 11: Cross-Border Transfer of Information; art. 12: Location of Computing Facilities; art. 16: Unsolicited Commercial Electronic Messages; art. 19: Cybersecurity US–Japan DTA.

[106] US–Japan DTA, art. 20.

[107] *Id.* art. 17.

[108] *Id.* art. 18. A side letter recognizes the differences between the US and Japan's systems governing the liability of interactive computer services suppliers and parties agree that Japan need not change its existing legal system to comply with art. 18.

in regard to ICT goods that use cryptography. Article 21 DTA specifies that for such goods designed for commercial applications, neither party shall require a manufacturer or supplier of the ICT good as a condition to entering the market to (a) transfer or provide access to any proprietary information relating to cryptography; (b) partner or otherwise cooperate with a person in the territory of the Party in the development, manufacture, sale, distribution, import, or use of the ICT good; or (c) use or integrate a particular cryptographic algorithm or cipher.[109] This rule is similar to Annex 8-B, Section A.3 of the CPTPP chapter on technical trade barriers. It is a reaction to a practice by several countries, in particular China, that impose direct bans on encrypted products or set specific technical regulations that restrict the sale of encrypted products, and caters for the growing concerns of large companies, like IBM and Microsoft, that thrive on data flows with less governmental intervention.[110]

Other minor differences that can be noted when comparing with the USMCA are some things missing in the United States–Japan DTA—such as rules on paperless trading, net neutrality, and the mention of data protection principles.[111] The exceptions attached to the United States–Japan DTA refer to the WTO general exception clauses of Article XIV of the GATS and Article XX of the GATT 1994, whereby the parties agree to their *mutatis mutandis* application.[112] Further exceptions are listed with regard to security,[113] prudential and monetary and exchange rate policy,[114] and taxation,[115] which are to be linked to the expanded scope of agreement including financial and insurance services.

3. The DEPA

The 2020 Digital Economy Partnership Agreement (DEPA) between Chile, New Zealand, and Singapore,[116] all parties also to the CPTPP, should be

---

[109] *Id.* art. 21.3.

[110] *See* Han-Wei Liu, *Inside the Black Box: Political Economy of the TPP's Encryption Clause*, 51 J. WORLD TRADE 309 (2017).

[111] Art. 15 merely stipulates that parties shall adopt or maintain a legal framework that provides for the protection of the personal information of the users of digital trade and publish information on the personal information protection, including how: (a) natural persons can pursue remedies; and (b) an enterprise can comply with any legal requirements.

[112] US–Japan DTA, art. 3.

[113] *Id.* art. 4.

[114] *Id.* art. 5.

[115] *Id.* art. 6.

[116] For details and the text of the DEPA, *see* Digital Economy Partnership Agreement, Sing.-Chile-N.Z., June 12, 2020, https://www.mfat.govt.nz/en/trade/free-trade-agreements/free-trade-agreements-concluded-but-not-in-force/digital-economy-partnership-agreement.

DIFFERENT PTA TEMPLATES FOR DIGITAL TRADE GOVERNANCE   283

mentioned as a new type of digital trade agreement, as it is not conceptualized as a purely trade deal but one that is meant to address the broader issues of the digital economy. In this sense, its scope is wide, open, and flexible and covers several emergent issues, such as those in the areas of AI and digital inclusion. The agreement is also not a closed deal but one that is open to other countries,[117] and the DEPA is meant to complement the WTO negotiations on e-commerce and build upon the digital economy work underway within APEC, the OECD, and other international forums. DEPA follows a modular approach, and the type of rules varies across the different modules. On the one hand, all rules of the CPTPP are replicated, some of the USMCA rules, such as the one on open government data[118] (but not source code), and some of the United States–Japan DTA provisions, such as the one on ICT goods using cryptography,[119] have been included too.

On the other hand, there are many other so far unknown for trade agreement rules that try to facilitate the functioning of the digital economy and enhance cooperation on key issues. For instance, Module 2 on business and trade facilitation includes next to the standard CPTPP-like norms,[120] additional efforts "to establish or maintain a seamless, trusted, high-availability and secure interconnection of each Party's single window to facilitate the exchange of data relating to trade administration documents, which may include: (a) sanitary and phytosanitary certificates and (b) import and export data."[121] Parties have also touched upon other important issues around digital trade facilitation, such as electronic invoicing (Article 2.5); express shipments and clearance times (Article 2.6); logistics (Article 2.4) and electronic payments (Article 2.7). Module 8 on emerging trends and technologies is also particularly interesting to mention, as it highlights a range of key topics that demand attention by policymakers, such as in the areas of fintech and AI.

With respect to AI, the parties agree to promote the adoption of ethical and governance frameworks that support the trusted, safe, and responsible use of AI technologies, and in adopting these AI Governance Frameworks parties

---

[117] DEPA, art. 16.2.

[118] *Id.* art. 9.4.

[119] *Id.* art. 3.4. The article also provides detailed definitions of cryptography, encryption, and cryptographic algorithm and cipher.

[120] *Id.* art. 2.2 (Paperless Trading); *id.* art. 2.3 (Domestic Electronic Transactions Framework).

[121] *Id.* art. 2.2(5). "Single window" is defined as a facility that allows Parties involved in a trade transaction to electronically lodge data and documents with a single-entry point to fulfil all import, export and transit regulatory requirements. *Id.* art. 2.1.

284 CREATING DATA FLOW RULES THROUGH PTAS

would seek to follow internationally recognized principles or guidelines, including explainability, transparency, fairness, and human-centered values.[122] The DEPA parties also recognize the interfaces between the digital economy and government procurement and broader competition policy and agree to actively cooperate on these issues.[123] Along this line of covering broader policy matters to create an enabling environment that is also not solely focused on and driven by economic interests, the DEPA deals with the importance of a rich and accessible public domain[124] and digital inclusion, which can cover enhancing cultural and people-to-people links, including between indigenous peoples, and improving access for women, rural populations, and low socioeconomic groups.[125]

Overall, the DEPA is a unique and future-oriented project that covers well the broad range of issues that the digital economy impinges upon and offers a good basis for harmonization and interoperability of domestic frameworks and international cooperation that adequately takes into account the complex challenges of contemporary data governance that has essential trade but also non-trade elements. Its attractivity as a form of enhanced cooperation on issues of data-driven economy has been confirmed by Canada's[126] and South Korea's[127] interest to join it. The DEPA's modular approach has been also followed in the Australia–Singapore Digital Economy Agreement, which is, however, still linked to the trade deal between the parties.[128]

B. The Digital Trade Agreements of the European Union

Apart from the generic differences between the EU and the U.S. approaches to PTAs, the EU template in regard to digital trade is not as coherent as that

---

[122] *Id.* art. 8.2(2)–(3).

[123] *Id.* arts. 8.3–8.4.

[124] *Id.* art. 9.2.

[125] *Id.* art. 11.2.

[126] Government of Canada, Global Affairs, Background: Canada's Possible Accession to the Digital Economy Partnership Agreement, Mar. 18, 2021, https://www.international.gc.ca/trade-commerce/consultations/depa-apen/background-information.aspx?lang=eng

[127] "South Korea Starts Process to Join DEPA," Oct. 6, 2021, https://en.yna.co.kr/view/PYH20211006124000325

[128] The DEA, which entered into force on Dec. 8, 2020, amends the Singapore–Australia FTA and replaces its Electronic Commerce chapter. See Australian Government, Department of Foreign Affairs and Trade, https://www.dfat.gov.au/trade/services-and-digital-trade/australia-and-singapore-digital-economy-agreement

of the United States.[129] It has also developed and changed over time. This can be explained by the EU's newly put stress on digital technologies as part of its innovation and growth strategy and with its new foreign policy orientation subsequent to the Lisbon Treaty, which includes PTAs as an essential strategic element.[130]

The agreement with Chile (signed in 2002) was the first to include substantial e-commerce provisions but the language was still cautious and limited to soft cooperation pledges in the services chapter[131] and in the fields of information technology, information society, and telecommunications.[132] In more recent agreements, such as the EU–South Korea FTA (signed in 2009), the language is much more concrete and binding. It imitates some of the U.S. template provisions and confirms the applicability of the WTO Agreements to measures affecting electronic commerce, as well as subscribes to a permanent duty-free moratorium on electronic transmissions. The EU, as particularly insistent on data protection policies, has also sought commitment of its FTA partners to compatibility with the international standards of data protection.[133] Cooperation is also increasingly framed in more concrete terms and includes mutual recognition of electronic signatures certificates, coordination on Internet service providers' liability, consumer protection, and paperless trading.[134]

The 2016 EU agreement with Canada—the Comprehensive Economic and Trade Agreement (CETA)—goes a step further. The CETA provisions concern commitments ensuring (a) clarity, transparency, and predictability in their domestic regulatory frameworks; (b) interoperability, innovation, and competition in facilitating electronic commerce; as well as (c) facilitating the use of electronic commerce by small- and medium-sized enterprises.[135] The EU has succeeded in deepening the privacy commitments and the CETA has a specific norm on trust and confidence in electronic commerce, which

---

[129] EU PTAs tend, for instance, to cover more WTO-plus areas but have less liberal commitments. For detailed analysis, *see* HENRIK HORN ET AL., BEYOND THE WTO? AN ANATOMY OF EU AND US PREFERENTIAL TRADE AGREEMENTS (2009), https://www.bruegel.org/wp-content/uploads/impor ted/publications/bp_trade_jan09.pdf.

[130] EU PREFERENTIAL TRADE AGREEMENTS: COMMERCE, FOREIGN POLICY, AND DEVELOPMENT ASPECTS (David Kleimann ed., 2013).

[131] EU–Chile FTA, art. 102. The agreement states that "[t]he inclusion of this provision in this Chapter is made without prejudice of the Chilean position on the question of whether or not electronic commerce should be considered as a supply of services",

[132] *Id.* art. 37.

[133] EU–South Korea FTA, art. 7.48.

[134] *Id.* art. 7.49.

[135] CETA, art. 16.5.

obliges the parties to adopt or maintain laws, regulations, or administrative measures for the protection of personal information of users engaged in electronic commerce in consideration of international data protection standards.[136] Yet, there are no deep commitments on digital trade; nor there are any rules on data flows.

Overall, the EU has been cautious when inserting rules on data in its free trade deals and presently none of its treaties has such rules of binding nature. It is only recently that the EU has made a step toward such rules, whereby Parties have agreed to consider in future negotiations commitments related to cross-border flow of information. Such a clause is found in the 2018 EU–Japan EPA[137] and in the modernization of the trade part of the EU–Mexico Global Agreement. In the latter two agreements, the Parties commit to "reassess" within three years of the entry into force of the agreement, the need for inclusion of provisions on the free flow of data into the treaty. This signaled a repositioning of the EU on the issue of data flows, which is now fully endorsed in post-Brexit agreement with the U.K., the recently signed agreements with New Zealand and with Chile, and EU's currently negotiated deals with Australia and Tunisia. These treaties include in their digital trade chapters norms that ensure the free flow of data. These newer commitments are, however, also linked with high levels of data protection.[138]

The EU wishes to permit data flows only if coupled with the high data protection standards of its GDPR. In the aforementioned trade deals, as well as in the EU proposal for WTO rules on electronic commerce,[139] the EU follows a distinct model of endorsing and protecting privacy as a fundamental right. On the one hand, the EU and its partners seek to ban data localization measures and subscribe to a free data flow; but on the other hand, these commitments are conditioned: first, by a dedicated article on data protection, which clearly states that "Each Party recognises that the protection of personal data and privacy is a *fundamental right* and that high standards in this regard contribute to trust in the digital economy and to the development

---

[136] *Id.* art. 16.4.

[137] EU-Japan EPA, art. 8.81.

[138] *See* EUR. COMM'N, HORIZONTAL PROVISIONS FOR CROSS-BORDER DATA FLOWS AND FOR PERSONAL DATA PROTECTION IN EU TRADE AND INVESTMENT AGREEMENTS, *in* EU TRADE AND INVESTMENT AGREEMENT (2018), https://trade.ec.europa.eu/doclib/docs/2018/may/tradoc_156884.pdf.

[139] Eur. Union, *Joint Statement on Electronic Commerce: EU Proposal for WTO Disciplines and Commitments Relating to Electronic Commerce, Communication from the European Union*, WTO Doc. INF/ECOM/22 (Apr. 26, 2019).

of trade,"[140] followed by a paragraph on data sovereignty: "Each Party may adopt and maintain the safeguards it deems appropriate to ensure the protection of personal data and privacy, including through the adoption and application of rules for the cross-border transfer of personal data. Nothing in this agreement shall affect the protection of personal data and privacy afforded by the Parties' respective safeguards."[141]

The EU also wishes to retain the right to see how the implementation of the FTA with regard to data flows impacts the conditions of privacy protection, so there is a review possibility within three years of the entry into force of the agreement and parties remain free to propose to review the list of restrictions at any time.[142] In addition, there is a broad carve-out, in the sense that "The Parties reaffirm the right to regulate within their territories to achieve legitimate policy objectives, such as the protection of public health, social services, public education, safety; the environment including climate change, public morals, social or consumer protection, privacy and data protection; or the promotion and protection of cultural diversity."[143] The EU thus reserves ample regulatory leeway for its current and future data protection measures. The exception is also fundamentally different than the objective necessity test under the CPTPP and the USMCA, or that under WTO law, because it is subjective and safeguards the EU's right to regulate.[144]

The new EU approach was first endorsed by the 2020 Trade and Cooperation Agreement (TCA) with the United Kingdom[145] that replicates all the above provisions, except for the explicit mentioning of data protection as a fundamental right—which can, however, be presumed, since the U.K. incorporates the European Convention on Human Rights (ECHR) through the Human Rights Act of 1998 into its domestic law (although the U.K. may be shifting away from the Strasbourg model post-Brexit[146]). The

---

[140] *See, e.g.*, draft EU-Australia FTA, art. 6(1) (emphasis added). The same wording is found in the EU-New Zealand FTA and the draft EU-Tunisia FTA.

[141] *See, e.g., id.* art. 6(2). The same wording is found in the EU-New Zealand FTA and the draft EU-Tunisia FTA.

[142] *See, e.g., id.* art. 5(2). The same wording is found in the EU-New Zealand FTA and the draft EU-Tunisia FTA.

[143] *See, e.g., id.* art. 2. The same wording is found in the EU-New Zealand FTA and the draft EU-Tunisia FTA.

[144] Svetlana Yakovleva, *Privacy Protection(ism): The Latest Wave of Trade Constraints on Regulatory Autonomy*, 74 U. MIAMI L. REV. 416, 496 (2020).

[145] Trade and Cooperation Agreement between the European Union and the European Atomic Energy Community, of the One Part, and the United Kingdom of Great Britain and Northern Ireland, of the Other Part, Dec. 30, 2020 [hereinafter TCA].

[146] *See Human Rights Act Reform: A Modern Bill of Rights – Consultation*, U.K. MINISTRY OF JUSTICE (July 12, 2022), https://www.gov.uk/government/consultations/human-rights-act-ref

288 CREATING DATA FLOW RULES THROUGH PTAS

rest of the EU digital trade template seems to include the issues covered by the CPTPP/USMCA model, such as software source code,[147] facilitation of electronic commerce,[148] online consumer protection,[149] spam,[150] and open government data,[151] not including, however, a provision on non-discrimination of digital products, and excluding audio-visual services from the scope of the application of the digital trade chapter.[152] It should also be underscored that the EU secures an essentially equivalent level of data protection in its PTA partners through the channel of adequacy decisions adopted unilaterally by the European Commission that are subject to monitoring and can be revoked in case that their requirements are not met.[153]

Despite the confirmation of the EU's approach through the TCA[154] and the 2022 FTAs with New Zealand and Chile, it could be that the EU would tailor its template depending on the trade partner. For instance, the agreement with Vietnam,[155] which entered into force on August 1, 2020, has

---

orm-a-modern-bill-of-rights/human-rights-act-reform-a-modern-bill-of-rights-consultation; *see also* Conor Gearty, *The Human Rights Act Comes of Age*, 2 Eur. Comm'n H.R. L. Rev. 117, 117–26 (2022).

[147] *See* TCA, *supra* note 185, art. 207. Again, with notable safeguards, specified in ¶¶ 2 and 3 of art. 207, including the general exceptions, security exceptions and a prudential carve-out in the context of a certification procedure; voluntary transfer of source code on a commercial basis, a requirement by a court or administrative tribunal, or a requirement by a competition authority pursuant to a Party's competition law to prevent or remedy a restriction or a distortion of competition; a requirement by a regulatory body pursuant to a Party's laws or regulations related to the protection of public safety with regard to users online; the protection and enforcement of IP; and government procurement related measures.

[148] *See id.* art. 205, 206.

[149] *See id.* art. 208.

[150] *See id.* art. 209.

[151] *See id.* art. 210.

[152] *See id.* art. 197.2.

[153] The European Commission has so far recognized Andorra, Argentina, Canada, Faroe Islands, Guernsey, Israel, Isle of Man, Japan, Jersey, New Zealand, Republic of Korea, Switzerland, the U.K. and Uruguay as providing adequate protection. With the exception of the U.K., these adequacy decisions do not cover data exchanges in the law enforcement sector. *See* European Commission, *Adequacy Decisions*, https://commission.europa.eu/law/law-topic/data-protection/internationaldimension-data-protection/adequacy-decisions_en; *see also* Christopher Kuner, Article 45 Transfers on the Basis of an Adequacy Decision, *in* The EU General Data Protection Regulation (GDPR): A Commentary, 771–96 (Christopher Kuner et al., eds. 2020), https://doi.org/10.1093/oso/9780198826491.003.0085; Anastasia Choromidou, *EU Data Protection under the TCA: The UK Adequacy Decision and the Twin GDPRs*, 11 Int'l Data Priv. L. 388 (2021), https://doi.org/10.1093/idpl/ipab021.

[154] Trade and Cooperation Agreement between the European Union and the European Atomic Energy Community, of the one part, and the United Kingdom of Great Britain and Northern Ireland, of the other part, 2020 O.J. (L 146) 10.

[155] Free Trade Agreement Between the European Union and the Socialist Republic of Viet Nam, E.U.-Viet., June 18, 2020, 2020 O.J. (L 186) 3, http://trade.ec.europa.eu/doclib/press/index.cfm?id=1437.

few cooperation provisions on electronic commerce as part of the services chapter, no dedicated chapter and importantly no reference to either data or privacy protection is made.[156] So while there is some certainty that in the deals with Australia and Tunisia, there will be digital trade provisions along the lines of the TCA, as well as in the FTAs with Chile and New Zealand, there is ambiguity as to the currently negotiated deals with India, Indonesia and the Association of Southeast Asian Nations (ASEAN).

C. The RCEP

An interesting and much anticipated development against the backdrop of the diverging EU and U.S. positions has been the recent Regional Comprehensive Economic Partnership (RCEP) between the ASEAN Members,[157] China, Japan, South Korea, Australia, and New Zealand. In terms of norms for the data-driven economy, the RCEP is certainly a less ambitious effort than the CPTPP and the USMCA, but still brings about significant changes to the regulatory environment and in particular to China's commitments in the area of digital trade. The RCEP provides only for conditional data flows, while preserving policy space for domestic policies, which may well be of data protectionist nature. The RCEP e-commerce includes a ban on localization measures[158] as well as a commitment to free data flows.[159] However, there are clarifications that give RCEP members a lot of flexibility, essentially undermining the impact of the made commitments. In this line, there is an exception possible for legitimate public policies and a footnote to Article 12.14.3(a), which says that "For the purposes of this subparagraph, the Parties affirm that the *necessity* behind the implementation of such legitimate public policy *shall be decided* by the implementing Party."[160] This essentially goes against any exceptions assessment, as we know it under WTO law, and triggers a self-judging mechanism.

---

[156] *See* Free Trade Agreement Between the European Union and the Socialist Republic of Viet Nam, E.U.-Viet., Mar. 30, 2020, 2020 O.J. (L 186) 63, https://policy.trade.ec.europa.eu/eu-trade-relati onshships-country-and-region/countries-and-regions/vietnam/eu-vietnam-agreement/texts-agreem ents_en.

[157] Brunei, Cambodia, Indonesia, Laos, Malaysia, Myanmar, Philippines, Singapore, Thailand, and Vietnam.

[158] RCEP, art. 12.14.

[159] *Id.* art. 12.15.

[160] Emphases added.

In addition, subparagraph (b) of 12.14.3 says that the article does not prevent a party from taking "any measure that it considers necessary for the protection of its *essential security interests*. Such measures shall not be disputed by other Parties."[161] Article 12.15 on cross-border transfer of information follows the same language and thus secures plenty of policy space, for countries like China or Vietnam, to control data flows without further justification. So, while in some senses, the RCEP's e-commerce chapter is built upon the CPTPP's framework, the treaty language is made more flexible in order to give the Parties leeway to adopt restrictive measures to digital trade and data flows.

IV. Conclusion

This chapter offers a mapping of developments in the area of digital trade governance with a deep dive on some more sophisticated templates that have been endorsed in recent years. It has become evident that PTAs have evolved into an important platform for rule-making in the area of digital trade, as well as that issues around data and data flows have moved to the center stage of trade negotiations. In the latter context, one could see that states have come up with new solutions that not only provide for legal certainty for data-driven businesses but also for policy space for the protection of vital public interests at home.

Yet, the question is still open as to whether this rule-making is adequate and sufficient to address the needs of the data-driven economy and our increasingly data-dependent societies. First, it must be acknowledged that preferential venues may not be ideal in this regard, as they create a complex and fragmented regulatory environment that does little to ensure seamless data flows, may be power driven and lacking in equality and equity. Furthermore, the above analysis revealed that the major stakeholders of the EU and the United States have adopted different approaches with regard to interfacing data protection and data-based innovation, and the EU as well as the RCEP Parties have been striving to carve out regulatory space and secure their digital sovereignty. This too may be suboptimal, as it does not provide for working reconciliation mechanisms and may undermine international

---

[161] *Id.* art. 12.14.3(b) (emphasis added). The "essential securiry interest" language has been endorsed by China also in the framework of the WTO e-commerce negotiations.

cooperation in advancing the data-driven economy. The calls for more regulatory cooperation and legal innovation that manages the interfaces and trade-offs feasibly appear at this stage better answered by the new agreements dedicated to digital trade, such as the DEPA and have been driven by legal entrepreneurs, such as Singapore. These agreements could pave the path toward better solutions, albeit in parts in soft legal form, in the domain of digital trade governance, possibly also under the multilateral forum of the WTO.

PART IV
DATA LOCALIZATION

12

Personal Data Localization and Sovereignty along Asia's New Silk Roads

Graham Greenleaf

This chapter focuses on countries at the heart of both the traditional and the modern "Silk Roads." It considers only one type of "data," personal data, and thus its focus is on data privacy laws. Data privacy laws can affect "sovereignty" in a variety of ways, all of which I argue can be related to the concept of data localization. The new Silk Road, like its historical predecessor, starts in China and proceeds primarily to the west and the southwest through two closely related Chinese initiatives, the "Belt and Road" and the "Digital Silk Road." This chapter therefore considers what impact data localization is having on the data privacy laws[*] of the countries of Central Asia and South Asia in closest proximity to China, some of which also have very strong historical and cultural ties to the Russian Federation.

Notions of "data sovereignty" in relation to personal data are expressed in four main forms of "data localization": requirements for local processing; requirements for copies to be held locally; conditional restrictions on data exports; and absolute or near-absolute prohibitions on such exports. Other impacts on sovereignty can also be viewed through the same lens of data localization: extraterritorial assertions of data privacy laws; and requirements for local representatives of overseas processors. So data privacy laws can involve at least six modulations of the exercise of sovereignty over processing of personal data for reasons to do with foreigners and foreign jurisdictions.

Data privacy legislation has newly arrived (or is in the legislative process of "arriving") in most countries of two branches of the "new Silk Roads," South

---

[*] This Chapter considers the laws of these countries, and other matters, as they were at September 9, 2021.

Graham Greenleaf, *Personal Data Localization and Sovereignty along Asia's New Silk Roads* In: *Data Sovereignty*. Edited by: Anupam Chander and Haochen Sun, Oxford University Press. © Oxford University Press 2023. DOI: 10.1093/oso/9780197582794.003.0013

Asia and Central Asia. We will examine the commonalities and differences in the approaches these laws take to (personal) data localization.

Finally, the chapter asks how important is it that various norms of international law, particularly those found in Free Trade Agreements (FTAs), are arguably inconsistent with some aspects of data localization found in various national or EU laws.

I. Types of "Data Sovereignty" and "Data Localization"

Authors have offered differing definitions and categorizations of "data localization," and many data privacy laws have implemented restrictions that exemplify some aspects of such data localization. Some governments and authors link some of these categories to concepts of "data sovereignty."

Svantesson, in a report for the OECD, defines "data localization" requirements narrowly, as requirements, directly or indirectly

"that data be stored or processed, exclusively or non-exclusively, within a specified jurisdiction."[1] Chander and Ferracane, for the World Economic Forum, take a broader view, and identify four types of "cross-border data transfer" regulations, which include conditional exports, local storage, local processing, and export bans.[2]

I propose a more systematic way of considering "data localization," anchored to the concept of sovereignty, by posing the question, "In what ways does a State exercise control over processing of personal data *such that* processing in another State is affected?" In other words, how do *local/national* rules about processing personal data affect what processing can be done *in other States*? To say "processing in another State is affected" also includes where it is negatively affected, by (for example), data not being allowed to be exported to it, or data only being allowed to be processed in the State where it is collected. If the rules enacted by one State purport to affect what actions may be taken in another State, then we can say that the sovereignty of that other State has been affected. Data localization has therefore been defined here in terms of effects on the sovereignty of other states.

---

[1] D. Svantesson, *Data Localisation Trends and Challenges: Considerations for the Review of the Privacy Guidelines*, OECD Digital Economy Papers No. 301, Dec. 2020.

[2] A. Chander & M. Ferracane, *Exploring International Data Flow Governance: Platform for Shaping the Future of Trade and Global Economic Interdependence*, WORLD ECONOMIC FORUM, Dec. 2019, <http://ww3.weforum.org/docs/WEF_Trade_Policy_Data_Flows_Report.pdf>.

TYPES OF "DATA SOVEREIGNTY" AND "DATA LOCALIZATION" 297

One strong advantage of this definition is that it is objective; it does not allow us to simply nominate various types of legislation of which we disapprove and call them (pejoratively) "data localization," while ignoring other forms of data localization to which we have no objection (or would prefer to ignore, because our country and/or its allies do them).

Taking this sovereignty-based approach, we can identify at least the following types of data localization, already implemented in at least some of the world's 145 national data privacy laws.[3] For convenient reference, they are numbered "loc #1," "loc #6," etc.

(1) *Local copy requirements* (loc #1): A copy of personal data, usually only in specified categories, must be stored in the local State. Whether or not the data is allowed to be exported is a separate question.

(2) *Local processing requirements* (loc #2): Requirements for "local processing" are a stronger version of local copy requirements, and also imply a local copy requirement (because storage is considered to be processing). An alternative is that a local copy may be required (loc #1), but the data may be exported (loc #3 or #4) and processed overseas.

(3) *Export allowed subject to conditions* (loc #3): Export of categories of personal data outside the State is allowed if and only if specified conditions are satisfied. Conditions may include approval by a State body (usually, government or data protection authority (DPA)). Such requirements were found in the laws of some European States from the 1970s and 1980s,but only became prominent with their inclusion as a requirement (the "adequacy" condition for data exports) in the EU's general data protection Directive of 1995, later continued in the EU's GDPR of 2016.

(4) *Export prohibited* (loc #4): Export of categories of personal data outside the State is prohibited.

(5) *Extra-territorial assertion/application of local data privacy law* (loc #5): Categories of processing of personal data about State citizens/residents by processors located outside the State must comply with the State's data privacy law (usually the entire law). This form of localization came to prominence with the EU's GDPR article 3(2), which it

---

[3] G. Greenleaf, *Global Tables of Data Privacy Laws and Bills* 169 (7th ed., Jan. 2021), *Privacy Laws & Business International Report* 6–19 <https://ssrn.com/abstract=3836261>.

298 DATA LOCALIZATION AND SOVEREIGNTY

has been suggested convinced the world to accept this form of restriction as acceptable and justifiable.

(6) *Local representation requirements* (loc #6): A foreign organization undertaking processing of personal data within the State (possibly only through online marketing) must establish a physical presence (a representative) within the State.[4] Examples can be found in the EU's GDPR (art. 27) and in the laws of Korea, Thailand, and some of the countries considered in this chapter.

For completeness, although it is not "localisation," "*outsourcing exemptions*" should be considered at the same time as forms of localization, in order to see the full picture of processing involving foreigners. Processing of data about categories of foreigners (noncitizens, nonresidents, etc.) by processors within the State are sometimes exempted from the operation of State data privacy laws. This is in effect an abdication of sovereignty by the State over personal data about specified categories of foreigners, even though the data is processed locally, usually for the purpose of attracting outsourced processing business from overseas countries. Examples have existed for the best part of a decade in the Philippines and Hong Kong and are now found in some of the Bills (Pakistan and India) discussed in this chapter.

"Categories of personal data" may refer to either specified categories (such as "sensitive data" or "critical data") or to all personal data. "Processing of personal data" may also refer to any processing, or only specific categories of processing.

De facto localization must also be considered. Both Svantesson and Chander and Ferracane note that there can be situations where conditions in localization #3 are so strict that only local copy retention or local processing (#1 or #2) is in fact feasible. These de facto forms should be identified whenever the whole position of a country is being assessed.

A State's law may combine all six types of localizations by limiting #3 and #4 to apply to only specific categories of personal data, because they cannot both apply to all personal data. Other combinations are common.

For example, the EU's GDPR combines #3 (conditional exports), #4 (extraterritoriality), and #5 (local representation). Some might argue that the restrictive nature of the *Schrems I* and *Schrems II* decisions are so extreme that a de facto version of #4 (no exports), rather that #3 applies. However, this is

---

[4] Svantesson (2020) p. 17 uses the term "rep localisation."

not so for so long as the adequacy decisions in favor of Japan's private sector, of the United Kingdom, and of Korea (proposed), and the other historical adequacy decisions under the Directive, still stand.

The USA's laws, as a generalization, include none of these data localizations (none of #1–#6), but no doubt there are some specific exceptions in sectoral laws. Therefore, while the USA can be seen as consistently opposed to all forms of personal data localization, the same cannot be said of the EU, which advocates some forms of localization and opposes others.

II. China, Russia, and Near Neighbors on the New Silk Roads

The historical "Silk Road" was in fact a confluence of many roads (and some sea routes), all physical, along which flowed many types of trade goods (famously including silk from China), slaves, technologies, and ideas. China was the eastern endpoint of these roads,[5] with Europe, Russia, India and Africa at other endpoints. Geographical imperatives required that, to reach the Chinese terminus, it was necessary for roads to traverse the lands of Central Asia, which were generally considered to be at the heart of the Silk Road.[6] These included the lands that subsequently became five Soviet Socialist Republics, now independent states ("the Stans");[7] "Chinese Turkestan," subsequently known as China's Xinjiang Province; and Mongolia. The countries that we sometimes group as "South Asia," or previously as "the Indian sub-continent" were also a vital part of this historical Silk Road due to their wealth at that time, and many goods and ideas flowed from there to China (and vice versa), of which Buddhism was the most important.

China's sprawling Belt and Road Initiative (BRI), announced in 2013, is well known, and is estimated to involve as many as 138 countries. Slightly less well known, Beijing launched the Digital Silk Road (DSR) initiative in 2015 "with a loose mandate" whereby "assistance goes toward improving recipients' telecommunications networks, artificial intelligence capabilities, cloud computing, e-commerce and mobile payment systems, surveillance

---

[5] Provided you ignore Korea and Japan, for sake of simplification, and because "roads" to those destinations were via China.

[6] From the voluminous literature on the historical Silk Roads, the most popular recent overview is P. FRANKOPAN, THE SILK ROADS (2015), which makes it clear that there were many Silk Roads.

[7] Kazakhstan, Kyrgyzstan, Tajikistan, Turkmenistan, and Uzbekistan.

300 DATA LOCALIZATION AND SOVEREIGNTY

technology, smart cities, and other high-tech areas.'"[8] As many as a third of the countries involved in BRI may be involved in DSR initiatives.[9]

While BRI and DSR are presented by China as a benign arrangement to increase trade, investment, and technical cooperation, others regard them as more malign, involving developing countries falling into debt traps to China, adopting Chinese surveillance technologies to use against their populations, and taking up Chinese 5G telecommunications technologies that pose cybersecurity risks.[10]

This chapter takes up only one small part of these debates, namely whether countries in the two regions most proximate to China that are involved in BRI and DSR initiatives, Central Asia and South Asia, are adopting data localization measures, and whether China's model of data localization may be having any influence on these developments.

A. China's Data Localizations

If China is the origin of these new Silk Roads, then it is useful to start an analysis of personal data localization with an understanding of China's position, to make it possible to assess its influence on the other countries under consideration.

The long-anticipated *Law of the People's Republic of China on the Protection of Personal Information*[11] ("PPIL") was enacted by the Standing Committee of the National People's Congress (SC-NPC), the second-highest legislative body in China,[12] on August 20, 2021. China utilizes all forms of data localization.

The forms of localization identifiable in the PPIL are as follows (articles 38–43).

---

[8] J. Kurlantzick, *China's Digital Silk Road Initiative: A Boon* , <https://thediplomat.com/2020/12/chinas-digital-silk-road-initiative-a-boon-for-developing-countries-or-a-danger-to-freedom/>.

[9] *Id.*

[10] *Id.*

[11] All quotations from the law are from the unofficial translations provided by ChinaLawTranslate. No official English translations are available. A detailed analysis of the first draft of PIPL is G. Greenleaf, *China Issues a Comprehensive Draft Data Privacy Law* (2020), 168 PRIVACY LAWS & BUSINESS INTERNATIONAL REPORT, 1, 6–10 <https://ssrn.com/abstract=3795001>.

[12] For the legislative hierarchy in China, *see* G. GREENLEAF, ASIAN DATA PRIVACY LAWS 193–94 (2014).

(1) If personal information collected or generated within the PRC is processed "at the volume provided for" by the State Internet Information Departments (i.e., the Cyberspace Administration of China (CAC)), then it must be stored within PRC territory (art. 40) (loc #1).

(2) To be exported, such data must have a CAC-organized security assessment, unless exempted (art. 40). This might be in effect a de facto export ban (as explained below), because the result might be that the data can only be stored (and thus processed) in China (loc #2).

(3) Personal information can only be exported "overseas"[13] when at least one of four conditions (loc #3) is satisfied (art. 38):

(a) "Passing a safety assessment organized by the national network information department" (CAC), unless exempt (under art. 40) from such an assessment by laws, regulations or provisions of the Cyberspace Administration of China (CAC), the highest-level regulatory body for Internet-related matters in China. The *Cybersecurity Law* (CSL)[14] of 2016 and the *Data Security Law* (DSL)[15] of 2021 also refer to more strict data localization and export rules that are to be developed to apply to "critical information infrastructure operators," and to other data handlers of "important" data, but these remain without definition as yet.[16]

(b) "Having a professional body conduct personal information protection certification in accordance with provisions of the State Internet Information Departments" (led by the CAC). A certification system will need to be established for this purpose, with clarification of whether certification is per transfer, per transfer type, or per business, and for what duration.[17]

(c) "Contracts concluded with the overseas recipient parties in accordance with standard contract drafted by the [CAC] [which]

---

[13] The first draft PIPL said, "outside the PRC," so it is possible but uncertain that this prohibition might also include Hong Kong.

[14] G. Greenleaf & S. Livingston, *China's New Cybersecurity Law – Also a Data Privacy Law?* (2016), 144 PRIVACY LAWS & BUSINESS INTERNATIONAL REPORT 1–7, <https://ssrn.com/abstract=2958658>

[15] J. Li and J.P. Tomaszewski, *China's New Data Security Law*, LEXOLOGY, July 9, 2021; a translation of the Data Security Law is available from China Law Translate.

[16] The *Regulations on Critical Information Infrastructure (CII) Security Protection*, which took effect on Sept. 1, 2021, has been described as "bizzarely" totally silent on the question of what implications a classification of "critical information infrastructure" will have for the export of personal data: Bird & Bird LLP, *'China Released Regulation on Critical Information Infrastructure Lexology*, Sept. 8, 2021.

[17] *See* DLA Piper, *China: New Draft National, Harmonised Data Protection Law for Mainland China*, LEXOLOGY, Oct. 26, 2020.

302 DATA LOCALIZATION AND SOVEREIGNTY

agree upon the rights and obligations of both parties."[18] It seems these will play an equivalent role to the GDPR's Standard Contract Clauses (SCCs).

(d) "Other conditions provided for by laws, administrative regulations, or provisions of the State Internet Information departments."

In addition (and not as alternative grounds for export), three other conditions must be satisfied: (i) the export must be necessary ("truly need") "due to business requirements" (art. 38); (ii) the consent of the individuals affected must be obtained, after provision of data about the overseas transfer (art. 39); and (iii) a "personal information protection impact assessment" must be conducted (art. 55), with specific requirements, and a copy retained (art. 56). The cumulative effect of these requirements may be prohibitive.

Another conditional basis for exports from the PRC is "requests for the provision of domestically stored personal information from foreign justice or law enforcement" authorities, information handlers (controllers) must not provide this information "without the permission of the competent organs of the PRC" (art. 41).[19]

(4) All of the above conditions for exports constitute localization #3, but if any of (a)–(c) are implemented in very restrictive manner by CAC, export would in effect be prohibited (de facto loc #4). Two clauses create new and uncertain types of prohibitions, by allowing retaliatory measures to be taken by China against overseas companies, countries, or regions. Where a foreign organization is involved in information-handling activities (not just statements) "that harm PRC citizens rights and interests, or endanger the PRC's national security and public interests," the CAC may put them on "the list of those restricted or limited in provision of personal information," which it can publish and "employ measures to restrict or stop the provision of personal

---

[18] The first draft referred to a contract with the overseas recipient where the rights and obligation, and oversight, comply with "standards provided for in this Law." The 2nd and 3rd drafts of the law tightened this condition very considerably. The 2nd draft appeared to say that standard clauses developed by the CAC would play an equivalent role to the GDPR's Standard Contract Clauses (SCCs) and would probably be compulsory. The 3rd draft went further, with some commentators interpreting it as requiring that the contract be tripartite, with the CAC also as a party (see Galaad Delval *op cit.*). This interpolation of the CAC into the contract formation process may have had a "chilling effect" on the enthusiasm of companies to use this option, but it does not appear in the final version enacted.

[19] The first draft provided that where it is necessary for "international judicial assistance or administrative law enforcement assistance," approval by the relevant regulatory authority is required, unless a treaty or agreement concluded by or participated in by the PRC provides authority. The enacted version of art. 41 is very different.

information to them" (art. 42). The PRC can also take "equal measures" against any country or region that "adopts discriminatory prohibitions, restrictions, or other similar measures against the PRC" (in the PRC's opinion) in relation to personal information (art. 43). "Corresponding measures" clauses are more common in international trade agreements and are an innovation in this context. They create a new type of risk for companies, that their own governments take actions that could result in their country becoming subject to Chinese retaliatory actions, which could adversely affect their company.

(5) The PPIL has extraterritorial application to processing outside the PRC (loc #5), including processing for the purpose of providing products and services (marketing) to persons in the PRC, or analyzing and assessing the conduct of such persons (like the GDPR), but unlike the GDPR "other situations provided for by law or administrative regulations" yet to be defined (art. 3). Extraterritoriality under China's law can therefore by expanded by other laws or regulations.

(6) Such extraterritorial processors must designate representatives within the PRC, and advise their identity to the relevant supervisory authorities (art. 53) (loc #6). Since such foreign processors are subject to all the requirements of this PRC law, this will be a significant risk factor for both them and their local representative. Will foreign processors do so, or will they ignore this requirement? Will organizations already present in China, but doing processing within article 3 overseas, have any realistic choice? Similar representation requirements apply to any party handling personal information at a volume specified by the CAC (art. 52), probably including platform operators.[20]

Are these export conditions (loc #3) "just Chinese adequacy"? There are no objective criteria for consent to export, no role for an independent Data Protection Authority (the PIPL does not provide for one), and no provisions for data controllers to appeal to a court against a CAC decision. CAC control over loc #3 conditions (a)–(d) equals CAC discretion to prohibit some categories of export completely. Some commentators conclude that this is likely to result in de facto export prohibition (loc #4) because "companies will

---

[20] Platforms must establish a local independent oversight body (art. 58). For discussion of the previous version, see PPIL 2nd draft; G. Greenleaf, *Asia's Privacy Reform Bills: Variable Speeds* (2021) 171 PRIVACY LAWS & BUSINESS INTERNATIONAL REPORT, 26–29.

greatly reduce cross-border transfers of personal information, as all available transfer mechanisms now require heavy administrative undertakings."[21] An unfettered government discretion to prohibit export of unspecified categories of personal data, such as the CAC can be argued to have, is one of the types of data localization about which opponents of data localization (including advocates of the "free flow of personal data" that accept conditional restrictions) have the highest concerns.

B. Russia's Data Localizations

Russia shared 150 years of common history until 1991 with Central Asian countries, when they were parts of the Tsarist Empire and then the Soviet Union. It continues to be a major cultural and economic influence in Central Asia generally, as discussed later. It may therefore be valuable to examine the extent to which its data privacy laws involve data localization.

Russia's Federal *Law On Personal Data* of 2006 was amended by the *Data Localisation Law* of 2014 (Law No. 242), one of the earliest laws requiring various forms of localization, mainly concerning local storage. Special requirements for specified "platforms" have now been added by Law No. 1176731-7 *"On the activities of foreign entities on the "Internet" telecommunications network in the territory of the Russian Federation,"*[22] enacted in June 2021, affecting requirements for local representatives, and prohibitions on exports. These are referred to herein as the "2006 law," "2014 law," and "2021 law."

The law in Russia on each of the forms of localization is as follows:

(1) *Local copy / storage* (loc #1)—Data operators must store personal data of Russian citizens, collected in Russia, on servers located within the territory of the Russian Federation (2014 law). This only applies to data collected directly from data subjects, by the company or its agent.

(2) *Local processing* (loc #2)—Specified processing in Russia is required by data controllers (not processors) before the data may be exported, but there is no requirement that all processing be in Russia.

---

[21] Galaad Delval *op cit.*

[22] Law No. 1176731-7 "On the activities of foreign entities on the 'Internet' telecommunications network in the territory of the Russian Federation," <https://sozd.duma.gov.ru/bill/1176731-7>

(3) *Data exports are allowed on conditions* (loc #3)—Exports are allowed (unless prohibited under loc #4) to:

    (i) All Parties to Council of Europe data protection Convention 108. This is an extremely unusual and broad "white-list" provision, as it is not decided by the national government or DPA.[23] Restrictions on such transfers may be imposed.

    (ii) All other Countries held by Russia's DPA to have laws that "conform to the provisions" of Convention 108 and are therefore considered to provide adequate protection. There are 23 such countries listed.[24] When the 55 Convention 108 parties in (i) above are added, this gives Russia the most extensive "white list" (78 countries) under any data privacy law globally.

    (iii) Organizations in countries that are not "adequate" under (i) or (ii), but meet at least one of five conditions: consent, international agreements, to protect the constitutional order and related interests, further to contracts, or emergency protection of data subject.

(4) *Data exports are prohibited* (loc #4) if:

    (i) The data are State secrets.

    (ii) The export would be allowed within 3(i) or (ii) as "adequate" but is prohibited for any of these reasons: protecting constitutional order; public morality and health; citizens' rights and interests; and national defense and state security.

    (iii) The export is by a "platform" for which local representation is required (loc #6), but the platform is prohibited from exporting personal data because of non-compliance, under the 2021 law.

(5) *Extraterritorial effect* (loc #5) emerges in two ways:

    (i) Local storage is required (loc #1), and Russian law applies, if data is processed abroad and targets persons in Russia, under the 2014 law. It applies to all foreign businesses that operate in Russia, whether through subsidiaries, representative offices, or

---

[23] A regulation under Israel's law is the only other known example of a blanket Convention 108 "white list": *Privacy Protection (Transfer of Data to Databases Abroad) Regulations, 5761–2001* (Israel).

[24] Listed in Part 7.2, I. Anyukhina & A. Petrova, *Russia–Data Protection Overview, Data Guidance,* Nov. 2020 (list at January 2019) Angola; Argentina; Australia; Benin; Canada; Chile; Costa Rica; Gabon; Israel; Japan; Kazakhstan; Malaysia; Mali; Mongolia; Morocco; New Zealand; Peru; Qatar; Singapore; South Africa; South Korea; and Tunisia.

through individual agents, to the extent they "collect, record, systematize, accumulate, store, correct (update, change), extract personal data of citizens of the Russian Federation."

    (ii) The law has a general extraterritorial effect, if targeting persons in Russia (Supreme Court decisions, 2020),[25] to be dealt with in civil proceedings, not administrative law.[26]

(6) *Local representation is required* (loc #6) by foreign owners of information resources with a daily audience in excess of 500,000 Russian users ("platforms"). Under the 2021 law they will have to open branches or representative offices or establish Russian legal entities that wholly represent the interests of the parent companies, which will have obligations including receiving complaints, court representation, and limiting access to information (or removing it) if in breach of Russian law. Failure to comply may lead to severe sanctions, including the blocking of the platform's content from online search results in Russia and prohibitions on data exports. The 2021 law has received strong criticism from Article 19[27] and from business groups, including on the grounds that content blocking cannot effectively be challenged in Russian courts. The 2021 law is operative from January 1, 2022.

Russia's law therefore includes all six forms of localization.

C. Comparison of Chinese and Russian Localizations

These provisions in Chinese and Russian laws are summarized and compared in the following:

---

[25] M. Ali and O. Novinskaya (Maxima Legal LLC), *Russia: 2019–2020 Results and Trends in Data Protection Regulation Data Guidance*, Dec. 2020; Decision of the Supreme Court of June 9, 2020 No. M-10004763/19 held that in a dispute between Russian Facebook users and Facebook, the terms of service were executed in Russia, there was potentially illegal collection of personal data in Russia, and Facebook intentionally targeted users in Russia.

[26] Ali & Novinskaya, *id.* Ruling of the Supreme Court of July 14, 2020, No. 58-KG20-2 held that a case initiated by the Roskomnadzor (DPA) on behalf of Russian citizens whose personal data was exposed on a website in the Bahamas, should be brought under the Civil Procedure Code, not as an administrative lawsuit.

[27] Article 19 "Russia: The Law on Activities of Foreign Internet Companies threatens freedom of expression," June 21, 2021, <https://www.article19.org/resources/russia-law-on-activities-of-foreign-internet-companies-threatens-free-expression/>.

CHINA, RUSSIA, AND NEAR NEIGHBORS ON THE NEW SILK ROADS   307

Table 12.1 Comparison of localisation measures in China and Russia

	Localization	China (Bill)	Russia (Law)
#1	*Local copy*	For high volume processing (rate decided by CAC)	PD of Russian citizens, collected in Russia; applies where extraterritorial jurisdiction applies.
#2	*Local processing*	If CAC refuses export conditional approvals, only processing in China possible	If export prohibited, or export conditions considered too onerous.
#3	*Export conditional*	Four conditions, all requiring CAC approval or approved processes; necessity, consent and risk assessment also required	Parties to Convention 108; listed countries complying with Convention 108; organizations meeting one of 5 conditions (consent, contracts etc.)
#4	*Export prohibited*	De facto prohibition if CAC implementation of loc #3 is too onerous; Prohibitions as retaliatory measures by China against companies or countries;	State secrets; exceptions on 4 grounds to loc #3 conditional exports; platforms requiring loc #6 representation, but exports prohibited for non-compliance.
#5	*Extraterritorial scope*	Foreign processors marketing to, or profiling, persons in China (like GDPR) or 'other circumstances' (unlike GDPR).	Court implies general extra-territorial effect if targeting persons within Russia; Act has similar provisions.
#6	*Local representation*	Extraterritorial processors bound by PPIL; also 'platforms' (local independent oversight body also)	Foreign-owned platforms with a daily audience in excess of 500,000 Russian users.
	Outsourcing exemption	N/A	N/A

Key: *"PD" = personal data; "white list" = list of countries to which exports are allowed without further conditions.*

Both countries implement all six forms of data localization to some extent but have done so in different ways, with little apparent influence of the provisions in one influencing the other. Their recent provisions concerning representation of foreign "platforms" (loc #6) have some similarities. Their implementation of extraterritoriality (loc #5) is most likely to be influenced by the EU's GDPR, rather than by each other. The actual extent of localization in China is very uncertain, because so much depends on what policies the Cyberspace Administration of China (CAC) will adopt once the PPIL is in force.

III. South Asia: Three Bills Include Localizations

Although China's Belt and Road Initiative (BRI) was initially greeted with considerable enthusiasm at its launch in 2013, observers argue that it "saw waning commitment in some of its South Asian members in 2019."[28] The Kashgar (China) to Gwadar (Pakistan) corridor project (China-Pakistan Economic Corridor—CPEC) was the flagship BRI initiative for South Asia, but the government of Imran Khan has been far less enthusiastic than the predecessor Nawaz Sharif government. Some observers are very skeptical about CPEC, pointing to local protests, political divisions, and suspension of project activity in 2021.[29] Other observers are more optimistic about BRI overall, considering that "despite many challenges, China remains steadfast in carrying out its Belt and Road vision in South Asia,"[30] and listing the "21st century Maritime Silk Road" involving Sri Lanka as one of four BRI sub-projects in South Asia. None of these involved India, which is often a critic of BMI.

A. Regional Agreements

SAARC (South Asian Area of Regional Cooperation), as a regional organization of which all three countries are members, has as yet expressed little interest in data privacy, but two regional developments are of some relevance. The SAARC Agreement on Trade in Services (2010) clause 23 is the same as article XIV(c)(2) of the GATS (discussed in part 5). There is a provision for India to become a party to the RCEP agreement (also discussed in part 5)), which is more permissive of data export restrictions, but no special provisions for other South Asian countries.

---

[28] S. Ramachandran, *A Bumpy Road Ahead for China in South Asia*, THE DIPLOMAT, Jan. 1, 2020, <https://thediplomat.com/2019/12/a-bumpy-road-ahead-for-china-in-south-asia/>

[29] M.A. Notezal, *What Happened to the China-Pakistan Economic Corridor?*, THE DIPLOMAT, Feb. 21, 2021, https://thediplomat.com/2021/02/what-happened-to-the-china-pakistan-economic-corridor/.

[30] A. Ghosal Singh, "China's Vision for the Belt and Road in South Asia," THE DIPLOMAT, Mar. 2, 2019, <https://thediplomat.com/2019/03/chinas-vision-for-the-belt-and-road-in-south-asia/>

B. India

India's Modi government submitted the *Personal Data Protection Bill, 2019*.[31] to India's lower house, the Lok Sabha. The government Bill is based on the draft Bill (and Report[32]) prepared by the committee chaired by former Supreme Court Justice Srikrishna, but almost every clause of the "Srikrishna Bill" is varied by this Bill.[33] Nevertheless, the structure of Srikrishna Bill, including its many influences from the EU's GDPR, is largely retained. The Bill was referred to a 30-member Joint Parliamentary Committee of both Houses, which called for submissions,[34] and whose report is delayed.[35]

India's Bill includes all of localisations #1–#5, omitting #6 on appointing representatives, and also includes "outsourcing exemptions." However, India's approach to limits on the export of personal data is very unusual. In effect, it divides personal data into four categories, with major differences in the treatment of sensitive and non-sensitive personal data (ss. 33–34). India's definition of 'sensitive personal data' (s. 3(36)) is unusual because it includes "financial data" (largely limited to account identifiers, and data concerning relationships with financial institutions: s 3(18)). The definition excludes racial or ethnic origin (while including "caste or tribe"), trade union membership, and criminal records. "Biometric data" (s. 3(7)) and "genetic data" (s. 3(19)) are both included and defined broadly. The government, after consulting the DPAI and any other relevant regulators, can by notification expand the categories of sensitive personal data (s. 15(1)).

The extent of data localization and exports depend on whether data is or is not sensitive personal data, so both the differences in its definition (from the GDPR and other laws), and the capacity for it to be expanded by regulations are significant. A major difference from other laws is that there are no restrictions on export of non-sensitive personal data (loc #3), and no

---

[31] Personal Data Protection Bill, 2019 (India), <https://prsindia.org/sites/default/files/bill_files/Personal%20Data%20Protection%20Bill%2C%202019.pdf>

[32] Committee of Experts under the Chairmanship of Justice B.N. Srikrishna, *A Free and Fair Digital Economy Protecting Privacy, Empowering Indians*, http://meity.gov.in/writereaddata/files/Data_Protection_Committee_Report.pdf.

[33] G. Greenleaf, *India's Data Privacy Bill: Progressive Principles, Uncertain Enforceability* (2020), 163 PRIVACY LAWS & BUSINESS INTERNATIONAL REPORT, 1, 6–9 <https://papers.ssrn.com/abstract_id=3572620 >.

[34] Lok Sabha Secretariat Press Communique Joint Committee on the Personal Data Protection Bill 2019, Jan. 22, 2020 <https://twitter.com/LokSabhaSectt/status/1220636832561369089>.

[35] It has been given an extension of time to submit its Report, until the monsoon session of parliament (July to August–September 2021) and has requested an extension to the winter session.

310 DATA LOCALIZATION AND SOVEREIGNTY

local storage requirements (loc #1), unless the data is deemed to be critical personal data (CPD) and prohibited from export (loc #4).

The types of "data localization" that result, are as follows, stated briefly:[36]

(1) *Local copy requirements* (loc #1): All sensitive personal data must be stored in India, whether or not it is allowed to be exported. There are also some separate sectoral controls.

(2) *Local processing requirements* (loc #2) implied where exports are prohibited by classification as CPD (loc #4) or under sectoral laws (important for financial information).

(3) *Export conditions* (loc #3) allow sensitive personal data be transferred outside India in four situations: (a) explicit consent; (b) transfers pursuant to contract or inter-group scheme approved by the DPAI (Data Protection Authority of India), with exporter remaining liable; (c) transfers to a country, class of entities,.

Etc.," which the government has found provides "adequate protection" (to be defined); (d) DPAI has allowed transfers "for any specific purpose."

(4) *Export prohibitions* (loc #4) are imposed on critical personal data (CPD), which will be defined by government. Export of CPD is allowed when exempted for emergency medical purposes, or exported to a jurisdiction that is adequate, and there is also government approval in the particular case.

(5) *Extraterritorial application* very similar to the EU's GDPR (s. 2(A)(c)) (loc #5).

(6) *Representative appointments* (loc #6) are not required.

(7) *Outsourcing exemption:* "The Government will have power to exempt specified processing of personal data of foreign nationals not present in India (s. 104). The EU would need to insist, as part of any adequacy discussions, that this provision does not apply to EU-origin personal data. Other countries such as the USA will be happy to have data originating there exempted. This is an undesirable provision, if India wishes to be seen as a global leader in the ethical processing of personal data.

---

[36] For details, see G. Greenleaf, "India's Personal Data Protection Bill, 2019 Needs Closer Adherence to Global Standards (Submission to Joint Committee, Parliament of India), Feb. 12, 2020, <https://ssrn.com/abstract=3539432>.

These complex provisions give the government and the DPAI a great deal of discretionary control (definitions of "sensitive personal data" and "critical personal data;" criteria for adequacy; many exemptions), with few legislative constraints and little room for judicial intervention. India's Bill is comparable to China's law, but the extent of similarity will depend significant on definitions and other discretionary elements adopted under each law.

C. Sri Lanka

The third draft of Sri Lanka's *Personal Data Protection Bill*[37] was released in July 2021 by the Ministry of Digital Infrastructure and Information Technology (MDIIT), following a first draft in 2019[38] and second draft in early 2021.[39] It will create a Data Protection Authority (DPA).

Sri Lanka provides for data localization #2 and #3 for data held by the public sector, and for localization #3 for data held by the private sector.

(1) *Local copies* (loc #1) are not explicitly required but are implied in relation to the public sector.

(2) *Local processing* (loc #2): Public authorities may only process personal data within Sri Lanka, unless the DPA and any relevant supervisory body classifies the data as being in a category permitted to be processed overseas, and "prescribed by the Minister pursuant to an adequacy decision" under s26(2) (s. 26(1)). This appears to be a dual condition: the data must be in a permitted category; and the country of processing must be "adequate." There is no such default local processing requirement applying to private sector data.

(3) *Export conditions* (loc #3): Private sector bodies may transfer personal data to a third country (or territory/sector within it) prescribed by the Minister in an adequacy decision (s. 26(3)(a)). The making of an adequacy decision requires the Minister, in consultation with the DPA, to take into account the third country's written law and

---

[37] *Personal Data Protection Bill* (Sri Lanka), <https://lnkd.in/gYa5KDJH>.

[38] Analyzed in G. Greenleaf, *Advances in South Asian DP Laws: Sri Lanka, Pakistan and Nepal* (2019), 162 PRIVACY LAWS & BUSINESS INTERNATIONAL REPORT, 22–25. See Draft Personal Data Protection Blll (Sri Lanka) http://www.mdiit.gov.lk/images/news/Data_Protection_bill/Data_Pr otection_Bill_3-10-2019_-_Amended_Draft_FINAL_-_LD_Release.pdf.

[39] G. Greenleaf, *Asia's Privacy Reform Bills: Variable Speeds* (2021), 171 PRIVACY LAWS & BUSINESS INTERNATIONAL REPORT, 26–29, <https://papers.ssrn.com/abstract_id=3899557>.

312 DATA LOCALIZATION AND SOVEREIGNTY

enforcement mechanisms, and the application in the third country of the equivalents of specific sections of Sri Lanka's law (establishing data subject rights, and controller obligations), and other prescribed criteria (s26(2)(a)), and also to be subject to periodic monitoring at least every two years, and able to be amended or revoked by the Minister in consultation with the DPA (s26(2)(b)). These conditions are similar to those applying to adequacy decisions under the EU's GDPR. Otherwise, private sector bodies are only permitted to process personal data outside Sri Lanka in countries that have not been held to be "adequate" if they ensure compliance with the same specified sections of the Act (s. 26(3)(b)), through a legally binding and enforceable instrument specified by the DPA (s. 26(4)).[40] These are the equivalent of binding contractual clauses (BCCs) under the EU's GDPR.

(4) *Exports prohibited* (loc #4): All public sector data is prohibited from export unless the DPA makes an exception under loc #3. No private sector exports are expressly prohibited.

(5) *Extraterritorial scope* (loc. #5) is defined in similar terms to the GDPR art. 3, but more narrowly requiring "specifically" offering to persons in Sri Lanka or "specifically" monitoring them (s. 3(1)(iv) and (v))), but only in situations specified by the DPA. It may therefore turn out to be rather narrow.

(6) *Local representation* (loc #6) is not required.

The changes to sections 25 and 26 in the course of the three drafts of the Bill have brought it into much closer alignment with provisions concerning "adequacy" in the EU's GDPR, and probably reflect the influence of submissions made by the European Commission.

D. Pakistan

Pakistan's Ministry of Information Technology and Telecommunications (MOITT) released a new "Consultation Draft" *Personal Data Protection Bill*

---

[40] Previous versions included the option of a binding instrument with the recipient in the third country. Such instruments will only allow enforcement by the exporting data controller, not the data subject, because the common law doctrine of privity of contract applies in Sri Lanka (even though its contract law is largely based on Roman–Dutch law).

SOUTH ASIA: THREE BILLS INCLUDE LOCALIZATIONS 313

2021 (PDPB)[41] in August 2021.[42] This is the latest in a series of consultations since 2017, which often referred to data sovereignty and data localization.[43] The Bill will create a data protection authority (National Commission for Personal Data Protection—NCPDP). The Bill has not yet reached the Federal Cabinet. Its data localisation elements are as follows.

(1) *Local copies (loc #1):* Two forms of data localization #1 are required. First, the DPA must "devise a mechanism for keeping some components of . . . sensitive personal data in Pakistan . . . provided that related to public order or national security' (cl. 15.2). This clause previously referred to "a copy of personal data in Pakistan," so it seemed to require a local copy to be kept of all data exported. The local copy requirement is now far more narrow.

(2) *Local processing* (loc #2): ' "Critical personal data shall only be processed in a server or data centre located in Pakistan" (cl. 14.2). "Critical Personal Data' is now defined as meaning 'data relating to public service providers, unregulated e-commerce transactions, and any data relating to international obligations' (cl. 2(d)).[44]

(3) *Conditional data exports* (loc #3): If personal data is to be transferred outside Pakistan 'it shall be ensured that the country where the data is being transferred offers personal data protection at least equivalent to the protection provided under this Act and the data so transferred shall be processed in accordance with this Act and, where applicable, the consent given by the data subject' (cl 14.1). Personal data exports (other than for critical personal data) may take place 'under a framework (on conditions) to be devised by the Commission' (cl. 15.1), but it is unclear whether this "framework) may provide additional methods for data exports, or whether transfers under clause 14 must comply with these conditions, or both. Also unclear is whether the government or the NCPDP decides which countries' laws are "at least

---

[41] *Personal Data Protection Bill 2021 (Pakistan)*, <https://moitt.gov.pk/SiteImage/Misc/files/25821%20DPA%20Bill%20Consultation%20Draft_docx.pdf>

[42] For an analysis of the draft of on Apr. 9, 2020, *see* G. Greenleaf, *Pakistan's DP Bill: DPA Will Have Powers but Lack Independence* (2020), 165 Privacy Laws & Business International Report 20–23, <https://papers.ssrn.com/abstract_id=3667396>.

[43] For example, Pakistan's Ministry of Commerce revised version of the country's e-commerce policy on Nov. 13, 2019.

[44] "Critical personal data" was previously "to be classified by the DPA with approval of the government."

314 DATA LOCALIZATION AND SOVEREIGNTY

equivalent," but if it uses rules (rather than regulations) to do so, it must have government approval.

(4) *Export prohibition* (loc #4): Data exports are prohibited for "critical personal data) (whatever that means), now with no exceptions.[45] This includes all public sector data, and some e-commerce data.

(5) *Extraterritoriality:* (loc #5): The Act will apply to a "'controller or processor digitally or non-digitally operational in Pakistan, but incorporated in any other jurisdiction and involved in commercial or non-commercial activity in Pakistan" (cl. 3.1(b)). This is a significant (but vague) extra-territorial application,[46] one quite different from the EU GDPR test of "marketing to or monitoring of" persons present in the EU. The Act will also apply to (any data subject present in Pakistan) (cl. 3.1(d)), which could mean that a data subject located in Pakistan will (in theory) be able to proceed under this law against any overseas processing of their data, or it might simply extend the scope of the law beyond Pakistani citizens.

(6) *Local representatives* (loc #6): The previous contentious requirement[47] for a foreign processor to have a local representative in Pakistan has been deleted.

(7) *"Outsourcing exemption"*: An unusual provision limits the applicability of the law to data about non-Pakistanis: "Foreign data subject shall have all his rights, if any provided under the laws of the country or territory where the foreign data has been collected or data subject resides in so far as consistent with this Act" (cl. 26). For example, if medical records of a U.S. citizen are sent to Pakistan for transcription, or a Karachi-based call center collects data from U.S residents, then those parts of Pakistan's which are also found in the relevant U.S. laws (federal or state) will apply, but if US law is minimal (as will often be the case), then the Pakistani law will give no protection. In contrast, in equivalent situations concerning a resident of a country in the EU, the whole of the GDPR will apply, giving wider protections than Pakistan's law. This is a convenient result for Pakistan-based companies doing outsourced processing, because it may satisfy both

---

[45] Previously, the government could make exceptions on "the grounds of necessity or strategic interests of the State" but perhaps not for sensitive data.

[46] It previously said that if "any of the data subject, controller or processor (either local or foreign) is located in Pakistan," the data controller and processor must comply with the law.

[47] This may be related to other proposals in Pakistan concerning "online harms," which would expose social media companies to substantial penalties.

US and EU customers. However, if a Pakistani processor is taking in content collected from data subjects in many countries, how will they know what are the "Rights, if any provided under the laws of the [foreign] country' or countries? Consistent compliance is unlikely, unless the processor in Pakistan applies the "highest common denominator" (GDPR) to all data. This would be one version of the Brussels Effect', where a de jure EU influence results in a wider de facto influence.

E. Comparison of South Asian Provisions

The following Table 12.2 compares the Bills in India, Sri Lanka, and Pakistan.

Table 12.2 Comparison of localisation measures in three South Asian Bills

	Localization	India (Bill)	Sri Lanka (Bill)	Pakistan (Bill)
#1	*Local copy*	√ All sensitive PD	√ Public sector PD	√ Some sensitive PD
#2	*Local processing*	√ Wherever export prohibited under #4 as 'critical' PD	√ Public sector PD, unless excepted	√ Critical PD – see definition
#3	*Export conditional*	√ All sensitive PD, unless #4 critical PD; 'adequate' whitelist (Govt. defined), other conditions X Non-sensitive PD – no conditions unless in #4	√ Public sector PD – Govt & DPA power to exempt from #2 and #4 √ Private sector PD – white list; other conditions	√ Critical PD – Govt. can make exceptions to #2 √ Private sector PD – white list; other conditions (DPA defined)
#4	*Export prohibited*	√ Critical PD – to be defined by Govt	√ Public sector PD – all unless exempted under #3 X Private sector PD – none specified	√ Critical PD – prohibition – implied by #2, unless exempted under #3; all public sector data, some e-commerce
#5	*Extraterritorial scope*	√ Similar to GDPR	√ Similar to GDPR	√ Specified connections with Pakistan
#6	*Local representation*	X Not specified	X Not specified	X (Now deleted)
	Outsourcing exemption	√ Govt. power to fully exempt	X N/A	√ Law where data collected etc applies

Key: "PD" = "personal data"; "white list" of countries to which exports are allowed without further conditions.

316   DATA LOCALIZATION AND SOVEREIGNTY

These South Asian Bills, although they differ a great deal, all include much more complex provisions concerning data localization than most existing data privacy laws in Asia. All three have extensive local copy provisions, and some local processing requirements. "White list" provisions allowing considerable government discretion are the basis of conditional exports. Provisions prohibiting export of "critical personal data" have been proliferating in Asian laws and Bills since China's *Cybersecurity Law* of 2016, with its references to "critical information infrastructure operators" (which still lacks definition). They are found India's Bill and Pakistan's Bill, and also in Vietnam's new Decree,[48] all without definition as yet, except for the latest version of Pakistan's Bill. All the Bills assert extraterritorial scope, and India and Sri Lanka follow the GDPR model of doing so, but not Pakistan.

IV. Central Asia: Five Laws Include Some Localizations

Central Asia is a region of great historical importance, and considerable economic significance. It has a population of about 72 million, spread over 4 million square kilometers of land in its five ex-Soviet republics known colloquially as "the Stans"[49] (or previously "Turkestan"): Kazakhstan (pop. 18 million), Kyrgyzstan (6 million), Tajikistan (9 million), Turkmenistan (6 million), and Uzbekistan (33 million).[50] Of these, 7 million are of Russian origin, and 500,000 Ukranian. With a total population of 72 million, they are a significant group of countries. They are all predominantly Muslim countries.

All five countries were parts of the Russian Tsarist Empire from the mid-nineteenth century until World War One, and after that became Soviet Socialist Republics as part of the Soviet Union (USSR), until its dissolution in 1991. Since then they are, to different extents, parties to post-Soviet regional agreements, and are affected to differing degrees by continuing Russian influences, and by China's "Belt and Road" initiatives.

---

[48] G. Greenleaf, *Vietnam: Data Privacy in a Communist ASEAN State* (2021) 170 PRIVACY LAWS & BUSINESS INTERNATIONAL REPORT, 1, 5–8, <https://ssrn.com/abstract=3874748 >
[49] "Stan" is an Iranian suffix for "land."
[50] Wikipedia: Central Asia, https://en.wikipedia.org/wiki/Central_Asia

None of the five countries have high rankings as liberal polities or as democracies.[51] They all have differing histories of post-Soviet authoritarian rule, with the Kyrgyz Republic as an increasingly democratic exception.[52] It is therefore somewhat surprising that all five of these Central Asian countries have now enacted data privacy laws of at least minimum international standard, with new or revised legislation since 2017:[53] Kyrgyz Republic (2008, revised 2017);[54] Kazakhstan (2013, revised 2016 and 2020);[55] Turkmenistan (2017);[56] Tajikistan (2018);[57] and Uzbekistan (2019).[58]

The Belt and Road initiative was launched by President Xi Jinping's during his September 2013 visit to Astana, capital of Kazakhstan. "With the BRI, Beijing's presence in Central Asia has been rapidly expanding, replacing Russia as the leading investor." 'Despite its growing impact, China cannot compete with Russia's institutional, cultural, and legal legacy in the region. A study of BRI investments in Kazakhstan concluded that there was "a solid basis for the assumption that Beijing does not insist on bringing its legal rules and prefers to operate BRI projects within the local legal framework."[59]

A study of changing perceptions of China in Central Asia since BRI/DSR concluded:

---

[51] S. Walker, "Democracy Was Hijacked. It Got a Bad Name": The Death of the post-Soviet Dream, THE GUARDIAN, Dec. 8, 2016, <https://www.theguardian.com/world/2016/dec/08/central-asia-taj ikistan-kazakhstan-kyrgyzstan-uzbekistan-turkmenistan>

[52] For an accessible account, *see* E. FATLAND, SOVIETISTAN (2014 with English translation and Afterword, 2019).

[53] The minimum standard is a law enforceable by some means of legal compulsion (i.e., not just self-regulation), which includes at least 9 of the 10 standards common to the OECD privacy Guidelines (1980) and the Council of Europe data protection Convention 108 (1981): for details, *see* G. Greenleaf, *Sheherezade and the 101 Data Privacy Laws: Origins, Significance and Global Trajectories'*(2014) 23(1) JOURNAL OF LAW, INFORMATION & SCIENCE, <https://ssrn.com/abstract= 2280877>.

[54] Law on Personal Information 2008, No. 58 (Kyrgyz Republic), as amended by the Law on Personal Data of July 27, 2017, No. 129.

[55] Law on Personal Data 2013 (Kazakhstan); as amended by Law on Amendments to Certain Legislative Acts on Informatization in Kazakhstan (referred to as the Informatization Law), published Nov. 16, 2015; and by Law No. 347-VI dated June 25, 2020, "On Amending Some Legislative Acts of the Republic of Kazakhstan on Regulation of Digital Technologies," in force July 7, 2020.

[56] Law on Information on Private Life and its Protection No. 519-V – 2017 (Turkmenistan); Was available in Russian from the Ministry of Justice site, <http://www.minjust.gov.tm/ru/>, but no longer.

[57] Law of 3 August 2018 No.1537 on Protection of Personnel Data (Tajikistan); available in Tajik <http://base.mmk.tj/view_sanadhoview.php?showdetail=&sanadID=609> and Russian <http:// base.mmk.tj/view_sanadhoview.php?showdetail=&sanadID=609&language=ru>.

[58] Law on Personal Data 2019, No. 3PY-547 dated 2 July 2019 (Uzbekistan).

[59] R. Nurgozhayeva, *How Is China's Belt and Road Changing Central Asia?*, THE DIPLOMAT, July 9, 2020, <https://thediplomat.com/2020/07/how-is-chinas-belt-and-road-changing-central-asia/>

Analysing the region's perceptions of China and BRI, we can see similar patterns across all five Central Asia countries. There are some differences, but they are not significant. Each country is attracted by Chinese economic projects and educational opportunities; but there is also a persistent anti-Chinese sentiment across Central Asia related to potential Chinese demographic and cultural expansion and increased financial debt dependence that may follow economic expansion.'

Although these data privacy laws have been enacted in all Central Asian countries, evidence of enforcement of their provisions is lacking. In some countries a "responsible state authority" may be appointed to administer and enforce the law (e.g., in Kyrgyzstan, Turkmenistan, Kyrgyz Republic), but other than in Kazakhstan (appointment of the Ministry of Digital Development, Innovation and Aerospace Industry, MDAI), no such appointments have been made as of mid-2021. In the absence of such appointment, enforcement is the responsibility of "the Cabinet of Ministers" (e.g., in Turkmenistan,). Lack of such appointments usually means that registration requirements are not yet enforced.

A. International and Regional Agreements

There is no regional international instrument (including trade agreements, FTAs) that deals with data protection issues. All Central Asian countries except Turkmenistan and Mongolia are members of the nine state Commonwealth of Independent States (CIS) grouping of Russia and other ex-Soviet states. The Commonwealth of Independent States Free Trade Area (CISFTA) includes all the Central Asian republics, plus Russia and other states. It does not include any provisions relating to personal data. There are other CIS treaties.[60]

The *General Agreement on Trade in Services* (GATS), article XIV of which imposes limits on data export restrictions, includes in its members Kazakhstan, Kyrgyzstan, and Tajikistan, but not Turkmenistan or Uzbekistan. As with the EU's GDPR, the compatibility of the data export limits in Central

---

[60] The Treaty on the Eurasian Economic Union came into force on Jan. 1, 2015. However, only Kazakhstan and Kyrgyzstan are parties to it.

Asian laws (see Part 5 following for details) with GATS article XIV could be questioned.

The only other international data protection instrument to which Central Asian countries could accede is the Council of Europe data protection Convention 108+. None have acceded or requested to become an Observer, although Kazakhstan did express interest to the Consultative Committee prior to its recent legislative amendments. The European Union, in partnership agreement with Kazakhstan, encouraged it to accede to Convention 108 (now 108+).[61] The lack of an independent DPA would be a major problem for accession, but not the only problem, because factors such as democracy and the rule of law are also relevant.[62]

Uzbekistan's law provides (art. 2) that where it is a Party to a treaty that establishes "other rules," those rules "shall be applied." This would apply if it acceded to Convention 108+. Kazakhstan's law has a similar provision (art. 4(2)).

B. Data Localization Measures in National Laws

How have these factors played out in relation to the adoption of data localization measures? Have the Russian or Chinese data localization provisions been influential? Each of the methods of localization is now considered, by comparing each Central Asian country.

---

[61] Yekaterina Khamidullina 'Kazakhstan – The impact of the GDPR outside the EU' 30 September 2019, Aequita law firm/Lexology: 'The Enhanced Partnership and Cooperation Agreement (the 'Agreement') between the European Union and its member states and the Republic of Kazakhstan was signed on 21 December 2015. The Agreement was ratified by Kazakhstan on 25 March 2016 . . . Pursuant to Article 237 of the Agreement: 'The Parties shall cooperate in order to ensure a high level of protection of personal data, through the exchange of best practices and experience, taking into account European and international legal instruments and standards. This may include, where appropriate and subject to applicable procedures, accession to, and implementation of, the Council of Europe Convention for the Protection of Individuals with regard to Automatic Processing of Personal Data and its additional Protocol by the Republic of Kazakhstan' ('Convention 108').'

[62] G. Greenleaf, How Far Can Convention 108+ "Globalise"?: Prospects for Asian Accessions, Feb. 3, 2020, *Computer Law & Security Review.* <https://ssrn.com/abstract=3530870>.

C. Local Processing and Storage (Loc #1 and #2)

Uzbekistan has made a number of rules concerning the location of servers, some processing and data, under its E-Commerce and Electronic Document Management laws,[63] summarized as:[64]

- the hosting of the main server and reservation of any level is allowed only in the territory of Uzbekistan;
- an information intermediary is required to place its information system on servers located in the territory of Uzbekistan;
- the seller is required to ensure the storage of electronic documents and electronic messages, and the electronic trading platform should securely exchange documents (messages) and store them on servers located on the territory of Uzbekistan; and
- the storage of documents, messages, and other information related to agreements concluded in electronic commerce should be carried out on the territory of Uzbekistan. The seller and/or the information intermediary is required to ensure the safety of personal data, both of buyers and other individuals who became known to them during the conclusion of electronic commerce agreements and the protection of their information systems, databases, means, and environment for storing electronic documents and messages from unauthorized access.

In *Uzbekistan*, some (not all) personal data databases are also subject to registration in the State Register of Personal Data Databases, by the data privacy law. However, there is no explicit requirement that a copy of the data be retained in the country.

Kazakhstan's law was amended in 2016[65] to require that owners and/or operators of databases containing personal data shall store that data on the territory of Kazakhstan (art. 12.2).[66] It is unclear whether this has

---

[63] "Rules on geographical location of the main servers" (Uzbekistan), made under the Law on Electronic Document Management, No. 611-II of 29 April 2004 (Uzbekistan) <https://lex.uz/docs/165074> (in Russian); and the Law on Electronic Commerce, No. 613-II of Apr. 29, 2004 < https://lex.uz/docs/165497> (in Russian) ("the Law on E-Commerce").

[64] Abdulaziz Jurajonov, *Uzbekistan – Data Protection Overview*, DATA GUIDANCE, Apr. 2020 https://www.dataguidance.com/notes/uzbekistan-data-protection-overview.

[65] *Law On Amendments to Certain Legislative Acts on Informatization in Kazakhstan* ('Informatization Law') Nov. 26, 2015, in effect from Jan. 1, 2016.

[66] M. Kahiani & L. Adbukhalykova *Kazakhstan - Data Protection Overview*, DATA GUIDANCE, Jan. 2020, <https://www.dataguidance.com/notes/kazakhstan-data-protection-overview>,

extraterritorial effect so as to apply to foreign companies without a legal presence in *Kazakhstan*, but whose operations target persons in Kazakhstan (and perhaps whose websites are accessible in Kazakhstan).[67] No administrative liability was assigned by the 2016 law for breach of the localization requirement.

Other Central Asian states do not have explicit local copy requirements. *Turkmenistan* does not require registration of databases or for records of processing to be kept.

Uzbekistan's law implies that processing of e-commerce transactions should take place on servers located in Uzbekistan. Kazakhstan's law is unclear about the need for local processing.

D. Data Export Conditions and Prohibitions (Loc #3 and #4)

All five laws allow data exports on the basis of compliance with conditions (loc #3), which in all cases allow export to jurisdictions providing some form of protection equivalent to the local law, variously expressed as "adequate" or "equal" or simply "ensure protection" or provide "data protection." Where such jurisdiction-wide conditions are not satisfied, limited other bases for transfers are sometime provided, including data subject consent or protection of vital interests. Although implemented in various ways, these conditional export restrictions appear to owe more to the EU's "adequacy" requirements in the 1995 DPD than they do to the Russian or Chinese provisions.

Both Uzbekistan and Tajikistan allow prohibitions on exports to protect broadly described interests, by regulations (localization #3). Kazakhstan allows this but possibly only by laws, not regulations. Neither of the other laws does so explicitly.

Uzbekistan limits data exports to transfers to states that provide for "adequate protection" (no definition or mechanism specified), or otherwise with data subject consent, or where necessary "to protect the constitutional order," or as provided by treaties. Uzbekistan also provides that cross-border transfers "may be prohibited or limited" to protect a wide range of interests, but no mechanism of limitation is specified.[68]

---

[67] These complexities are discussed in Nataliya Shapovalova, *Personal data storage in Kazakhstan: amendments to come into effect on 1 January 2016*, Dentons website / Lexology, Dec. 4, 2015.

[68] Uzbekistan, art. 15: "The cross-border transfer of personal data may be prohibited or limited in order to protect the foundations of the constitutional order of the Republic of Uzbekistan, morality,

322 DATA LOCALIZATION AND SOVEREIGNTY

Kazakhstan's local storage requirement does not prevent personal data being exported from Kazakhstan in accordance with the Act's cross-border transfer provisions. Under Kazakhstan's 2013 law, data exports may only be to countries whose laws also ensure data protection, or to other countries with data subject consent in some cases, or if authorized by treaties, or by other laws, or to protect the rights of others where consent is impossible (A 16). No data is explicitly prohibited from being exported. These provisions were not changed by the 2016 or 2020 amendments. There is no specification of the level of the "data protection" that other countries must provide. Commentators have suggested that the level of protection might be indicated by article 22, which states the security and data breach obligations of data system owners/operators, but this argument does not take into account the broader obligations imposed on them under art. 25.[69] Kazakhstan's law also allows cross-border transfers to be "or prohibited or restricted" by other Kazakh laws, so complete bans on exports of some categories of data are possible, but may need to be specified in laws, not regulations.

Tajikistan's law provides for both data export conditions and prohibitions. Cross-border transfers may be to processors in foreign states that provide "adequate protection" (undefined) (art. 18(1)), or otherwise with the consent of the data subject, according to treaties, or as stipulated by legislation (where necessary to protect specified interests), or where to protect interests of other citizens but obtaining consent is not possible (art. 18(2)). Prohibitions or other limitations on exports are allowed to protect a variety of State and public interests (art. 18(1)),[70] by regulations made or approved by the president.

In its 2008 law (and continued in the 2017 law), *Kyrgyzstan* allowed "transboundary transfer of personal data" on the basis of an "international treaty between the parties according to which the receiving party shall provide level of protection of rights and freedoms of the personal data subjects and the personal data security equal to that of established in the Kyrgyz Republic" (art. 25(1)); or otherwise with the "obviously expressed consent" of the data subject, or if necessary to protect their vital interests, or if in "publicly

---

health, rights and legitimate interests of citizens of the Republic of Uzbekistan, ensure the national defense and state security."

[69] Kahiani & Adbukhalykova, cited above.

[70] Tajikistan, art. 18(1) allows prohibitions "in order to protect the foundations of the constitutional order of the Republic of Tajikistan, morality, health, rights and legitimate interests of citizens, ensure the defense of the country and the security of the state."

available personal data files" ("intended for general public use") (art. 25(3)). There are no provisions explicitly prohibiting export of categories of personal data, but the Law "On protection of the state secrets of the Kyrgyz Republic" would be likely to have such effect concerning state secrets.

In *Turkmenistan* data exports are only permitted to states that "ensure protection" (like Kazakhstan) of the information, but there are no explicit prohibitions on data being exported.

E. Extraterritoriality and Local Representation (Loc #5 and #6)

It is unclear whether *Kazakhstan*'s law, as amended in 2016, has extraterritorial effect such that it applies to foreign companies without a legal presence in Kazakhstan, but whose operations target persons in Kazakhstan.[71] The laws of *Tajikistan*, *Krygyzstan*, and *Uzbekistan* do not provide for extraterritorial effect or require local representation.

F. "Outsourcing Exemptions"

None of the Central Asian States have provisions allowing the selective exemption of data originating in specified countries from their laws.

G. Comparison of Central Asian Provisions

The following table compares the five Central Asian laws.

Provisions for conditions for personal data exports are found in all five countries, based on equivalent protections, and three countries prohibit some exports as well. Otherwise, data localization measures are uncommon in Central Asia, with only two countries requiring some local storage of personal data, and none clearly asserting extraterritorial jurisdiction.

---

[71] These complexities are discussed in Nataliya Shapovalova, *Personal data storage in Kazakhstan: amendments to come into effect on 1 January 2016*, Dentons website / Lexology, Dec. 4, 2015.

324 DATA LOCALIZATION AND SOVEREIGNTY

Table 12.3 Comparison of localisation measures in five Central Asian Laws

	Localization	Uzbek	Kyrgyz	Tajik	Turkmen	Kazakh
#1	*Local copy*	√ e-commerce PD	N/A	N/A	N/A	√ All PD local storage
#2	*Local processing*	√ e-commerce PD	X N/A	X N/A	X N/A	X N/A
#3	*Export conditional*	√ equivalence	√ equivalence	√ equivalence	√ equivalence	√ equivalence
#4	*Export prohibited*	√ by regs	X N/A	√ by regs	X N/A	√ by other laws; none yet
#5	*Extraterritorial scope*	X N/A	X N/A	X N/A	X N/A	? unclear
#6	*Local representation*	X N/A	X N/A	X N/A	X N/A	X N/A
	Outsourcing exemption	X N/A	X N/A	X N/A	X N/A	X N/A

Key: "PD" = "personal data"; "white list" = list of countries to which exports are allowed without further conditions; "equivalence" = a requirement of similar quality laws, without a white list.

V. How Relevant Are Free Trade Agreements?

This chapter has focused on national laws, with only brief reference to international commitments. However, free trade agreements (FTAs) often purport to constrain national laws. A considerable literature exists on the tensions between data privacy protections and provisions in FTAs that aim to restrict data export limitations and other forms of data localization.

A. Adequacy and the GATS

Where data localization provisions exist in national laws, their effect is direct and immediate on businesses trading or intending to trade in those countries. In contrast, the effect of any FTA restrictions on enactment of data export restrictions (including data localization provisions) is as yet hypothetical because there have not yet been any legal challenges under any FTA to data export or localization provisions. The General Agreement on Trade in Services (GATS) article XIV(c)(ii) is the oldest such provision, and the one with potentially the broadest scope, because all members of the WTO are parties to the GATS. All countries discussed in this chapter are WTO members, except Uzbekistan.

The most important national (and regional) law imposing restriction on data exports is the 1995 EU data protection Directive (DPD), and now, its successor the GDPR, because of their requirements that personal data may not be exported to destinations which do not provide adequate protection to such personal data or satisfy alternative criteria. Yakovleva and Irion[72] set out the various ways in which the DPD/GDPR "adequacy" provisions may be inconsistent with the GATS: it may violate the EU's nondiscrimination commitments under the GATS by giving favored treatment to countries receiving positive adequacy findings; and it may apply a double standard in relation to its own members' surveillance practices, compared with what it accepts by states such as the USA. They argue that these violations may not be excusable under the "necessity test" required by the exceptions in article XIV(c)(ii), because the adequacy requirement is not the least trade-restrictive of all "reasonably available" alternatives. Perhaps the EU has no choice but to take this approach,[73] but that is not in issue here except that it indicates that the EU will not back off from "adequacy" without a fight.

The GATS article XIV(c)(ii) has existed since 1994, so there have been over 25 years during which the arguably inconsistent 1995 DPD and now GDPR provisions could have been challenged. No country has mounted such a challenge, but during that time 115 countries have enacted data privacy laws,[74] and over 100 of them restrict data exports based at least in part on the laws of the recipient country of the personal data to be exported (i.e., something resembling "adequacy" requirements). While time does move slowly in international law, it can sometimes be overtaken by events. Data export restrictions, and more recently, other forms of data localization, have obtained many more "boots on the ground," a situation which, in practice, is increasingly difficult to undo.

---

[72] S. Yakovleva & K. Irion, TOWARD COMPATIBILITY OF THE EU TRADE POLICY WITH THE GENERAL DATA PROTECTION REGULATION, 2020, 114 AJIL UNBOUND 110–15.

[73] Yakovleva and Irion argue that "The adequacy approach—the most questionable from a trade law perspective—is thus, in theory, the only personal data transfer mechanism that fully complies with [the EU's] constitutional requirements."

[74] G. Greenleaf, *Countries with Data Privacy Laws – By Year 1973-2019*, unpublished May 2019, https://ssrn.com/abstract=3386510.

326 DATA LOCALIZATION AND SOVEREIGNTY

In relation to the countries which are the subject of this chapter, two other FTAs are relevant.

B. The Comprehensive and Progressive Agreement for Trans-Pacific Partnership (CPTPP)

The *Comprehensive and Progressive Agreement for Trans-Pacific Partnership* (CPTPP) has strong restrictions on data export limitations, and on local processing or storage requirements (i.e., localizations #1–#4). CPTPP has 11 signatories but came into force on December 30, 2018, once six Parties ratified it.[75] Nine other APEC economies have announced interest in joining CPTPP,[76] including China in May 2020.[77] In February 2021 the United Kingdom became the first country to apply to accede to the CPTPP.[78] Any South Asian or Central Asian country that wished to accede would also have apply. The major unknown is whether the Biden administration will seek to negotiate U.S. accession to CPTPP.[79]

In summary,[80] the CPTPP's implications for privacy legislation can be summarized as follows:

- It imposes *a Four-Step-Test for any exceptions to its prohibition on data export limitations* (i.e., localisations #3 or #4). States have the onus to prove that their legislation (i) is "to achieve a legitimate public policy objective"; (ii) "is not applied in a manner which would constitute a means of arbitrary or unjustifiable discrimination"; (iii) is not applied so as to be "a disguised restriction on trade"; and (iv) "does not impose restrictions on transfers of information greater than are required to

[75] Mexico, Canada, Japan, New Zealand, Australia, and Singapore ratified. Vietnam subsequently did so, giving seven current Parties. The other four original signatories (Brunei, Chile, Malaysia, and Peru) have signed but not yet ratified, although they may still do so at any time (CPTPP art. 3(2)).

[76] Any other country, or customs territory may also ratify, with the consent of all the parties, and subject to any conditions agreed (CPTPP, art. 5).

[77] For references for each expression of interest, see Wikipedia: Comprehensive and Progressive Agreement for Trans-Pacific Partnership.

[78] H. Channer & J. Wilson *Expanding the CPTPP: A Form Guide to Prospective Members*, THE INTERPRETER, Feb. 22, 2021,<https://www.lowyinstitute.org/the-interpreter/expanding-cptpp-form-guide-prospective-members>.

[79] The Trump administration pulled out of its proposed predecessor, the TPP, in 2017.

[80] *See* G. Greenleaf, *Asia-Pacific Free Trade Deals Clash with GDPR and Convention* 108 (2018) 156 PRIVACY LAWS & BUSINESS INTERNATIONAL REPORT 22–24; *see also* Greenleaf, *Looming Free Trade Agreements Pose Threats to 2018*, 152 PRIVACY LAWS & BUSINESS INTERNATIONAL REPORT, 23–27, and earlier articles cited therein.

achieve the objective." This is arguably stricter than GATS article XIV(c) (ii).

- There are *similar data localization prohibitions*: a prima facie ban on requiring use of computer facilities (i.e., processing, localization #2) within a party's territory to conduct business within that territory, subject to the same tough four-step test to overcome the ban.
- *Government exceptions*—It does not apply to information held or processed by or on behalf of a government, or measures related to it. The provisions only apply to "trade by electronic means" and not to non-trade processing of information.

CPTPP includes two provisions that go beyond diplomatic means of enforcement. *State party dispute settlement* provisions can result in a panel awarding monetary assessments against a party, in lieu of the suspension of CPTPP benefits. *Investor-state dispute settlement (ISDS) provisions* could apply in limited situations, particularly where a provision could be argued to constitute direct or indirect expropriation of investments.

Are these CPTPP provisions likely to result in attacks on data localization provisions in national laws? U.S. accession would increase the likelihood of enforcement of CPTPP's data export and data localization provisions, because the United States opposes export restrictions and localization, and is likely to be subjected to data export restrictions (as the *Schrems* cases have shown). It is difficult to see other countries attempting to enforce these provisions, because three of the Parties have also succeeded in obtaining a positive "adequacy" finding from the EU (Japan, Canada, and New Zealand), and the remaining parties all have relatively strong data protection laws and are relatively unlikely to be subjected to export restrictions. Two potential new accessions to the CPTPP, Korea and the United Kingdom,[81] have adequacy applications near-finalized or finalized. It is therefore difficult to see parties or prospective parties to the CPTPP having a strong incentive to wish to demonstrate that other Parties' localization provisions are in breach of CPTPP, or (indirectly) in breach of GATS (by being non-compliant with article XIV(c)(ii)). They would also be reluctant to have their own data export restrictions attacked via the CPTPP provisions. No South Asian or Central Asian countries are parties to the CPTPP. It is unknown whether their data localization provisions would become an issue if they so applied.

---

[81] Channer & Wilson *op cit.*

328 DATA LOCALIZATION AND SOVEREIGNTY

C. The Regional Comprehensive Economic Partnership (RCEP)

The *Regional Comprehensive Economic Partnership* (RCEP) had 16 countries as signatories on November 15, 2020: the 10 members of ASEAN plus the 6 countries with which ASEAN has free trade agreements (the ASEAN free trade partners).[82] China is the only one directly relevant to this chapter, and a leading RCEP participant. India is entitled to a fast-track accession process at a later date. "Even without India, RCEP will still be the world's largest free trade agreement."[83] For RCEP to come into force requires nine ratifications, but there are none as yet.

RCEP's electronic commerce chapter (Chapter 12),[84] does have provisions on data exports and local processing (localizations #1–#4), but they are far more permissive than those in CPTPP.[85] Cross-border transfer restrictions are superficially subject to a "4 step test" for allowed exceptions, which is superficially similar to that in the CPTPP. However, the question of whether measures are those "that [a Party] considers necessary to achieve a legitimate public policy objective" is to be decided solely by that party (RCEP, Ch. 12, art. 12.15(3)(a) and footnote 14). Measures that a Party considers necessary for "protection of its essential security interests" also "cannot be disputed by other Parties" (RCEP, Ch. 12, art. 12.15(3)(b)). These are significant reductions in the CPTPP restrictions.

In similar fashion, the prohibition on requirements to use or locate computing facilities on a Party's territory is subject to the familiar "4 step test" for exceptions, but the question of what measures are "necessary to achieve a legitimate public policy objective" is left solely to the decision of the implementing Party (RCEP, Ch. 12, art. 12.14 and footnote 12). There is also a "completely self-judging and non-disputable national security exemption"[86] for such data localization. This too is weaker than the CPTPP data localization provision.

---

[82] New Zealand Foreign Affairs and Trade "RCEP Overview," https://www.mfat.govt.nz/en/trade/free-trade-agreements/agreements-under-negotiation/regional-comprehensive-economic-partnership-rcep/rcep-overview/#countries.

[83] Australia (DFAT), *About the Regional Comprehensive Economic Partnership Agreement (RCEP)*, <https://www.dfat.gov.au/trade/agreements/not-yet-in-force/rcep>.

[84] Australia (DFAT) RCEP Text, <https://www.dfat.gov.au/trade/agreements/not-yet-in-force/rcep/rcep-text>.

[85] For the history of the RCEP negotiations, see Jane Kelsey, *Important differences between the final RCEP electronic commerce chapter and the TPPA and lessons for e-commerce in the WTO*, BILATERALS.ORG website, Feb. 2020, <https://www.bilaterals.org/?important-differences-between-the>.

[86] Terminology used by Kelsey, *op cit.*

The exclusion of government use of data in RCEP is broad. Also, Chapter 12 is not subject to state-to-state dispute settlement procedures, only negotiations (Ch. 10, art. 12.17). In contrast CPTPP is subject to such procedures, and with limited ISDS provisions. RCEP therefore offers very limited opportunity for its data localization provisions to be attacked, and there is seems to be no obvious incentive for any of its Parties to do so.

D. FTAs and the Future of Data Localization

Finally, it is too early to say what the E-commerce treaty at present under discussion at the WTO will add to this discussion, but leaked documents indicate that a wide spectrum of positions are being put forward, including those similar to the permissive clauses in RCEP.

Based on the history of FTAs since 1994, it seems unlikely that the GATS, the CPTPP, and the RCEP (when in force) will have any major impact on whether countries in Central Asia or South Asia enact, or retain, legislative provisions concerning data localization.

VI. Conclusion

This chapter has proposed a somewhat different way of looking at the question of data localization, characterizing it as the ways by which a State exercises control over processing of personal data *such that* processing in another State is affected. Six distinct forms of localization are identified. The laws (or in three countries, proposed laws) of ten countries relevant to the "new Silk Road" are then examined against these six criteria: China, Russia, three South Asian countries, and five Central Asian countries. This has proven to be a useful method of analysis.

The first and broadest conclusion to be drawn is that data localization is much more common than many expect—particularly those who use it as a pejorative expression. In China, Russia, and the three South Asian states, all six forms of data localization are found in relation to some categories of data. In Central Asia only a version of conditions for data exports, loosely similar to the concept of "adequacy" are found in all five states, and other forms of localization are hardly present at all.

330 DATA LOCALIZATION AND SOVEREIGNTY

The more detailed comparative position is as follows, and it shows little uniformity despite the high use of data localization provisions:

1. *Local copy*—In China this depends on the volume of transactions. Russia requires local copies of all personal data of Russian citizens that are collected directly from them. India requires local storage of all sensitive personal data, and Pakistan an undefined subset of sensitive data relating to public order or national security. Sri Lanka implies such a requirement for public sector data. Uzbekistan requires local storage for e-commerce data, and Kazakhstan for all personal data, but other Central Asian countries do not.

2. *Local processing*—*Data* export bans (loc #4) will result in *de facto* local processing. In China, exports can be banned for many largely discretionary reasons. In default, public sector data must be processed in Sri Lanka. "Critical personal data" (undefined as yet) must be processed in Pakistan. Russia requires some processing steps before exports are allowed. Uzbekistan's law implies something similar, and Kazakhstan may do likewise.

3. *Export conditional*—*Nine* of the countries impose conditions on any personal data exports, except India does not do so with non-sensitive data (but has a broad definition of "sensitive"). Every country, except China, includes some condition where the quality of data protection available in the recipient country is a determining factor, but only some have procedures for a government or DPA to predetermine which countries meet the criteria. The criteria are often not well-defined, and vary between "adequate," "equal," "ensure protection." The EU notion of "adequacy" has spread widely but found many different forms of expression. The broadest expression is in Russia, where both all parties to Convention 108 and a long list of specific countries satisfy the Russian DPA's "white list" criteria.

4. *Export prohibited*—Eight of the countries allow exports to be banned, but there is little consistency. All public sector data is prima facie banned from export in Sri Lanka. Russia has a short list of state secrets and national interests, plus bans for non-compliance with other requirements. China's bans can be for expressly retaliatory reasons, or failure to meet demanding criteria. As yet undefined "critical personal data" are the basis of bans in India and Pakistan. Uzbekistan, Tajikistan, and Kazakhstan each have broadly described grounds for prohibitions.

5. *Extraterritoriality*—Since the EU's GDPR provisions became known in 2016, it has become very common for new laws to have extraterritorial application, often with criteria similar to the EU (marketing or profiling) as in China, Russia, India, or Sri Lanka. However, Pakistan's criteria are very different, and China adds the ability to define new grounds by regulations. Broad extra-territoriality is now almost unremarkable, having previously been exceptional.

6. *Local representation*—China and Russia are able to impose this requirement on foreign countries, but none of the other eight countries do so.

Patterns of influence are difficult to ascertain, except for the general proposition that all of the countries' laws show the influence of the EU's GDPR, less so in the Central Asian countries. China's substantial economic influence on the countries of the new Silk Road are not at this stage matched by equivalent influence on the data privacy laws of proximate countries.

13

Lessons from Internet Shutdowns Jurisprudence for Data Localization

Kyung Sin Park

Data is external manifestation of a sentient being's perception. Transfer of data from one sentient being to another is speech.[1] Collection of data by a sentient being is knowledge. Regulation of data transfer and collection, and therefore, regulates speech and knowledge acquisition, constituting a form of censorship. Then, what is national sovereignty over data—other than state censorship on speech and perception?

Under the flags of "data sovereignty" and "digital sovereignty,"[2] a full spectrum of data localization schemes has appeared from arguably the adequacy scheme of the General Data Protection Regulation (GDPR)[3] to China's 2017 Network Security Law[4] and South Korea's latest but failed server localization bill[5], Trump's attempts to kick TikTok off the U.S. market,[6] and Brazil's shutdown of WhatsApp for refusal to cooperate with local criminal investigations[7]

---

[1] *See* Jane Bambauer, *Is Data Speech?*, 66(1) STANFORD LAW REVIEW 57 (2014), for an extrapolation from this insight into the First Amendment jurisprudence.

[2] *See* ANUPAM CHANDER & HAOCHEN SUN, SOVEREIGNTY 2.0, Georgetown University Law Center (2021), for a valuable comprehensive catalogue of data/digital sovereignty initiatives.

[3] General Data Protection Regulation, Article 45.

[4] https://www.newamerica.org/cybersecurity-initiative/digichina/blog/translation-cybersecurity-law-peoples-republic-china/ Article 37; Anqi Wang, *Cyber Sovereignty at Its Boldest: A Chinese Perspective*, 16 OHIO ST. TECH. L.J. 395, 403 (2020); http://www.china.org.cn/government/whitepaper/2010-06/08/content_20207978.htm

[5] Business Korea, *Controversy over Server Localization: Debates Heating Up over Google Tax*, Nov. 29, 2018, http://www.businesskorea.co.kr/news/articleView.html?idxno=27017. *See* NOHYUNG PARK, A KOREAN APPROACH TO DATA LOCALIZATION, https://carnegieendowment.org/2021/08/17/korean-approach-to-data-localization-pub-85165 for the preexisting requirement of consent for cross-border data transfer.

[6] Riya Bhattacharjee, Amanda Macias, & Jordan Novet, *Trump Says He Will Ban TikTok through an Executive Action*, CNBC (July 31, 2020), https://www.cnbc.com/2020/07/31/trump-says-he-will-ban-tiktok-through-executive-action-as-soon-as-saturday.html.

[7] Jacqueline de Souza Abreu, *Disrupting the Disruptive: Making Sense of App Blocking in Brazil*, 7 INTERNET POL'Y REV. 1 (2018)

Kyung Sin Park, *Lessons from Internet Shutdowns Jurisprudence for Data Localization* In: *Data Sovereignty.*
Edited by: Anupam Chander and Haochen Sun, Oxford University Press. © Oxford University Press 2023.
DOI: 10.1093/oso/9780197582794.003.0014

LESSONS FROM INTERNET SHUTDOWNS JURISPRUDENCE 333

and other regional blockings of social media platforms. Although they are different in their subjective intent and ostensible relationship to democracy and values constitutive of rights-respecting systems, they are based on the idea that *geolocation or geolocational origin of data matters*: *People should be exposed and contribute only to the online data hosted or copy-stored in domestic or other "adequate" places*." The Brazilian court wishes that communicative data were located within Brazil so that they can be subject to warrants for criminal investigations on its users. The U.S. government believes that TikTok having its servers in China may be subject to the higher risk of unwieldy data breaches.[8] GDPR's adequacy scheme is based on the idea that there are better places for protection of EU citizens' data. The end results remain the same: *communication inevitably involves transfer of data and data localization schemes by definition attempt to fix the location of data hampering its transfer and therefore speech*, and ultimately, the availability of data for knowledge and communication are subject to ever-increasing levels of collectivistic or other external control, whether benign or baneful, which go against the radical pluralism[9] through which the Internet has contributed to democracy and economic growth in the past several decades.

Sovereignty, by definition, requires control on things under it. When defamation takes place between its own citizens, nations often exercise their sovereignty by providing civil damages as binding remedies for the harms arising therefrom. When incitation of violence or disclosure of official secrets takes place, nations sometimes offer criminal punishment as sovereign solutions. When privacy of its subjects is infringed, nations also offer civil damages as remedies. So in a sense data sovereignty (or equivalently sovereignty over transfer of data) has existed in the past already. What we see under the recent banners of "data sovereignty" is expansion beyond the Westphalian notion of sovereignty[10], that is, *ex ante* regulation on location of data. As long as we could regulate intraterritorial activities ex post, we did not complain loss of Westphalian sovereignty.

Data localization demands, ex ante, that, in order to make that regulation easier, all the subject activities should take place within the territory. Some other sovereignty measures go even beyond that and require the activities

---

[8] New York Times, "Trump Approves Deal Between Oracle and TikTok," Sept. 19, 2020.

[9] John P. Barlow, *The Declaration of the Independence of Cyberspace*, Electronic Frontier Foundation.

[10] Cf. Andrew Keane Woods, *Litigating Data Sovereignty*, 128 YALE L.J. 328, 366–71 (2018).

334 LESSONS FROM INTERNET SHUTDOWNS JURISPRUDENCE

to take place on the equipment of certain geo-locational origin, e.g., Trump trying to sanitize the U.S. processing of Huawei equipment.[11] Other sovereignty measures are even more extreme to be blatantly protectionist, e.g., European Parliament's 2020 study identifying the U.S. origin of dominant platforms as "depriving EU Member States of their sovereignty in areas such as copyright, data protection, taxation or transportation."[12] Since when was import considered threatening to sovereignty?[13]

They are in need of a stable norm for evaluating data localization schemes. Some data localizations have been roundly criticized as barriers to trade.[14] However, as I shall show below, the applicable WTO trade norms, namely *free flow of information*, do not produce a stable norm for justifying or evaluating data localizations. For one, WTO rules are subject to exceptions such as protection of public morals, life, health, privacy under which cross-border acquisition or transfer of data can be readily restricted.

It is important to produce an effective norm otherwise it allows the race to the bottom: As I shall show below, claims of digital sovereignty by one country (e.g., U.S.) end up rationalizing and thereby escalating other countries' (e.g., China) localization efforts. It is important for us to find a coherent, unified international Internet governance norm under which data localization schemes and other data sovereignty claims can be properly evaluated. As much of data sovereignty or digital sovereignty implicates greater censorship, benign or baneful, we look to human rights as a source of norm for evaluating data localization in this article.

Having said that, we notice that data localization is a measure of requiring all data to be located within the territories of a country, the converse of which is that data located overseas will be blocked from its domestic users. In that sense, data localization is enforced by and necessitates Internet shutdowns, namely *platform blockings administered against those data located overseas*. Although human rights jurisprudence on data localization is scarce, the number of cases and rules on Internet shutdown are in relative abundance. For that reason, we would like to use the emerging UN human rights norms

---

[11] ANDROID AUTHORITY, THE HUAWEI BAN EXPLAINED: A COMPLETE TIMELINE AND EVERYTHING YOU NEED TO KNOW, Dec. 25, 2021.

[12] EUROPEAN PARLIAMENT THINK TANK, DIGITAL SOVEREIGNTY FOR EUROPE (2020), available at https://www.europarl.europa.eu/thinktank/en/document.html?reference=EPRS_BRI(2020)651992.

[13] CHANDER & SUN, *supra* note 2, at 25.

[14] Stuart Lauchlan, *Data Localization Rules Damage the Global Digital Economy, Says Us Tech Thinktank*, DIGINOMICA (May 3, 2017), http://diginomica.com/2017/05/03/data-localization-rules-damage-global-digital-economy-says-us-tech-thinktank.

on Internet shutdown to compare, analyze, and evaluate various data localization schemes.

I. Motivations of Data Localization

A. Cybersecurity—Protection (Control) of Domestic People

Data localizations are one form of data sovereignty measures. Chander et al. classifies nations' digital sovereignty measures by three motivations:[15] to protect one's own citizens, to build one's domestic digital economy, and finally control one's own citizens. We can apply the same classifications for data localizations but one challenge with this classification is that it is difficult to fathom motivations of the nations. For instance, if a nation requires all content providers to place their main servers so that the police or other censorship bodies can directly order contents down, the motivation is to control *bad* uploaders as well as protect the public who may suffer harm from the harmful information. China, given its paternalist approaches derived from the overarching communist ideology, will find it difficult to distinguish control of the public from their protection.[16] China's 2017 Network Security Law includes a data wall through which Internet traffic in and out of country can be gatekept ostensibly for purposes of protecting Chinese people's data but has been also useful for internal surveillance and censorship purposes.[17]

There are times that protection and control can be distinguished. GDPR's adequacy scheme is wholly to enhance data protection for EU citizens for it does not require the data to remain within the reach of domestic surveillance and censorship and therefore does not increase the vulnerability to the same. However, after the Snowden revelations, Germany's data protection authorities requested Deutsch Telecom to keep Internet traffic within Germany as much as possible and was creating a Bundes Cloud, a cloud infrastructure for all data held by governments by 2022 and proposed a data

---

[15] CHANDER & SUN, *supra* note 2, at 8.

[16] *See* CHANDER & SUN, *supra* note 2, 11, for an objective genealogy of China's conceptions of data sovereignty.

[17] ADRIAN SHABAZ ET AL., USER PRIVACY OF CYBER SOVEREIGNTY: ASSESSING THE HUMAN RIGHTS IMPLICATIONS OF DATA LOCALIZATION, FREEDOM HOUSE (2020), https://freedomhouse.org/report/special-report/2020/user-privacy-or-cyber-sovereignty.

network only for EU.[18] Such German effort does increase vulnerability to sovereign surveillance while presumably enhancing sovereign data protection. Brazil likewise attempted to pass a data localization law as a clear response to the Snowden revelations, that is, out of concern for protection, but failed and ended with Marco Civil da Internet under concern about enhanced risk of surveillance.[19] Distinguishable or not, protecting and controlling the subjects seems to be at the heart of almost all data localizations.

B. Nurturing Domestic Digital Players and Tax Revenues

Martin Shulz, a former European Parliament chairperson, warned that "digital giants"' dominance over data market will not be just that of economic problems but also social problems.[20] GDPR's data portability provisions were an attempt to mitigate such dominance when EU Data Retention Directive was declared invalid by Court of Justice of the EU (CJEU) in 2014.[21] The more direct declarations of the desire to promote domestic companies have been abundantly made by the political and economic leaders of Europe.[22] However, it is not clear whether GDPR's adequacy scheme, the only comprehensive data localization for Europe, is an appropriate vehicle for such data mercantilism.

Some localizations are motivated by taxation efforts. Access to the Internet is done remotely via telecommunications, and taxing remote servers is against general rules of taxation. Therefore, foreign Internet companies are taxed at a much lower rate than domestic companies. While EU Commission decided to address that by bending tax rules,[23] Southeast Asian countries required servers to remain within their borders.[24]

---

[18] ALBRIGHT STONEBRIDGE GROUP, DATA LOCALIZATION: A CHALLENGE TO GLOBAL COMMERCE AND THE FREE FLOW OF INFORMATION 8 (2015), https://www.albrightstonebridge.com/files/ASG%20Data%20Localization%20Report%20-%20September%202015.pdf.

[19] Law360, *Brazil Nexes Data Localization Mandatae from Internet Bill*, Mar. 20, 2014, https://www.law360.com/articles/520198/brazil-nixes-data-localization-mandate-from-internet-bill.

[20] Martin Schulz, President of the European Parliament, Keynote Speech at CPDP2016 on Technological, Totalitarianism, Politics and Democracy (Jan. 28, 2016), https://edpl.lexxion.eu/article/edpl/2016/1/4/display/html.

[21] Philippe Bradley & Mark Young, *EU Data Retention Directive Declared Invalid by Court of Justice of the EU*, INSIDE PRIVACY (Apr. 8, 2014), https://www.insideprivacy.com/international/european-union/eu-data-retention-directive-declared-invalid-by-court-of-justice-of-the-eu.

[22] CHANDER & SUN, *supra* note 2, at 24–25.

[23] Jennifer Rankin, *EU to Find Ways to Make Google, Facebook and Amazon Pay More Tax*, THE GUARDIAN (Sept. 21, 2017), https://www.theguardian.com/business/2017/sep/21/tech-firms-tax-eu-turnover-google-amazon-apple.

[24] https://www.asiasentinel.com/p/indonesia-web-giants-local-data-centers.

Although protectionist or nationalist origins of data localizations are undeniable, those blindly protectionist localizations can be squarely evaluated and hopefully remedied as well by international economic law as shown below. On the other hand, data localizations motivated by protection(control) of domestic people are more in need of a stable governing norm as they are not easily governable by international economic law.

II. Trade Rules Applied to Data Localizations

A. Applicability of Trade Rules

When people use YouTube, for instance, often the data is provided remotely from servers overseas. Also, when local businesses purchase advertising time on YouTube, the eyeballs may be those of local residents but they are gathered around the advertisements provided remotely from servers overseas. In either sense, such usage constitutes a trade in services from the locus of the YouTube server to that of the advertisers. Trade in services through cross-border supply via the Internet is increasing a great deal. Data localization is a requirement that the remote server providing the content or the services be located within the country.

The most contentious obligations of state parties to WTO are market access and national treatment under the General Agreement on Trade in Services (GATS). They are prohibited from violating these two obligations listed in their respective Schedule of Specific Commitments under GATS. According to GATS classification of services[25], data localization requirements will affect the services falling under "value-added services"[26] and "computer and related services."[27] A majority of WTO members have made liberalizing commitments on both of the services.

Although these commitments were made at the Uruguay Round before the Internet became pervasive and popular, these liberalization commitments should be deemed still effective with respect to the Internet, according to the *US-Gambling* Panel that announced intra-modal technological neutrality

---

[25] Services Sectoral Classification List, WTO Co. MTN.GNS/W/120 (July 10, 1991).

[26] Value added services means, according to W/120, electronic mail, voice mail, on-line information and database retrieval, EDI (Electronic Data Interchange), enhanced facsimile services, code and protocol conversion, and on-line information and/or data processing services.

[27] CRS consists of, according to W/120, Consultancy Services, Software Implementation Services, Data Processing Services, Database Services, and Other.

338 LESSONS FROM INTERNET SHUTDOWNS JURISPRUDENCE

in cross-border supply mode[28] and the Appellate Body's decision on *China-Publications and Audio Visual Products* that interpreted China's liberalizing commitment on sound recording distribution services to include online as well as offline services.[29]

First, as to market access, Article XVI:2 of GATS provides an exhaustive list of quantitative restrictions that can be sustained only by explicitly itemizing them in the Schedule of Commitments.[30] Data localization is not explicitly on this list as it is not a quantitative restriction but may be deemed one of them as the nationality requirement was deemed equivalent to "zero quota" imposed on overseas service providers[31] as done by the U.S.-Gambling decision.[32] Data localization effectively bans cross-border supply of services as a mode of service trade and forces foreign service providers to move into the commercial presence mode[33] and is likely to be considered a "zero quota" that violates GATS Article XVI.

Secondly, national treatment norm governed by Article XVII of GATS bans both *de jure* discrimination and *de facto* discrimination based on

---

[28] Appellate Body Report, *United States-Measures Affecting the Cross-border Supply of Gambling and Betting Services (US-Gambling)*, ¶¶ 227–33, WTO Doc. WT/DS285/AB/R (adopted Mar. 23, 2005) [hereinafter Appellate Body Report, *US Gambling*].

[29] Appellate Body Report, *China–Measures Affecting Trading Rights and Distribution Services for Certain Publications and Audiovisual Entertainment Products (China-Publications and Audio Visual Products)*, ¶ 412, WTO Doc. WT/DS363/AB/R (adopted Jan. 19, 2010).

[30] In sectors where market-access commitments are undertaken, the measures which a Member shall not maintain or adopt either on the basis of a regional subdivision or on the basis of its entire territory, unless otherwise specified in its Schedule, are defined as: (a) limitations on the number of service suppliers whether in the form of numerical quotas, monopolies, exclusive service suppliers or the requirements of an economic needs test; (b) limitations on the total value of service transactions or assets in the form of numerical quotas or the requirement of an economic needs test; (c) limitations on the total number of service operations or on the total quantity of service output expressed in terms of designated numerical units in the form of quotas or the requirement of an economic needs test; (d) limitations on the total number of natural persons that may be employed in a particular service sector or that a service supplier may employ and who are necessary for, and directly related to, the supply of a specific service in the form of numerical quotas or the requirement of an economic needs test; (e) measures which restrict or require specific types of legal entity or joint venture through which a service supplier may supply a service; and (f) limitations on the participation of foreign capital in terms of maximum percentage limit on foreign shareholding or the total value of individual or aggregate foreign investment.

[31] MARKUS KRAJEWSKI, NATIONAL REGULATION AND TRADE LIBERALIZATION IN SERVICES-THE LEGAL IMPACT OF THE GENERAL AGREEMENT ON TRADE IN SERVICES (GATS) ON NATIONAL REGULATORY AUTONOMY 86 (2003).

[32] Appellate Body Report, *US-Gambling*, *supra* note 28, at 133.

[33] The two other available modes are *consumption abroad* and natural persons. For instance, in KORUS FTA, the mode of commercial presence belongs to the investment chapter while the three other modes belong to the cross-border trade chapter. Relevantly, KORUS FTA prohibits state parties from requiring service providers to shift into the commercial presence mode. "Article 12.5 Neither Party may require a service supplier of the other Party to establish or maintain a representative office or any form of enterprise, or to be resident, in its territory as a condition for the cross-border supply of a service."

nationality. Here, it is important to note that substance is more important than form: formally equal treatment may be de facto discriminatory and therefore violate the norm.[34] The WTO adjudication bodies have consistently held that the "aims" of a certain measure does not cure the discrimination since the *EC-Banana III* decision to the *Argentina-Financial Services* decision.[35] For instance, even if some measures have such purposes of privacy protection or national security, the crux is whether measures treat foreign service providers less favorably.

One may argue that foreign online content providers are not like domestic content providers to begin with because their content is transmitted from remote locations. However, in the *U.S.-Gambling* decision, Antigua argued[36] that services should not be considered "unlike" just because they are provided through different modes of supply. The Panel did not explicitly rule on this[37] but Antigua prevailed in the decision. Also, in the *Canada-Autos* decision, the WTO Panel also found "likeness" between the services provided on the Canadian soil through commercial presence and movement of natural persons and the services provided remotely through cross-border supply and consumption abroad.[38] Then, data localization can be said to be applicable to two like services, namely content provided remotely and content provided domestically through local servers, and on that ground we can ask whether there is a violation of a national treatment norm.

Based on the aforesaid framing, we can posit that, while most data localization measures do not explicitly single out foreign content providers and therefore do not constitute de jure discrimination, they do impact foreign-based content providers only, possibly committing de facto discrimination in violation of Article XVII of GATS.

This is not the end of the story. Article XIV lit. a) of the GATS allows the adoption of measures considering the protection of public morals and the maintenance of public order and Art. XIV[bis] of the GATS allows security

---

[34] Panel Report, *China-Certain Measures Affecting Electronic Payment Services (China- Electronic Payment Services)*, ¶ 7.687, WTO Doc. WT/DS413/R and Add.1 (adopted Aug. 31, 2012); Appellate Body Report, *Argentina-Measures relating to Trade in Goods and Services (Argentina-Financial Services)*, ¶ 6.34, WTO Doc. WT/DS453/AB/R (adopted Apr. 14, 2016) [hereinafter Appellate Body Report, *Argentina-Financial Services*].

[35] Appellate Body Report, *European Communities-Regime for the Importation, Sale and Distribution of Bananas (EC-Bananas III)*, ¶ 241, WTO Doc. WT/DS27/AB/R (adopted Sept. 25, 1997); Appellate Body Report, *Argentina-Financial Services*, *supra* note 139, ¶ 6.106.

[36] Appellate Body Report, *US-Gambling*, *supra* note 28, at133, ¶ 3.150.

[37] *Id.* ¶ 6.287.

[38] Panel Report, *Canada-Certain Measures Affecting the Automotive Industry (Canada-Autos)*, ¶ 10.307, WTO Doc. WT/DS139/R, WT/DS142/R (adopted Feb. 11, 2000).

340 LESSONS FROM INTERNET SHUTDOWNS JURISPRUDENCE

exception, subject to the condition in the chapeau to Article XIV that[39] it be "applied in a manner which would constitute a means of arbitrary or unjustifiable discrimination between countries where the like conditions prevail, or a disguised restriction on international trade." For example, in *U.S.-Gambling*, prohibition of online gambling services from Antigua and Barbuda was held to violate the chapeau because it tolerated U.S. domestic Internet operators to provide the same services.[40]

Since then, scholars have tried to figure out what constitutes a violation or satisfies the exception in the context of restrictions on free flow of data but without not much success.[41]

B. Trade-Rules-Based Arguments against Data Localization

As with other trade issues, the possibility that data localization may violate WTO rules has not dissuaded various countries from engaging in data localization. In the field of international trade law where WTO cases are far and between (i.e., *US-Gambling, China-Publications and Audio-Visual Products*), it is trade talks through which the rules are made.

In 2013, the United States began including "data localization" as a list of digital protectionist measures along with censorship, filtering, privacy regulations, and sometimes even absence of intellectual property enforcement.[42] Starting in 2015, the EU criticized Russia's and China's data localization requirements as disproportionate to national security concerns and therefore digital protectionism.[43] After much deliberation in 2018, the EU announced its trade strategy toward digital protectionism taking into account

---

[39] General Agreement on Trade in Services, Apr. 15, 1994, Manakesh Agreement Establishing the World Trade Organization, Annex 1B, 1869 U.N.T.S. 183, 33 I.L.M. 1167 (1994); World Trade Organization, "WTO Analytical Index: GATS – Article XIV (Jurisprudence)," World Trade Organization, https://www.wto.org/english/res_e/publications_e/ai17_e/gats_art14_jur.pdf. Also see World Trade Organization Appellate Body Report, "US—Gambling," Paragraph 339

[40] Sacha Wunsch-Vincent, *The Internet, Cross-Border Trade in Services, and the GATS: Lessons from US-Gambling*, 5 WORLD TRADE REV. 319, 320–22 (2006).

[41] Rolf H. Weber & Rainer Baisch, *Revisiting the Public Moral/Order and the Security Exceptions under the GATS*, 13 ASIAN J. WTO & INT'L HEALTH L & POL'Y 375 (2018).

[42] U.S. INT'L TRADE COMM'N, DIGITAL TRADE IN THE U.S. AND GLOBAL ECONOMIES, PART 1 (2013), https://www.usitc.gov/publications/332/pub4415.pdf; RACHEL F. FEFER ET AL., CONG. RESEARCH SERV., R44565, DIGITAL TRADE AND US TRADE POLICY (2019), https://fas.org/sgp/crs/misc/R44 565.pdf.

[43] *Report from the Commission to the European Council on Trade and Investment Barriers Report 2015*, COM (2015) 127 final (Mar. 17, 2015), http://trade.ec.europa.eu/doclib/docs/2015/march/tradoc_153259.pdf.

its data protection concerns. In its trade agreements (e.g., the renegotiated EU—Mexico Global Agreement), the EU proposed the following three pillars: (1) free flow of data, (2) a ban on data localization, and (3) language that excludes data protection regulations from the list of barriers to trade.[44] According to a study, data localization regulations cost EU citizens about $193 billion per year, in part due to higher domestic prices.[45]

By 2016, the United States and EU have been able to agree on three measures as clearly protectionist, one of which was data localization and the other two being taxes on digital flows and forced technology transfers.[46] These measures can lead to unanticipated side effects, including reduced Internet stability, generativity, and access to information.[47] However, we have yet to confirm if these measures truly hamper trade.[48] Most importantly, the EU and United States do not agree as to when trade restrictions on information are protectionist. Furthermore, they themselves have trade-restrictive policies and practices.[49]

At least on data localization, the United States and EU may agree on its protectionist nature.[50] However, it still lacks a broad general normative context in which data localization is evaluated. No trade agreement discussing cross-border data flows mentions other supposedly protectionist measures such as censorship, filtering, or Internet shutdowns as impermissible barriers to trade.[51] This means that it does not provide a sufficient normative force to discourage other countries from enacting data localizations.

---

[44] European Comm'n, Horizontal Provisions for Cross-border Data Flows and for Personal Data Protection, in EU Trade and Investment Agreements (2018), https://trade.ec.europa.eu/doclib/docs/2018/may/tradoc_156884.pdf.

[45] Matthias Bauer et al., *Tracing the Economic Impact of Regulations on the Free Flow of Data and Data Localization* (Centre for International Governance Innovation, GCIG Paper No. 30, 2016), https://www.cigionline.org/publications/tracing-economic-impact-regulations-free-flow-data-and-data-localization.

[46] Office of the U.S. Trade Representative, Promoting Digital Trade (2015), https://ustr.gov/sites/default/files/TPP-Promoting-Digital-Trade-Fact-Sheet.pdf.

[47] Jonah Force Hill, *The Growth of Data Localization Post Snowden: Analysis and Recommendations for US Policymakers and Industry Leaders*, 2 Lawfare Res. Paper Series 1 (2014), https://lawfare.s3-us-west-2.amazonaws.com/staging/Lawfare-Research-Paper-Series-Vol2No3.pdf.

[48] Anupam Chander & Uyên P. Lê, *Breaking the Web: Data Localization vs. the Global Internet* (Univ. of Cal. Davis Sch. of Law, Working Paper No. 378, 2014).

[49] Susan A. Aaronson, *Why Trade Agreements are not Setting Information Free: The Los History and Reinvigorated Debate over Cross-Border Data Flows, Human Rights and National Security*, World Trade Review, Available on CJO 2015 doi:10.1017/S1474745615000014.

[50] World Trade Organization, Ministerial Decision of 13 December 2017, WT/MIN(17)/65 (2017).

[51] Susan A. Aaronson, *Data Is Different, and That's Why the World Needs a New Approach to Governing Cross-Border Data Flows*, 21 Digital Pol'y, Regulation & Governance 441 (2019).

342 LESSONS FROM INTERNET SHUTDOWNS JURISPRUDENCE

For instance, the United States has not fully endorsed EU's stringent data protection schemes such as right to be forgotten.[52] In practice, the right to be forgotten works in the form of geo-blocking and therefore a loose form of data localization.[53] As some complain, it is not clear even whether and when privacy regulations can be exempted under GATS's public order or national security exceptions.[54]

This is important because many data localizations are enacted for the two contradictory purposes: enhancing data privacy and deprecating privacy. The enacting state wants to make it easier to access user data for criminal investigation or national security surveillance purposes but also wants to protect the privacy of data subjects by not making the data available to foreign bad actors.

Given the lack of robust normativity, state parties can fall into a vicious cycle of digital protectionism begetting further digital protectionism.[55] One clue is the differences between data and other commodities,[56] but it is not clear how those differences translate into a stable theory of what is protectionist, that is, a GATS violation is not clear. One meaningful attempt is to reconfigure the trade talks as the rights talk: any restriction to data-based service is also interfering with freedom of speech, and "free flow of information" had been the motto of the U.S. State Department for a long time already. The uniqueness of data is more relevant to the rights talk than to the trade talk. While some scholars are finding even such reconfiguration ineffective and sometimes hypocritical[57], this may be the only way to find a sufficiently stable norm.

This leads us to a discussion on constructing a full-fledged human rights framework. If data localization is a human rights violation, it is also more likely to be considered protectionist since the interest protected by data

[52] Olivia Solon, *EU 'Right to Be Forgotten' Ruling Paves Way for Censorship*, WIRED (May 13, 2014), https://www.wired.co.uk/article/right-to-be-forgotten-blog; Alex Hern, *Wikipedia Swears to Fight "Censorship" of "Right to Be Forgotten" Ruling*, THE GUARDIAN (Aug. 6, 2014), https://www.theguard ian.com/technology/2014/aug/06/wikipedia-censorship-right-to-be-forgotten-ruling.

[53] Peter Fleischer, *Adapting Our Approach to the European Right to Be Forgotten*, GOOGLE (Mar. 4, 2016), https://blog.google/around-the-globe/google-europe/adapting-our-approach-to-europ ean-rig.

[54] Aaronson (2015), *supra* note 49, at 19.

[55] Sarah Box, *Internet Openness and Fragmentation: Toward Measuring the Economic Effects* (Ctr. for Int'l Governance Innovation & Chatham House, Paper Ser. No. 36, 2016). OECD, *Economic and Social Benefits of Internet Openness* (OECD, OECD Digital Econ. Papers No. 257, 2016), https:// www.oecd-ilibrary.org/docserver/5jlwqf2r97g5-en.pdf?expires=1627013567&id=id&accname= guest&checksum=A48F2980AF21769C38E43E107B46CACF.

[56] *See* Aaronson (2019), *supra* note 51.

[57] See Aaronson (2015), *supra* note 49.*Id.*

localization is outweighed by the loss of human rights and is therefore not weighty enough to justify the trade barrier. Full convergence of human rights law and trade rules is beyond the scope of this chapter but we can obtain a relatively robust norm governing data localization based on human rights, as we shall see.

III. Regulating Internet Shutdowns through Human Rights Norms

KeepItOn Report 2018 defines Internet shutdown as follows, including social media platforms, and therefore, the definition is compatible with this research:[58]

> An internet shutdown can be defined as an "intentional disruption of internet or electronic communications, rendering them inaccessible or effectively unusable, for a specific population or within a location, often to exert control over the flow of information."[3] They include blocks of social media platforms, and are also referred to as "blackouts," "kill switches," or "network disruptions."

The extremely distributed architecture of the Internet has a civilizational significance of having given all powerless individuals an agency in mass communication previously available only to newspapers and broadcasting or other powerful individuals and entities hoarding their attention, and also has given them power of knowledge previously available only to governments and businesses. It has become tools for political equality and democracy for many around the world. In the words of one highest court, "[The] Internet, rapidly spreading and reciprocal, allows people to overcome the economic or political hierarchy off-line and therefore to form public opinions free from class, social status, age, and gender distinctions, which make governance more reflective of the opinions of people from diverse classes and thereby further promotes democracy. Therefore, . . .speech in the Internet, though fraught with harmful side-effects, should be strongly protected in view of its constitutional values."[59]

---

[58] KeepItOn 2018, page 3.
[59] Korean Constitutional Court, 2010 Hun-ma 47, August 2012.

344 LESSONS FROM INTERNET SHUTDOWNS JURISPRUDENCE

Given its relationship to democracy and human rights, it is only dialectically befitting that the first major Internet shutdown threatening democratization movements also took place during the Egypt uprising in 2011.[60] Increasingly, successive regimes have resorted to Internet shutdowns or blockage of major social media platforms, from 75 in 2016, 106 in 2017, 196 in 2018,[61] and 213 in 2019[62] a majority of which has been enacted for the actual purpose of most of them for suppressing communications during political protest or instability, military actions, or elections.[63]

Their impact is beyond political. "People routinely depend on the Internet to stay in touch with family and friends, create local communities of interest, report public information, hold institutions accountable, and access and share knowledge".[64] Also economies suffer greatly: Brookings Institute estimated the impact on the combined GDP of 19 countries practicing Internet shutdowns to be 2.4 billion USD between June 2015 and June 2016, working back from the countries of GDP figures and the estimated percentage of contribution from Internet, mobile, and major apps.[65] The impact on social, cultural, and educational rights are far-reaching.[66]

Most internet shutdowns have taken place in India which cover 134 out of 196 in 2018 and 121 out of 213 in 2019. In OECD countries, you can find almost none showing the disproportionate impact the shutdowns are having on the less developed sectors.

---

[60] http://www.telegraph.co.uk/news/worldnews/africaandindianocean/egypt/8288163/How-Egypt-shut- down-the-internet.html

[61] https://www.accessnow.org/the-state-of-internet-shutdowns-in-2018/

[62] TARGETED, CUT OFF, AND LEFT IN THE DARK, The #KeepItOn report on internet shutdowns in 2019 available at https://www.accessnow.org/cms/assets/uploads/2020/02/KeepItOn-2019-report-1.pdf

[63] Id., and The State of Internet Shutdowns around the World: The 2018 #KeepItOn Report available at https://www.accessnow.org/cms/assets/uploads/2019/06/KIO-Report-final.pdf

[64] Internet Society, Internet Shutdowns: An Internet Society Public Policy Briefing, December 2019.

[65] Brookings Institute, "Internet Shutdowns Cost 2.4 Billions Last Year", October 2016 https://www.brookings.edu/wp-content/uploads/2016/10/intenet-shutdowns-v-3.pdf ; See also CIPESA, Economic Impact of Internet Disruptions in Sub-Saharan Africa, September 2017 (employing similar methods as the Brookings Institute for 10 African countries), https://cipesa.org/2017/09/economic-impact-of-internet-disruptions-in-sub-saharan-africa; Deloitte, The economic impact of disruptions to Internet connectivity, October 2016, https://globalnetworkinitiative.org/wp-content/uploads/2016/10/GNI-The-Economic-Impact-of-Disruptions-to-Internet-Connectivity.pdf (using similar methods as Brookings but granulating for different levels of connectivity); EXX Africa, Special Report: The Cost of Internet Shutdowns in Africa, https://www.exxafrica.com/special-report-the-cost-of-internet-shutdowns-in-africa.

[66] Disconnected: A Human Rights-Based Approach to Network Disruptions. Global Network Initiative. June 2018. https://globalnetworkinitiative.org/wp-content/uploads/2018/06/Disconnected-Report-Network- Disruptions.pdf

Most shutdowns are taking place in Asia and Africa, with the exceptions such as Turkey, Russia, and Venezuela although Brazil's famous *Whatsapp* blocking took place only too early to be added here.

The most worrying trend is lack of transparency about why the internet is shut down:

> [In 2018],. . . when governments shut down the internet citing "public safety [91 cases]," it is often evident to observers that, in reality, authorities may fear protests and cut off access to the internet to limit people's ability to organize and express themselves [one third (⅓)]. . . when authorities cite "fake news," rumors, or hate speech [33 cases], they are often responding to a range of issues including communal violence [20], protests[5], elections [4], political instability [3], among others (numbers in bracket provided by this author).[67]

> [In 2019], in China, the highly complex system of censorship made it extremely hard to detect and verify any instances of internet shutdowns. In the lead-up to the 30th anniversary of the Tiananmen Square protest, state-owned internet service providers (ISPs) in many provinces — including Guangdong, Shanghai, and Chongqing — reported brief internet shutdowns "due to technical problems."[68]

Also, in 2019, more than half of 24 shutdowns motivated by 'public safety' were actually attempts to quell protests while more than half of 30 shutdowns taken as precautionary measures were done to shutter people's criticism and knowledge of military actions. Again, fake news and hate speech cases (33) were also part of military actions, or responses to protests, and other community happenings.

In a stark example, post-election shutdown, ostensibly aimed at abating "fake news" about election results, turned out to be a cover-up for election rigging as in DRC.[69] More than one half of national security shutdowns (40) were actually responses to political instability.[70]

Actually, research has shown that internet shutdowns, ostensibly enacted to protect the public, often occur in conjunction with higher levels of state

---

[67] KeepItOn 2018, 5.
[68] KeepItOn 2019, 3.
[69] KeepInOn 2018.
[70] *Id.*

346 LESSONS FROM INTERNET SHUTDOWNS JURISPRUDENCE

repression.[71] In 2018, there were at least 33 incidents of state violence reported during internet shutdowns. It appears that in some cases, governments and law enforcement may cut off access to the internet to unleash violence on citizens with impunity. In Sudan, protesters have become victims to state violence under the "cover" of shutdowns.

Moreover, even innocuous shutdowns affect the state's sensitivity to other shutdowns, KeepItOn Report states that, among the shutdown incidents between 2014 and 2018, "the countries that shut down the internet for exams are more likely to cut access during protests, elections, and for information control."[72]

"Geographically targeted shutdowns can be an especially obvious attempt at discrimination, exclusion, and censorship of voices speaking out against harmful government practices"[73] as in Myanmar's and Bangladesh's case on Rohingyas, India's case on Kashmir and Jammu, and Indonesia's case on Papua.[74]

Likewise, blocking specific social media platforms may be more pernicious in intent than taking down the whole Internet as in case of Venezuela:

> Whenever Guaidó livestreams, the National Assembly convenes, or opposition leaders and groups develop public activities, Maduro's government blocks social media and streaming services. The minute the activity concludes, the blocking ends.[75]

Data localization is a measure of requiring all data to be located within the territories of a country, the converse of which is that data located overseas will be blocked from its domestic users. In that sense, data localization is enforced by and interchangeable with a subset of Internet shutdowns, namely platform blockings administered against those data located overseas. Although jurisprudence on data localization is scarce, the number of cases and rules on Internet shutdown and platform blockings are in relative abundance in the human rights field.

---

[71] Anita R. Gohdes, *Pulling The Plug Network Disruptions and Violence in Civil Conflict*, 52(3) JOURNAL OF PEACE RESEARCH, 352–67 (2015).

[72] KeepItOn 2018, 7.

[73] KeepInOn 2019, 5.

[74] KeepInOn 2019, 5–6.

[75] KeepInOn 2019, 7.

A. United Nations

The UN Human Rights Committee warned about the use of Internet shutdowns as early as 2011 in its seminal General Comment 34, noting that there is a presumption that Article 19 of the International Covenant on Civil and Political Rights[76] will be infringed where there is any broad restriction placed on an entire site or an entire system of media

> 43. Any restrictions on the operation of websites, blogs or any other internet-based, electronic or other such information dissemination system, including systems to support such communication, such as internet service providers or search engines, are only permissible to the extent that they are compatible with paragraph 3. Permissible restrictions generally should be content-specific; generic bans on the operation of certain sites and systems are not compatible with paragraph 3 . . . (citing Concluding observations on the Syrian Arab Republic (CCPR/CO/84/SYR))[77]

Also, the UN Human Rights Council has affirmed on four different occasions, that "the same rights that people have offline must also be protected online, in particular freedom of expression, which is applicable regardless of frontiers and through any media of one's choice, in accordance with article 19 of the Universal Declaration of Human Rights and of the International Covenant on Civil and Political Rights."[78] This proposition, first noted in 2012 and repeated afterward put to rest the issue of whether new rights must be devised for the Internet.[79] In order to protect offline rights in equal stead with online rights, the Internet must be made available "as a precondition."[80] This is why the Human Rights Council in its first resolution addressing this issue in

---

[76] While it does not specifically say "the Internet," it states "in writing or in print, in the form of art, or through any other media of his choice."

[77] See U.N. Human Rights Committee, General Comment No. 34, Article 19: Freedoms of Opinion and Expression, U.N. Doc. CCPR/C/GC/34 (Sept. 12, 2011), http://www2.ohchr.org/english/bodies/hrc/docs/GC34.pdf [https://perma.cc/876X-JFF3].

[78] Human Rights Council Res. 38/7, U.N. Doc. A/HRC/RES/38/7 (July 5, 2018); Human Rights Council Res. 32/13, U.N. Doc. A/HRC/RES/32/13 (July 1, 2016) [hereinafter Human Rights Council Res. 32/13]; Human Rights Council Res. 26/13, U.N. Doc. A/HRC/RES/26/13 (June 26, 2014); Human Rights Council Res. 20/8, U.N. Doc. A/HRC/RES/20/8 (July 5, 2012) [hereinafter Human Rights Council Res. 20/8].

[79] Matthias C. Kettemann, *UN Human Rights Council Confirms that Human Rights Apply to the Internet*, EJIL: Talk! (July 23, 2012), https://www.ejiltalk.org/un-human-rights-council-confirms-that-human-rights-apply-to-the-internet.

[80] *Id.*

2012 "call[ed] upon all States to promote and <u>facilitate access to the Internet</u> and international cooperation aimed at the development of media and information and communications facilities in all countries" (emphasis added).[81] Four years later, when it was recognized that the access issue can arise also in the countries that already have Internet access, the UN Human Rights Council finally "<u>condemn[ed] unequivocally measures to intentionally prevent or disrupt access to or dissemination of information online in violation of international human rights law and calls on all States to refrain from and cease such measures</u>" (emphasis added).[82]

B. UN Special Rapporteurs on Freedom of Expressions

In addition, the most explicit statements of guidance have come from reports of the two successive UN Special Rapporteurs on Freedom of Expressions Frank La Rue and David Kaye whose focus was timely shifted to the freedom of expression in the digital space when the Human Rights Council's resolution emphasized that the right to freedom of expression must be equally protected both offline and online.

Most relevantly, in his 2011 report, which predates both the Human Rights Council's first Internet freedom resolution and the Human Rights Committee's General Comment 34, La Rue stated that "[t]he Special Rapporteur is deeply concerned by increasingly sophisticated blocking or filtering mechanisms used by States for censorship. The lack of transparency surrounding these measures also makes it difficult to ascertain whether blocking or filtering is really necessary for the purported aims put forward by States. As such, the Special Rapporteur calls upon States that currently block websites (1) *to provide lists of blocked websites and full details regarding the necessity and justification for blocking each individual website.* An explanation should also be provided on the affected websites as to why they have been blocked. (2) <u>Any determination on what content should be blocked must be undertaken by a competent judicial authority or a body which is independent of any political, commercial, or other unwarranted influences</u> (emphasis added)."[83]

---

[81] Human Rights Council Res. 20/8, *supra* note 60.
[82] Human Rights Council Res. 32/13, *supra* note 60.
[83] Frank La Rue (Special Rapporteur on the Promotion and Protection of the Right to Freedom of Opinion and Expression), *Report of the Special Rapporteur on the Promotion and Protection of the*

In the same 2011 report, La Rue also stated that "While blocking and filtering measures deny users access to specific content on the Internet, States have also taken measures to cut off access to the Internet entirely." The Special Rapporteur considers "cutting off users from Internet access, regardless of the justification provided, . . . to be disproportionate and thus a violation of article 19, paragraph 3, of the International Covenant on Civil and Political Rights." La Rule went as far as to call "upon all States to (3) ensure that Internet access is maintained at all times, including during times of political unrest."[84] It is significant to note that La Rue was condemning the so-called three-strike copyright laws of France, United Kingdom, and ACTA, which presumably affect a relatively small number of individuals.[85]

In the report, La Rue explains as follows the strong language he uses regarding the right to Internet access:

> Very few if any developments in information technologies have had such a revolutionary effect as the creation of the Internet. Unlike any other medium of communication, such as radio, television and printed publications based on one-way transmission of information, the Internet represents a significant leap forward as an interactive medium. Indeed, with the advent of Web 2.0 services, or intermediary platforms that facilitate participatory information sharing and collaboration in the creation of content, individuals are no longer passive recipients, but also active publishers of information. . . . More generally, by enabling individuals to exchange information and ideas instantaneously and inexpensively across national borders, the Internet allows access to information and knowledge that was previously unattainable.[86]

It is significant that La Rue's main concern was the effects on individuals cut off from the "revolutionary" communication facilities—revolutionary because they become active publishers and attain access to unprecedented knowledge. This is a rare moment where international soft law explains rather than advocates for the ban against Internet shutdowns.

Right to Freedom of Opinion and Expression, ¶ 70, U.N. Doc. A/HRC/17/27 (May 16, 2011) [hereinafter, "La Rue 2011 Report"].

[84] *Id.* ¶¶ 78–79.
[85] *Id.* ¶¶ 49–50.
[86] *Id.* ¶ 19.

350 LESSONS FROM INTERNET SHUTDOWNS JURISPRUDENCE

Finally, the UN General Assembly also resolved in its resolution adopted by consensus in 2017 on the Safety of Journalists and the Issue of Impunity[87] to condemn ". . . unequivocally measures in violation of international human rights law <u>aiming to or that intentionally prevent or disrupt access</u> to or dissemination of information online and offline, aiming to undermine the work of journalists in informing the public, and calls upon all States to cease and refrain from these measures, which cause irreparable harm to efforts at building inclusive and peaceful knowledge societies and democracies."

C. Joint Declarations of Special Rapporteurs on Freedom of Expression

The 2011 Joint Declaration on Freedom of Expression and Internet signed by freedom-of-expression special mandate holders of various human rights institutions confirmed the almost global consensus that the blocking of a whole site is disproportionate and not compatible with the protection of human rights online, regardless of the reasons given: "mandatory blocking of entire websites, IP addresses, ports, network protocols or types of uses (such as social networking) is an extreme measure—analogous to banning a newspaper or broadcaster— which can only be justified in accordance with international standards, for example where necessary to protect children against sexual abuse."[88]

It is important to consider the blocking of Internet sites through the analogy of "banning a newspaper or broadcaster." The Declaration clarifies that such a ban works prospectively, prohibiting the publication of future articles or shows to appear in that newspaper or broadcasting channel and is therefore a "prior restraint,"[89] which is generally most strictly scrutinized as the most pernicious suppression on free speech in all jurisdictions. Similarly, the blocking of websites prohibits the publication of future content, again a "prior restraint."

Given the deficiency of due process[90], it is apt that the Special Rapporteurs direct "greater attention . . . to developing alternative, tailored

---

[87] G.A. Res. 72/175 (Dec. 19, 2017).

[88] U.N. Special Rapporteur on Freedom of Opinion and Expression et al., *Joint Declaration on Freedom of Expression and the Internet*, ¶ 3a, ORG. FOR SEC. & CO-OPERATION IN EUR. (June 1, 2011) [hereinafter "2011 Joint Declaration on Freedom of Expression and the Internet"], https://www.osce.org/fom/78309?download=true.

[89] *Id.* ¶ 3b.

[90] Alpana Roy & Althaf Marsoof, *The Blocking Injunction: A Comparative and Critical Review of the EU, Singaporean and Australian Regimes*, 38 EUR. INTELL. PROP. REV. 9 (2016).

approaches . . . for responding to illegal content" instead of shutting down part or whole of the Internet.[91]

Procedural safeguards are even more important when entire sites are blocked: "The State must at all times require products intended to facilitate filtration by end users to be accompanied by clear information intended to inform those users on how the filters work and the possible disadvantages should filtering turn out to be excessive."[92]

Since then, the Special Rapporteurs have continued to issue joint statements in the same light:

2014 joint declaration: "States should actively promote <u>universal access to the Internet</u> regardless of political, social, economic or cultural differences, including by respecting the principles of net neutrality and of the centrality of human rights to the development of the Internet (emphasis added)."[93]

2015 joint declaration: "<u>Filtering of content on the Internet, using communications "kill switches" (i.e. shutting down entire parts of communications systems)</u> and the physical takeover of broadcasting stations are measures which can never be justified under human rights law (emphasis added)."[94]

2019 Joint declaration: "The exercise of freedom of expression requires a digital infrastructure that is robust, universal and regulated in a way that maintains it as a free, accessible and open space for all stakeholders. Over the coming years, States and other actors should:

 a. Recognise the right to access and use the Internet as a human right as an essential condition for the exercise of the right to freedom of expression.

 b. Protect freedom of expression in accordance with international human rights law in legislation that can have an impact on online content.

---

[91] 2011 Joint Declaration on Freedom of Expression and the Internet, *supra* note 70, ¶ 3c.
[92] *Id.*
[93] U.N. Special Rapporteur on Freedom of Opinion and Expression et al., *Joint Declaration on Universality and the Right to Freedom of Expression*, ORG. FOR SEC. & CO-OPERATION IN EUR. (May 6, 2014), https://www.osce.org/files/f/documents/f/e/118298.pdf.
[94] U.N. Special Rapporteur on Freedom of Opinion and Expression et al., *Joint Declaration on Freedom of Expression and Responses to Conflict Situations*, ORG. FOR SEC. & CO-OPERATION IN EUR. (May 4, 2015), https://www.osce.org/files/f/documents/a/0/154846.pdf.

352 LESSONS FROM INTERNET SHUTDOWNS JURISPRUDENCE

c. <u>Refrain from imposing Internet or telecommunications network disruptions and shutdowns.</u>"[95]

D. Europe

Article 10 of the European Convention on Human Rights stipulates the right to receive and impart information. Included within its scope are the methods by which information is transmitted and received, since any restriction imposed on the means necessarily interferes with the right to receive and impart information.[96] As noted by the European Court of Human Rights (ECtHR), "[a]s a new and powerful information tool, the Internet falls undoubtedly within the scope of Article 10."[97]

Accordingly, the ECtHR has recognized the importance of the Internet and has also condemned the blocking of Internet access.[98] The Court in Times Newspapers Ltd v. the United Kingdom stated this:

> In light of its accessibility and its capacity to store and communicate vast amounts of information, the Internet plays an important role in enhancing the public's access to news and facilitating the dissemination of information generally. The maintenance of Internet archives is a critical aspect of this role and the Court therefore considers that such archives fall within the ambit of the protection afforded by Article 10.[99]

Later, the Court in Yıldırım v. Turkey stated that blocking Internet access may be "in direct conflict with the actual wording of paragraph 1 of Article 10 of the Convention, according to which the rights set forth in that Article are

---

[95] U.N. Special Rapporteur on Freedom of Opinion and Expression et al., *Joint Declaration on Challenges to Freedom of Expression in the Next Decade*, ORG. FOR SEC. & CO-OPERATION IN EUR. (July 10, 2019), https://www.osce.org/files/f/documents/9/c/425282.pdf.

[96] EUROPEAN COURT OF HUMAN RIGHTS, INTERNET: CASE-LAW OF EUROPEAN COURT OF HUMAN RIGHTS 44–46 (2015), https://www.echr.coe.int/documents/research_report_internet_eng.pdf (citing Autronic AG v. Switzerland, 178 Eur. Ct. H.R. (ser. A), ¶ 47 (1990); De Haes and Gijsels v. Belgium, App. No. 19983/92, ¶ 48 (Feb. 24, 1997), http://hudoc.echr.coe.int/eng?i=001-58015; News Verlags GmbH & Co. KG v. Austria, App. No. 31457/96, ¶ 39 (Jan. 11, 2000), http://hudoc.echr.coe.int/eng?i=001-58587) [hereinafter, "2015 ECtHR Memo on Internet"].

[97] 2015 ECtHR Memo on Internet at 44.

[98] *Id.* at 44–46.

[99] Times Newspapers Ltd (Nos. 1 and 2) v. United Kingdom, App. Nos. 3002/03, 23676/03, ¶ 27 (Mar. 10, 2009), http://hudoc.echr.coe.int/eng?i=001-91706.

secured 'regardless of frontiers.'"[100] In this case, a Turkish court blocked access to all *Google Sites*, the websites made by the users and hosted by Google, for all persons in Turkey. In a criminal proceeding against a third party's Google Site under a law prohibiting insults against the memory of Atatürk, all access to Google Sites were blocked, including the plaintiff's website.

Although this blocking was conducted by an independent judiciary, the Court found a violation of Article 10 for the following reasons (§§ 66–68): (1) failing to examine whether a method could have been chosen whereby only the offending Google Site was made inaccessible; (2) failing to take into consideration "*a significant collateral effect*" of rendering large quantities of information inaccessible to all Internet users; and (3) not having domestic legal safeguards to ensure that a blocking order in respect of a specific site is not abused as a means of blocking access in general.

The Court emphasized that "the Internet has now become one of the principal means by which individuals exercise their right to freedom of expression and information, providing as it does essential tools for participation in activities and discussions concerning political issues and issues of general interest," rejecting Turkey's argument that the Internet is only one of the means of accessing and imparting the information.

In another ECtHR case Akdeniz v. Turkey,[101] however, the Court found no violation on a copyright blocking order on "*myspace.com*" and "*last. fm*," reasoning that "the users of those websites concerned were deprived of only one among many means of listening to music and could easily access a whole range of musical works in many other ways without infringing copyright laws."

The Research Division of the ECtHR explained the difference between the 2012 *Yıldırım* blocking of all Google Sites and the 2014 *Akdeniz* blocking of myspace.com as follows:[102]

> State interference in the form of blocking or restricting access to the Internet is subject to strict scrutiny by the Court. Recent case-law shows that the extent of the States' obligations in the matter depends on the nature of the information posted online, the subject matter, and the status

---

[100] Ahmet Yildirim v. Turkey, App. No. 3111/10, ¶ 67 (Dec. 18, 2012), http://hudoc.echr.coe.int/eng?i=001-115705.

[101] Akdeniz v. Turkey (dec.), App. No. 20877/10 (Mar. 11, 2014), http://hudoc.echr.coe.int/eng?i=001-142383.

[102] 2015 ECtHR Memo on Internet, *supra* note 78, at 46.

354 LESSONS FROM INTERNET SHUTDOWNS JURISPRUDENCE

of the applicant (owner or user of a site). <u>Where infringements of *"copyright protection"* are concerned which do not raise any important question of general interest, the Court considers that the domestic authorities enjoy a particularly wide margin of appreciation (Akdeniz v. Turkey (dec.), cited above, § 28). This also applies to users of commercial websites, but the margin of appreciation enjoyed by the States must be put in perspective when what is in issue is not a strictly *"commercial"* message but one that contributes to a debate on matters of *"general interest"* (*Ashby Donald and Others*, cited above, § 41)</u> . . . In such a case, in order to comply with Convention standards it is necessary to adopt a particularly strict legal framework—one that limits the restriction and provides an effective safeguard against possible abuse. In [*Yıldırım*], the blocking of Internet access produced a serious *"collateral censorship"* effect. In this case the Court acknowledged and upheld the *"rights of Internet users"* and the need for the national authorities—including the criminal courts—to weigh up the competing interests at stake. Any restrictions must be limited to what is strictly necessary to achieve the legitimate aim pursued.

On a casual look, the Strasbourg Court's ruling seems to diverge from UN Special Rapporteur La Rue's guidance of applying the same high standard to copyright-protective Internet blocking[103] even in circumstances where only a small number of people are affected who have repeatedly infringed on copyright, as in "three strikes' situations. However, La Rue's intervention can be distinguished by the fact that the "three strikes" law stops the affected users from using *all* of the Internet while the Akdeniz order blocks the users from only one site that deals only in music files. Such distinguishing is consistent with La Rue's and other UN documents that establish opposition to Internet shutdowns on the basis of their overbreadth and *previous* character, that is, shutting down diverse communications including the ones that have not yet taken place.

Europe's relative leniency on website blocking aimed at intellectual property protection is also shown through a CJEU case Telekabel Wien GmbH v. Constantin Film Verleih GmbH (Telekabel) where the court approved a national court's order on an Internet service provider (Telekabel) to block a

---

[103] La Rue 2011 Report, *supra* note 65, at ¶¶ 78–79.

sharing and streaming website (kino.to) for reason of two pirated contents on the website, though, under the following condition:[104]

> [T]he measures adopted by the internet service provider must be strictly targeted, in the sense that they must serve to bring an end to a third party's infringement of copyright or of a related right but without thereby affecting internet users who are using the provider's services for lawful access. Failing that, the provider's interference in the freedom of information of those users would be unjustified in the light of the objective pursued.

Arguably, it is difficult to understand how lawful users would not be affected when a website is blocked in its entirety as presumably many files shared and streamed on kino.to are lawful copies. This again shows the importance of "shutdown of general communication" as an element of unlawful shutdown.

The UK case Cartier Int'l AG v. British Sky Broadcasting shows the difficult balancing between the intellectual property rights guaranteed by Article 17(2) and the freedom of information of Internet users under Article 11 of the EU Charter[105] on a trademark-related website blocking order:

> (i) neither Article as such has precedence over the other; (ii) where the values under the two Articles are in conflict, an intense focus on the comparative importance of the specific rights being claimed in the individual case is necessary; (iii) the justifications for interfering with or restricting each right must be taken into account; (iv) finally, the proportionality test— or "ultimate balancing test"—must be applied to each.

The lower court in *Cartier*[106] had approved the blocking order under the following safeguards: (1) if there is a material change in circumstances, target websites and ISPs (Internet Service Providers) may apply to courts for a discharge of the blocking order; (2) the page shown to users who try to access blocked content must include details such as names of parties that obtained the order and inform users of their right to appeal such an order; and (3) when possible, such orders must carry a "sunset" clause. *Cartier* seems to advocate that it is impossible to avoid interference with lawful use when an

---

[104] Case C-314/12, UPC Telekabel Wien GmbH v. Constantin Film Verleih GmbH, ECLI:EU:C:2014:192, ¶¶ 55–56 (Mar 27, 2014).

[105] Cartier Int'l AG v. British Sky Broadcasting [2016] EWCA Civ 658.

[106] Cartier Int'l AG v. British Sky Broadcasting [2014] EWHC 3354 (Ch).

356 LESSONS FROM INTERNET SHUTDOWNS JURISPRUDENCE

entire platform is blocked and, in such case, the focus should be on ensuring there is an appeals process. This lower court's order was neither approved nor disapproved but was left intact. One takeaway for our project may be that presence of appeal process may justify a blocking on the border line on communications of *general interest* or specific commercial interest.

In Cengiz and Others v. Turkey,[107] a case concerning the wholesale blocking of access to YouTube, a website enabling users to send, view, and share videos, the applicants, who were active users of the website, complained of an infringement of their right to freedom to receive and impart information and ideas.

The Court found a violation of Article 10 (freedom of expression) of the Convention, reasoning that the applicants, all academics in different universities, had been prevented from accessing YouTube for a lengthy period of time and that, as active users, having regard to the circumstances of the case, they could legitimately claim that the blocking order in question had affected their right to receive and impart information and ideas. The Court also observed that YouTube was a single platform that enabled information on political and social matters to be broadcast and citizen journalism to emerge. The Court further found that there was no provision in the law allowing the domestic courts to impose a blanket blocking order on access to the Internet, and in the present case to YouTube, on account of one of its contents.

E. Turkish Domestic Courts

"Twitter.com" judgment: In March 2014, following several decisions in which the Turkish courts had found that Twitter was hosting content that was damaging to a person's private life and reputation, the Directorate of Telecommunication and Communication (TİB) ordered the blocking of access to the site. In its judgment of March 25, 2014, the Ankara Administrative Court stayed the implementation of the TİB's order. In the meantime, on March 24 and 25, 2014, three individuals, including the second and third applicants, had applied to the Constitutional Court to challenge the blocking order.

---

[107] Cengiz v. Turkey, App. Nos. 48226/10, 14027/11 (Dec. 1, 2015), http://hudoc.echr.coe.int/eng?i=001-159188.

On April 2, 2014 (no. 2014/3986), the Constitutional Court held that the TİB's decision to block access to Twitter interfered with the applicants' right to receive and impart information and ideas. It noted, in particular, that delaying the posting of information or opinions shared via this medium, even for a short time, risked making the site devoid of all topical value and interest and that as a result, the applicants, who were active users of the site, had an interest in having the blocking order lifted promptly. Referring to the ECtHR's 2012 *Yıldırım* case (cited above), it also held that the measure in issue had had no legal basis.

"YouTube" judgment: On March 27, 2014, the TİB issued an order blocking access to YouTube, particularly in the light of a judgment of the Gölbaşı Criminal Court of First Instance that certain content hosted on the site violated state secrets and honor of Ataturk. On May 2, 2014, the Ankara Administrative Court stayed the implementation of the TİB's order. Following the non-enforcement of that judgment, the YouTube company, the second and third applicants, and six other individuals applied to the Constitutional Court.

On May 29, 2014 (no. 2014/4705), the Constitutional Court set aside the blocking order. Before addressing the merits of the case, it determined whether the applicants had the status of victims and held:

> 27. . . . It appears from the file that . . . Yaman Akdeniz, Kerem Altıparmak and M.F. taught at different universities. These applicants explained that they carried out research in the field of human rights and shared the research via their YouTube accounts. They also stated that through the website they were able to access written and visual material from the United Nations and the Council of Europe . . . The applicant, E.E., for his part, explained that he had a [YouTube] account, that he regularly followed users who shared files, as well as the activities of non-governmental organisations and professional bodies, and that he also wrote critical comments about the shared content . . .
>
> 28. In the light of those explanations, it can be concluded that the applicants were direct victims of the administrative decision ordering the blocking of all access to www.youtube.com . . ."

As to the merits of the case, with reference to the ECtHR's 2012 *Yıldırım* case (cited above), the Constitutional Court found that the measure in issue had had no legal basis, particularly in the light of Law no. 5651,

358 LESSONS FROM INTERNET SHUTDOWNS JURISPRUDENCE

which did not authorize the wholesale blocking of an Internet site. It held as follows:

> 52. In modern democracies, the Internet has acquired significant importance in terms of the exercise of fundamental rights and freedoms, especially the freedom of expression. Social media constitute a transparent platform . . . affording individuals the opportunity to participate in creating, publishing and interpreting media content. Social-media platforms are thus indispensable tools for the exercise of the right to freedom to express, share and impart information and ideas. Accordingly, the State and its administrative authorities must display considerable sensitivity not only when regulating this area but also in their practice, since these platforms have become one of the most effective and widespread means of both imparting ideas and receiving information.

F. Americas

The American Convention on Human Rights states in Article 13 that "Everyone has the right to freedom of thought and expression," and in paragraph 4 bans "prior censorship" except for the purpose of "protection of children."

The OAS Declaration of Principles on Freedom of Expression contains 13 principles for the protection of freedom of expression. It recognizes in Principle 5 that "prior censorship, direct or indirect interference in or pressure exerted upon any expression, opinion or information transmitted through any means . . . must be prohibited by law."[108]

The Inter-American Commission on Human Rights (IACHR) Special Rapporteur of Freedom of Expression appears to align with the United Nations' overall approach:[109] restrictions on the rights to freedom of expression and access to knowledge on the Internet *even in connection to copyright protection* must comply with the requirements established in the American

---

[108] Inter-American Commission on Human Rights, *Declaration of Principles on Freedom of Expression*, http://www.oas.org/en/iachr/expression/showarticle.asp?artID=26 [https://perma.cc/G7HA-8NKX].

[109] Edison Lanza (OAS Special Rapporteur on Freedom of Expression), *Standards for a Free, Open, and Inclusive Internet*, ¶¶ 155–59, OAS Doc. OEA/Ser.L/V/II (Mar. 15, 2017).

Convention.[110] These limitations must pass the same three-prong test: (1) formal and material legality and legitimate objective, (2) necessity in a democratic society, and (3) proportionality. Moreover, there must be sufficient judicial control over the restriction in all cases with respect to due process guarantees, including user notifications.[111]

As a result, IACHR's Special Rapporteur specifically states that punishing users for violating copyright by disconnecting them is a disproportionate and radical measure that is not compatible with international human rights law, even when a gradual mechanism is employed (three strikes, for example, in which the Internet is disconnected after three violations).[112] Also, the measure should be "subjected to a strict balance of proportionality and be carefully designed and clearly limited so as to not affect legitimate speech that deserves protection."[113]

Blocking is exceptional, that is, "war propaganda, hate speech inciting violence, genocide incitement, child pornography", and when allowed, it should be applied only to illegal content "without affecting other content."[114] At this strict standard, any form of Internet shutdown, website blocking, or any other non-content-based (as opposed to forum-based) action is illegitimate under the Convention.

IACHR Special Rapporteur's strict approach appears to rely on the belief that website blocking constitutes "prior censorship."[115] No matter how proportionate and necessary the limitations on freedom of speech are, they should not be applied through prior censorship and can only be prosecuted after the dissemination of the information through the subsequent and proportional imposition of liability.[116] Blocking access to or removing a link is considered to be prior censorship[117] because it prevents all contents on the web page destined by that link from being accessed by anyone, and therefore constitutes prior censorship on those contents. Therefore, website blocking constitutes prior censorship.

---

[110] Catalina Botero Marino (OAS Special Rapporteur for Freedom of Expression), *Annual Report of the Inter-American Commission on Human Rights 2013* , ¶ 76, OAS Doc. OEA/Ser.L/V/II.149. Doc. 50. (Dec. 31, 2013).

[111] *Id.* ¶ 55.

[112] *Id.* ¶ 81.

[113] *Id.* ¶ 85.

[114] *Id.* ¶ 86.

[115] Catalina Botero Marino (Special Rapporteur for Freedom of Expression), *Inter-American Legal Framework Regarding the Right to Freedom of Expression*, OAS Doc. CIDH/RELE/INF.2/09 (Dec. 30, 2009).

[116] *Id.* ¶ 91.

[117] *Id.* ¶ 148.

360   LESSONS FROM INTERNET SHUTDOWNS JURISPRUDENCE

The Inter-American Court of Human Rights, although lacking any case law directly on website blocking, is likely to support the IACHR Special Rapporteur's position given that the Court has stated "Article 13(4) of the Convention establishes an exception to prior censorship, since it allows it in the case of . . . moral protection of children . . . In all other cases, any preventative measure implies the impairment of freedom of thought and expression."[118]

Overall, the Inter-American Commission does not seem to accept that website blocking or Internet shutdown is consistent with the Inter-American Convention of Human Rights under any circumstances, a position stronger than that of the European judiciaries.[119]

G. Brazil Domestic Courts

Brazil is unique in that social media blockings have originated from the judiciary, generally designed to punish overseas social media platforms for not complying with court orders either demanding user data or content takedowns.[120]

Most famously, WhatsApp was shut down three different times for not fulfilling data access orders that the judiciary had issued for criminal investigation purposes. The information sought was stored on servers outside Brazil. WhatsApp Inc. refused to execute the orders, arguing that it was a foreign company operating in the United States and therefore that it was not under an obligation to comply with direct requests for user data made by Brazilian judges under Brazilian Law and insisted that authorities had to resort to the process under mutual legal aid treaties.

Three courts then ordered the ISPs to block WhatsApp.[121] The provisions authorizing these orders are not clear. Some judges made explicit reference

[118] Olmedo-Bustos v. Chile, Merits, Reparations and Costs, Judgment, Inter-Am. Ct. H.R. (ser. C) No. 73, ¶ 70 (Feb. 5, 2001).
[119] SUBHAJIT BANERJI ET AL., THE "RIGHT TO BE FORGOTTEN" AND BLOCKING ORDERS UNDER THE AMERICAN CONVENTION: EMERGING ISSUES IN INTERMEDIARY LIABILITY AND HUMAN RIGHTS 65 (2017), https://www-cdn.law.stanford.edu/wp-content/uploads/2017/09/The-_Right-to-Be-For gotten_-and-Blocking-Orders-under-the-American-Convention-Emerging-Issues-in-Intermedi ary-Liability-and-Human-Rights_Sep17-.pdf.
[120] Jacqueline de Souza Abreu, *Disrupting the Disruptive: Making Sense of App Blocking in Brazil*, 7 INTERNET POL'Y REV. 1 (2018).
[121] Justiça Estadual do Rio de Janeiro (July 17, 2016). Inquérito Policial 062-00164/2016, 2a Vara Criminal de Duque de Caxias, judge Daniela Barbosa Assumpção de Souza, July 17, 2016; Justiça Estadual de São Paulo (Dec. 6, 2016). Processo de Interceptação Telefônica n. 0017520-08.2015.8.26.0564, 1a Vara Criminal de São Bernardo do Campo, judge Sandra Regina Nostre

to art. 12, III of the Marco Civil da Internet, which provides for "temporary suspension" as a sanction to application providers for violations of art. 10 and art. 11, to justify the blocking orders. However, art. 10 and art. 11 concern the ISPs' and app providers' obligations to protect privacy. The underlying investigations were not for privacy violations taking place on WhatsApp but rather for child abuse, drug trafficking, and organized crime.

At any rate, it seems that the higher courts still accepted art. 12 of Marco Civil da Internet as a legitimate legal basis for the blocking but blocking orders were reversed by appellate courts, because of their "disproportionality."[122]

The Federal Supreme Court also issued a preliminary decision in a constitutional challenge against the 2016 Duque de Caxias criminal court's blocking order.[123] In granting the preliminary injunction, the president of the Federal Supreme Court reasoned as follows:[124]

> the Law 12,965/2014 (Marco Civil da Internet) [the law commandeered to justify the blocking order] provides that the discipline of internet use in Brazil has, as one of its principles, the "guarantee of freedom of expression, communication and manifestation of thought, under the Federal Constitution." In addition, this legal framework is concerned with "preserving the stability, security and functionality of the network."

Justice Lewandowski highlighted the importance of instant messaging even to subpoenas and court decisions and emphasized that the messaging application has more than one billion users worldwide, and that Brazil has the second largest number of users. He suspended what he saw as an act apparently not "reasonable and proportionate," which "would leave millions of Brazilians without this communication tool."[125]

Marques; Justiça Estadual de Sergipe (Apr. 26, 2016). Processo n. 201655090143, Vara Criminal da Comarca de Lagarto, judge Marcel Maia Montalvão.

[122] Tribunal de Justiça do Piauí (Feb. 26, 2015). Mandado de Segurança n. 2015.0001.001592-4, rapporteur Desembargador Raimundo Nonato Costa Alencar; Tribunal de Justiça de São Paulo (Dec. 17, 2015). Mandado de Segurança n. 2271462-77.2015.8.26.0000, rapporteur Xavier de Souza; Tribunal de Justiça de Sergipe (May 3, 2016). Mandado de Segurança n. 201600110899, rapporteur Ricardo Múcio Santana de Abreu Lima.

[123] Supremo Tribunal Federal (July 17, 2016). Medida Cautelar na ADPF 403, Justice Ricardo Lewandowski (order suspending ban on WhatsApp).

[124] *Id.*

[125] *Id.*

362 LESSONS FROM INTERNET SHUTDOWNS JURISPRUDENCE

In 2012 and 2016, orders were issued to ISPs to block Facebook for failing to take down posts that violated local election laws, but these orders were not carried out because Facebook removed the posts, after facing the threat of blocking orders.[126]

H. Africa

The fundamental right to freedom of information and expression is enshrined in Article 9 of the African Charter on Human and Peoples' Rights (the African Charter). The African Commission on Human and People's Rights issued a resolution in 2016 referring to the UN Human Rights Council's 2012 Resolution "[c]all[ing] on States Parties to respect and take legislative and other measures to guarantee, respect and protect citizen's right to freedom of information and expression through access to Internet services."[127]

In 2019, the African Commission on Human and Peoples' Rights issued a public statement "express[ing] concern on the continuing trend of Internet shutdowns in Africa, including in Chad, Sudan, the Democratic Republic of Congo (DRC), Gabon and Zimbabwe" and explained that "internet and social media shutdowns violate the right to freedom of expression and access to information contrary to Article 9 of the African Charter on Human and Peoples' Rights."[128]

For the first time in Africa, in January 2019, the Zimbabwe High Court in Zimbabwe Lawyers for Human Rights v. Minister of State in the President's Office ruled in a provisional order that the government had no power to order an Internet shutdown that coincided with widespread protests in January.[129] In a terse ruling not explicit in its reasoning, Judge Owen Tagu ordered full Internet access to be restored, stating verbally that "it has become very clear that the minister had no authority to make that directive."[130] The application included a constitutional argument under the Fundamental

---

[126] Abreu, *supra* note 102.

[127] Afr. Comm'n on Human and Peoples' Rights Res. 362, ACHPR/Res.362(LIX)2016 (Nov. 4, 2016).

[128] Press Release, Special Rapporteur on Freedom of Expression and Access to Information in Africa, The Continuing Trend of Internet and Social Media Shutdowns in Africa (Jan. 29, 2019), https://www.achpr.org/pressrelease/detail?id=8.

[129] Zimbabwe Lawyers for Human Rights v. Minister of State in the President's Office (unreported, HC 265/19, Jan. 21, 2019) (Zim.).

[130] AFP, *Zimbabwe Protests: Court Rules Against Internet Shutdown*, THE SOUTH AFRICAN (Jan. 22, 2019), https://www.thesouthafrican.com/news/zimbabwe-news-internet-access-returns.

Human Rights and Freedom of the country's Constitution, to which the government responded:

> The information that was being circulated on the popular communication platforms such as Whatsapp, Skype, Twitter and Facebook had far reaching consequences to national peace and security as evidenced by the violence that was perpetrated. The platforms had become mediums of inciting violence to the general populace. Their use for business purposes was outweighed by the threats of violence that was communicated. . . . The subject rights were being abused and infringed on the rights of others in a violent and abusive manner. Any disgruntlement by the affected citizens should have prompted them to seek dialogue with the government.[131]

I. Asia

There is no regional human rights body in Asia. However, India which has conducted the lion's share of the world's shutdowns in 2019 witnessed one of the most important legal developments in shutdowns in Jammu and Kashmir designed to pacify protests against new citizenship laws in late 2019.

In Anuradha Bhasin v. UoI [WP(C) 1031/2019] and Gulam Nabi Azad v. UoI [WP(C) 1164/2019], the Indian Supreme Court laid down the law on the issue of the Internet. Firstly, the Court held that *"the right to freedom of speech and expression under Article 19(1)(a), and the right to carry on any trade or business under 19(1)(g), using the medium of internet is constitutionally protected."* This meant that any curtailment of Internet access would need to be reasonable and within the boundaries laid down by Arts. 19(2) and 19(6) of the Constitution.

Then, the Court ordered that all shutdown orders must be published in accordance with "a settled principle of law, and of natural justice," as it "affects lives, liberty and property of people."

Also, the Court required that every shutdown order be "reasoned" and the necessity of the measure as well as the "unavoidable" circumstance

---

[131] *Id.*; Opposing Affidavit of Abigail Tichareva, ¶¶ 6.2–7.4, Zimbabwe Lawyers for Human Rights v. Minister of State in the President's Office (unreported, HC 265/19, Jan. 21, 2019).

necessitating such order. The Court held that suspending Internet services indefinitely is impermissible, although it refused to strike down the five-month-long ongoing shutdown in Kashmir. The Court gave the government an opportunity to prove that a shutdown was "preventive" as opposed to reactive to a danger but ruled that such danger should be in the nature of an "Emergency." Further, the enabling law cannot be used to suppress expression of opinion. Any shutdown order must state material facts to enable judicial review. The Court further stressed that principles of proportionality should be used and the least intrusive measure applied. The Court held that there should not be repetitive use of the enabling law either as this would amount to abuse of power.

Finally, the Court held that any curtailment of fundamental rights should be proportional and that the least restrictive measures should be resorted to by the State. Although the State opposed selective access to Internet services based on a lack of technology, the Court held that if such a contention was accepted, the government would have a free pass to place a complete blockage on the Internet each time and that such complete and indefinite blocking/prohibition cannot be accepted. The Court further held that complete broad suspension of Telecom services, be it the Internet or otherwise, is a drastic measure that must be considered by the State only if "necessary" and "unavoidable" and that the State must assess the existence of an alternate less intrusive remedy.

However, the only relief granted was a direction given to the State to review all orders suspending Internet services forthwith. The Software Freedom Law Center has observed that "*the Court has laid down the law on Internet shutdowns with emphasis on proportionality and reasonableness. The need to issue reasoned orders along with the mandate to make all orders public could result in reduction of arbitrary shutdowns. Removing the veil of secrecy from shutdowns itself could help in reducing the number of shutdowns.*"[132]

---

[132] *Safeguards for Shutdown, Limited Relief for Kashmir*, SOFTWARE FREEDOM LAW CENTER (Jan. 11, 2020), https://sflc.in/sc-judgment-safeguards-shutdown-limited-relief-kashmir.

IV. Adaptation of the Internet Shutdown Jurisprudence for Data Localization

A. Synthesis of Jurisprudence on Internet Shutdowns

Given the absolute languages used by international human rights bodies and regional and domestic courts, shutting down the entire Internet in any region is a clearly excessive measure -- even if it is done for innocuous purposes of preventing cheating at examinations -- since it shuts down the full variety of communications enabled by the Internet that are not related to the purpose of the shutdown, and is therefore deemed a violation of human rights.

Also, the UN, Inter-American, and African human rights bodies seem to agree that blocking an entire social media platform also can never be a measure proportionate to the purpose desired, for it always blocks communication not related to the purpose of the blocking. Blocking of a social media platform, the topic of this research effort, is especially more disproportionate than blocking of an ordinary website since the social media platform is interactive and therefore has much more diversity of authors and contents that are not related to the purpose of the blocking. The only exception, out of Europe, is the blocking of a special purpose platform such as music sharing executed for the purpose of protecting intellectual property rights, under which communications of "general interest" are not blocked.

Indeed, human rights bodies report that, even when social media platforms are shut down to respond to the fake news causing hate crimes against minorities, research indicates that shutdown only makes the situation more volatile[133] and takes away information that can save lives.[134] As Access Now states, "Whether they are justified as a measure to fight "fake news" and hate speech or to stop cheating during exams, the facts remain the same: internet shutdowns violate human rights."[135]

Furthermore, as pointed out by European and Inter-American human rights bodies, Internet shutdown or social media platform works as a "prior censorship" as to the contents that have not yet appeared online or on that blocked website. The prior censorship argument has been effective in invalidating shutdowns and blockings in major court cases.

---

[133] Rydzak, J. "Of Blackouts and Bandhs: The Strategy and Structure of Disconnected Protest in India." Available at SSRN: https://ssrn.com/ abstract=3330413.

[134] KeepItOn 2018, page 6.

[135] KeepItOn 2018, page 2.

The above case law also requires that, if a platform-wide blocking takes place, the overbreadth problem be ameliorated by appeals process whereby the contents not related to the purpose of blocking may be exempt from the effects of the blocking. Also, the administrative authorities, being under the influence of the ruling political elites, are not very transparent about the reason for the blocking. To address mismatch between actual reasons and announced reasons, it will be preeminently important that the platform blockings require judicial approval. Such requirements for the judiciary's involvement will naturally include an appeal process.

To summarize, platform blockings are problematic for human rights mostly for the following reasons: First, platform blockings almost always block too much innocuous information. Second, the overbreadth problem is especially acute for platforms supporting communications of general interest, as opposed to special purpose platforms. Third, platform blockings intercept information before being available to the public. Fourth, the overbreadth problem must be ameliorated procedurally by availability of appeals process where contents unrelated to the purpose of the blocking may be exempted. Fifth, platform blockings effected by administrative bodies, as opposed to judiciary, must be scrutinized with more caution due to their lack of transparency on the motives of the blocking. These factors will form the main standard by which platform blocking will be evaluated.

B. Adaptation to Data Localization

Data localization is implemented by Internet shutdown[136] although sometimes enforced at a penalty of financial burden.[137] Under the typical data localization rule, unless data is stored domestically, that data becomes inaccessible domestically. In that sense, data localization is equivalent to a subset of Internet shutdowns that is administered in accordance with location of data and that does not affect the whole Internet but particular non-localized platforms through which data are processed: platform blockings. Since platform blocking is the other side of the same coin that is data localization,

---

[136] Maria Elterman, "Why LinkedIn Was banned in Russia", Jan 23, 2017, INTERNATIONAL ASSOCIATION OF PRIVACY PROFESSIONALS, https://iapp.org/news/a/why-linkedin-was-banned-in-russia/.

[137] *Facebook Pays Russia $50K Fine for Not Localizing User Data*, MOSCOW TIMES (Nov. 26, 2020), https://www.themoscowtimes.com/2020/11/26/facebook-pays-russia-50k-fine-for-not-localizing-user- data-a72152.

human rights evaluation of a data localization measure requires treatment as a platform blocking.

Of course, we should be careful that *actual* data localizations are not directed at particular platforms or particular data hosted and stored by those platforms unlike *actual* platform blocking. Actual data localizations discriminate simply based on the geolocation of data while actual platform blocking operates on some definitions of "harmful data to be blocked." Platform blocking by definition targets the substance of certain platforms, therefore changing the location of the data does not save the target platform from the blockage. Data localization applies across many platforms and contents to leave out the non-localized ones, regardless of the substance and contents of the platforms.

In that sense, the relationship between platform blocking and data localization can be likened to the relationship between content regulation and content-neutral time-place-manner regulation in the American First Amendment jurisprudence. The American constitutional law takes a differential approach to content regulation and time-place-manner regulation of speech whereby the former is subject to strict scrutiny and the latter intermediate scrutiny.[138] By strict scrutiny, we mean the requirement that the regulation necessarily achieves compelling public interest and restricts not a bit more than necessary for that purpose. By intermediate scrutiny, we mean the requirement that the regulation substantially promotes important public interest maintaining some measure of proportionality to the extent of restriction on human rights. Proportionality means a balance between the private harm created by a state action and the public benefit created by that state action.[139] We can use this methodology to build a broad framework under which various forms of data localizations can be evaluated, adapting the multi-factor standard applied to platform blocking.

As a result, the following observations are in order: First, the overbreadth problem, that is, that innocuous information unrelated to the purpose of localization is forced into localization, can be given a more leeway than platform blocking since the same platform can be made accessible simply by changing the location. Still, there must be a proportional relationship

---

[138] Ashcroft v. ACLU, 542 U.S. 656 (2004); Ward v. Rock Against Racism, 491 U.S. 781 (1989).

[139] Kyung Sin Park, *Mysteries of American Constitutional Law Explained by Comparison to the Korean Principle of Proportionality*, 2 KOREA UNIV. L. REV. 52 (2007).

between the public benefit achieved by the measure and its cost on free speech and privacy. The goal of data localizations is also to protect (and control) domestic people and their data and communicative experiences, that is, provide sovereign protection. Yet many data on the localized platform do not necessarily require sovereign protection (via surveillance, censorship, or not) that the administering authority aimed to provide by the localization measure.

Second, just as in platform blocking, data localizations affecting special categories of data must be more freely allowed than the ones affecting communications of general interest. Third, since the regulation is content neutral, prior censorship argument does not fit as it only affects the location of the data and does not completely block the data from reaching the marketplace of ideas. Fourth and fifth, as data localizations are often effected by blanket statutory enactments, rather than discretionary process, we should scrutinize the proportional relationship between the cost and benefit that arises out of the statutory text in lieu of demanding judicial supervision and appeals process.

In balancing the cost on free speech and privacy against the data protection benefit, it is important to note that actual data localizations come in different forms: hard localization requiring all storage of the subject data to be localized; soft localization requiring storage of a *copy* of the subject data to be localized; and hybrid localization that requires all permanent storage of the subject data to be localized but allows temporary storage of the same for processing.[140] These variations related to the private cost on free speech and privacy. Also, we should also note that the scope of data localizations can vary between "all personal data," "sensitive personal data," "(personal or impersonal) critical data," "(personal or impersonal) financial data," and so on. Just as evaluation of platform blocking is affected by whether the platform is a general platform carrying communications of general interest or a special purpose platform carrying specific types of communication, for example, files, that of data localization should change as its scope of data affected varies.

---

[140] Lindsey R. Sheppard, Erol Yayboke, & Carolina G. Ramos, The Shift Toward Data Localization, CENTER FOR STRATEGIC AND INTERNATIONAL STUDIES, July 2020. The authors make the extra category of de facto data localization and categorize the GDPR adequacy scheme as such, but GDPR explicitly bans the data from being transferred to "inadequate" jurisdictions and is therefore de jure data localization.

ADAPTATION OF THE INTERNET SHUTDOWN JURISPRUDENCE   369

For instance, India's data protection bill enhance sovereign power to conduct surveillance by localizing "critical data" and "sensitive personal data" and thereby having the data within the reach of domestic investigation authorities.[141] However, in conducting the proportionality test, we note that the measure does not interfere with freedom of speech because it simply requires a *copy* of the information to be stored domestically so that they can be inspected by domestic authorities. This means that the foreign-based servers can continue to be accessed by domestic users as long as a copy of the data accessed remains within the country. The measure does have the negative impact on surveillance vulnerability (privacy) since the data thus accumulated domestically either in original form or in duplication will be subject to government surveillance.[142] Also, it is only "critical data" and "sensitive personal data" that is localized, so the impact on surveillance vulnerability may be minimized. Therefore, the human rights scrutiny of India's data protection bill should not result in a low mark compared to hard localizations of all personal data.

GDPR's adequacy scheme is one such hard localization of all personal data. It aims to increases the public interest—the need to protect the citizens' data from infringement of data privacy—while it does enhance the EU jurisdictions' sovereign power to conduct surveillance and censorship. In balancing between the two, we can make the following observations. First, it does not increase highly the risk of sovereign surveillance and censorship for it does not mandate localization in specific national jurisdictions but only within EU and the non-EU "adequate" jurisdictions. Second, the harm resulting from the adequacy scheme depends on the severity of sovereign surveillance and censorship. There is no evidence that sovereign surveillance and censorship is particularly severe in the EU jurisdictions and the non-EU "adequate" jurisdictions. Third, the benefit achieved by the adequacy scheme depends on the relative level of data protection of the EU/non-EU adequate jurisdictions compared to the non-EU inadequate jurisdiction. Fourth, the adequacy scheme has the extra benefit of enhancing cross-border data

---

[141] India's draft Personal Data Protection Bill, chapter 8, available at https://www.meity.gov.in/writereaddata/files/Personal_Data_Protection_Bill,2018.pdf; Pakistan's draft Personal Data Protection Bill, section 15, available at https://www.huntonprivacyblog.com/wp-content/uploads/sites/28/2020/05/Personal-Data-Protection-Bill-2020-Updated1.pdf.

[142] However, the U.S. CLOUD Act has profoundly changed the discourse on whether people should have the right to expect the preexisting level of privacy and protection from government surveillance from the use of overseas servers as communication platforms. Post-CLOUD Act, people cannot avoid (supposedly heightened) domestic surveillance by using overseas communication platform because now the data can be directly accessed by the domestic investigation authorities.

transfer among the EU and non-EU adequate jurisdictions. However, what data protection benefit EU citizens obtain from the measure will be determined by the objectivity and efficiency of the adequacy scheme.

China's Network Security Law (another hard localization) deepens the vulnerability to sovereign censorship and surveillance by localizing all personal data within the territory, the extent of which depends upon the quality of the laws administering state censorship and surveillance. Whether it enhances data protection of the Chinese people under the recently adopted data protection law will depend on the quality of that data protection law. It is important to note that the human rights assessment of China's current laws (data protection law and state surveillance law) influence both sides of the equation, and these two groups of laws are closely related to each other. The track record of China's data protection practice and state surveillance practice will determine the score on Network Security Law.

Trump's proposed TikTok ban (another hard localization) does not deepen the vulnerability to sovereign censorship and surveillance because it does not attempt to place the data within U.S. soil but simply outside China or outside the oversight of the Chinese Communist Party. Also, what data protection benefit American people draw from the localization measure will be determined by the risk of state surveillance under CCP's supervision.

V. Conclusion

Data localizations have been evaluated under the trade rules that do not produce a sustainable governance model, given the public interest/national security exception built into the trade rules, where most data localizations are effected for the ostensible purpose of protecting the data and communicative experiences of the domestic population.

Much of human rights jurisprudence has denounced Internet shutdowns as serious human rights violations. Platform blockings were also considered just as harmful to democracy as broad Internet shutdowns.

Now many shutdowns, especially platform blockings, are necessary corollaries of data localizations. Therefore, if we adapt our rich, already existing human rights inquiry on Internet shutdowns, we will be able to establish an effective governance model for data localizations under which we can evaluate concretely various data localization attempts.

14

European Digital Sovereignty, Data Protection, and the Push toward Data Localization

Theodore Christakis

When Jean-Claude Juncker,[1] then president of the European Commission, proclaimed in 2018 that now is the "The Hour of European Sovereignty,"[2] "half of Europe criticized" him, notes Paul Timmers before adding: "In the words of Bob Dylan, the times they are a-changin.'"[3] Today hardly a day goes by in Europe, without a politician talking about "digital sovereignty." The European Council itself openly uses now the term "digital sovereignty." In the conclusions of a special meeting held in October 2020, the Council explained that:

> To be digitally sovereign, the EU must build a truly digital single market, reinforce its ability to define its own rules, to make autonomous technological choices, and to develop and deploy strategic digital capacities and infrastructure. At the international level, the EU will leverage its tools and regulatory powers to help shape global rules and standards. The EU will remain open to all companies complying with European rules and standards. Digital development must safeguard our values, fundamental rights and security, and be socially balanced. Such a human-centred approach will increase the attractiveness of the European model."[4]

---

[1] This Chapter covers developments until August 2022.

[2] Jean-Claude Juncker, President, Eur. Comm'n, State of the Union 2018: The Hour of European Sovereignty (Sept. 12, 2018), https://ec.europa.eu/commission/presscorner/detail/en/SPEECH_18_5808.

[3] Paul Timmers, *When Sovereignty Leads and Cyber Law Follows*, DIRECTIONS/CYBER DIGITAL EUROPE (Oct. 13, 2020), https://directionsblog.eu/when-sovereignty-leads-and-cyber-law-follows.

[4] *European Council Special Meeting (1 and 2 October 2020) – Conclusions*, ¶ 7, EUCO 13/20 (Oct. 2, 2020), https://www.consilium.europa.eu/media/45910/021020-euco-final-conclusions.pdf.

Theodore Christakis, *European Digital Sovereignty, Data Protection, and the Push toward Data Localization* In: *Data Sovereignty*. Edited by: Anupam Chander and Haochen Sun, Oxford University Press. © Oxford University Press 2023. DOI: 10.1093/oso/9780197582794.003.0015

As shown by this declaration the concept of European Digital Sovereignty has two major dimensions. First, "digital sovereignty" is seen as the **power to regulate** what is going on in cyberspace and in the digital sphere, including the activities of big tech. Second, it is used as the means to achieve **strategic autonomy** in the digital sphere and to boost European competitiveness in tech. I have discussed extensively these two dimensions in my study on "European Digital Sovereignty"[5] where I tried to show that the initiatives undertaken under the banner of this concept create important opportunities for Europe, but they also entail potential pitfalls. I also argued that the EU and Member States should carefully study the risks and successfully navigate around them or, at least, make decisions in an informed way, after sufficiently weighing the potential negative impact of a specific measure.

One of these measures, on which this chapter[6] will focus exclusively, concerns the current trends toward "data localization" and the idea that "European data must be stored and processed in Europe." Part I of this chapter will recall how certain influential political voices in Europe were pushing in favor of data localization even before the *Schrems II* Judgment of the Court of Justice of the European Union (CJEU). Part II will try to discern the exact reasons that motivated such calls for data localization. Part III will discuss in depth the major influence of the July 2020 *Schrems II* Judgment of the CJEU and will show that, ultimately, the numerous calls in favor of strict data localization of personal data as a response to this judgment, were not able to be balanced by those calling for the adoption of a "risk-based approach" to international data transfers. I will end with a few thoughts about the necessity, for Europe, to study further the possible adverse effects of soft[7] or strict data localization mandates and to find solutions that enable the main objective of data protection to be achieved without necessarily engaging in severe and disproportionate restrictions to transnational data flows that might be disruptive for European business and the global economy.

---

[5] THEODORE CHRISTAKIS, "EUROPEAN DIGITAL SOVEREIGNTY": SUCCESSFULLY NAVIGATING BETWEEN THE "BRUSSELS EFFECT" AND EUROPE'S QUEST FOR STRATEGIC AUTONOMY (2020), https://ssrn.com/abstract=3748098.

[6] This chapter covers developments until March 2022.

[7] Anupam Chander introduced the term "soft data localization" in order to refer to "a legal regime that puts pressure on companies to localize, not by directly requiring localization of data or processes, but by making alternatives legally risky and thus potentially unwise." Anupam Chander, *Is Data Localization a Solution for Schrems II?*, 23 J. INT'L ECON. L. 771, 772 (2020).

I. The Push Toward Data Localization in Europe

The discourses on "digital sovereignty" in Europe have been marked by calls for "data sovereignty" and strict data localization requirements. The European Commissioner for the Internal Market, Thierry Breton, who is in charge of digital affairs, is by far the most important proponent of data localization. Already in 2018, one year before becoming Commissioner and while he was still a CEO of Company Atos in France, T. Breton declared:

> we must go further and demand that European data be stored, processed and handled in Europe, in accordance with procedures to be determined by Europe. In other words, the information space must be structured in the same way as territorial, maritime and air space have been organised in the past. The Gafa have tried to make digital technology a "no man's land" for which they would write the law. This has now come to an end. It is time to relocate this information space by opting to process our data on European soil.[8]

After his appointment as Commissioner, T. Breton continued his calls for data localization. In an interview with French TV, for instance, he said on August 25, 2020:

> As far as we Europeans are concerned, our data is the most valuable industrial asset we have. I have always said that I want Europeans' data to be processed, stored and processed in Europe. I have a feeling that Donald Trump is saying the same thing. The Chinese and the Russians are doing it, we will do it too."[9]

And in an interview with *Politico* on September 1, 2020, he reaffirmed that: "European data should be stored and processed in Europe because they belong in Europe," adding that "he understands U.S. President Donald

---

[8] Bertille Bayart & Jacques-Olivier Martin, *Thierry Breton: "C'est aux Gafa de s'adapter à nos règles, pas l'inverse»,»* LE FIGARO (Apr. 10, 2018), http://www.lefigaro.fr/secteur/high-tech/2018/04/06/32001-20180406ARTFIG00280-thierry-breton-c-est-aux-gafa-de-s-adapter-a-nos-regles-pas-l-inverse.php.

[9] Hugues Garnier, *Thierry Breton: "Je souhaite que les données des européens soient traitées et stockées en Europe,"* BFM BUS (Aug. 25, 2020), https://www.bfmtv.com/economie/thierry-breton-je-souhaite-que-les-donnees-des-europeens-soient-traitees-et-stockees-en-europe_AD-202008250281.html.

374 DIGITAL SOVEREIGNTY, DATA PROTECTION AND LOCALIZATION

Trump's concerns about TikTok." "The Trump administration is right to finally recognize that there is ownership on data," he concluded.[10]

Other members of the European Commission seem to hesitate more on this, insisting on the need for free flow of data. For instance, the European Commissioner for Justice, Didier Reynders, seemed to adopt a more nuanced approach during a conference on October 1, 2020, when he declared that:

> It's not to say that we are just using data located in Europe. I know that there are many discussions about the localization of data. I of course support the process to invest more in Europe in data management and data storage and many other things but we are also open to receive products and services from abroad."[11]

Indeed, there seems to be a lot of "discussions about the localization of data" within the European Union and one could even guess that there is a real split between Commission's members on these issues. There is thus a real need to understand the reasons behind calls in Europe for data localization.

II. The Need to Better Understand the Reasons behind Calls for Data Localization

Some commentators have expressed concern that one potential reason could merely be protectionism. Alex Roure, for instance, of the Computer & Communications Industry Association (CCIA) lobby group, observed that "he has not seen a single case where data localization benefits privacy, security or the economy," and he added that: "If it's to protect local incumbents, that would be problematic."[12] Equally perplexing for some is the contrast between politicians' declarations and the perceived lack of demand for data localization within Europe. "Where is the demand for this?" said Alex Roure,[13] while M. Bauer noted that "cloud providers that tout their local

---

[10] Laura Kayali & Florian Eder, *Thierry Breton "Understands" Trump on TikTok, Wants Data Stored in Europe*, POLITICO (Sept. 1, 2020), https://www.politico.eu/article/breton-wants-tiktok-data-to-stay-in-europe.

[11] *EU Justice Chief Reynders Pushes Back on Talk of European Data Localization*, POLITICO (Oct. 1, 2020).

[12] Vincent Manancourt, *Europe's Data Grab*, POLITICO (Feb. 19, 2020), https://www.politico.eu/article/europe-data-grab-protection-privacy.

[13] *Id.*

credentials already exist, but the market for them is small. If localization is a key concern, more people would be buying these services."[14]

A second hypothesis is that Europe is just following, in a rational or more irrational way, a more general trend of several countries to take physical control of the network architecture. Indeed, Europe is far from being the first global actor to call for data localization. As the Global Data Alliance[15] (a cross-industry coalition of companies created to lobby against data localization mandates) "there is a trend to impose data localization requirements and restrict cross-border transfers, including in India, China, Russia, Indonesia, and Vietnam".[16] It could well then be that Europe is either retaliating (albeit that European calls for data localization seem to present this as something rather "positive"—rather than a measure to counter an illegitimate policy) or trying to imitate others based on the idea that data control requires data localization.

A third hypothesis, and undoubtedly a very valid one, is that what motivates calls for data localization in Europe is essentially data protection/privacy considerations. Developments after the July 16, 2020, *Schrems II* judgment of the CJEU are very relevant in this respect and will be discussed extensively in the next section. But, as we will show in the conclusion, in Europe the trend toward localization of personal data is now followed by similar trends in favor of localization for non-personal data. This shows that there is a fear of foreign snooping of data having economic value. At a time when Europe is seeking to catch up with China and the United States in terms of technology, "a strategy that rests heavily on the hope of leveraging pools of industrial data into new AI applications," the European authorities feel "the need to keep such highly valuable data, which may be produced by German carmakers or French banks, secure from industrial espionage by storing it on the Continent."[17] This has also been emphasized by the Director of the French Cybersecurity Agency ANSSI, Guillaume Poupard, who said that "data should probably remain in Europe just because we want only European laws and rules to apply to it."[18] As a consequence, ANSSI has revised its cybersecurity certification and

---

[14] *Id.*

[15] GLOBAL DATA ALLIANCE, https://www.globaldataalliance.org (last visited Aug. 30, 2022).

[16] GLOBAL DATA ALLIANCE, ABOUT THE GLOBAL DATA ALLIANCE, https://globaldataalliance.org/wp-content/uploads/2021/06/aboutgda.pdf (last visited Aug. 30, 2022). For a mapping of data localization measures in place or proposed in different countries until 2015, *see* Anupam Chander & Uyên P. Lê, *Data Nationalism*, 64 EMORY L. REV. 677 (2015). This "classic" study needs update in the light of the very important trends toward data localization during the last five years.

[17] Manancourt, *supra* note 11.

[18] Laurens Cerulus, *French Cyber Czar Promotes European Tech Sovereignty*, POLITICO (Feb. 10, 2020), https://subscriber.politicopro.com/article/2020/02/french-cyber-czar-promotes-european-tech-sovereignty-1876769.

labeling program (known as SecNumCloud)[19] in order to introduce an "immunity from non-EU laws" requirement that will effectively preclude foreign cloud firms from providing services to government agencies as well as 600-plus firms that operate "vital" and "essential" services.[20] France is also advocating that the European Union Agency for Cybersecurity (ENISA) include an identical rule of "immunity from non-EU laws" in its draft EU Cloud Security Scheme (EUCS), which aims to standardize the proliferation of cloud security schemes and procurement standards across Europe.

III. The Influence of the *Schrems II* Judgment of the CJEU

Let's turn now to the very important judgment issued by the CJEU on July 16, 2020,in order to analyze its effects on the debate about data localization in Europe. I have five observations to make on this subject, following a chronological order.

A. The Starting Point: Data Localization Is Not in the GDPR's DNA

First, and as a matter of principle, it must be emphasized that, when it comes to personal data protection, the European approach has never been that personal data should not travel (that is, before *Schrems II*). Instead, the principle has always been that European personal data should travel with protections. Recital 101 of the GDPR is very clear in this respect:

> Flows of personal data to and from countries outside the Union [. . .] are necessary for the expansion of international trade and international cooperation. The increase in such flows has raised new challenges and concerns with regard to the protection of personal data. However, when personal

---

[19] *See L'ANSSI actualise le référentiel SecNumCloud*, ANSSI, https://www.ssi.gouv.fr/actualite/lanssi-actualise-le-referentiel-secnumcloud (last visited Aug. 30, 2022).
[20] *See* Nigel Cory, *"Sovereignty Requirements" in France—and Potentially EU—Cybersecurity Regulations: The Latest Barrier to Data Flows, Digital Trade, and Digital Cooperation Among Likeminded Partners*, Cross Border Data Forum (Dec. 10, 2022), https://www.crossborderdataforum.org/sovereignty-requirements-in-france-and-potentially-eu-cybersecurity-regulations-the-latest-barrier-to-data-flows-digital-trade-and-digital-cooperation-among-likemi.

data are transferred from the Union to controllers, processors or other recipients in third countries [. . .], the level of protection of natural persons ensured in the Union by this Regulation should not be undermined, [. . .]. A transfer could take place only if, subject to the other provisions of this Regulation, the conditions laid down in the provisions of this Regulation relating to the transfer of personal data to third countries [. . .] are complied with by the controller or processor.

It is impossible to enter here into a detailed analysis of all the GDPR mechanisms and provisions for international data transfers. It is enough to note that nowhere does the GDPR present data localization as the only means of protecting personal data. Data localization could of course be, in some situations, one of the means to do so, when for instance there is no legal basis whatsoever to transfer data outside of the EU and when local storage and processing could appear as a necessary and proportionate measure in light of important existing risks. However, the GDPR offers a series of other solutions compatible with the GDPR's idea of "free data flows with protection." These include transfers on the basis of adequacy decisions (Article 45 GDPR); use of "appropriate safeguards" (Article 46) or "binding corporate rules" (Article 47); transfers on the basis of international agreements (Article 48); and even exceptional transfers based on the different "derogations for specific situations" under Article 49.

B. Calls for Data Localization After Schrems II

The *Schrems II* judgment issued by the CJEU in July 2020 constituted an extremely important development in this respect. In this judgment the Court affirmed "strongly the importance of maintaining a high level of protection of personal data transferred from the European Union to third countries dealing in a comprehensive way with the issue of government access to data not only by the United States but also by any other country."[21] The Court not only invalidated the Privacy Shield arrangement between the EU and the United States but also imposed several conditions on the use of Standard

---

[21] *Cf.* Theodore Christakis, *After Schrems II: Uncertainties on the Legal Basis for Data Transfers and Constitutional Implications for Europe*, Eur. L. Blog (July 21, 2020), https://europeanlawblog.eu/2020/07/21/after-schrems-ii-uncertainties-on-the-legal-basis-for-data-transfers-and-constitutional-implications-for-europe.

Contractual Clauses ("SCCs") as the legal basis for transfers to all countries for which the European Commission had not already adopted adequacy decisions. On July 16, 2020, the CJEU thus mostly closed the door on personal data being allowed to leave Europe without an adequacy decision, but left some windows open to enable data to find their way out of the bloc.

Immediately after *Schrems II*, some DPAs in Europe started calling for data localization as the only credible solution. For instance, the Berlin data commissioner Maja Smoltczyk called, on July 17, 2020, for data currently stored in the U.S. to be relocated to the EU stating that: "Now is the time for Europe's digital independence."[22]

However, following the *Schrems II* judgment, everybody was awaiting for the guidance to be given on its application by the European Data Protection Board (EDPB), which unites all European DPAs. As we will now see, the initial EDPB guidance, published on November 2020, pushed for a de facto strict localization of data in Europe but, following widespread criticism, the EDPB seemed to adopt a more flexible approach in its final guidance in June 2021.

C. Initial EDPB Guidance: Toward De Facto Data Localization

The EDPB published on November 11, 2020, a set of post-*Schrems II* "Recommendations" which created a huge level of anxiety on the future of international data transfers. I have discussed extensively the EDPB guidance on three different posts published at the European Law Blog.[23] It is impossible to reproduce this analysis in the limited space available here. I will only

---

[22] Press Release, Berliner Beauftragte für Datenschutz und Informationsfreiheit, "Nach „Schrems II: Europa braucht digitale Eigenständigkeit" (July 17, 2020), https://www.datenschutz-berlin.de/fileadmin/user_upload/pdf/pressemitteilungen/2020/20200717-PM-Nach_SchremsII_Digitale_Eigenstaendigkeit.pdf ("According to 'Schrems II': Europe needs digital independence").

[23] Theodore Christakis, *"Schrems III"? First Thoughts on the EDPB Post-Schrems II Recommendations on International Data Transfers (Part 1)*, Eur. L. Blog (Nov. 13, 2020), https://europeanlawblog.eu/2020/11/13/schrems-iii-first-thoughts-on-the-edpb-post-schrems-ii-recommendations-on-international-data-transfers-part-1; Theodore Christakis, *"Schrems III"? First Thoughts on the EDPB Post-Schrems II Recommendations on International Data Transfers (Part 2)*, Eur. L. Blog (Nov. 16, 2020), https://europeanlawblog.eu/2020/11/16/schrems-iii-first-thoughts-on-the-edpb-post-schrems-ii-recommendations-on-international-data-transfers-part-2; Theodore Christakis, *"Schrems III"? First Thoughts on the EDPB Post-Schrems II Recommendations on International Data Transfers (Part 3)*, Eur. L. Blog (Nov. 17, 2020), https://europeanlawblog.eu/2020/11/17/schrems-iii-first-thoughts-on-the-edpb-post-schrems-ii-recommendations-on-international-data-transfers-part-3.

present very briefly the main conclusions of this analysis before submitting some additional thoughts in relation to the subject matter of this study.

The first conclusion of my analysis was that third countries might rarely if ever meet the requirements set by the EDPB's "European Essential Guarantees" (EEG) Recommendations."[24] This means that, beyond the 10 States/14 entities that have the opportunity of benefiting today from an EU adequacy decision[25], few other countries might be considered as offering a protection "essentially equivalent" to that offered by EU law.[26]

The second conclusion was that if third countries are not considered as "adequate/essentially equivalent," then data transfers to them are lawful only if supplemental measures are adopted by the data exporter. The EDPB initial guidance seemed nonetheless to prohibit almost all such transfers when the personal data is readable in the third country if there was a risk that the intelligence or law enforcement agencies of this third country might request the data from the data importer (through a mechanism of compelled access) or, indeed, access them directly (direct or covert access). Indeed, the EDPB "Recommendations on Supplementary Measures"[27] clearly indicated that, if there was such a risk, no data transfer should take place to non-adequate/ non-essentially equivalent countries unless the data is so thoroughly

---

[24] I refer here to one of the two documents published by the EDPB on Nov. 11, 2020, entitled: "Recommendations 02/2020 on the European Essential Guarantees for surveillance measures" (EEG Recommendations). Eur. Data Prot. Bd., Recommendations 02/2020 on the European Essential Guarantees for Surveillance Measures (2020), https://edpb.europa. eu/sites/default/files/files/file1/edpb_recommendations_202002_europeanessentialguaranteessurv eillance_en.pdf. The objective of these Recommendations is to provide data exporters with a guide, based on the two European Courts' jurisprudence, in order to determine whether foreign countries surveillance laws meet the European human rights requirements and could thus be considered as offering an "essentially equivalent protection."

[25] See Adequacy Decisions: How the EU Determines If a Non-EU Country Has an Adequate Level of Data Protection, Eur. Comm'n, https://ec.europa.eu/info/law/law-topic/data-protection/internatio nal-dimension-data-protection/adequacy-decisions_en (last visited Aug. 30, 2022).

[26] This conclusion seems to be shared by the Danish Data Protection Agency which, in its March 2022 "Guidance on the use of cloud" notes (at 20) that "it is the opinion of the DDPA that (controllers) may take a "worst case scenario" as the basis of (their) assessment i.e. base (their) assessment on the assumption that all the concerned third countries have "problematic" legislation and/or practice. . . "
See Danish Data Prot. Agency, Guidance on the Use of Cloud (2022), https://www.datat ilsynet.dk/Media/637824108733754794/Guidance%20on%20the%20use%20of%20cloud.pdf.

[27] This is the second document adopted on Nov. 11, 2020, by the EDPB. Its full title is "Recommendations 01/2020 on measures that supplement transfer tools to ensure compliance with the EU level of protection of personal data" ("Recommendations on Supplementary Measures"). Eur. Data Prot. Bd., Recommendations 01/2020 on Measures That Supplement Transfer Tools to Ensure Compliance with the EU Level of Protection of Personal Data (2020), https:// edpb.europa.eu/sites/default/files/consultation/edpb_recommendations_202001_supplementa rymeasurestransferstools_en.pdf. This guidance had been eagerly expected since Schrems II in order to understand what kind of measures could allow to continue data transfers from the EU to the United States and to other countries that do not offer an "equivalent" level of protection.

380 DIGITAL SOVEREIGNTY, DATA PROTECTION AND LOCALIZATION

encrypted or pseudonymised that it cannot be read by anyone in the recipient country, not even the intended recipient. If European data has almost no way of leaving Europe (that is, in a readable format) that means that it needs to remain in Europe. Without actually labeling it "data localization," the EDPB's initial guidance was inevitably leading in that direction.

Promoters of "digital sovereignty" in France hailed the EDPB guidance as a "an opportunity that we have rarely seen in the past" for "Europeans to regain control of their digital sovereignty" and "for European Cloud providers and startups in Europe".[28]

These enthusiastic statements contrasted sharply with the position of business organizations and companies all over Europe that strongly criticized the EDPB guidance as being "very restrictive" and "unrealistic"—to quote just the position of the main French business organization, Medef, which added that:

> By recommending measures that are not feasible in practice, especially for very small and medium-sized businesses that do not have sufficient resources, the development of French and European companies internationally is hampered"[29]

Indeed, as shown in a *SchremsII Impact Survey* published on November 26, 2020, by four major pan-European business organisations, European business could be greatly affected by the restrictive interpretation of SchremsII proposed by the EDPB. According to this survey, 75% of companies using SCCs for transfers of data out of Europe are European (against only 13% U.S. companies). The survey concluded that:

> "It seems to us that in its current form such guidance would make it very difficult for businesses to rely on SCCs. This is not only in conflict with the European Commission's new draft set of SCCs, but even with the *Schrems II* decision itself."[30]

---

[28] *See* CHRISTAKIS, *supra* note 4, at 70.

[29] *See* MEDEF, SUBMISSION OF MEDEF TO THE EU COMMISSION'S DRAFT SCCs 3 (Dec. 10, 2020), https://ec.europa.eu/info/law/better-regulation/have-your-say/initiatives/12741-Data-protection-standard-contractual-clauses-for-transferring-personal-data-to-non-EU-countries-implementing-act-/F1305807_en.

[30] *See* BUS. EUR. ET AL., SCHREMS II - IMPACT SURVEY REPORT 3 (2020), https://www.businesseurope.eu/publications/schrems-ii-impact-survey-report.

THE INFLUENCE OF THE *SCHREMS II* JUDGMENT OF THE CJEU   381

This initial EDPB guidance opened a debate about whether such strict restrictions to transborder flows of personal data and data localization are a necessary and proportionate response to the existing risks. The initial EDPB guidance rejected the so-called risk-based approach. The EDPB seemed to consider that, even if the risk of a foreign government accessing a specific category of data is almost inexistent in practice, data should not be transferred in a readable format if the foreign country's legal system does not offer, as a matter of principle, a protection equivalent to the one suggested by the EDPB's "EEGs".

To understand better the debate, let's take the example of a European company transferring human resources data to its branch in the United States, a transfer necessary for its everyday operations—for instance, in order to allow U.S. executives to consult the agenda of European colleagues so as to be able to fix a call. The company in our example has never received orders to disclose HR (or other) data under FISA 702 and has never otherwise provided personal data to U.S. intelligence agencies. Based on existing practice and also the assurances given by the U.S. government in the post-Schrems II White Paper published in September 2020,[31] the lawyers of this European company could conclude that the risk to receive a request in relation with this HR data is negligible, despite being subject to FISA 702 requests at a purely theoretical level. Thus they could decide to permit such HR data transfers, providing for additional organizational and contractual safeguards and on the basis of the commitment that such data transfers will stop immediately if they receive in the future a FISA 702 request or if they learn that other companies, in a similar situation, received such requests. This risk-based approach would sound like a logical solution in conformity with Chapter V of the GDPR and the principle of proportionality. It would also sound as compatible with the *Schrems II* judgment that invited for transfers to continue "in the light of all the circumstances of that transfer" (§ 121, 146) and "on a case by case basis" (§ 134).

The initial EDPB guidance, however, explicitly prohibited such intragroup transfers of readable data for shared business purposes in its "Use Case 7." It seemed to consider that the theoretical possibility that a U.S. intelligence agency might present in the future a FISA 702 request for this type

---

[31] *See* U.S. DEPT. OF COM. ET AL., INFORMATION ON U.S. PRIVACY SAFEGUARDS RELEVANT TO SCCS AND OTHER EU LEGAL BASES FOR EU-U.S. DATA TRANSFERS AFTER SCHREMS II (2020), https://www.commerce.gov/sites/default/files/2020-09/SCCsWhitePaperFORMATTEDFINAL5 08COMPLIANT.PDF.

382 DIGITAL SOVEREIGNTY, DATA PROTECTION AND LOCALIZATION

of data, however improbable its effective realization might be, prohibits the transfer.[32] Faced with criticism, the EDPB revised, nonetheless, its position on this point and adopted a more flexible approach in its final guidance published in June 2021.

D. The New Model SCC's and EDPB's Final Guidance: A Degree of Room for a Risk-Based Approach?

Despite the considerable initial hostility of the EDPB regarding a "risk-based approach," the European Commission seemed to accept this approach to a certain degree. Its new model Standard Contractual Clauses for international transfers, published on June 4, 2021, permitted, subject to several safeguards, the data exporter to take into consideration the "laws and practices of the third country of destination" including "prior instances of requests for disclosure from public authorities, or the absence of such requests." The Commission added that: "Where this practical experience is relied upon to conclude that the data importer will not be prevented from complying with these Clauses, it needs to be supported by other relevant, objective elements, and it is for the Parties to consider carefully whether these elements together carry sufficient weight, in terms of their reliability and representativeness, to support this conclusion."[33]

A few days later, on June 21, 2021, the EDPB adopted its *"Final version of Recommendations on supplementary measures,"* which followed the same line as the Commission, by leaving a degree of room for a risk-based approach. Indeed, the EDPB noted that "among the main modifications are: the emphasis on the importance of examining the practices of third country public authorities in the exporters' legal assessment to determine whether the legislation and/or practices of the third country impinge in practice—on the effectiveness of the Art. 46 GDPR transfer tool; [and] the possibility that the exporter considers in its assessment the practical experience of the importer, among other elements and with certain caveats." More importantly,

---

[32] For a detailed analysis of this issue, *see* CHRISTAKIS, *supra* note 4, at 72–74.

[33] *See* Commission Implementing Decision on Standard Contractual Clauses for the Transfer of Personal Data to Third Countries Pursuant to Regulation (EU) 2016/679 of the European Parliament and of the Coun, Annex, at 22–23, C (2021) 3972 final (June 4, 2021), https://commission.europa.eu/system/files/2021-06/1_en_annexe_acte_autonome_cp_part1_v5_0.pdf.

the EDPB noted in the section of its final guidance for the attention of data exporters conducting a Transfer Impact Assessment that:

> Alternatively, you may decide to proceed with the transfer without being required to implement supplementary measures, if you consider that you have no reason to believe that relevant and problematic legislation will be applied, in practice, to your transferred data and/or importer. You will need to have demonstrated and documented through your assessment, where appropriate in collaboration with the importer, that the law is not interpreted and/or applied in practice so as to cover your transferred data and importer, also taking into account the experience of other actors operating within the same sector and/or related to similar transferred personal data."[34]

The EDPB followed this guidance with a series of conditions and safeguards intended to "objectivise" the process and prevent abuse. Nevertheless, by referring to the "practice related to the transferred data," the EDPB left a degree of room for a risk-based approach to international data transfers. However, a few recent DPAs decisions in Europe seem to reject this approach.

E. Intensification of Enforcement of *Schrems II* by European DPAs and Rejection of a Risk-Based Approach

During the first weeks of 2022, an intensification of the enforcement of the *Schrems II* judgment by European DPAs emerged. Among other cases, two decisions issued by DPAs, the first issued by the European Data Protection Supervisor (EDPS) on January 5, 2022,[35] and the second issued by DPS, the Austrian DPA, on January 13, 2022,[36] found that two websites, one run by a European Parliament (EP) contractor, and the other by an Austrian company, had unlawfully transferred personal data to the United States merely by enabling cookies (Google Analytics and Stripe) provided by two U.S.-based

---

[34] *Id.* at 18.

[35] Eur. Data Prot. Supervisor, Decision of the European Data Protection Supervisor in Complaint Case 2020–1013 Submitted by Members of the Parliament Against the European Parliament (Jan. 5, 2022), https://noyb.eu/sites/default/files/2022-01/Case%202020-1013%20-%20EDPS%20Decision_bk.pdf.

[36] A translation of the decision can be found here: https://noyb.eu/sites/default/files/2022-01/E-DSB%20-%20Google%20Analytics_EN_bk.pdf.

384 DIGITAL SOVEREIGNTY, DATA PROTECTION AND LOCALIZATION

companies on the devices of their visitors. Both decisions looked at the various technical and legal safeguards put in place by the data controllers and found them to be either insufficient—in the case against the EP, or ineffective—in the Austrian case.

Interestingly, in both cases the data controllers claimed that the "risk-based approach" was appropriate and that the likelihood of the U.S. government requesting this kind of cookie-related data should be taken into consideration. However, the two DPAs rejected this argument in an implied way, without even mentioning their motivations for rejecting it.

These two decisions were considered veritable landmarks and the "first two pieces that fell" in the "Transatlantic data transfers domino." As explained by Gabriela Zanfir Fortuna, referring to 101 other similar complaints concerning Google Analytics from the Austrian NGO NoyB: "a series of similar decisions will be successively published in the short to medium future, with small chances of seeing significant variations."[37]

Indeed, just a few days after the DPS decision, it emerged that the French DPA CNIL was about to prepare its own decisions concerning the use of Google Analytics by certain websites in France, one of them being, for instance, the French website Sephora.fr, which specializes in beauty creams and products.

At the same time, Google published a blog in response to the DPS decision, in which it emphasized that:

> Google has offered Analytics-related services to global businesses for more than 15 years and in all that time has never once received the type of demand the DPA speculated about. And we don't expect to receive one because such a demand would be unlikely to fall within the narrow scope of the relevant law.[38]

Taking all of these elements into consideration, one could ask this: What is the likelihood that the NSA or other U.S. Intelligence agencies will try to access Sephora cookie-related data (to use this website known to have been targeted by a NoyB complaint as an example)? If one believes Google's

---

[37] See Gabriela Zanfir-Fortuna, *Understanding Why the First Pieces Fell in the Transatlantic Transfers Domino*, FUTURE OF PRIVACY FORUM (Jan. 27, 2022), https://fpf.org/blog/understanding-why-the-first-pieces-fell-in-the-transatlantic-transfers-domino.

[38] See Kent Walker, *It's Time for a New EU-US Data Transfer Framework*, GOOGLE (Jan. 19, 2022), https://blog.google/around-the-globe/google-europe/its-time-for-a-new-eu-us-data-transfer-framework.

statement concerning previous practice and looks carefully at the Sephora website (which is certainly not some terror or foreign spies honeypot), one might conclude, in good faith, that the chances of this happening *in this specific case* are extremely unlikely. This seem to demonstrate the benefit of a case-by-case risk-based approach to international data transfers, which would be much more justifiable than a strict data localization mandate.[39] This is all the more compelling when one considers that websites using Google Analytics also have the option to activate a function enabling strong technical measures such as IP anonymization.

On February 10, 2022, the CNIL published indeed its decision[40] concerning one of NoyB's complaints against websites using Google Analytics. The website is not mentioned in the decision, which means that it could well be the one used in my example above (Sephora.fr). In a disappointing way, the CNIL decision does not include any analysis on the risk-based approach or the issue of the likelihood of access discussed above. It becomes then clear that, in all these recent European DPAs' decisions on enforcing *Schrems II*, the *mere theoretical possibility* that U.S. intelligence agencies might request Google Analytics cookie data from any website in Europe is enough to prohibit the use of Google Analytics by European websites, without the need to undertake any specific or case-by-case risk assessment.

IV. Conclusion

As we have seen in this chapter, there is an increasing trend in Europe in favor of data localization.

This trend, which mostly concerns personal data following the *Schrems II* judgment, is now being followed by similar trends in favor of localization of non-personal data. For example, an initial leaked draft of the "Data Governance Act" (DGA) Regulation (an ambitious proposal aiming to boost data sharing at the EU level and to drive the development of Common European Data Spaces and the wider data sharing ecosystem) included

---

[39] One should bear in mind however that, as the EDPB guidance and the model SCCs published by the Commission show, the burden of proof that the "the law is not interpreted and/or applied in practice so as to cover" a specific category of transferred data, lies with the data exporter. It is therefore essential to deal adequately with this question in the Transfer Impact Assessment (TIA).

[40] *See* COMMISSION NATIONALE INFORMATIQUE & LIBERTÉS, DÉCISION N° [...] DU [...] METTANT EN DEMEURE [. . .] (Feb. 10, 2022), https://www.cnil.fr/sites/default/files/atoms/files/med_google_analytics_anonymisee.pdf.

wording that the processing of public sector data "should be limited to the European Union" and intended to create a new blocking statute, for non-personal data, which goes far beyond that which is already provided for personal data by Article 48 of the GDPR.[41] To be more precise, the draft included a provision as follows:

> The provider of data sharing services shall have adequate safeguards in place, including of a technical, organizational and legal nature, that prevent it from responding to requests from authorities of third countries with a view of obtaining access to non-personal data relating to companies established in the Union and Union public administration, unless the request is based on a judicial decision from the Member State in which the company to which the data relate is established.[42]

These provisions met with strong reaction[43] and finally disappeared in the official draft published by the Commission less than a month later.[44] However, as discussed elsewhere, this official draft also included *indirect* and *complex* mechanisms that might result in some form of "soft" data localization.[45] Ken Propp published more recently a critical comment on the "restrictive data transfer features" of the final version of the DGA, as well as the more recent "Data Act" proposed by the European Commission on February 23, 2022. According to Propp:

> The Commission has not yet explained in any detail why existing protections against intellectual property theft and industrial espionage are insufficient for international flows of non-personal data. Borrowing the data transfer safeguards originally developed to protect individuals' privacy seems a cumbersome and imprecise solution, in any case. The immediate consequence, as the Data Act begins to wind through the legislative

---

[41] *See* Theodore Christakis, *Transfer of EU Personal Data to U.S. Law Enforcement Authorities after the CLOUD Act: Is There a Conflict with the GDPR?, in* Cybersecurity and Privacy in a Globalized World - Building Common Approaches 60 (Randal Milch et al. eds., 2019).

[42] This leaked draft is available here: Melissa Heikkilä, *Read the Commission's Proposal on the Data Governance Act*, Politico (Oct. 28, 2020).

[43] Vincent Manancourt & Melissa Heikkilä, *Legal Experts: EU Data Proposals Break International Law*, Politico (Nov. 4, 2020), https://www.politico.eu/article/legal-experts-eu-data-proposals-break-international-law.

[44] *Commission Proposal for a Regulation of the European Parliament and of the Council on European Data Governance (Data Governance Act)*, COM (2020) 767 final (Nov. 25, 2020).

[45] *See* Christakis, *supra* note 4, at 74–80.

labyrinth, could be a foreign concern that the EU's bid for greater autonomy in the data economy is once again headed in a protectionist direction.[46]

European calls in favor of data localization are often motivated by genuine and legitimate concerns, related to data protection, privacy considerations, and the fear of foreign snooping into European personal and industrial data.

Nevertheless, it is well known that data protection considerations can sometimes be misused as a vehicle to further domestic business interests and protectionism. Christopher Kuner has rightly stressed that "the distinction between rights protection and protectionism can often be in the eye of the beholder, and it is thus difficult to differentiate the constitutional and legal issues raised by restricting data flows from the hidden economic agendas that may be at play."[47]

While data localization solutions can sometimes be the only way to effectively protect European data, in other situations such strict localization mandates, used instead as a tool for protectionism, can become counterproductive. Before engaging in data protectionism, Europe should study the potential adverse effects and costs of such policies for European companies, the consequences in terms of cybersecurity,[48] and the potential impact of such policies on global human rights. Data localization measures, initially promoted by countries like Russia, are now being adopted by other countries. NGOs have indicated that this is "alarming" for the future of the free, open and global Internet. What would the message be to other countries if Europe embraces data localization?[49]

It is very probably because of these considerations that the European Data Protection Supervisor (EDPS) Wojciech Wiewiórowski declared that he wasn't "keen" on the idea of data localization, while a key EDPS lawyer, Anna Buchta, said that the EDPS "would not support a general trend towards data localization."[50] Similarly, members of the European Commission have

---

[46] Kenneth Propp, *Cultivating Europe's Data Garden*, LAWFARE (Mar. 4, 2022), https://www.lawf areblog.com/cultivating-europes-data-garden.

[47] Christopher Kuner, *Data Nationalism and Its Discontents*, 64 EMORY L. J. ONLINE 2089, 2097 (2015).

[48] *See* PETER SWIRE & DE BRAE KENNEDY-MAYO, THE EFFECTS OF DATA LOCALIZATION ON CYBERSECURITY (2022), https://peterswire.net/wp-content/uploads/Swire-Mayo-Effects-of-Data-Localization-on-Cybersecurity-Draft-SSRN-Feb-2022-.pdf.

[49] For a detailed analysis of all these issues, *see* CHRISTAKIS, *supra* note 4, at 80–86 and the bibliography appearing there. *See also* Nigel Cory & Luke Daskoli, *How Barriers to Cross-Border Data Flows Are Spreading Globally, What They Cost, and How to Address Them*, INFO. TECH. & INNOVATION FOUND. (July 19, 2021), https://itif.org/publications/2021/07/19/how-barriers-cross-border-data-flows-are-spreading-globally-what-they.cost.

[50] According to the Politico's Newsletter Cyber Insights of Oct. 9, 2020.

388 DIGITAL SOVEREIGNTY, DATA PROTECTION AND LOCALIZATION

emphasized that *Schrems II* should not usher in an era of data localization. "That has not changed with the judgment. We believe in free data flows," said Ralf Sauer Deputy Head of Unit for International Data Flows for the Commission on October 1, 2020,[51] while his boss, Bruno Gencarelli, stressed several times recently that "data localisation has never been in the GDPR's DNA."[52] Similarly, Commissioner Margrethe Vestager insisted that it is "important that data can travel, into and out of the union."[53]

To avoid strict data localization mandates, the EU could opt for a risk-based approach that focuses on whether restrictions to transnational data flows are proportionate to the risks presented, taking into account the nature of the data and a series of other considerations. Strict data localization regimes may not constitute a necessary, proportionate, or adequate response to ensuring that data is protected in cases where the likelihood of foreign access to data is very low and where other, more satisfactory and less disruptive, solutions exist. This seems to be the approach suggested by the OECD Privacy Guidelines, which state that "Any restrictions to transborder flows of personal data should be proportionate to the risks presented, taking into account the sensitivity of the data, and the purpose and context of the processing."[54] But a risk-based approach may only help *mitigate* the consequences of the problems created by situations in which data localization appears the only way to achieve effective data protection. It cannot be a solution to the underlying problems.

In order to definitively resolve these problems, priority should be given to international negotiations and agreements in order to reach commonly agreed solutions. The conclusion, by the EU and United States, of a satisfactory and long-lasting adequacy arrangement, capable of addressing the deficiencies highlighted by the CJEU in its *Schrems II* judgment,[55] is of paramount importance but will not be enough. Indeed, at the transatlantic level,

---

[51] Vincent Manancourt & Melissa Heikkilä, *EU Eyes Tighter Grip on Data in 'Tech Sovereignty' Push*, POLITICO (Oct. 29, 2020), https://www.politico.eu/article/in-small-steps-europe-looks-to-tighten-grip-on-data.

[52] Digital Sovereignty conference, Sciences Po, November 18, 2020.

[53] *Id.*

[54] *OECD Guidelines on the Protection of Privacy and Transborder Flows of Personal Data*, ¶ 18, OECD, http://www.oecd.org/sti/ieconomy/oecdguidelinesontheprotectionofprivacyandtransborderflowsofpersonaldata.htm (last updated 2013).

[55] For a recent proposal on how to do that see our two recent articles at the European Law Blog with Ken Propp and Peter Swire, *see* Theodore Christakis et al., *EU/US Adequacy Negotiations and the Redress Challenge: How to Create an Independent Authority with Effective Remedy Powers*, EUR. L. BLOG (Feb. 16, 2022), https://europeanlawblog.eu/2022/02/16/eu-us-adequacy-negotiations-and-the-redress-challenge-how-to-create-an-independent-authority-with-effective-remedy-powers.

the negotiation of an EU/U.S. Agreement on Law enforcement access to data is equally important in order to restore trust and avoid conflicts of laws in transatlantic relations.[56] At the bilateral/regional level it is important to continue the trend toward the creation of "regional networks" and other actions that enable "bridges to be built" between "a number of common principles and safeguards."[57] And at more of a global level, it is crucial that a process as important as that which the OECD has embarked on since December 2020 be supported, with the aim of restoring trust in international data transfers by formulating common principles concerning government access, for national security and law enforcement purposes, to personal data held by the private sector.[58]

---

[56] *See* Theodore Christakis & Fabien Terpan, *EU-US Negotiations on Law Enforcement Access to Data: Divergences, Challenges and EU Law Procedures and Options*, 11 Int'l Data Privacy L. 81 (2021).

[57] *See* Gabriela Zanfir Fortuna, *Dispatch from the Global Privacy Assembly: The Brave New World of International Data Transfers*, Future of Privacy Forum (Nov. 10, 2021), https://fpf.org/blog/dispatch-from-the-global-privacy-assembly-the-brave-new-world-of-international-data-transfers.

[58] Theodore Christakis et al., *Towards OECD Principles for Government Access to Data: Can Democracies Show the Way?*, Lawfare (Dec. 20, 2021), https://www.lawfareblog.com/towards-oecd-principles-government-access-data-can-democracies-show-way. This Chapter covers developments until August 2022.